Homeland Security Handbook

PUBLIC ADMINISTRATION AND PUBLIC POLICY

A Comprehensive Publication Program

EDITOR-IN-CHIEF

EVAN M. BERMAN

Huey McElveen Distinguished Professor
Louisiana State University
Public Administration Institute
Baton Rouge, Louisiana

Founding Editor

JACK RABIN

Professor of Public Administration and Public Policy
The Pennsylvania State University—Harrisburg
School of Public Affairs
Middletown, Pennsylvania

Available Electronically

Principles and Practices of Public Administration, edited by Jack Rabin, Robert F. Munzenrider, and Sherrie M. Bartell

PublicADMINISTRATION*netBASE*

Homeland Security Handbook

Edited by

Jack Pinkowski
Nova Southeastern University
Fort Lauderdale, Florida, U.S.A.

CRC Press
Taylor & Francis Group
Boca Raton London New York

CRC Press is an imprint of the
Taylor & Francis Group, an **informa** business

CRC Press
Taylor & Francis Group
6000 Broken Sound Parkway NW, Suite 300
Boca Raton, FL 33487-2742

© 2008 by Taylor & Francis Group, LLC
CRC Press is an imprint of Taylor & Francis Group, an Informa business

---

Library of Congress Cataloging-in-Publication Data

Homeland security handbook / Jack Pinkowski. -- Public administration and
    public policy.
        p. cm.
    Includes bibliographical references and index.
    ISBN-13: 978-0-8493-7926-0 (alk. paper)
    ISBN-10: 0-8493-7926-1 (alk. paper)
    1. Terrorism--United States. 2. National security--United States. I. Pinkowski,
Jack.

HV6432.H663 2008
363.325'17--dc22   2007046425

Visit the Taylor & Francis Web site at
http://www.taylorandfrancis.com

and the CRC Press Web site at
http://www.crcpress.com

In Memoriam

Dr. Terrance A. Johnson passed away on November 10, 2007. Dr. Johnson, along with Dr. Nathaniel A. Wilkinson, was responsible for Chapter 3, "Homeland Security: A 'One-Stop Shop' Approach." It makes all of us realize that our contribution to the literature is a legacy that will survive long after our earthly pursuits. Hopefully, his involvement with this project will contribute to greater understanding of the challenges facing us and make a meaningful difference in our attempts to structure workable solutions.

Dedication

To all the innocent victims

Contents

SECTION I: INTRODUCTION AND THEORETICAL CONSTRUCTS

SECTION II: TERRORISM, EXTREMIST MOVEMENTS, AND WEAPONS OF MASS DESTRUCTION

SECTION III: PLANNING, PREVENTION, PREPAREDNESS, RECOVERY, AND ASSISTANCE

SECTION IV: CASE STUDIES

SECTION V: FINANCIAL AND ECONOMIC IMPACTS

Preface

Shortly after Ali Farazmand and I finished our work on the *Handbook of Globalization, Governance, and Public Administration*, we began discussing future projects. Among many other things, Ali said that he was going to work on a second edition of the *Handbook of Crisis and Emergency Management* wherein I had contributed two chapters. I expressed a strong interest in the developing field of homeland security and felt that the literature was lacking a good practitioner and policy resource incorporating homeland security and disaster management. I thought that these should be treated as global problems incorporating many points of view to understand the challenges and opportunities and ultimately to reduce or eliminate destructive consequences for life, property, and economies. Subsequently, I submitted a book proposal to Jack Rabin, the then executive editor of the Public Administration and Public Policy Book series, and he and I had several in-depth conversations regarding how best to approach these subjects. The conclusion that we reached was that two separate volumes would be appropriate: one dedicated to homeland security; the other, more broadly focused, on disaster management in general.

A serious consideration of homeland security in the United States has only been underway since the terrorist attacks of September 11, 2001 that shocked the nation. Previously, the Department of Defense and the intelligence agencies worked somewhat independently to counter such threats. The creation of the Department of Homeland Security and the USA Patriot Act has provided new impetus for accumulation of studies and analysis focused on the terrorist threat more broadly conceived than military action and nation-state aggressors. A lot of this literature has been focused on government documents. Analysis of policy results and lessons learned has been sorely lacking.

What I envisioned was a comprehensive book dealing with national security and what it entails to defend a way of life and economic system in the face of opponents who are intent on inflicting personal and economic destruction on a society. This concerns border and transportation security, emergency preparedness and response, science and technology, information analysis, and infrastructure protection, among others. However, because these are not limited to the United States, I reached out for contributions and experiences from colleagues across the globe for contributions to this new handbook. The result is this reference work that is useful as a textbook to understand the interrelated issues of national preparedness, emergency response, disaster recovery, and threat mitigation in dealing with prevention and the aftermath of attempted and successful attacks. We rely on the concept of *praxis*, which combines theory and practice resulting in the practical application of learning from experience and applied theoretical scenarios. This handbook is a valuable means to communicate lessons learned among professionals in the field as well as a library resource.

I am most grateful to the contributors of the handbook not only for their valuable contributions to this work and their individual expertise but also for their considerable patience over the extended time since the call for proposals. It will be approximately two years from concept statement to the availability of the published handbook. This has taken intensive coordination and attention to many details. Frankly, it was beyond my ability to do it alone. Fortunately, in the beginning I had the assistance of Mary Fenney who helped immensely with organization of the database and spreadsheets relating to the distribution of the call for manuscripts. The support of my associate dean, J. Preston Jones, of the H. Wayne Huizenga School of Business and Entrepreneurship at Nova Southeastern University has been really invaluable including financial support when needed to advertise the call for manuscripts. And I have been blessed with a patient, understanding, and encouraging publisher, Rich O'Hanley at Taylor & Francis. It was only with all of their help that I was able to finally finish editing this project.

To conclude, I want to make special note of the passing of Jack Rabin. He encouraged me, inspired me, coaxed me, and believed in me, even though he had so many other authors in the field of public administration. The literature in the field today is what it is in large part because of his unceasing desire to expand the body of knowledge and his vision for the growing book and journal series dedicated to public administration and public policy. His presence and influence will be profoundly missed.

Jack Pinkowski

Introduction

The *Homeland Security Handbook* is intended to serve as a comprehensive reference work and theoretical analysis covering the interrelated issues of preparedness, response, recovery, and mitigation in dealing with the worldwide challenge posed by the increasing threat of terrorism. Our ambitious goals for this work are that, ultimately, such a collection of lessons learned and thoughtful analysis of the issues and challenges will lead to a workable policy that will contribute to prevention of needless loss of life, maintenance of sovereign democratic states, financial stability, and ultimately world peace. It affects a global community of all races, religions, and developed societies.

Certainly the terrorist attacks on the United States on September 11, 2001 were a tipping point for America in the challenge of the modern terrorist threat. It has led to substantial changes in the American way of life and continues a robust policy debate in responding to and preventing future attacks, no matter where the protagonists or their funding may originate. The response to homeland security must be a multidisciplinary approach that involves various perspectives, assets, and skill sets. It is an evolving discipline that will benefit from collaboration and cross-information comparisons by sharing experiences and approaches across disciplines. Until now, there has been no single point of reference to serve such sharing of accounts and lessons learned. The *Homeland Security Handbook* meets this need and presents real-world experiences on the part of practitioners, as well as analysis and policy proposals by academics.

Although focused principally on homeland security in the United States, cross-border issues and foreign accounts are also included as they provide real-life examples and affect immigration, international travel, and the capacity for inter-diction and prevention. The more the issue of homeland security becomes a global dialog the better all countries will be in cooperating and identifying behaviors and organizations that can offer safe harbor to protagonists. This will lead to better understanding and prevention, which will help us all.

The chapters in the handbook are divided into five sections of related chapters. In Section I, Introduction and Theoretical Constructs, the contributions to the literature include a reflection on where we are in this discipline and suggestions for future developments in terms of policy. We include an overview of the worldwide threat of terrorism and historical trends that have led to a significant change in American society in the chapter titled "The New Normal." In the contribution "Lessons Learned: A Comparison of the Uniform Militia Act of 1792 and the Homeland Security Act of 2002," the law that created the U.S. Department of Homeland Security (DHS) is juxtaposed with legislation for national defense shortly after the U.S. Constitution was adapted. A constraint for both models of national security is the federal system of government itself that stipulates limited roles for the national and subnational levels of government. The conclusion is that, when under attack, intergovernmental collaboration is a key challenge to effectiveness. Today, this also includes the required cooperation of private sector and nongovernmental organizations. Communication and coordination of disparate parts are still areas of preparedness and response plans that are in need of further development to achieve standardization while maintaining overlapping authority.

In "Homeland Security: 'A One-Stop Shop' Approach," the inherent inequities in historical patterns of law enforcement are highlighted. Suitable caution is advised regarding conclusions reached too quickly based on superficial patterns and racial profiling that have repeatedly had negative societal impacts in the past. The merger of local public safety efforts with national and local law enforcement authorities under the new umbrella agency (DHS) is challenged by previous criticisms wherein maintaining a separation of authority actually served the system of checks and balances that protects innocent minorities from biased overzealousness. Another area considering historical precedents deals with the complexity of contemporary issues to deal with terrorism in the face of the lack of policies for specific issues that are germane today regarding the impact on immigration and national borders. "Securing Homeland Security: Immigrant Responses to State and Citizenship" suggests that the most daunting challenge for the United States is its receptivity to immigrants and its open, perhaps porous, borders. Globalization has facilitated worldwide information and monetary exchange and it also serves terrorists who can easily infiltrate liberal societies under the cloak of assimilation. Although tightening border immigration policy is warranted, past disparate impact has been shown by governmental policies resulting in negative effects on indigenous populations although intended for immigrants.

Border policy regarding immigration and homeland security is particularly relevant in the southern states with extensive coastline and miles of international land borders. In "Homeland Security Agencies in Selected Southern States: Case Studies in Politics, Organizations and Policies," the different perspectives of agencies depending on organizational focus and locus in the federal system are examined. The conclusion is that no matter the difference in state structure and the lead agency, ultimately, the response in a crisis situation will depend on the federal agency's lead. Consequently, state homeland security agencies must be linked and coordinated with the Federal Department of Homeland Security including financial resources and contingency plans. This may best be achieved through regional security zones that supersede traditional state boundaries. But it confronts the constitutionally defined roles of traditional federalism.

Section I concludes with a chapter titled "Homeland Security: Emerging Discipline, Challenges, and Research" that attempts to frame the context for future research in the policy and management arenas. The spectrum of potential disciplines involved with homeland security is extensive and its development must be multi-disciplinary. The chapter explores possibilities for future studies in the field and significant areas for investigation and offers suggestions for several research questions.

In Section II, Terrorism, Extremist Movements, and Weapons of Mass Destruction, we explore specific examples of threats to homeland security and the challenges associated with them. "Understanding New Global Multicellular Terrorism" asserts that terrorism has fundamentally changed in that a multinational presence of organized terrorism relies on globalization and technological progress to transcend geographical constraints. This has included support from outwardly appearing legitimate international charities for financial dealings. Even if the leadership and chief protagonists of al-Qaeda are eventually rooted out, its methods of using terrorism to spread a cause are likely to continue because they rely on using liberal Western societies against themselves. This includes vulnerable borders, openness to immigration, permissiveness regarding freedom of expression and religion, and inadequate antiterrorism surveillance because of general opposition to "the police state" and "big brother."

International maritime terrorism, as differentiated from maritime piracy, and coordinated terrorist movements in Southeast Asia are the subject of "The Abu Sayyaf Group and Maritime Terrorism." And organized terrorism on the African continent is highlighted in the chapter, "Promise and Perils of Politicized Islam in Africa." These are seen as attempts by Muslim countries in the Middle East to reestablish religious domination in the former Islamic empire. They point to the financial strength of oil-rich nation states as a significant aspect of the politicized spread of theocracy. Defending the American homeland and understanding the terrorist threat need to begin with understanding the driving forces behind the politicized theological as well as secularist movements.

Terrorism, ecoterrorism, and broader threats to the environment are described in the context of weapons of mass destruction in "Environmental Terrorism: A Weapon of Mass Destruction for the Future." Because the natural environment may connect people to the land and to their culture, to damage the environment is to inflict lasting impact on a way of life. In the terrorist mindset, the destruction of the environment is merely collateral damage in a war. It serves as a political hostage just as well as the innocent victims who taken by force to publicize demands. Another area of the potential for widespread pain and suffering relates to pandemics and animal-borne infectious diseases. These potential threats along with other chemical and biological agents pose new challenges for public health officials resulting in new needs for cross training and increased surge capacity. These are discussed in "Pandemics and Biological/Chemical Terrorism Attacks: A New Role for Disaster Mental Health." A key focus of this chapter is the recommendation for appropriate preparation to deal with the emotional response to such terror.

Because of the violence associated with terrorist acts, the social, psychological, and economic impacts resulting from the acts themselves, and the fear of anticipation of such acts, the viewpoint that one must meet force with force is proffered in the chapter "Terrorism as Societal Conflict Resulting in Response." But the launching of armies in distant lands to search for alleged weapons of mass destruction (WMDs) and the nebulous terrorist movement leaders may achieve little more than "striking at windmills." The distinct advantage of small bands of terrorist cells remotely controlled and coordinated cannot be efficiently eliminated by modern armies. And the enormous consumption of financial and material resources will take its toll on the defending aggressor in terms of its economy, public opinion of the leadership, and psychological impact. In the end, psychoterrorism and the price in terms of the defender's economy actually serve the terrorists' objectives.

In Section III, Planning, Prevention, Preparedness, Recovery, and Assistance, several concrete recommendations are offered as practical advice. These include "Profiling," with clear debate as to the cure being worse than the illness, coordinated medical response teams, in "Metropolitan Medical Response Systems: Coordinating the Healthcare Response to Terrorist Incidents," and the use of databases for knowledge management to contribute to safe public events, which represent very substantial economic impacts, in "eSAFE: The Knowledge Management System for Safe Festivals and Events."

A key component for coordinating medical and emergency response has been increasing in popularity and development for several years through formalized mutual aid agreements. However, homeland security expands the necessity and utility of such prearranged memorandums of understanding to cross-jurisdictional and multijurisdictional considerations, involving different levels of government to include federal funding for local governments. This trend mandates the use of the Incident Command System (ICS) or Incident Management System (IMS) in cases of multiagency response to effectuate a clear order of lines of authority and reporting. The original ICS in the U.S. Forest Service has evolved from the IMS in many different agencies to ultimately the National Incident Management System (NIMS), which is a component of the National Response Plan for the Department of Homeland Security.

In the case of local festivals and celebrations with significant economic impact, coordination must be focused on planning to assure safe events instead of relying on response to bad situations. With many private participants and stakeholders, this becomes much more difficult compared to emergency services professionals who can practice tabletop exercises and "what-if" scenarios. The chapter suggests a solution may be an online knowledge management database for event management professionals and others involved with safety and security concerning event planning. This involves knowledge sharing and ready availability of others' lessons learned and acquired expertise. In another example of preparedness education and information sharing, the DHS has created the Ready public information campaign. It is an example of reaching out to nonresponders and nonemergency services by contributing to heightened public awareness to ways that they can be more vigilant and self-sufficient. This collaborative partnership with government and the advertising community is described in "Collaborative Preparedness: The U.S. Department of Homeland Security's Ready Campaign."

Case Studies are the focus of Section IV. These include local governments in "Homeland Security Preparedness and Planning in City Governments: A Survey of City Managers"; an example of a foreign government in "Reorganizing for Homeland Security: The Case of Norway"; behavior modification as a result of changes in border immigration policy from "Behavioral Change and Border Crossing: The Effects of 9–11 on Cross-Border Traffic Five Years Later"; and the case of victim assistance described in "Continuity and Change in Disaster Response: Victim Management in the Case of the World Trade Center Collapse."

Results of the survey of city managers in communities of 100,000 and more residents indicate that there is no clear consensus on what threats they face. Consequently, local spending has focused on response preparedness instead of efforts at prevention or mitigation. But most city managers reported little local support for the acceptance of increased taxation to pay for greater preparedness. The case of Norway explores proposals for the reorganization of administration for homeland security from a flat hierarchy with a great deal of cross-communication on the peer level to one of vertical hierarchy, reminiscent of the command and control form that is embodied in the incident command response structure. Ultimately, Norway settled on a hybrid model. It is interesting that the 9/11 tragedy in the United States had little impact on the ultimate changes adopted in Norway. The authors attribute this to political factors because organization theory generally prescribes less hierarchical designs under more unstable conditions. This would call for greater decentralization of authority and less emphasis on formal structure because of the time required for communicating up the unity of command and down the span of control paradigm in classic bureaucracy. Unstable environments require flexibility and rapid decision making at the level of execution. The Agency Model that was adopted in Norway involves a hybrid to give agencies in the field semiautonomous status along with some coordinating power to superior ministries.

Coordination and involvement of many stakeholders also seem to be part of the findings of the participatory approach to evaluation in Afghanistan. At the same time, the declining health of the population is highlighted as an ancillary outcome of prolonged conflict and the resulting diminished infrastructure, which international aid is intended to mitigate. The case study points out a fatal flaw in any intervention strategy, that for the evaluation to be useful it ultimately must incorporate post-evaluation steps and constructive actions actually put to use to improve the deficiencies uncovered by the evaluation.

The chapter on modifications of behavior for cross-border traffic between the United States and Mexico highlights the terrorist watch strategy implemented after

9/11. In the case of traffic from Mexico, the policy shift was diametrically opposed to earlier thinking. This encouraged Mexican–American trade as a vital component of the North American Free Trade Agreement (NAFTA) and now it is one of vulnerability to terrorist infiltration across porous borders, which previously was not thought of as a national security threat. The result has been longer delays and a swing from a free-economy perspective to a police mentality on the southern border. There was a shift from pedestrian traffic to individuals stuck in vehicles at border crossings. This has resulted in increased air pollution and decreased retail business in border communities. No apparent change in unauthorized entry has been apparent although the behavioral shift in law-abiding border crossers has resulted in negative economic impacts. The conclusion reached is that the processes implemented may reinforce political positions but do not seem to provide solutions to the fundamental issues of homeland security.

The chapter on the immediate response to the collapse of the buildings of the World Trade Center on 9/11 identifies the ways in which response policy changed regarding victim assistance in the aftermath of the tragedy. In times of great uncertainty and changeable facts day by day, when many disparate agencies were involved in the disaster response and assistance, it is natural that many details may be unclear and the best approach is at best a fluid conception. Still with the large amount of public monies at stake, it is important to learn from the experience to better serve the victims in the future and minimize disaster relief lost to administrative inefficiency. Future questions resulting from this study include, for example, how future efforts will be coordinated, whether by formal mechanisms, informal sharing, or by emergent relationships. And, does the extent of information sharing affect decision making and benefit distribution?

In our concluding Section V, Financial and Economic Impacts, we include two chapters that quantify some of the costs resulting from the new focus on homeland security. Surprisingly, the chapter "Homeland Security Administration and Finance: A Survey of Texas County Officials" reveals a general sense of satisfaction of the self-perceived level of preparedness for homeland security that is being funded from reallocation of existing revenues and, to a limited degree, from external grants. It also reinforces previous findings regarding the unwillingness of the local populations to bear a greater tax burden to pay for it. The chapter "Border Closures in the Southern United States: Measuring the Economic Impact of a Sustained Crisis" looks at the hypothetical scenario of complete closure of the border with Mexico incorporating a multitude of competitive issues. The authors conclude that economic collapse may be more important in this context than weapons of mass destruction. The trade between the United States and Mexico is reportedly in excess of $250 billion and 85 percent of Mexico's manufactured goods are destined for the United States. Consequently, border policy is not unilateral but a subject of vital concern to both nations to protect national security and economic vitality for both sides.

Editor

Jack Pinkowski, PhD, has more than 30 years of experience as a successful business entrepreneur. To share this experience for the betterment of communities, he pursued graduate education later in life in the fields of public administration and government management. Now, Professor Pinkowski combines real-world experience with academic credentials that enhance teaching in the classroom and in applied research. His business entities have capitalized on global trade and local economic development. This includes the import–export trade with Southeast Asia, Central America, and Europe; manufacturing, sales, and distribution; retail outlets and marketing; and real estate investment and management.

In the academic realm, Professor Pinkowski is a principal researcher or facilitator on many local government projects including public/private economic development initiatives, strategic community visioning processes, transportation planning for urban redevelopment, and emergency management needs analysis, among others. He has been appointed to several local government and nonprofit boards and has been a consultant for local governments on these issues. Professor Pinkowski teaches the capstone course in the master of public administration (MPA) program and other masters level and doctoral courses at the H. Wayne Huizenga School of Business and Entrepreneurship at Nova Southeastern University in Fort Lauderdale, Florida, where his students are primarily working adults. He regularly teaches graduate courses on government budgeting, public financial management, organization theory, ethics, economic systems, economic development, and comparative government and economic systems. His research interests include various issues in public finance, economic development, globalization, international economic and organizational impacts of the Internet, the evolution of e-commerce and its impacts on state and local government finance, and other issues of public policy.

Professor Pinkowski earned his PhD from Florida Atlantic University in Boca Raton, Florida, a master of public administration (MPA) degree from Georgia Southern University in Statesboro, Georgia, and a bachelor of arts (BA) degree from Temple University in Philadelphia, Pennsylvania.

Contributors

Moye Bongyu
Department of Law and Political
  Science
Dschang University
Dschang, Cameroon

and

Department of Public Policy
Jackson State University
Jackson, Mississippi

Thom Curtis
Department of Sociology
University of Hawaii-Hilo
Hilo, Hawaii

Howard A. Frank
School of Public Administration
Florida International University
Miami, Florida

Heather Getha-Taylor
Department of Political Science
University of South Carolina
Columbia, South Carolina

John M. House
School of Business and Technology
  Management
North Central University
Prescott, Arizona

Clark Hu
National Laboratory for Tourism
  and eCommerce
  School of Tourism and Hospitality
  Management
Temple University
Philadelphia, Pennsylvania

Eric D. Johnson
Charleston Southern University
Charleston, South Carolina

Terrance A. Johnson (Deceased)
Sociology and Anthropology
  Department
Lincoln University
Lincoln University, Pennsylvania

Dale Jones
L. Douglas Wilder School of
  Government and Public Affairs
Virginia Commonwealth
  University
Richmond, Virginia

Kalu N. Kalu
Department of Political Science and
  Public Administration
Auburn University Montgomery
Montgomery, Alabama

Per Lægreid
Department of Administration and
    Organization Theory
University of Bergen
Bergen, Norway

Mathew McElroy
Institute for Policy and Economic
    Development
University of Texas at El Paso
El Paso, Texas

Tatah Mentan
Institute for Global Studies
University of Minnesota
Minneapolis, Minnesota

DeMond S. Miller
Department of Sociology
Rowan University
Glassboro, New Jersey

Carlos Olmedo
Institute for Policy and Economic
    Development
University of Texas at El Paso
El Paso, Texas

Ronald W. Perry
School of Public Affairs
Arizona State University
Phoenix, Arizona

Jack Pinkowski
H. Wayne Huizenga School of Business
    and Entrepreneurship
Nova Southeastern University
Fort Lauderdale, Florida

Thomas E. Poulin
Department of Urban Services and
    Public Administration
Old Dominion University
Norfolk, Virginia

Pradeep Racherla
National Laboratory for Tourism
    and eCommerce
School of Tourism and Hospitality
    Management
Temple University
Philadelphia, Pennsylvania

Christopher G. Reddick
Department of Public
    Administration
University of Texas at San Antonio
San Antonio, Texas

Jason D. Rivera
Liberal Arts and Sciences
    Institute
Rowan University
Glassboro, New Jersey

Synnøve Serigstad
Department of Administration and
    Organization Theory
University of Bergen
Bergen, Norway

Robert W. Smith
Department of Political Science
Clemson University
Clemson, South Carolina

Dennis L. Soden
Institute for Policy and Economic
    Development
University of Texas at El Paso
El Paso, Texas

Scott C. Somers
Department of Technology
    Management
Arizona State University
Mesa, Arizona

Glenn L. Starks
Department of Political Science
Georgia Southern University
Statesboro, Georgia

Steven D. Stehr
Department of Political Science and
 Criminal Justice
Washington State University
Pullman, Washington

Nathaniel A. Wilkinson
Sociology and Anthropology
 Department
Lincoln University, Pennsylvania

Joel C. Yelin
Liberal Arts and Sciences Institute
Rowan University
Glassboro, New Jersey

INTRODUCTION AND THEORETICAL CONSTRUCTS

I

Chapter 1

The New Normal

Jack Pinkowski

CONTENTS

Introduction

The *new normal* refers to the establishment in the national psyche of an awareness of vulnerability to terrorism and a willingness to accept the individual burdens necessary to meet the challenge of homeland security. This extends to personal inconveniences, additional waiting times, greater scrutiny of all kinds of activities, and increased skepticism about apparent innocence. Examples of ways in which daily life has changed in America pervade our society. For instance, we now accept that there will be long lines and the possibility of personal searches at airports and cross-border checkpoints [1]. Citizens and visitors are inconvenienced in many activities based on identity checks and restrictions on entry. Previously, open buildings such as historical sites and sightseeing attractions are now subject to restricted access or even closed to visitors. We now have to pass through metal detectors and offer our bags and pockets to be searched at guarded entrances to many public facilities. New concrete barriers have been placed surrounding buildings to prevent possible destruction from vehicle bombers [1]. Entire streets have been closed to traffic for the same reasons. There is a heightened awareness of the potential danger associated with unattended packages that include luggage but is extended to restrictions on sending a carton through the U.S. mail. Gone are the days when we could just drop them off at unattended mailboxes. The concern with security extends to how international freight is shipped and inspected. There is a new vulnerability in advanced economies from shipments that originate in far-off lands where there is little ability for the recipient nation to control the remote steps in the global supply chain [1,2].

Collectively, the need for increased vigilance has resulted in a historic increase and realignment in the federal bureaucracy to create the Department of Homeland Security (DHS), principally concerned with borders, immigration, transportation, and emergencies [3–5]. The new normal involves security review and personal searches to join large public gatherings such as sporting events. To identify those who may pose a threat, we have new technology invading our privacy in the form of facial recognition cameras utilizing biometrics when we are on streets and in public places [1,6]. There is now a long list of prohibited items for entrance to many public venues such as arenas, Times Square on New Year's Eve, the Super Bowl, and other celebrations. This even extends to commemorating our democracy on the Fourth of July. Some have even asserted that democracy encourages terrorism [7]. People who disagree with majority rule may resort to terrorism because they feel that the right to vote and freedom of speech has not resulted in enough political power to win over the establishment to their views.

Americans and citizens of free societies everywhere seem to be willing to accept governmental imposition as a new normal even if it extends to personal liberties. The First Amendment to the U.S. Constitution guarantees freedom of speech but making any untoward remark, even in jest, at an airport about hijacking or terrorism will result in detention and interrogation. In the aftermath of 9/11 all travelers face stricter airport security measures that impinge on these rights [8]. The Fourth Amendment protects against unwarranted search and seizure but under the new normal we accept personal searches and its invasion of privacy [1]. We need to prove our identity in many more routine circumstances.

More than 500 men are being held at the U.S. Naval Station Guantanamo Bay in Cuba without judicial process even though the Fifth Amendment prohibits incarceration without criminal charges being filed [9]. And the Sixth Amendment guarantees speedy and public trial with assistance of counsel for ones defense. Even the Geneva Convention provides protection of prisoners of war that is not being observed at Guantanamo Bay, and possibly other secret locations around the world [1]. The courts initially ruled that detainees have no constitutional rights but subsequent decisions challenge that ruling and the Supreme Court may be the ultimate arbiter of executive branch authority in this case [9]. The new normal has resulted in bending the rules and new interpretations of what constitutes probable cause regarding constitutionally guaranteed freedoms and rights in America [3,4,6,10].

Unauthorized wiretaps now seem to be acceptable if there is a suspicion of terrorism [1]. The free society that the United States is known for has become less free. Yet it is apparently generally accepted on a daily basis. A big part of this lack of universal abhorrence of such gross violations of democratic rights must be due to lack of understanding of just who the enemy is and a willingness to cooperate with the U.S. government's declared Global War on Terror (GWT) even if the threat is nebulous and the enemy ill defined. The fear is real and we realize that open, democratic societies are particularly vulnerable. Although many nations join the United States in condemning the terrorist attacks of 9/11, there is a substantial fear among the international community that the massive and unilateral response by the United States presents a fundamental challenge to international law [11]. It also represents a challenge to our own laws.

The Tipping Point for the United States

Certainly, the new normal is due in part to the shock of 9/11 on the United States. The actions of a small group of Islamic extremists were successful in destroying the World Trade Center on September 11, 2001. After that event, perhaps we moved from the post-cold-war era into the Age of Terror; everything has changed [12]. The perpetrators of the 9/11 attacks on the World Trade Center cited Islam as the inspiration for their attacks [13]. But Islamic extremists struck the same towers before, in 1993, and six people died as a result of that bombing. Yet the result of that extremists' attack was without the same impact on the national consciousness or perception of national vulnerability as we have seen following 9/11. Even though that assault resulted in a six-floor-large hole in the immediate vicinity of the underground blast, the buildings remained standing with little long-term impact. It actually had the effect of buoying confidence in the structural integrity of the World Trade Center buildings [14]. In 2001, the Osama bin Laden-led plotters would learn a valuable lesson in how to use the initial event as a precipitating force to cause cascading greater destruction. It would become more than they imagined a small group could inflict [11].

In the previously most deadly terrorist event ever committed on U.S. soil, April 19, 1995, a truck bomb destroyed the Alfred P. Murrah federal building in Oklahoma City, Oklahoma, killing 168 citizens and injuring hundreds. Property damage was assessed in hundreds of millions of dollars. The FBI classified that incident as a known act of terrorism and it attracted considerable public attention. But it too did not engender the kind of shift in public opinion concerning national vulnerability as that which grew after 9/11. In both incidents, Oklahoma City and the World Trade Center in 1993, the protagonists were eventually hunted down by law enforcement and arrested. Timothy James McVeigh and Terry Lynn Nichols, both Americans, were charged with the Oklahoma City bombing. Ramzi Ahmed Yousef, the alleged mastermind of the World Trade Center bombing, and 14 suspected terrorists were foreigners. In the 9/11 assault, the attackers all died in pursuit of their objective. But after 9/11, the dialog turned to a worldwide network of support instead of local splinter groups or individuals capable of actions leading to great destruction.

Both incidents were intended to instill terror and take many innocent lives. But they pointed out our vulnerability to such actions both from our own citizens and others from outside the country. So we have come to reassess our readiness concerning preparedness. We have new concerns for the identification of individuals as well as groups who are intent on using terror for their own means in the name of a cause. The new normal is a result of an appreciation that innocent individuals are at great risk. The great military might of the United States and its geographical isolation from much of the world that had experienced turmoil previously are no longer enough to ensure the security of the country and its citizens [12]. To stop terrorists, domestic and foreign, it requires more attentive and vigilant citizens who must cooperate with law enforcement rather than merely relying on the ability of the criminal justice system to do the job alone.

The New Threat

Civil Defense concerning national security in the United States used to be predicated on the model of attack by organized state actors utilizing overwhelming force against the country [5,15,16]. It did not account for primarily individual actions, suicide protagonists, or non-state combatants. The former defense paradigm presumed that the intended targets of lone individual actions would be other persons or focused objectives, unless they were covert military operatives, but not widespread destruction or devastation. During World War II, German infiltrators had spent years in the United States and made extensive plans to destroy key infrastructure across the nation [17]. The saboteurs were convicted and put to death under the legal description of enemy combatants instead of prisoners of war (ibid.). This established the different treatment that the country would take regarding state-directed terrorism that has led to the new challenge to traditional civil liberties [1,18].

Homeland security is different from national defense, which involves maintaining military forces around the world to facilitate actions against governmental authorities, armies, and organized militaristic factions. Homeland security involves defensive measures, such as hardening potential targets and more intensive screening of passengers and immigrants. It also extends to proactive measures wherein transnational terrorists are monitored and identified in their home countries, including dispatching the U.S. military to their turf as in Iraq and Afghanistan. Transnational terrorism impacts the United States as both state victim and as a fertile ground for raising funds to support violent groups against U.S. allies and innocent civilians elsewhere around the world [17].

Most civilians never experience the terror or the possibility of death, their own and others, in war as soldiers do. But those who died or were injured in the World Trade Center and in the Murrah federal office building were just ordinary people going about their routines. Now ordinary folks, even bystanders at tragic events, have personally experienced the horror akin to war. The GWT makes all people citizen-soldiers in the GWT. With that comes a greater personal appreciation that the terror is real. Citizens are asked to accept sacrifices in personal freedoms as citizen-combatants to achieve greater security in the face of the enemy whose identity is now so imprecise. Essential to acceptance of the new normal is the desire to protect and perpetuate the American way of life.

But because we do not have a profile of the antagonists, the enemy remains unclear and hard to identify. We have seen that they can include homegrown individuals and coordinated groups and can be either domestic or foreign. Among the untrained citizen-soldiers this has led to greater suspicion and perhaps greater tendency for accusations of "guilt by association." Some have posed the threat as "terrorism versus democracy" calling for a unique "liberal state response" [19]. Other free societies have been dealing with the threat of terrorism for many years resulting in counter-terrorism policies in countries such as Belgium, Britain, France, Germany, Ireland, Israel, and Italy [20].

But now, homeland security has become a new issue for the United States that specifically focuses on threats in North America and countermanding potential violence from any quarter. The intention is to preserve and protect democratic freedoms and citizens from personal harm and organized violence such as terrorist acts. It also includes purposeful disruption of the economic system and its vitality, which extends to critical infrastructure.

The new threat includes widespread fear and a cascading economic impact throughout the country. Ultimately, the economy is just as much victim as the individuals killed and maimed [21]. Growing poverty and the gap between advanced economies and the third world have led many to desperation, which has been cited as an impetus for new terrorist recruits [22].

When faced with change, even cataclysmic change, people have always been asked to accept the new direction instead of maintain status quo. History is replete with convulsions, revolutions, schisms, reinvention, and new regime politics. A reasonable question to understand the current state of affairs and the new normal that we apparently are willing to accept is to consider: How did we get to where we are? What makes the United States and its capitalistic economy the target now? The quick answer as to why the United States is so hated and why Islam is so feared is that "the United States is hated because it is feared, while Islam is feared because it is hated" [11]. But we need to frame these issues with greater depth to understand such simple answers. Who are the enemies? What significant actions or trends have been going on heretofore worldwide? And, perhaps, what have we done about them?

Past Accounts of Terrorism on American Soil

Terrorism as a method of violence that serves political motives is not new. As one example of political motives, anarchists in 1914 precipitated World War I at Sarajevo. In one interpretation, World War I was a manifestation of the Ottoman influence against the British Empire in an Islamic Holy War [12]. Nevertheless terrorism has become a worldwide phenomenon. The terrorism in America that inflicts death and destruction is not new either. Long before the United States entered a new era of homeland terrorism by foreign aggressors on September 11, 2001, the pattern of murdering innocents and even suicidal behavior in the name of a cause was an established political strategy [23].

Nineteenth century America has several examples of organized terrorism. The Molly Maguires were a group in support of the Irish labor movement in the coal regions of Pennsylvania that carried out a campaign of intimidation and murder against anthracite coal mine owners in the 1860s and 1870s [24,25]. The Ku Klux Klan had been targeting blacks in the name of white supremacy in the southern states since before the civil war [25]. And even earlier, there were attacks and murders by colonists and by Native Americans that were designed to terrorize and promote political causes. Groups in favor of Puerto Rican independence resorted to violence in the 1950s [26].

The turbulent 1960s had many examples of violence and killing in the name of a cause. The Minutemen in the 1960s practiced terrorism against alleged communists and traitors. Other groups in the 1960s that used violence for political motives, some of which constituted hate crimes, included the Palestine Liberation Organization (PLO), the Jewish Defense League (JDL), the Black Panthers, the Weather Underground, and the Red Army Faction [27]. They shared a theme of anarchy and revolutionary violence [25,26]. Airplane hijackings and associated bomb threats were a regular feature of the evening news in the 1960s following the Cuban revolution.

The kidnapping of heiress, Patty Hearst, in 1974 highlighted the violence and planned bombings organized by another revolutionary group, the Symbionese Liberation Army (SLA). In the 1990s we saw other hate groups that advocated violence including murder by the White Supremacists, the Aryan Nation, The Convenant, the Sword and the Arm of the Lord (CSA), and the White Patriot Army [28].

What is new is the spread of the Middle-Eastern brand of terrorism and Islamic jihad to American soil. The motivation for terrorism is not solely religious zealotry on behalf of extremist organizations. It includes personal vendettas, ideology and rebellion, brainwashing, and hostage taking. Many lone actors have perpetrated terrorist crimes on targeted individuals or groups as hate crimes [28]. Ted Kaczynski (aka. Kazinski), the Unabomber, had a personal vendetta against industry, as the embodiment of the negative consequences of the Industrial Revolution and technology (Unabomber's Manifesto) [25]. The actions of a lone bomber, Eric Robert Rudolph, at the Atlanta Olympics in 1996 turned out to be an individual who was opposed to abortion as against fundamental religious beliefs [25,26]. The paradox in such examples is that these actions frame the argument that in the perpetrators' minds it is justified to take innocent life to protest the taking of innocent life. Now we have seen those willing to take their own life as well if it causes much greater harm to others, including society and its institutions.

The earlier terrorists' acts in America were against targeted groups and individuals, not indiscriminant victims. We have seen that even individuals with the right knowledge and access can be effective from the perspective of instilling widespread fear, even if not annihilation. Some perpetrator, still unknown, sent anthrax through the U.S. mail in 2001 to members of Congress, news anchors, and various public figures to spread terror for an apparently personal vendetta [3,25]. Single-issue terrorists obsessed with their focused issues today include, for example, Green Peace; People for the Ethical Treatment of Animals (PETA); and anti-abortion proponents. During prohibition and continuing their influence for decades, the Mafia and organized crime have employed terror for personal economic gain [29]. The Mafia embodies a very strong internal code amongst a small circle of confidants and promotes a basic distrust of everyone else. They believe they have to take advantage of everyone outside of their immediate family because they consider the outsiders to be intent on taking advantage of them [30]. These movements have characteristics and attributes that can help us understand today's international terrorists. They have a strategic component as well as a psychological basis regarding aberrant behavior [23]. The culture of ones surroundings and the strength of family bonds influence how we view others and our perception of their aggression toward us [31].

Today, the American threat runs the gamut from indiscriminate publicity-seeking murderers, to lone actors with specific targets, and state-aided terrorist organizations. State-sponsored and state-supported terrorists cross over sovereign borders [19,32]. Now state terrorism and political violence have the intention of using global psychology on the entire society by instilling fear of annihilation from weapons of mass destruction (WMD) [29,33,34]. The danger of a small handful of people with their hands on the components for nuclear weapons, the mother of WMDs, which could destroy whole cities, has been known since the beginning of the Nuclear Age. Still today, small quantities of dangerous material can enter the country largely undetected [35]. State-sponsored terrorist groups that seek to acquire and deploy WMDs for use against civilian targets are perhaps the greatest threat to the world today [36].

Terrorism as a Global Movement

The United Nations first addressed the issue of terrorism in 1972 [20]. Combating terrorism has proved to be a difficult challenge. Nation-states can sponsor non-state actors to carry out terrorist actions in other countries, across international boundaries. Ideological terrorism has been perpetrated in many regions of the world including Europe, e.g., Germany, Italy, Ireland; in the Middle East [23,28,31–34], in Latin America; in East Asia; and on the African continent [32,23]. The PLO spread terrorism worldwide with the support of the Soviet Union in the 1970s [19]. In the approach advocated by Karl Marx in breaking the chains of oppression by violent means the modern day terrorists believe that their intense desire for change necessitates violent behavior [29,37].

The hijacking of an Israeli airliner in 1968 by Palestinian terrorists has been cited as the advent of the modern era of international terrorism [32]. The "Great Terror" of the French Revolution first gave rise to the term "terrorist," which now pales in comparison to modern day threats to national security, democracy, and the future of pluralistic societies everywhere [1,38,39]. Robespierre led a Reign of Terror in the eighteenth century and defended the use of terrorism against the enemies of democracy to suppress internal and external threats to the new government [27,40].

Around the world there are nationalist terrorists who seek self-determination, such as in Chechnya; ideological terrorists who seek to change the entire political, societal, and economic systems, such as al-Qaeda; and religiopolitical terrorists, such as Hezbollah and Hamas [19,32]. In World War II, the Nazis in Germany inflicted state-sponsored terrorism against the Jews in Warsaw, Poland [40]. The German blitzkrieg amounted to waging a war of terror on the citizens of London, England [39]. Stalin led a brutal state terror campaign in Russia to impose communist rule [27]. In the twenty-first century organized terror takes many forms, both domestic and international.

Incidents of terrorism and organized political violence are recorded in many disparate countries, for example, many of the Arab states, Algeria, Argentina, many countries in Asia, Australia, Germany, India, Italy, Northern Ireland, Libya, Pakistan, South Africa, countries in South America, and Spain [38,41–44]. Extremists believe that they can affect change by gaining attention through terrorism. As a global movement, it followed dissatisfaction of nonviolent methods in Russia in the nineteenth century [23,45], in the twentieth century in Ireland [44–48], and in the Israeli–Palestinian struggle that continues to this day [45,49].

In March 1995, the Japanese religious sect, Aum Shinrikyu (aka. Aum Shinrikyo), was responsible for the Sarin nerve gas attack on the Tokyo subway system.

Cults are known to copy the examples set by others and may be even more dangerous than the originators [50]. One outcome of that attack is that the Washington DC Metro has now been equipped with chemical weapon sensors, the first subway system in the world to do that [18]. The Tokyo attack resulted in more than 5,000 innocent victims exposed to the deadly agent, 12 of whom died as a result [25,41]. The domestic terrorist's attack was directed against the Japanese government.

The Tokyo subway incident called attention to the fact that small groups anywhere could have access to weapons and materials with which to make WMDs. It makes it relatively easy for a few to attempt to kill as many people as possible [51]. The Japanese cult has also expressed its intent to plot against the United States [17]. In March 2004, nearly 200 people were killed and more than 1,000 were wounded when, according to the Spanish government, members of the Basque separatist group ETA coordinated the explosion of ten bombs at three of Madrid's train stations [52,53]. In July 2006, four British natives, alleged al-Qaeda operatives, coordinated bombing London's trains and busses with the intention of harming non-Muslims in Britain as a protest of Great Britain's troop involvement with the war in Iraq. This represents an evolution of extremists' movements utilizing terrorism around the world [43,48,49]. Global super powers are particularly desirable as targets because they are the beneficiaries and the proponents of globalization as an extension of capitalism [47,54].

But a new type of terrorism, which threatens the world, is driven by an ideology that is very strong in every culture and across cultures [29,55–57]. Religious fanaticism is dependent on its successful efforts to attract supporters. It now may incorporate a determination to inflict maximum civilian and economic damages on the infidels, or nonbelievers [21,58].

Religious Fanaticism

The communal strife between Muslims and non-Muslims is a centuries old struggle. The remarks of Pope Benedict the XVI in his lecture on "faith and reason" on September 12, 2006 at the University of Regensburg, Germany are further proof of the power of religious devotion to incite conflict in defense of one's beliefs. The pope was widely criticized in protest by Islamic politicians and religious leaders for reciting a passage from the fourteenth century Byzantine emperor Emanuel II Palaiologos. He viewed holy war, i.e., jihad, and forced-conversion "under the sword," as directly ensuing from Islam according to the teachings of Muhammad and said it was an irrational behavior that was contrary to God's nature. The fact the Muhammad's teachings were characterized as bad and inhuman rests in the contradiction that in following God anyone could behave irrationally. Prelates in the West Bank, Gaza, Mogadishu, Turkey, Pakistan, Afghanistan, Chechnya, and elsewhere called for violence by the Muslim faithful in response to the alleged blasphemy by the pope. Historically, even the Crusades of the twelfth century were motivated by earlier Catholic popes' attempts to defeat Islam [40]. It is representative of the centuries-old Christian–Western bias against Islam that dated from its birth in the seventh century. Still, one has to realize that both sides have extremists. The majority of Muslims and the majority of mainstream Christians are opposed to violence and are pluralistic. But most Islamic culture differs from other world cultures in that it rejects not only Western policies but also is opposed to religious tolerance [30].

The global jihad is a worldwide religious movement that expresses the goal of reestablishing past Muslim glory from "Morocco to the Philippines" [58]. This has given rise to transnational nationalism as a worldwide community of Muslims based on religion [59]. Islamist fundamentalism is a twentieth century phenomenon that purports to be the true voice of Islam [60]. The worldwide networks that support terrorism today are collections of links connecting isolated nodes of followers [58,61]. Globalization has facilitated this spiderweb structure and its effectiveness [41]. Because financing and control are remote and the actors so disbursed, it makes the paper trail more unclear, which favors the objectives of the organization to live on even if their suicide bombers do not. Terrorism today is an outgrowth of the earlier model of state-sponsored terrorism but now transcends sovereign states [29,44,54]. Although states that offer terrorist organizations safe harbor are a problem for the international community, the fact that terrorist organizations are both subnational and supranational means that formal sovereign-state support is merely one of many sources of funding for these organizations.

An example of cross-border support for religious fundamentalism is well illustrated by the case of Pakistan. The Mujahidin regime in Afghanistan concerned itself with power struggles among rival factions, including ethnic and religious groups— Pashtuns, Tajikis, Uzbekis, and Shiite Hazaras—which led to ongoing conflict in the society that was fueled by outside instigation from Iran and elsewhere [56]. Outside involvement from Pakistan led to the Taliban movement whose members came from Islamic schools there. The Taliban did not believe that the Mujahidin practiced the laws of Islam properly and called on Afghan refugees to return from Pakistan and Iran to form the kind of new Islamic state that they had fought for from the Soviet Communists (ibid.). But their efforts in turning Afghanistan into a true Islamic state did not overcome the anarchistic reality that has led to breeding ground for religious zealots who were raised in a culture of fighting with a violent passion for their religion. Islamist fundamentalism poses a threat to many countries because it preaches hatred and urges the destruction of infidel societies from within those societies themselves but it also advocates the takeover of Muslim countries by fundamentalists, as in Afghanistan [60].

The leadership of Pakistan provided principal support for Tajik rebels in Uzbekistan, which evolved into a source of support for the Pakistan–Taliban– al-Qaeda network [62]. Uzbekistan is one of five new countries that arose in Central Asia following the collapse of the Soviet Union: Turkmenistan, Uzbekistan, Kazakistan, Kirghizstan, and Tajikistan. Their individual cultures had been suppressed for decades [38]. The small Muslim principality of Chechnya, in Russia, for example, has a unique language and 7,000-year long history and established culture. But it struggled for its own identity under human rights abuses at the hands of the Russians. Consequently, these oppressed cultures are very open to support from anywhere to regain their identity.

It is no surprise that Osama bin Laden and al-Qaeda could find refuge and support amongst the leadership of Pakistan. Pakistan has been a breeding ground for militancy for decades, perhaps since its founding in 1947, resulting from its profound social inequities, repeated outside interference, and government policies [63]. Osama bin Laden has called for a holy war in his Fatwah urging Jihad against Americans because the United States insulted Islam by establishing military bases in the Holy Land of Saudi Arabia. The United States, he says, has occupied the holiest places to plunder the riches of the Arabian Peninsula, i.e., oil, and dictate to its rulers. He viewed this as a crime against Islam to which all devout Muslims have the duty to kill Americans to restore honor and dignity to the Middle East and Islam [13]. The principal purpose of al-Qaeda is to end the American occupation of the Arabian Peninsula [64].

Poor Muslims are being taught hatred of non-Muslims in some of the madrasahs in Pakistan and elsewhere [49]. Madrasahs (aka. madrasas), or Islamic schools, are allegedly responsible for training most of the world's terrorists including the 9/11 hijackers [13,61]. Such schools thrive because of abject poverty, impressionable youth, and religious conviction that instill a belief in a path to a better life for ones family through martyrdom. It also is a way that a poor man can educate his son, which might not be possible otherwise. Terrorist organizations have a systematic recruiting methodology that even addresses six–seven year olds in the indoctrination into their ideology [62]. The youth-bulge in some countries has contributed to joblessness and the attractiveness of political violence including terrorism [20].

Richard Clark, a national counter-terrorism expert for the National Security Council in the Clinton and Bush administrations, has characterized Osama bin Laden's efforts to drive the United States out of the Muslim world as essentially an effort to replace moderate Western regimes in Muslim countries with theocracies modeled along the line of the Taliban [51]. Jihadi groups have built strong relations with individual politicians, intelligence agencies, and various factions of divided governments [57]. Four-fifths of the Muslim-majority nation-states are ruled by nondemocratic regimes [57]. However, much of the superpower interference is motivated by the energy-rich resources of these countries [38].

In return for Saudi Arabian oil and support for the United States in the Middle East peace talks and in the U.S. confrontation with Iraq, the United States let the Saudis run their government in any way that they wanted, which resulted in the growth and export of Islamic militancy by Osama bin Laden and others. It deflected criticism away from their own regimes and toward the United States and Israel [55]. But Archbishop Demond Tutu has said that Washington has supported some of the world's worse dictators, who have followed wholesale policies of state terrorism [49].

Countries that perpetrated terrorism on their own citizens were supported by Washington in Latin America, Africa, Asia, and the Middle East in the name of anticommunism policy (ibid.). On the basis of earlier possibly errant judgment, or unintended outcomes of U.S. support for select regimes, such as Saddam Hussein's in Iraq and the Taliban in Afghanistan, the GWT must be especially wary to not create more terrorists in the states that allow cruelty, ignore moral principles, and human rights of their citizens. The United States has to be especially careful in its support of those countries that practice state terrorism or repress human rights at the same time it joins international efforts to punish them [39,49].

The clash of Islam and Christianity is not the only passionate religious fervor that has resorted to violence. Consider the Protestant–Roman Catholic violence in Northern Ireland [46,48], the Palestinian–Israeli conflict [20], and the Taliban's campaign against Indian Buddhism [56]. The American public has much to be wary of. Besides al-Qaeda there is Hezbollah and Hamas, and others that constitute demonstrated anti-American terrorist capability around the world [54].

Hezbollah claimed responsibility for the bombing of the U.S. Marines' barracks in Beirut in 1983 [25]. Yasir Arafat, chairman of the PLO headquartered in Beirut, awakened the Western world to international terrorism in the 1970s. He ordered the Black September terrorists in 1973 to kill two U.S. and one Belgian diplomat in the Saudi Embassy in Khartoum, Sudan where they were held hostage, which led to the U.S. no-concessions policy [51]. The Black September group held Israeli athletes hostage at the Summer Olympics in Munich in 1972 and massacred 11 of them [36]. These groups have shown that they are predisposed to endorsing terrorism against Westerners wherever they are.

Al-Qaeda operatives were involved in simultaneously bombing American embassies in Dar es Salaam, Tanzania, and Nairobi, Kenya in 1998 that killed more than 200 people [57]. Sudan, in the Horn of Africa, remains on the U.S. terrorist watch list as a state-sponsor of terrorism and is considered a key to combating terrorism in Africa and the Middle East [42]. Many Islamic groups have a presence in Sudan where there is a culture of humanitarian and human rights abuses. The crisis involving the brutal ethnic cleansing in Darfur is a representative of the nexus between chaotic and anarchistic societies and receptivity to Middle-Eastern radical groups where their training grounds may thrive. Africa has become "an enclave of Islamic extremism and anti-American sentiment" [57]. There have been many political movements based on ethnic separatism such as Bosnia in the former Yugoslavia and Kashmir in India for which the rise of terrorism serves to de-institutionalize democratic institutions [62].

The threat facing the world today is far greater than any one terrorist leader or any one religious movement. Terrorist operatives use many different approaches to achieve their objectives including ambushes, sabotage, kidnappings, antiaircraft missiles, hijackings, bombings, and suicide attacks [17,32,64]. The ultimate terrorist organization consists of "networks, franchises, and freelancers" [57]. The Arabic word, al-Qaeda, means a base or foundation that supports a column [63]. Such a column is the phalanx of volunteer soldiers whose sacred duty is to go forth anywhere Muslims are oppressed and further the cause of radical Islam. The common strategy of suicide campaigns is to compel democracies to withdraw military forces from the terrorists' homelands [64]. Al-Qaeda has been successful in recruiting locals to participate in attacks and carefully grooming operatives in sleeper cells [57]. Its network of largely autonomous cells makes the al-Qaeda organization particularly resistant to targeted removal of its leadership [10,17]. The central leadership of al-Qaeda is said to consist of no more than 30 senior officials although they have tens of thousands of followers [61]. The new normal encapsulates the fear of and willingness to combat threats from a small cadre of "shadowy figures in distant lands" [35].

The Clash of Cultures

To understand the new normal requires an understanding of the GWT in the context of cultural differences. The decline and fall of the Holy Roman Empire has been described as a confrontation between a mature and decadent empire and politicized religion [12]. Christianity was the radical sect who rallied against Rome [65]. Early Islam overthrew Byzantium. And the Hapsburg Empire faced the religious fundamentalist challenge from Martin Luther in the sixteenth century [12]. Samuel Huntington proposed that after the end of the cold war civilizations have replaced nations as the driving force of global politics [66]. Terrorism was used by early religious leaders to maintain control by warning that departure from beliefs would lead to unimaginable terror. Throughout history many cultures have had a reputation for violence, including the Tartars, Huns, Romans, Barbarians, and Jewish Zealots in the first century [50].

The view today is that to achieve desired change requires violent actions against a society, a culture, and a way of life. The economic culture encompasses the beliefs, attitudes, and values that bear on economic activities [67]. Western culture incorporates economic success in its value system. The "age of reason" that began in France in the eighteenth century established the idea that a successful society is one that patterns behavior on the rationality of man [68]. The concept of "laissez faire" embodies government noninterference to give free reign to the market [69]. But what if your world view is encapsulated in your religious beliefs and you abhor capitalism and the economic market as the epitome of decadence?

Perhaps the American ethos is blind to this additional world view. For a long time we have been on a worldwide march to spread our culture through our business institutions. A significant contribution to the postwar expansion was the symbiotic relationship between big business and American government policy. General Motors president, Charles Wilson, is famous for saying before Congress: "What's good for General Motors is good for the U.S." It literally meant that America was pro-business and it led many to believe that American business was also good for the world.

The age of globalization has provided new power for hegemony of the United States through the global economic policy managed by the International Monetary Fund, the World Bank, and other international financial institutions that "put the interests of Wall Street ahead of that of the poorer nations that they serve" [70]. Transnational Nongovernmental Organizations (NGOs) are the facilitators of economic movement both for positive change and development as well as for clandestine money-raising to fuel partisan terrorism [11,60].

The consumption economy and consumerism culture of the United States was the driving force for attempts at the McDonaldization and Disneyization of the world [71–74]. The same phenomenon, that is replication and duplication of sameness no matter the cultural circumstances, has been ongoing within the United States throughout the postwar era. Wal-Mart has displaced family stores and independent pharmacies. McDonalds and a few competitors have all but eliminated the independent burger joint. Pizza chains have become routinized and nondistinct. There appears to be a Walgreens or Eckerd (or both) on every corner, along with a Starbucks in every shopping center. They take the place of the family druggist and neighborhood coffee shop. Americans themselves have been victimized by consumerism and the diminishing appreciation for uniqueness and genuine differences in choice. Restaurant chains are alike, frozen food offerings and convenience marketing contribute to spending less quality time with family and appreciating differences in our own society, let alone genuinely valuing others. The conversation-filled dinnertime is a thing of another era [72].

Globalization and the increasing power of the Internet for spreading worldwide ideology including corporate, social, and religious perspectives, also contributes to the imposition of Western ideas on indigenous cultures because the leaders have a vested interest in the maintenance of the status quo or promotion of change. This is not to say that one side is totally right and the other side is totally wrong. What it calls into question is the ability to be open to the other side's viewpoints. After all, the fast food restaurants and branded merchandise eventually fail or succeed in the foreign element only if the firms are successful in the market there. But it is the elevation of the market economy to such prominence that is offensive in other cultures. In the quest for sameness there is likely to be displacement. The uniqueness is exactly what gives character to different cultures. Once lost it cannot be regained. Americans have become desensitized to this phenomenon of which they are a victim. But in the Middle East especially, the effort to displace indigenous culture with Westernized commercialism is readily apparent.

The New Normal and the New Imperialism

Terrorism involves more than religious strife. It has resulted from a fundamental negative reaction to capitalism and embodies the unwelcome spread of American, industrial, capitalism, which is rejected by many less developed societies [59,73]. As such, its progenitor was the era of colonialism that took from resource-rich areas to fuel industrially talented but resource-dependent colonizers [74]. Americans should be uniquely qualified to understand this fundamental struggle as the cry of "taxation without representation" was the clarion call for the declaration of independence from the British crown.

The actions of Western states to occupy other countries have increased in recent years. The new imperialism has been defended as intervention, e.g., to halt ethnic cleansing in Kosovo; to increase stability in Sierra Leone; to liberate Iraq from an oppressive regime; and to capture Osama bin Laden and rout the Taliban in Afghanistan. Tony Blair justified this as not amounting to imperialism because the intervention is not intended to exploit economically; it intends to prevent the occupied state from harboring terrorism or from menacing its neighbors [12].

State aggression during the period of mercantilism was merely the effort of nation-states to subvert indigenous populations to serve their own economic self-interests. Consequently, American policy is misdirected if leaders think that the protagonist is one man or his followers. The issues and motivations are much deeper than Osama bin Laden, al-Qaeda, or the Taliban. These are just representative actors in a broader political resistance movement to globalization; Western oppression for the sake of Western corporate profits, culture, and domination. The attempts at imposition of Western democratic values on occupied societies, and so-called freedom, are still oppression of the subjects, albeit in the name of altruism and generosity. The successful societies are still imposing their will and values on the less technically advanced societies.

The root of the growth of fundamentalism is the encounter with Western culture, including many aspects, cultural foreignness, and modernism that present repercussions for traditional life in Eastern and Middle-Eastern cultures [56]. These encounters generally take the perspectives that the Islamic East is inferior to the West. Eastern cultures are very strongly based on their ethnic groups. The heterogeneity of Eastern cultures, which prefer to keep their own identity, is not the same as the Western concept of diversity and assimilation. Consequently, we have seen the attempts at domination of the Kurds and Shiite Muslims by the Sunni Muslims in Sadam Hussein's Iraq. In Afghanistan, the regime in Kabul had attempted to suppress the demographic balance that was kept under control during the communist time as part of the Soviet system [56]. Viewed in this context, it is easier to understand Saudi businessmen supporting terrorist organizations whose success would contribute to their own financial domination of the world economy, which would be further enhanced by diminished Western hegemony.

From this perspective, the resolution may be both economic as well as religious tolerance. Over the past 25 years, the standard of living has not advanced in the majority of Muslim-majority states but for many it has actually fallen [57]. Typical radical propaganda accuses the West as being responsible for their plight. But it is more a case of poor governance and inadequate protection of civil liberties and human rights that have allowed the extremists to thrive and spread their message.

Essentially terrorism today, the sort that has engendered the new concerns on the part of the American public, is related to political motives that use or threaten violence that are designed to have far-reaching psychological impacts, conducted by an organization with worldwide reach and networks that constitute non-state entities [44]. The effects of terrorism go beyond the state where the terrorism occurs. It demonstrates the global interdependence of nations. Terrorism can contribute to the overall distribution of political power; affect the civil liberties of citizens, the political behavior of the populace, and the prospects for continuation of violence [48]. It is the deliberate creation of a state of fear and exploitation using the threat of violence with impacts far exceeding those immediately victimized. It uses noncombatants as the near-term victims but the societal system as the ultimate target [54]. It is more than the jihad that makes global terrorism networks work. The strong social bonds among friends and relatives of terrorists assist them in financing and in hiding. They offer means of communications and support for training. A prime example of such a community of interest is the membership in the growing number of mosques in the Western world. These various influences and interconnections based on the social fabric constitute "human bridges" [58].

The rage against America in particular and Western societies in general is an outcome of the actions of the weak or authoritarian governments that has resulted in extreme and growing poverty, that may actually be supported by Western policy to maintain the status quo in the Arab and Islamic world to uphold a consistent and inexpensive supply of oil.

Conclusion

The essential challenge that we face is our own belief in our way of life as being superior to all others. That somehow anyone who would come to live in the United States would universally adopt the American way of life as the best in the world. The 9/11 attacks proved that assumption wrong as the terrorists lived here and plotted their actions for months or years but did not become pro-Western [57]. They were not dissuaded by the standard of living or the land of opportunity.

We still believe that we can fight a GWT by leading with the U.S. military might against the enemy. But it is the failing states where terrorists thrive that represent the greatest danger because they are breeding groups of recruits who follow the cause in part out of desperation [20,57]. When you have very little, you feel you have little to lose. The value of human life becomes diminished when you see so little regard for its preservation all around you. Even though the deliberate murder of innocent civilians is counter to every mainstream religion, even the Qur'an forbids taking a life, the articulation of the grievance that is instilled in the terrorist recruits is so strong that they are willing to violate normal moral rules in the name of the cause to redress the grievance for the sake of God [57]. From the perspective of the Middle-Eastern fanatics, suicide or death in battle is not a tragedy, and not the consequence of despair, but rightful if it serves the purposes of the greater cause [43].

Globalization has heightened in the less-developed world an appreciation for their plight. It involves susceptibility to "seductive pastimes of the West" [57]. Another viewpoint is that globalization has contributed to the migration of dreams and as the gap between expectations and achievements grows, so does a sense of deprivation that contributes to rising violence [47]. Devout followers of Islam are repulsed by America's materialism, racism, promiscuity, and feminism, which they view as vulgar and unacceptable in accordance with their teachings.

Imam Samudra, the leader of the Indonesian group that blew up a nightclub in Bali in 2002, reportedly said that they did so because he was disgusted by the "adulterous practices" of the white people that he saw there [63]. All terrorist groups believe that they are creating a more perfect world by purifying the world of injustice, cruelty, and other behaviors that they believe are antihuman while they themselves utilize cruelty in the form of indiscriminate killing and maiming innocent civilians. They persuade themselves that even their heinous crimes are justified and morally right because those that they aim to help are so deprived and helpless and have been made more so by the enemy aggressors who are stealing the very identity of the oppressed [57]. The West has been the historical enemy of Islam during the crusades, for the duration of mercantilism, all through colonialism, and the cold war [57]. Many cultures believe that globalization, transnational corporations, and international financial institutions are imposing capitalism and secular ideas on them and are attempting to exterminate traditional values.

Another remnant of the cold war is the stockpiles of enriched uranium and plutonium and scientists willing to profiteer on the black market from thefts at former Soviet nuclear sites. They represent a new threat in the potential for a dirty bomb that might become available to a rogue state or well-financed terrorist group [43]. The terrorist organizations that abhor technology would use it against modern societies just as they use the Internet for propaganda, financial solicitations, and communications with their far-flung cells [50].

The tools of empowerment for the population in the developing world are the same as in the West: clean drinking water, adequate sanitation, healthcare, food, and education. Because the United States has these tools, for the most part, in abundance, we find it hard to understand societies that are in such dire need of them. Although many communities in our own midst are lacking in these same empowerment tools, in the lesser-developed world, there is a growing sense of "being violated by the realization that they may be less than equal." They become angry, which can lead to violence [47].

The growing view of the United States as the Lone Ranger, self-arbiter of morals, entrepreneur of capitalism in which the world is both supplier and market, but not necessarily beneficiary, will continue to engender resentment and hostility as the gap between the haves and have-nots grows wider. Even well-intended U.S. policy has resulted in growing isolation of the United States, which erodes its position in the world. The liberation of Iraq from Sadam Hussein's reign that turned into the occupation of Iraq in the eyes of the Arab world is just an example of overstaying our welcome and failure to understand the human desire to maintain self-identity and culture and not to accept assimilation.

Globalization provides new breeding grounds for terrorism because it leaves people behind [47]. The market economy and the worldwide factory concept accept failure and the consequences of not being competitive. But those who fail in globalization do not accept the condition. As one consequence they can be more prone to join those who would do something about it by violent means, as a last resort. The public interest has become subordinate to the corporate drive for profits. When government becomes the protector of corporations instead of the protector of the basic needs of human beings, the global setting can spawn violence and terrorism [47].

The economic position of oil as crucial to the world economy has resulted in military policy to enforce its continued availability from the Middle East at all costs [64]. This has engendered much of the hatred in the Persian Gulf states who view the Western military force as an occupation. This is only going to change when we substantially reduce the dependence on Arabian oil and the necessity of defending its supply to the Western economies.

The new normal may appear to be a world of difference. But as the foregoing dialog has chronicled, it reflects behavior and results from developments throughout history. It does represent substantial differences for behavior and freedoms in American society today to defend against the current threat from terrorism. But the concept of homeland security does not speak to a solution. What has been presented here may answer some of questions posed in the introduction: "How did we get to where we are?"; "What makes the U.S.A. and its capitalistic economy the target now?"; and "What significant actions or trends have been going on heretofore worldwide?" But a clear recognition of "Who are the enemies?" is still nebulous. It is a multilevel threat that involves people, cultures, strategic objectives, public, and corporate policy, and the reactions to it.

But the answer to the final question posed, "What have we done about them?" is Not enough. We can accept the new normal and resign ourselves to accepting these changes, reduced freedoms, and increased financial burdens, along with growing hatred aimed at our culture in many parts of the world, as a consequence of our actions. Or we can address the real issues that relate to imposition of the market economy, insensitivity to indigenous culture, and the desperation of many people in the world regarding opportunity and education, which have made them susceptible to other choices offered to them by charismatic leaders. They appeal to faith and established dogma and advocate resorting to violence. The great wealth of the United States can be channeled better to address worldwide needs and concerns that in the end directly impact the American homeland. The new normal has made all residents of the U.S. citizen-soldiers in a GWT. But beneficial change can come from it only when those citizen-soldiers get nearer to understanding that they need to look at how they are perceived as citizens of the world and make appropriate changes in economic and military policy that make them better neighbors in the global village.

References

1. Purpura, P.P., *Terrorism and Homeland Security: An Introduction with Applications*. 2007, Amsterdam, The Netherlands/Boston, Massachusetts: Butterworth-Heinemann.
2. Flynn, S.E., *America the Vulnerable: How Our Government Is Failing to Protect Us from Terrorism*. 2004, New York: Harper Collins.
3. Kettl, D.F., *System under Stress: Homeland Security and American Politics*. 2nd edn. 2007, Washington, DC: CQ Press.
4. Nakaya, A.C., Ed. *Homeland Security*. 2005, Detroit, Michigan: Greenhaven Press.
5. Bullock, J. et al., Ed. *Introduction to Homeland Security*. 2nd edn. 2006, Amsterdam, The Netherlands/Boston, Massachusetts: Butterworth-Heinemann.
6. Torr, J.D., Ed. *Homeland Security*. 2004, San Diego, California: Greenhaven Press.
7. Rapoport, D.C., *Democracy Encourages Terrorism*, in *Terrorism Opposing Viewpoints*, Egendorf, L.K., Ed. 2000, San Diego, California: Greenhaven Press, pp. 73–76.
8. Egendorf, L.K., Ed. *Terrorism Opposing Viewpoints*. 2000, San Diego, Caliofornia: Greenhaven Press.
9. Leonnig, C.D., *Judge Rules Detainee Tribunals Illegal*, *Washington Post*. 2005, Washington, DC. p. A1.
10. White, J.R., *Defending the Homeland: Domestic Intelligence, Law Enforcement, and Security*. 2004, Belmont, California: Wadsworth/Thomson Learning.
11. Booth, K. and Dunne, T., Eds. *Worlds in Collision: Terror and the Future of Global Order*. 2002, Houndmills, Basingstoke, Hampshire/New York: Palgrave Macmillan.
12. Talbott, S. and Chanda, N., Eds. *The Age of Terror: America and the World after September 11*. 2001, New York: Basic Books.
13. Friedman, L.S., Ed. *What Motivates Suicide Bombers?* 2005, Detroit, Michigan: Greenhaven Press.
14. Ede, B. and Green, S., Eds. *Why the Towers Fell: An Exclusive Investigation into the Collapse of the World Trade Center*. 2002, British Broadcasting Corporation (BBC).
15. Waugh, W.L., *Living with Hazards, Dealing with Disasters: An Introduction to Emergency Management*. 2000, Armonk, New York: M.E. Sharpe.
16. Drabek, T.E. and Hoetmer, G.J., *Emergency Management: Principles and Practice for Local Government*. 1991, Washington, DC: International City Management Association.
17. Sauter, M.A. and Carafano, J.J., *Homeland Security: A Complete Guide to Understanding, Preventing, and Surviving Terrorism*. 2005, New York: McGraw-Hill.
18. Smith, N. and Messina, L.M., Eds. *Homeland Security*. 2004, Bronx, New York: H.W. Wilson Co.
19. Wilkinson, P., *Terrorism versus Democracy: The Liberal State Response*. 2001, London/Portland, Oregon: Frank Cass.
20. Bjorgo, T., Ed. *Root Causes of Terrorism: Myths, Reality, and Ways Forward*. 2005, London/New York: Routledge.
21. Enders, W. and Sandler, T., *The Political Economy of Terrorism*. 2006, Cambridge, England/New York: Cambridge University Press.
22. Hammond, A., *Economic Distress Motivates Terrorists*, in *Terrorism Opposing Viewpoints*, Egendorf, L.K., Ed. 2000, San Diego, California: Greenhaven Press, pp. 77–80.
23. Reich, W., *Origins of Terrorism: Psychologies, Ideologies, Theologies, States of Mind*. 1990, Washington, DC/Cambridge, England/New York: Cambridge University Press.

24. Pinkowski, E., *Lattimer Massacre*. 1950, Philadelphia, Pennsylvania: Sunshine Press.
25. Anderson, S. and Anderson, S.K., *Terrorism: Assassins to Zealots*. 2003, Lanham, Maryland: Scarecrow Press.
26. Hewitt, C., *Understanding Terrorism in America: From the Klan to Al Qaeda*. 2003, London/New York: Routledge.
27. Miller, D.A., Ed. *Terrorism*. 2003, San Diego, California: Greenhaven Press.
28. Ronczkowski, M., *Terrorism and Organized Hate Crime: Intelligence Gathering, Analysis, and Investigations*. 2007, Boca Raton, Florida: CRC Press.
29. Laqueur, W., *The New Terrorism: Fanaticism and the Arms of Mass Destruction*. 1999, New York: Oxford University Press.
30. Fukuyama, F., *History and September 11*, in *Worlds in Collision: Terror and the Future of Global Order*, Booth, K. and Dunne, T., Eds. 2002, New York: Palgrave Macmillan, pp. 27–36.
31. Harrison, L.E. and Huntington, S.P., Ed. *Culture Matters: How Values Shape Human Progress*. 2000, New York: Basic Books.
32. Hoffman, B., *Inside Terrorism*. 1998, New York: Columbia University Press.
33. Kushner, H.W., Ed. *Essential Readings on Political Terrorism: Analyses of Problems and Prospects for the 21st Century*. 2002, New York/Lincoln, Nebraska: Gordian Knot Books.
34. Maniscalco, P.M. and Christen, H., *Understanding Terrorism and Managing the Consequences*. 2002, Upper Saddle River, New Jersey: Prentice Hall.
35. Allison, G.T., *Nuclear Terrorism: The Ultimate Preventable Catastrophe*. 2004, New York: Times Books/Henry Holt.
36. Dershowitz, A.M., *Why Terrorism Works: Understanding the Threat, Responding to the Challenge*. 2002, New Haven, Connecticut: Yale University Press.
37. Marx, K.M. and Moore, S., *Communist Manifesto*. 1985, Chicago, Illinois: Gateway Editions.
38. Chopra, V.D., Ed. *Global Challenge of Terrorism*. 2002, New Delhi, India: Gyan Publishing House.
39. Primoratz, I., *Terrorism: The Philosophical Issues*. 2004, Houndmills, Basingstoke, Hampshire/New York: Palgrave Macmillan.
40. Houle, M.E., Ed. *Terrorism Opposing Viewpoints*. 2005, Farmington Hills, Michigan: Greenhaven Press.
41. Das, D.K. and Kratcoski, P.C., *Meeting the Challenges of Global Terrorism: Prevention, Control, and Recovery*. 2002, Lanham, Maryland: Lexington Books.
42. Rotberg, R.I., Ed. *Battling Terrorism in the Horn of Africa*. 2005, Cambridge, MA/Washington, DC: Brookings Institution Press.
43. Whittaker, D.J., *Terrorism: Understanding the Global Threat*. 2002, London: Longman.
44. Whittaker, D.J., *The Terrorism Reader*. 2003, London/New York: Routledge.
45. Crenshaw, M., Ed. *Terrorism in Context*. 1995, University Park, Pennsylvania: Pennsylvania State University Press.
46. O'Day, A. and Alexander, Y., Ed. *Ireland's Terrorist Trauma: Interdisciplinary Perspectives*. 1989, New York: St. Martin's Press.
47. Nassar, J.R., *Globalization and Terrorism: The Migration of Dreams and Nightmares*. 2005, Lanham, Maryland: Rowman & Littlefield.

48. Crenshaw, M., Ed. *Terrorism, Legitimacy, and Power: The Consequences of Political Violence.* 1983, Middletown, Connecticut/Scranton, Pennsylvania: Wesleyan University Press.

49. Gareau, F.H., *State Terrorism and the United States: From Counterinsurgency to the War on Terrorism.* 2004, Atlanta, Georgia: Clarity Press.

50. Sloan, S., *Terrorism: The Present Threat in Context.* 2006, Oxford/New York: Berg.

51. Naftali, T.J., *Blind Spot: The Secret History of American Counterterrorism.* 2005, New York: Basic Books.

52. Fox. *Madrid Train Station Blasts Kill 190.* 2004, March 11. Cited 2007; Available from: http://www.foxnews.com/story/0,2933,113887,00.html.

53. CNN. *Police Search for Madrid Bombers.* 2004. Cited 2007; Available from: http://www.cnn.com/2004/WORLD/europe/03/11/spain.blasts/.

54. Pillar, P.R., *Terrorism and U.S. Foreign Policy.* 2001, Washington, DC: Brookings Institution Press.

55. Benjamin, D. and Simon, S., *The Age of Sacred Terror.* 2002, New York: Random House.

56. Shay, S., *The Endless Jihad: The Mujahidin, the Taliban and Bin Laden.* 2002, Herzliya, Israel: International Policy Institute for Counter-Terrorism.

57. Stern, J., *Terror in the Name of God: Why Religious Militants Kill.* 2003, New York: Ecco.

58. Sageman, M., *Understanding Terror Networks.* 2004, Philadelphia, Pennsylvania: University of Pennsylvania Press.

59. Hershberg, E. and Moore, K.W., *Critical Views of September 11: Analyses from Around the World.* 2002, New York: New Press.

60. Elshtain, J.B., *Just War against Terror: The Burden of American Power in a Violent World.* 2003, New York: Basic Books.

61. Abuza, Z., *Militant Islam in Southeast Asia: Crucible of Terror.* 2003, Boulder, Colorado: Lynne Rienner Publishers.

62. Raju, A.S., Ed. *Terrorism in South Asia: Views from India.* 2004, New Delhi, India: India Research Press.

63. Burke, J., *Al-Qaeda: Casting a Shadow of Terror.* 2003, London/New York: I.B. Tauris.

64. Pape, R.A., *Dying to Win: The Strategic Logic of Suicide Terrorism.* 2005, New York: Random House.

65. Gibbon, E., *The Decline and Fall of the Roman Empire.* 1963, New York: Washington Square Press.

66. Huntington, S.P., *The Clash of Civilizations and the Remaking of World Order.* 1996, New York: Simon & Schuster.

67. Porter, M.E., *Attitudes, Values, Beliefs, and the Microeconomics of Prosperity,* in *Culture Matters: How Values Shape Human Progress,* Harrison, L.E. and Huntington, S.P., Eds. 2000, New York: Basic Books. pp. 14–28.

68. Sowell, T., *A Conflict of Visions: Ideological Origins of Political Struggles.* 2002, New York: Basic Books.

69. Smith, A., *An Inquiry into the Nature and Causes of the Wealth of Nations.* 1776/1981, Indianapolis, Indiana: Liberty Classics.

70. Stiglitz, J.E., *Globalization and its Discontents.* 2002, New York: W.W. Norton.

71. Bryman, A., *The Disneyization of Society*. 2004, London/Thousand Oaks, California: Sage Publishers.
72. Ritzer, G., *The McDonaldization of Society*. 2004, Thousand Oaks, California: Pine Forge Press.
73. Barber, B.R., *Jihad vs. McWorld*. 1996, New York: Ballantine Books.
74. Friedman, T.L., *The Lexus and the Olive Tree*. 2000, New York: Anchor Books.

Chapter 2

Lessons Learned: A Comparison of the Uniform Militia Act of 1792 and the Homeland Security Act of 2002

Thomas E. Poulin

CONTENTS

Introduction

At the end of the American Revolution, the new government began to debate the most effective means of protecting the nation from domestic and foreign threats, while simultaneously safeguarding the liberal democratic values the nation developed during the rebellion. The solution created by the First Congress was embodied in the Uniform Militia Act of 1792. During the first large-scale, defensive challenge faced by the nation, the War of 1812, the system proved largely inefficient and ineffective.[1] Consequently, after nearly three years of war the conflict ended without a conclusive victory, although the U.S. forces were fighting mainly on their home ground and had overwhelming numerical superiority.[2]

After the terrorist attacks of September 11, 2001, the present-day government began similar discussions on the most effective means of defending the nation, ending with the passage of the Homeland Security Act of 2002. This article examines parallels behind the two legislative acts, separated by almost two centuries, and examines the effectiveness of the Uniform Militia Act in preparing the nation for the War of 1812 as a means of predicting the ability of the Homeland Security Act to provide an effective framework for the defense of the nation through an intergovernmental collaborative approach.

The Uniform Militia Act of 1792

During the constitutional convention, the leaders of the fledgling republic engaged in a great debate regarding the proper roles of the federal and state governments. Having just vanquished a foreign monarchy they believed had held unbearable sway over their lives, few were willing to grant strong powers to the newly established central government for fear they might only be exchanging a foreign tyrant for a domestic one. The opposing views in this debate were expounded upon in *The Federalist Papers*, revolving around the philosophical argument of how best to provide the federal government sufficient power necessary for the provision of sound governance without infringing upon the rights of either the states or the individual. Few phases of the discussions were more heated than those revolving around the military. Great Britain had enforced its rule with its troops, and few Americans wanted to see a large standing military force on U.S. soil (Hill 1964, p. 8). Many legislators held dear the ideological view that America would always be safe in the hands of her citizen-soldiers. Finally, after much argument, Congress elected to divide military powers between the federal and state governments (Mahon 1960, p. 13).

The Second amendment to the constitution was illustrative of this ideal. The existence of a well-ordered militia was considered to be an adequate safeguard against the potential threats faced by eighteenth century America. The militia was viewed as an adequate defense against foreseeable threats, while simultaneously providing a diffusion of military power that lessened the possibility that the federal government would have sufficient armed forces to act in a preemptory manner. Congress viewed the primary role of the militia as being a guarantor of freedom, rather than as a potential enforcer of unpopular government policies (Hart 1998, p. 77). Consequently, the structure of the military was designed not to assure organizational effectiveness and efficiency, but carefully and deliberately to diffuse any military power that could be used in a coercive manner against the citizens of the United States.

In 1792, Congress enacted the Uniform Militia Act. The law was intended to provide guidance to the individual state militias so they would be sufficiently similar in structure and ability to be capable of coalescing into a single, effective entity in times of national crisis. The law called for each state to establish a militia structured along similar lines through an organization comprised of divisions, brigades, regiments, battalions, and companies (Mahon 1960, p. 19). Each state was to appoint an adjutant general to be responsible for the training of the militia using Baron Stueben's 1779 Rules of Discipline as the national training standard (Mahon 1960, p. 20). The law called for all free, white, able-bodied men between the ages of 18 and 45 to join the militia, providing their own arms and supplies (Mahon 1960, p. 19). Congress believed this law would create a national military force of 13 distinct units that, being structured, trained, and equipped in a common fashion, would be able to function as a single force when necessary. Although the intent of the Uniform Militia Act was to create a military force comprised of disparate units that could quickly be called into service in times of national crisis, such was not to be. The failure of the militia system to produce a coherent system of defense was due in large part to the Uniform Militia Act itself, which concluded with the phrase " . . . if the same be convenient (Mahon 1960, p. 19)." The Uniform Militia Act included no penalties for the states should they fail to comply with the act and the convenient phrase permitted each state to determine in what manner it would comply, should it choose to do so (Mahon 1960, p. 20).

The states responded to the Uniform Militia Act in different ways. In New Hampshire, the militia was organized precisely along the lines of the Uniform Militia Act, but the legislature directed that the militia could only be called out of the state with their consent (Mahon 1960, p. 22). Several states had such laws, and Congress responded to the perceived shortcoming by enacting the Calling Forth Act of 1792, authorizing the President to call the state militias into national service, but it failed to include any penalty to the states should they refuse to comply (Mahon 1960, p. 22). Each state legislature created its own militia act based upon its perceptions of the potential threat conjoined with what was thought to be the most appropriate means of responding to such crises. To retain civilian control over the military, officers in the New Hampshire militia had to have their commissions approved by the legislature, while in other states, officers were elected by the members of their units (Mahon 1960, p. 23). The Massachusetts Militia Act did not require members to obey orders, and merely recommended that they comply with the directives of their elected officers (Galvin 1967, p. 67). African-Americans were not permitted to be members of the militia in many northern states but in the south they served as support troops (Mahon 1960, p. 22). In many states, men could be exempted from militia service by paying a set fee or by hiring a substitute (Mahon 1960, p. 22). Federal laws included no enforcement powers, no funding for state militias, and offered little in the way of leadership. Consequently, the states felt little compunction to adhere to the guidelines established by Congress. Militia laws were enacted to guarantee the autonomy of state governments over their military units, and ideological values often won out over military concerns for efficiency and effectiveness (Hart 1998, p. 110; Hill 1964, p. 9).

In the late eighteenth and early nineteenth centuries, the regular army of the United States served primarily as guardians of the frontier. On the borders, they served as explorers and protectors. Along the seaboard, they served as engineers constructing defensive works along the coast. A large standing army was considered unnecessary. Congress believed the state militias could coalesce into a functional, unified force capable of withstanding any threat at a moment's notice. This belief was in some part due to the legend of the Revolutionary War minutemen. Many legislators viewed the minutemen of the revolution as self-disciplined, organized units comprised of well-equipped and well-trained men who were ready at a moment's notice, which had emerged from their communities without the need for government oversight or control when danger threatened (Duncan 1997, p. 28). This view ignored the fact that many of the minutemen were former members of the Royal Militia, created by the Massachusetts Militia Act of 1636, which created a mandatory, formalized system of organization, training, equipment, and discipline for the colonists to prepare them for military action when needed, and which was capable of mustering 30 percent of their forces within the first half-hour (Galvin 1967, p. 12; Whisker 1979, p. 8). Earlier, the abilities of the minutemen in the Revolutionary War were largely based upon the standards to which they had adhered in past years. Later in the war, newly created militia units were looked upon with less favor. Their role was largely relegated to serving as a short-term, stopgap measure until regular troops could arrive, instead of being viewed as a force to fight a sustained action against an armed force (Whisker 1979, p. 10). This two-army system of defense was the basis for defending the United States for decades (Hart 1998, p. 97).

The first large-scale, external challenge requiring the two-army system to respond was the War of 1812. Simmering tensions led to the outbreak of war, and President Madison called up the state militias to face the enemy. In response to this call, the governors of several states refused to send their militias into national service because they felt their states were not threatened and that the national government was attempting to use the military resources of the individual states to achieve political ends. The Governor of Connecticut refused to call up his militia for the war, and the Governor of Vermont quickly followed suit (Whisker 1999,

p. 326). Louisiana had just become a state and had no militia law in effect when the war began; consequently, there was a delay in their creating a unit. When it was created, over 1000 troops were African-American, who were not permitted to serve with the federal forces (Whisker 1999, p. 326).

There was a great deal of confusion concerning the lines of authority in the two-army system. Senior men in the standing army often found themselves outranked by the elected officers of state militias, who sometimes were voted to higher rank by their units solely to increase their authority over the regular army personnel (Berton 1980, p. 94). This is not to say that militia officers were followed in an unquestioning manner. In many instances, militia officers who disappointed their units were deposed by their subordinates for minor slights (Berton 1980, p. 94). Berton (1980, p. 22) wrote that the relationships between regular army officers and those of the militias were often marked with petty jealousies and infighting that hindered collaborative efforts. The confusion was exacerbated by role ambiguity between the civil and military roles of elected officials in a democratic society. Civilian leaders occasionally attempted to take direct command over operational forces at the spur of the moment. During the British attack on Washington, President Madison was seen riding along the front lines trying to personally direct an attack, and Secretary of State Monroe attempted to take command of a unit of Maryland's militia during the Battle of Bladensburg (Hill 1964, p. 13). The system of command was often ineffectual because it was so disjointed, and in the Battle of Bladensburg, a patchwork of militia units led in a disorganized manner lost to an enemy force less than one-half its size (Whisker 1999, p. 326).

Many military historians are of the opinion that the system of state militias was so uncoordinated that to categorize it as a system seems to be an error. One author described the Uniform Militia Act as more of a means to conduct a census of available forces than as a system of defense (Hill 1964, p. 9). If so, it was a poor census system because no one was cognizant of the number of men in the militia at any given time. In 1811, the aggregate rolls of the state militias reported 719,499 men in the enrolled militias, comprising 1000 regiments led by 300 generals (Hill 1964, p. 11). In truth, there is no way to determine the accuracy of those numbers because participation in training was sporadic, and militia members believed they were free to leave at any time. Militia members thought nothing of leaving their units for any reason, and often were not subject to discipline for their departure because the states were dedicated to the ideal of the militia man being a citizen first and a soldier second (Berton 1980, p. 22; Hart 1998, p. 78). One historian estimated the peak strength of the militia on active duty at any time during the War of 1812 to be approximately 67,000 (Hill 1964, p. 17). Although some records provide much higher numbers, one must understand that hundreds of militia members were only called to duty for between one and twelve weeks, making it impossible to know the precise numbers on duty at a specific time during the conflict (Hill 1964, p. 15).

The number of militia available was not the only weakness of the system; militia members often lacked sufficient training to act as part of a military unit. Although the militia was required to conduct training at least once every year, it was not uncommon for local militias to never drill, and rarer for two units to drill together (Whisker 1999, p. 96). The militia drills that were conducted were often viewed more as social gatherings rather than as the military readiness functions they were intended to be, and were frequently marked by heavy drinking, socializing, and picnics (Mahon 1960, p. 40). Many militia commanders developed and adopted their own set of tactics, using them as the basis for training their troops, creating a system where neighboring militia units operated in differing manners (Whisker 1999, p. 157). Because members of the militia were required to provide their own arms and equipment, there was a great disparity between the resource needs of differing units, making effective supply impossible (Whisker 1999, p. 97). Additionally, although residents of frontier communities often possessed arms and the ability to use them proficiently, urban dwellers often found little need for weaponry and, even if they owned them, were often unable to fire muskets with any degree of skill (Whisker 1999, p. 97). The effectiveness of any militia unit depended on its manpower, and the wide variance in personal capabilities led to the disparity between differing militia units, further inhibiting their ability to coalesce into an effective force.

The effectiveness of militias in the early years of the country was inconsistent. In the Revolutionary War, the militias ran from the field at the Battle of Long Island and the Battle of Camden, but fought with distinction at the battles of Bennigton and Cowpens (Mahon 1960, p. 5). Several planned attacks on British forces in Canada during the War of 1812 failed because militia forces refused to cross the border into another nation, stating that their role was solely defensive in nature (Berton 1980, p. 127). In November 1812, two-thirds of one militia unit refused to cross the border into Canada during an attack, and a few weeks later less than one-third of the Pennsylvania militia obeyed the order to enter Canada during another invasion attempt (Whisker 1999, p. 325). In contrast, in one of the greatest U.S. victories of the War of 1812, General Andrew Jackson led a composite force comprised of federal troops, militias from several states, pirates, Native Americans, and free African-Americans to a stunning victory against British forces with more than twice his numbers. Jackson's victory illustrates how strong leadership could overcome seemingly overwhelming odds.

Governmental leaders found there was no way to accurately predict how well the militia might perform in any circumstances; therefore, their role in battle plans was often minimized. Illustrative of the ambiguous view of militias held by army officers, when responding to a question about the abilities of the Continental Army and the militias in 1780, George Washington wrote, "If in all cases ours was one army, or thirteen armies allied for the common defense, there would be no difficulty in solving your questions; but we are occasionally both, and I should not be much out if I were to say we are sometimes neither but a compound of both" (Hill 1964, p. 6).

The War of 1812 generally provided strong evidence that a disjointed, unco-ordinated collection of state militias could not easily be combined into a single effective force, capable of defending the nation (Mahon 1960, p. 69). A lack of common training, procedures, equipment, coordination, and leadership hampered the development of an effective fighting force, leading to the inability of U.S. forces to achieve tactical supremacy. Whisker (1999, p. 225) estimated that the total U.S. forces during the War of 1812 numbered just under 400,000, but they were effectively held in check for nearly three years by British forces approximately one-eighth their number. This, though the United States was fighting a war mainly on their home soil, possessed numerous fixed defensive fortifications, and did not face the same logistical challenges faced by Great Britain, which was attempting to supply a large-scale military operation an ocean away.[3] Consequently, in 1815 when the war ended, there had been no conclusive victor, and the relations between the nations returned to the status quo ante.

The Homeland Security Act of 2002

In 2002, after the September 11th terrorist attacks, Congress began to explore means of developing a system to prepare the nation for the consequences of another terrorist attack. Unlike the time-consuming ideological debates that characterized the development of the Uniform Militia Act, the Homeland Security Act was passed rapidly, considering the complexity of the task, spurred by perceptions of eminent danger. Congressional debates culminated in the Homeland Security Act of 2002, which has several parallels with the Uniform Militia Act of 1792. Most notably, it attempted to create a homeland security system based upon a federal model, with distinct roles for local, state, and federal agencies. Those efforts were aligned with Executive Order 12612, signed by President Ronald Reagan in 1987. That order called for all federal agencies to act under the presumption that local and state agencies were primarily responsible for local services, and federal agencies should not excessively intrude into local affairs. The system developed provided limited federal leadership and funding, with few sanctions for agencies or governments that failed to participate.

In the Homeland Security Act, Congress tried to develop a homeland security system built on existing agencies and networks that had previously been viewed as only tangentially concerned with meeting the terrorist threat, such as local fire and health departments. Many of these agencies had previously not been engaged in planning or preparing for a terrorist event, at least not as a primary response agency. Consequently, their individual agency mission statements and extant interorganizational relationships were often insufficient to fully support their newly defined roles. Homeland security legislation called for shared authority and responsibility at all levels of government, presuming that a common threat would be met with a common effort from all concerned. However, those networks were generally perceived to be inadequate before the attack, notably because they were not linked by a cogent national strategy (USGAO 2001, p. 51). In recent emergency management exercises, the Department of Homeland Security noted emergency plans often called for a degree of intergovernmental communication and coordination that does not exist (USDHS 2003, p. 3).

Goal ambiguity has been an issue in system development. After September 11th, the federal government initially appeared to be moving towards the forefront of any potential response system. However, the federal government continues to view the immediate response to terrorist events to be primarily a local responsibility, with local government resources being supported by state and federal resources as requested, if available, without consideration of what the impact on response would be if resources were not forthcoming (USGAO 2001, p. 5, 25). In December 2004, the Department of Homeland Security reaffirmed this concept of operations, modifying it to permit federal agencies to actively participate if they shared primary responsibility for delivery of a specific service, had concurrent jurisdiction, or under specified circumstances when the President directs the Secretary of Homeland Security to assume control over a domestic incident (USDHS 2004, p. 4). Although the revised National Response Plan does provide for direct federal involvement in events designated as being of national significance, it is likely that significant resources will not be available in the immediate aftermath of a terrorist event.

Federal, state, and local agencies have often developed their own disaster plans in isolation, and duplication in the planned allocation of resources is rampant (USFEMA 1999, p. 15). Some local and state agencies have adopted boiler-plate plans that neither reflect the needs of their communities nor the capabilities of their agencies (USFEMA 1999, p. 19). The revised National Response Plan does not call for a change in the planning process, or for the development of a vetting system for plans in existence. Instead, it leaves much of the responsibility for developing a network of coordinated plans at the local level (USDHS 2004, p. 8). The homeland security focus in each state varies, and governors have assigned the role to different agencies in each state, including existing emergency management agencies, law enforcement agencies, and the National Guard (Poulin 2004, p. 9). Most governors have appointed a coordinator of homeland security efforts within their state, but there is no system for coordinating the efforts of these officials at this time and, like the adjutant generals of the militias of 1792, they are relatively free to organize for response as they see fit. Consequently, many professional organizations have called for the federal government to assume a stronger leadership role, and to foster a common vision for all (International Association of Fire Chiefs 2002, p. 10).

Earlier to the passage of the Homeland Security Act, there were over 40 federal agencies that played a role in homeland security; many of their responsibilities overlapped and there had been little done in an attempt to coordinate them with a national strategy (USGAO 2000, p. 18). Although the Act has given the Department of Homeland Security a leading role, many federal agencies remain dispersed within the federal structure, generally free to prepare and train independently. The Department of Homeland Security is still in a normalizing phase, and the system is not fully coherent. States have developed homeland security plans to meet their own perceived needs, and there are vast disparities in structure, funding, and activity (Poulin 2004, p. 14). Most local governments use their fire departments as their first responders to disasters, and the fire department is considered to be an integral part of the nation's homeland security (White House 2001b).

The U.S. Fire Service is similar to the militia of the early nineteenth century in several ways. Local fire protection has been considered strictly a matter of local concern. The federal government did not become involved in the fire service until 1974 when President Nixon appointed the National Commission on Fire Prevention and Control to assess the fire problem in the nation. The National Commission on Fire Prevention and Control found the U.S. Fire Service was generally an unknown. There were no records of such basic information as the numbers of firefighters or fire departments in the country, and they determined the incidence and cost of fire was ineffectually documented (NCFPC 1973, p. x). On the basis of the final report of the Commission, *America Burning*, Congress enacted the National Fire Prevention and Control Act of 1974 (Public Law 93–498) to address the identified issues. The legislation stressed that fire was an issue of local concern and that the proper role of the federal government was to be as a coordinator of local activities. The Act did not include legislative mandates, continuous funding, training, and equipment standards, or a formalized central leadership. Therefore, like the Uniform Militia Act of 1792, there exists today a multitiered system of response to a recognized national problem, with federal, state, and local elements acting in an independent manner. During the War of 1812, there was some debate on the number of militia units available, and with the levels of training and equipment each possessed. Today, although it is estimated that the fire service is comprised of over 30,000 departments staffed by more than one million firefighters, of which approximately 75 percent are volunteers, the U.S. Fire Administration reports that they really have no idea how many fire departments or firefighters there are in the country at this time (USFA 2001, p. 28). Like the Uniform Militia Act, the present laws do not provide a clear view of resource availability or capability.

The Uniform Militia Act did not provide funding for insuring the readiness of local militia units. Similarly, the federal government today does not financially support local fire protection on a consistent basis. President Ronald Reagan, in 1982, and President George W. Bush, in 2001, made efforts to reduce or dismantle the U.S. Fire Administration, with Bush's budget proposal to reduce funding stating that financial support of local fire departments " . . . did not represent an appropriate responsibility of the federal government" (White House 2001a). This has left local governments to staff and equip their local emergency response organs on their own, and in a study of hazardous materials response team readiness the federal government found that there was a wide disparity in the availability and capability of local chemical emergency response units across the nation (USNIST 1999, p. 3). This lack of coordination is exacerbated because of a lack of consensus on the resources necessary to effectively mount a response. For example, one government study found that no one is sure what equipment and staffing would be needed to respond to a large-scale chemical emergency in an urban area (USGAO 1999, p. 3). If local resources are overwhelmed and federal assets are requested, it may take over four hours to get the first federal units to the scene (ESDP 2001, p. 3). This has created a system where many urban areas have highly developed and capable emergency response organizations, but leaves large areas of the country without even rudimentary response capabilities (USFEMA 1999, p. 3). As under the Uniform Militia Act, the Homeland Security Act does not provide for a standard level of emergency response across the nation. The Homeland Security Act does not mandate compliance with national standards, but instead recommends that local and state agencies comply with voluntarily established standards (Homeland Security Advisory Council 2003, p. 6). One of the most persistent calls for improvement has included a call for the development of a national system of mandatory standards (ESDP 2001, p. 5; Rudman et al. 2003, p. 4).

Conclusions

The Uniform Militia Act was an attempt to structure a national defense with a two-army system: one state based, and one federal. During the War of 1812, the militia forces proved ineffective through a combination of a lack of training, coordination, and funding. The system proved ineffective and the problems were eventually rectified in 1903 with the formation of the National Guard. The revised system placed military units under state control, but with clear recruiting, promotional, logistical, operational, and training standards established at the national level (Hill 1964, p. 9).

The Homeland Security Act was an attempt to structure a national system of defense using a three-tiered system: federal, state, and local. There has been a call for more federal funding for first responders under homeland security legislation, and President Bush requested and received over $35 billion for homeland security, with $3.5 billion allocated for first responders at the local level (White House 2002). This is undoubtedly a positive move in creating an effective system, but only if it is continued. There is, however, a lack of standardized training and coordination between local governments, and between the local, state, and federal governments. A large-scale terrorist attack, such as was seen on September 11th, would require the integrated and coordinated efforts of local, state, and federal agencies, as well as the efforts of many private and nongovernmental actors. Although many local, state, and federal agencies are capable of performing well within the normal scope of their operational responsibilities, there is sufficient documentation to indicate that they do not always work efficiently and effectively when called together at the scene of a disaster. To make this disparate group of individual entities work together in a cohesive and collaborative manner requires some means of coordinating response, standardizing training, and providing equitable funding. At the present, most of federal, state, and local agencies do not even possess compatible radio systems that would permit them to speak with each other on the scene of an emergency (ESDP 2001, p. 5).

The Uniform Militia Act of 1792 sought to create a national system that placed a premium on the autonomy of state governments over the efficiency of the national defense system. In many respects, it failed because it was an attempt to build a system out of heterogeneous components, without providing a means of uniting the disparate parts. The militia system in the United States has not always led to a failure or stalemate. The overall pattern in other conflicts was for early failures to be followed by stalemates and, ultimately, to overall victory. The militias in the Mexican-American War, the civil war, and the Spanish-American War all served well and, while they experienced difficulties in the early stages of each conflict, they ultimately were honed into effective military forces that led to the ultimate victory of U.S. forces. Often, the turning point in each conflict was when the federal government provided strong leadership, standards, logistics, and funding as a means of melding individual parts into an effective whole. At some point during the conflict, for a variety of reasons, the militia units solidified into effective fighting units. However, their inadequacies during the early stages of each conflict were costly. In the twenty-first century, when terrorists have the ability to bring weapons of mass destruction to bear against the nation at any time, the country has much to lose while catching up to the learning curve once hostilities have begun.

The Homeland Security Act of 2002 has many of the same shortcomings as the Uniform Militia Act. It is possible that, in their haste to enact the Homeland Security Act, Congress had insufficient time to ponder the potential outcomes of attempting to meld so many distinct agencies into one functional entity. To insure that an effective response is available should a terrorist attack occur, the nation must learn from its own history and develop a better system of protecting local communities. Any such system shall require the development of mandatory standards, the establishment of a strong leadership, and a means of promoting collaborative relationships between local, state, and federal actors.

It is possible that the issues noted in this article could be addressed through structural approaches that more clearly delineate the role and responsibilities of each of the actors in the federal system. Such actions should not require the relinquishment of local or state autonomy by creating a federal system, but it must require some form of standardization in recruitment, training, funding, and equipment for state and local agencies, such as was seen when the National Guard was organized in 1903. The federal system of government was designed to share power for reasons linked to ideology and politics. Issues concerning intergovernmental management were not a notable concern to the founding fathers. It is not likely that the intergovernmental framework will change dramatically in the near term. Consequently, the federal government must establish a strong leadership position, even if formal authority is not always present. It must provide adequate funding to support the efforts of state and local governments to meet clear, realistic, and achievable national standards. Perhaps most importantly, the federal government needs to foster a collaborative environment for governmental leaders, facilitating more effective intergovernmental management within the present federal system.

Failure to take positive steps towards remediation may place the populace at risk from the consequences of a terrorist attack, indicating that the United States has failed to learn from its own history.

References

Berton, P. 1980. *The Invasion of Canada*. Boston, Massachusetts: Little, Brown and Company.

Duncan, S.M. 1997. *Citizen Warriors*. Novato, California: Presidio.

ESDP (Executive Session on Domestic Preparedness). 2001. *Memo to Governor Tom Ridge, United States Office of Homeland Security on the Intergovernmental Dimensions of Domestic Preparedness*. (November 2, 2001). Taubman Center for State and Local Government, John F. Kennedy School of Government, Harvard University, Cambridge, Massachusetts.

Galvin, J.R. 1967. *The Minute Men*. New York: Hawthorn Books.

Hart, G. 1998. *The Minutemen*. New York: The Free Press.

Hill, J.D. 1964. *The Minuteman in Peace and War*. Harrisburg, Pennsylvania: Stackpole.

Homeland Security Advisory Council. 2003. Statewide Template Initiative. Washington, DC: President's Homeland Security Advisory Council.

International Association of Fire Chiefs. 2002. *A Time to Lead: A Vision for the Future of the Fire Service*. International Association of Fire Chiefs.

Mahon, J.K. 1960. *The American Militia*. University of Florida Monographs. Social Science Number 6, Spring 1960, Gainesville, Florida.

NCFPC (National Commission on Fire Prevention and Control). 1973. *America Burning*. Emmitsburg, Maryland: United States Fire Administration.

Poulin, T.E. 2004. Defending the Homeland: A Comparison of State-Mandated Police, Fire, and Emergency Medical Training in the Southeast U.S. A paper presented at the annual meeting of the Southern Political Science Association Intercontinental Hotel, New Orleans, Louisiana, January 8, 2004. Available on-line at http://archive.allacademic.com/publication/search.php.

Rudman, W.B., Clarke, R.A., and Metzel, J.F. 2003. *Drastically Underfunded, Dangerously Unprepared*. New York: Council of Foreign Relations.

USDHS (United States Department of Homeland Security). 2003. TOPOFF 2 after Action Report. The after action report for a disaster management exercise conducted for top officials in Seattle, Washington, and Chicago, Illinois, May 12–16, 2003.

—— 2004. National Response Plan. Washington, DC: United States Department of Homeland Security.

USFA (United States Fire Administration). 2001. Report on the National Volunteer Fire Summit. USFA publication number FA-212. Emmitsurg, Maryland: United States Fire Administration.

USFEMA (United States Federal Emergency Management Agency). 1999. Report of the Federal Emergency Management Agency Hazardous Materials Summit: Working Better Together. Washington, DC: Federal Emergency Management Agency.

USGAO (United States Government Accountability Office). 1999. Combating Terrorism: Use of National Guard Response Teams Is Unclear. GAO publication number GAO/T-NSIAD-99-184. Washington, DC: General Accounting Office.

—— 2000. Combating Terrorism: Federal Response Teams Provide Varied Capabilities: Opportunities Remain to Improve. GAO Publication number GAO-01-14. Washington, DC: General Accounting Office.

—— 2001. Combating Terrorism: Selected Challenges and Related Recommendations. GAO publication number GAO-01-822. Washington, DC: General Accounting Office.

USNIST (United States National Institute of Standards and Technology). 1999. Fire Service Needs Workshop Proceedings. National Institute of Standards and Technology publication number NISTIR 6538. Gaithersburg, Maryland: National Institute of Standards and Technology.

Whisker, J.B. 1979. *The Citizen Soldier and United States Military Policy.* Croton-on-Hudson, New York: North River Press.

—— 1999. *The Rise and Decline of the American Militia System.* Cranbury, New Jersey: Associated University Press.

White House. 2001a. *A Blueprint for New Beginnings: The 2002 Federal Budget.* Available at http://whitehouse.gov/news/usbudget/blueprint/bud32.html.

—— 2001b. *Executive Order Establishing the Office of Homeland Security.* Available at http://whithouse.gov/new/releases/2001/20/2011108.2html.

—— 2002. 2003 Federal Budget: Homeland Security. Available at http://whitehouse.gov/homeland/homeland.security?book.html.

Endnotes

1. Although the War of 1812 was one of the first, major external threats to the United States, the first threat requiring a response by the two-army system created by the Uniform Militia Act was the Whiskey Rebellion of 1794. During the rebellion, the U.S. government faced the internal threat of widespread insurrection along the entire western frontier.

2. There were a number of factors that contributed to the outcome of the War of 1812. The war was not universally popular, and many in the nation believed that President Madison was pursuing his own agenda. This led to internecine squabbling among the nation's political leaders, which undoubtedly was a contributing factor to the outcome of the war. Although the Constitution had been in effect for some time, the roles and relationships of the federal and state governments were still unclear. Additionally, the British fleet was still the most potent naval force in the world, which was unquestionably an inhibiting factor to U.S. military efforts. Consequently, although this article focuses on issues pertaining to the militia system during the War of 1812, readers should appreciate that it was only one of the many factors that impacted the course of events, several of which were highly significant in their own right.

3. The British retained control of Canada throughout the war, using it as a source of supplies and as a base of naval operations. Their fleets also used ports in the West Indies as staging and refitting points. Still, readers should understand that during the bulk of the war, British forces were attempting to invade and control their enemy' territories, which militarily placed them in a disadvantageous position.

Chapter 3

Homeland Security: A "One-Stop Shop" Approach

Terrance A. Johnson* and Nathaniel A. Wilkinson

CONTENTS

The subtitle of this chapter came from meetings hosted by the U.S. Department of Transportation during 1998–2000 to consolidate the functions of the Disadvantaged Business Enterprise Program for each state, regional, and local certifying authority.
* Terrance A. Johnson is deceased.

Introduction

Although the Tenth Amendment to the Constitution delegates the power to regulate (Gaines and Kappeler, 2003) to the states, recent terrorist attacks raise questions about which level of government should proactively manage, coordinate, and allocate public safety and emergency preparedness resources for homeland security. Before the terrorist attacks, the federal government provides direct funding to state and local police agencies, and takes on a mentorship approach in helping state and local entities coordinate a nationwide public safety effort (see the COPS Fact Sheet on Training and Technical Assistance, 1999). However, the events of 9/11 have forced the U.S. government to take a forefront, hands-on approach in public safety matters. Many argue that these activities require a national proactive approach, i.e., one that is led by the federal government but still involves state and local governments, and even private entities (Cohen et al., 2002; Comfort, 2002; Donley and Pollard, 2002; Glendening, 2002; Kirlin and Kirlin, 2002; Walker, 2002; Wise and Nader, 2002). The nation, with no real fear of international terrorism as seen around the world, may have been lulled into believing that the public safety community reflected the entire concept of homeland security. This may have produced a narrowed theoretical perspective on what homeland security really means, without actually using the term. The use of the term "homeland security" to replace "public safety" is more than mere semantics. The term homeland security expands the concept of safety beyond the narrow barriers of the police, firefighters, paramedics, and other enforcement emergency response personnel. Homeland security enlarges the traditional public safety concerns and includes a proactive effect to address natural events such as floods, wildfires, hurricanes, and volcanoes, and the protection of man-made and natural assets.

Before 9/11, the federal government had in place what it believed is a solid strategy for dealing with acts of terrorism (see the Omnibus Crime Bill of 1994, 18 U.S.C.A. § 1033(e)). The Federal Bureau of Investigation (FBI) has been the lead federal law enforcement agency for this endeavor (Vise and Adams, 2000). However, 9/11 has left some doubt to the FBI's ability to continue to oversee domestic terrorism, and to expand into international waters because of several highly publicized and mishandled investigations (such as Ruby Ridge, WACO, Los Alamos Laboratory investigations) that have been labeled as major foul-ups (*Houston Chronicle*). Despite recent problems within the FBI, it is still regarded as one of the premiere law enforcement agencies in the world. Moreover, the very system design of a law enforcement organization is that it is rigid and discourages creativity through cultural and structural barriers. If this is true, then the FBI and other like organizations are unlikely to be able to address this concern. The creation of the Office of Homeland Security (OHS) and later DHS is to effectively and efficiently manage all homeland security resources under one office (and later department). This is a sound management practice; however, the creation of the DHS has resulted in a "hodge-podge" of cultures and subcultures competing with each other under one roof because DHS has been formed from existing federal law enforcement and nonlaw enforcement agencies (Cox, 2004). Ervin (2006) states that these very cultural and subcultural differences are so pronounced that they have resulted in the entities being dysfunctional before the merger with DHS. The leading theorists on culture (and subcultures) advance the idea that culture helps to shape the norms, values, and traditions within an organization. Organizational culture helps to set parameters for behavior of individuals attempting to carry out the mission and goals and objectives (Shafritz and Ott, 1992; Argyris, 1999; Johnson, 2001, 2003; Johnson and Cox, 2004/2005).

Homeland Security: The Effort before September 11th

The New FBI

The bureau has been a part of American crime fighting since the late 1920s. Over the last six decades in particular, the FBI has had tremendous success in crime fighting (Peak, 2004/2005). Most of its effort is in the area of domestic terrorism (Vise and Adams, 2000). From investigating major organized crime activities to white-collar crimes involving insider trading; bank robberies; the Communist plots to overthrow the government; and the rise, rebirth, and remaking of hate groups, the FBI has responded to the challenge. However, during this same period, the FBI has been involved in spying on political and civil rights leaders in the United States (*Denver Post*, 2002). The Ruby Ridge and WACO investigation have helped to weaken the FBI's clean boy image (*Houston Chronicle*, 2002). The Robert Hanssen spy investigation, the failure to properly investigate the Oklahoma City bombing incident before it occurred, and the Wen Ho Lee (the Los Alamos laboratory scientist) inquiry are just some examples of the bureau's misleading high-profile investigations (*Houston Chronicle*, 2002; San Francisco Chronicle, 2002). These continuously systemic problems within the FBI have lead to organizational changes by director Mueller (*Boston Globe*, 2001). This has led some congressional leaders to accuse the bureau of failing to coordinate its efforts to effectively investigate international terrorism (Vise and Adams, 2000). Even the law enforcement community has blamed the FBI for not having a clear line of communications with sister federal law enforcement agencies as well as those at the state and local levels (*Houston Chronicle*, 2002).

Because the bureau's senior management ignored information from the field division that foreign nationals were attending flight school, Director Mueller reorganized the bureau to have a better internal communications system. The FBI's Intelligence Program allowed it to meet current and emerging national security threats by becoming more proactive in its efforts to stop internal terrorism. The bureau is now employing a concerted effort to gather and analyze information that is relevant to national threats. There is a better effort to share the bureau's information with sister federal, state, and local law enforcement agencies and the intelligence community (www.fbi.gov/counterterrism).

The Office of Intelligence within the FBI will now coordinate all these types of matters directly with the field offices, breaking the old bureaucratic chain-of-command (*Houston Chronicle*, 2002). Externally, however, the FBI has had problems coordinating its efforts with other federal law enforcement agencies regarding this matter, and with state and local law enforcement involving traditional investigative issues. It is a common knowledge throughout the law enforcement arena that the FBI considers itself the premiere law enforcement agency, not only in the United States but also in the world. This FBI's narcissistic attitude is the main reason that it meets resistance from other law enforcement agencies (*Boston Globe*, 2001).

Consolidation of the Federal Law Enforcement Effort

The United States Commission on the Advancement of Federal Law Enforcement (Webster Commission) was charged with examining the idea of consolidating federal law enforcement efforts in 2000. According to Vise and Adams (2002), William Webster, the chairman of the Commission (and former director of the FBI and Central Intelligence Agency), recommended that the Drug Enforcement Administration (DEA) and Bureau of Alcohol, Tobacco, and Firearms (BATF) become one mega law enforcement agency under the control of the FBI. His justification was that the federal government possessed 148 separate law enforcement units and that this lack of a real coordinated effort made the nation susceptible to terrorist attacks.

In essence, the former director of the FBI advocated giving his old agency power over two of the elite federal law enforcement agencies. Strong congressional resistance was evident. Senator Schumer echoed the sentiments of the Founding Fathers when he noted his reluctance to transfer law enforcement functions from several law agencies to one and thereby, creating a national police force (Vise and Adams, 2002, p. 2). Senator Schumer did acknowledge the need to streamline so many agencies; yet, he still resisted any idea of placing the FBI over the DEA and

BATF. He also noted that the report had been a start in the right direction toward realigning federal law enforcement, and should be further examined (Vise and Adams, 2002). Although many of the suggestions made in Webster's Commission were good, there were those in the Clinton administration who rejected the realignment of the FBI, DEA, and BATF. The issue remained until the following administration.

The terrorist attacks have presented a far-reaching question that extended beyond the country's ability to detect and prevent such occurrences from happening (Wise and Nader, 2002). Is the federal government and its massive bureaucracies organized in such a way as to detect, prevent, and deter further attacks, especially abroad? *Time magazine* argues that in Iraq, explosive weapons are far more advanced. Explosive devices—homemade bombs also known as improvised explosive devices (IEDs)—have caused more than half of the 2300 U.S. troop deaths (Barry, et al., 2006). In terrorist attacks in Madrid and London, those devices were the conspirators' weapons of choice, and bomb experts believe it is only a matter of time before an IED strike takes place in the United States. But Washington has done little to prepare a national strategy for the threat. Sadly, the plans to deal with these issues were compromised because of "inexperienced leadership and bureaucratic infighting." The Bush administration created a national IED Task Force, but it met only once—in November 2006 in Washington—and provided no clear steps forward.

One National Homeland Security Agency

The federal government is not structured to deal solely with terrorism. To effectively fight terrorism, the agencies of government must be coordinated (Freedberg, 2001). These very sentiments were echoed in the report from The U.S. Commission on National Security/21st Century 2001 (the Hart–Rudman Commission). The current resources dedicated to homeland security needs are spread out among more than 24 agencies. Therefore, it will take a number of changes to correct this major flaw in the system. There are a number of federal law enforcement agencies with overlapping jurisdiction. The FBI has overall responsibility for enforcement of all of Title 18 USC Statues; however, they are not alone. In the area of terrorism, the National Security Agency, Department of Defense, Defense Intelligence Agency, the BATF, U.S. Department of State, and now the DHS are involved in this issue. There are numerous other federal law enforcement agencies with responsibility for national security. The lack of coordination does not stop at the federal law enforcement system. Prior to 9/11, the Federal Emergency Management Agency (FEMA) was the lead agency to handle natural disasters (such as floods, wildfires, hurricanes, and tornadoes). Depending upon where the natural disaster occurred (in urban or rural areas), the Departments of Agriculture and Housing and Urban Development had concurrent or overlapping jurisdiction to assist the affected population. Posner says that the lack of coordination and redundancy in efforts results in fragmentation within a system. Fragmentation, duplication, and disparity seem to be a mainstay in the federal government (see Advancing the Management of Homeland Security: Managing Intergovernmental Relations for Homeland Security, 2004).

The lack of a real synchronized effort within one department perhaps is a result of the politics that prohibit agencies and bureaus of that department from working together. This is why Newmann (2002) notes that the interagency model is more suited for the current atmosphere because it is impossible to expect one agency to handle the massive undertaking of homeland security. Intergovernmental associations appear to cause inefficiencies and other dysfunctional problems (see Advancing the Management of Homeland Security: Managing Intergovernmental Relations for Homeland Security, 2004).

Rather than a harmonized effort, there seems to be a reconfiguration of the federal system. The events of September 11th have resulted in a federalization of airport security initiatives (Gould, 2002). Congress has adopted and President Bush has signed the Aviation Security Act (Act). The Act has established the Transportation Security Administration (TSA), then under the Department of Transportation. A new undersecretary for the transportation security position was created. TSA assumed the responsibility of passenger and baggage screening from the airlines. Each airport has an airport security director and the occupant of this position will work to improve landside aspects of airport security. The Federal Aviation Administration (FAA) will still handle all aspects of airport security airside (Frederickson and LaPorte, 2002) and the sky marshal service. The U.S. Commission on National Security/21st Century 2001 (Hart–Rudman Commission) has been established to examine the need for a national homeland security agency. Cochaired by former senators Gary Hart and Warren Rudman, the Commission submitted its report on homeland security on February 15, 2001, to the president with suggestions that a person be accountable to the president for homeland security issues. Specific homeland security efforts now being performed by a number of federal law enforcement agencies would thus be consolidated.

The Hart–Rudman Commission report has recommended that a National Homeland Security Agency (NHSA) be established and its director possess cabinet-level status under the executive branch. The NHSA should be modeled after the FEMA. The transfer of the United States Customs Service (USCS), the Border Patrol (BP), and Coast Guard (CG) should comprise the nucleus of this organization. Although the USCS would retain its small investigative unit of special agents, the NHSA would function as a well-armed, uniform agency. All of NHSA's units would continue to wear uniforms and patrol the air, land, and sea creating a substantial and frightening presence at American borders.

The Hart–Rudman Commission's report was released on February 15, 2001. The Bush administration had been in office less than a month. As a result, this report was placed on a hold status. Its importance was not truly appreciated until nine months later. William Webster believed that the duplication of responsibility of the FBI and DEA for drug investigations would lead to trouble. However, the Clinton administration rejected the idea of merging the FBI, DEA, and BATF due to political turf wars (Vise and Adams, 2000).

State and Local "Security" Initiatives

Soon after former Pennsylvania Governor Ridge left Pennsylvania to become the director of the OHS, his replacement, former Governor Mark Schweiker, created the state branch of the OHS and appointed retired FBI special agent Earl Freilino as the first director. Pennsylvania's OHS was created as a resource for public safety, coordinating emergency management services. The current Governor Edward Rendell appointed retired General Keith Martin as the office's current director (http://www.homelandsecurity.state.pa.us/homelandsecurity/cwp/view.asp? a=445&q=168038&homelandsecurityNav=|7312|). The Pennsylvania OHS has been given specific duties. Pennsylvania also has established Homeland Security Advisory Council (Council), which is charged with coordinating a logical response to terrorist attacks. The purpose of the council is to advise the governor on matters relating to homeland security.

According to Advancing the Management of Homeland Security: Managing Intergovernmental Relations for Homeland Security (2004), many other states have also created their own version of a homeland security organization within the executive branch of government that includes emergency or crisis management. These state jurisdictions have designated homeland security czars who answer directly to the governor, while others have been separated from the chief executive. Some homeland security executives have been placed within existing agencies such as the state police and emergency management (Advancing the Management of Homeland Security: Managing Intergovernmental Relations for Homeland Security, 2004, p. 9). Even with the states creating homeland security offices, they will still rely on the federal government for guidance. There are numerous federal agencies that possess some responsibility for homeland security. However, state and local governments are skeptical of new federal plans.

The Public Sentiment toward a Sole National Security Agency

The initial response to the terrorist attacks was widely supported by the public (Gould, 2002). Polls conducted in 2001 by *Newsweek, NBC/Wall Street Journal* showed that the respondents were willing to accept changes in civil liberties to combat terrorism. In early 2002, the Greenberg poll revealed that Americans agreed that the country would have to accept the new restrictions on civil rights. However, *Time/CNN* polls conducted in March 2002 showed that respondents were concerned that the government might go too far in an attempt to thwart terrorism.

Rehnquist (1998) stated that when there is a national crisis, the evenness between "freedom" and "order" tips toward order so that the government can restore peace (p. 222). Congress responded to the 9/11 by passing legislation that removes many of the constitutional safeguards found in the Bill of Rights. Attorney General (AG) John Ashcroft has described the USA PATRIOT Act (Act) as a parcel of tools desperately needed to combat terrorism (McGee, 2001). The Act, in its original form, allowed the FBI to obtain court orders based on a significant purpose instead of the old standard of primary purposes. This permitted people who are merely suspected of acting in concert with terrorists to be wiretapped. The FBI can share information about suspected terrorists with intelligence agencies without judicial oversight as long as the information is related to terrorism. The bureau can access a person's Internet communications as long as they certify to the court that the information is part of a criminal investigation. This standard was significantly lower than the probable cause standard for arrest. Financial institutions must monitor their daily activities and share the information with intelligence agencies. Law enforcement may gain access to an individual's credit report without a court order. Noncitizens subject to deportation may be held for an indefinite period once the AG designates the person as a danger to national security (Gould, 2002).

According to de Rugy, V (2005), international terrorism is probably the greatest security challenge America faces today. Policymakers have responded in two ways: going after terrorists abroad and improving security against terrorism at home by boosting homeland security funding. Regarding the latter, total spending directed to homeland security activities will be at least $50 billion for fiscal year 2006. Yet, the important question is whether America is getting the maximum level of benefit in exchange for this increase in spending. Because of the media blitz, there is a fear that the police will overreact to the added pressures of solving these new homeland security crimes by racial profiling all Arabs and Muslims. The 9/11 concerns may spark the racial profiling of young Middle Eastern males (Gould, 2002). Arabic and Muslim communities, because of public perceptions of their religious beliefs, may have to endure added scrutiny by law enforcement (Dubnick, 2002; Gould, 2002). There are many documented stories that Arabic and Muslim communities are experiencing the same aggressive police tactics that law enforcement traditionally uses in minority neighborhoods when investigating crimes. Even though many Arab and Muslim Americans are voluntarily cooperating with law enforcement in the aftermath of the terrorist attacks, they are targets for surveillance. They are a part of random and frequent stops and pat downs, and some have been incarcerated under material witness warrants because of accusations of being associates of terrorists (Gould, 2002). However, a *Newsweek* poll right after September 11th indicates that 68 percent of the respondents believe it would be wrong to target Arabs and Arab-American males.

The Aftermath of 9/11: A New Perspective on Homeland Security

The New Conception of a Homeland Security Organization

Homeland security should be a cooperative effort, not only between the federal departments and agencies but also between the state and local authorities as well as the private sector. This means that the country must now think from a national coordinated view and not the old fragmentized approach, which caused much confusion and duplication of efforts in government operations in the past. Wise and Nader (2002) argue that homeland security means that a major redeployment of the public service resources (law enforcement and emergency preparedness) dedicated to absolute public safety needs to be addressed. Wise (1990) has echoed these same views in the past by looking not only at how the public sector resources are supervised but also in the private sector as well. Because homeland security is the first basic service provided to the nation, all of its resources must be thoroughly handled (Wise and Nader, 2002). Homeland security should be seen as a web that is used to capture the "concept, incorporating arranging of goals and objectives, missions, means, components, and threats related to the security of the United States" (Donley and Pollard, 2002, p. 139).

For any intergovernmental cooperation on homeland security to be effectively led by the federal government, it may need to consider a reorganization of its agencies that currently handle this issue on a piecemeal basis. Donley and Pollard (2002) say that the federal government is exploring how to reconfigure homeland security. The first step in this endeavor was the creation of the OHS.

Office of Homeland Security

On October 8, 2001, President Bush, by executive order, created the OHS and appointed Pennsylvania Governor Tom Ridge as its director. President Bush told the American people that the OHS's mission was to oversee all aspects of a comprehensive federal plan to protect the United States against terrorist attacks. (http://www. whitehouse.gov/news/releases/2001/10print/20011008.html). Donley and Pollard contended that the development and coordination of an overall national strategy to address threats of terrorism or actual attacks was a crucial mandate of this new office.

The placing of the OHS in the Executive Office of the President appeared to send the proper message to the entire executive branch of government under the jurisdiction of the president that he fully supported the OHS. However, without cabinet-level status, statutory authority, an independent budget, and most importantly, the senators and representatives of the key subcommittees, the foundation of developing a clear plan was in jeopardy. The strategy should include the goals, capabilities, and requirements (Donley and Pollard, 2002, p. 140) necessary to carry out the mission. President Bush addressed these concerns by noting that the OHS was a prelude, although the process of making homeland security a cabinet-level department within the executive branch of government endured the legislative process (http://www.whitehouse.gov/news/releases/2001/10print/20011008.html).

The Department of Homeland Security

On November 25, 2002, President Bush signed the Homeland Security Act of 2002 (the Act) establishing the DHS (http://www.dhs.gov/dhspublic/display?theme=10&content=11). On January 22, 2003, the U.S. Senate confirmed former Pennsylvania Governor Tom Ridge as DHS' first secretary. On January 24, 2003, OHS Director Tom Ridge was sworn in as DHS secretary (http://www.bens.org?HSDSynthh.html).

The main objectives of the DHS are to prevent terrorist attacks within the United States, reduce the vulnerability to attacks, and minimize the effects of such attacks should they occur. The DHS is responsible for border and transportation security, protecting critical infrastructure, coordinating emergency response activities, and overseeing research and development for homeland security efforts. The new department also responds to natural disasters (Homeland Security, *World Almanac & Book of Facts*, 00841382, 2004). The DHS is organized into five directorates: border and transportation security, emergency preparedness, science and technology, information analysis and infrastructure protection, and management, the administrative arm of the department. The U.S. Coast Guard, Secret Service, and Bureau of Citizenship and Immigration Services (formerly part of the INS) became part of DHS as discrete entities, separate from the directorates. The fiscal year 2004 budget for the new department was $36.2 billion (Homeland Security, *World Almanac & Book of Facts*, 00841382, 2004).

The DHS unifies 22 separate agencies and bureaus from existing federal departments. Secretary Ridge has revealed a plan to regionalize DHS and have the regional directors pass on information to state and local officials. Specifically, the regional executives will serve as the point-of-contact for the mayors (see Advancing the Management of Homeland Security: Managing Intergovernmental Relations for Homeland Security, 2004).

As outlined in the Commission Report, the USCS, BP, and CG are a part of DHS. In addition, the Immigration and Naturalization Service, the United States Secret Service, other current federal agencies are separate function of DHS (http://www.dhs.gov/dhspublic/theme_home1.jsp).

For DHS to be successful, the policymakers will need to reconfigure the nation's intergovernmental relation system in the context of homeland security. The following summarize the issues in this endeavor (see Advancing the Management of Homeland Security: Managing Intergovernmental Relations for Homeland Security, 2004):

- City and state personnel do not possess a basic understanding of the overall process and their specific roles in the homeland security effort.
- State and local governments do not trust each other and this hampers homeland security proposals.
- Fragmentation of government systems is sometimes intentional.
- Government networks are very complicated.
- Restrictions on legal and political authority stymie the top–down management approach.
- Serious situations cannot be predicted and create the need for constant change.
- There are federal, state, and local agencies that lack the ability to act as cooperative associates.
- Planning for homeland security promotes the Achilles' heel.
- Partners outside the intergovernmental community extended the level of difficulties in forming successful relations.

Since September 11, Congress has appropriated nearly $180 billion to protect Americans from terrorism. Estimated spending on homeland security in 2006 will be at least $50 billion—roughly $450 per American household. Ironically, the money is being used for other reasons than keeping the U.S. secure. States and cities are using this much needed money on meaningless pet projects that have nothing to do with homeland security; state and local officials fight over who will get the biggest share of the money, regardless of whether they have a rightful claim to it. When Congress is not recklessly giving out money, it is overreacting to yesterday's attacks instead of concentrating on cost-effective defenses against the most likely current threats (Rugy, 2006). The most recent literature written on addressing homeland security assets seems to take the position of a nationally coordinated effort led by the federal government to include state and local governments and the private sector, especially those dealing with the manufacturing of natural resources into energy (Cohen et al., 2002; Comfort, 2002; Donley and Pollard, 2002; Glendening, 2002; Kirlin and Kirlin, 2002; Walker, 2002; Wise and Nader, 2002). According to Posner (2002), the General Accounting Office has noted that a national plan is necessary, whereby the federal government joins hands with the state and local governments to develop a plan that will achieve maximum readiness and provide the best resources to allow government (with its private partners) to achieve the goal of national safety.

Organizational Culture and "Security" Structures

Evolving Cultures

The concept of culture has been adopted from the field of anthropology and has been defined in many ways and from different perspectives. It is the unique configuration of norms, values, beliefs, and so forth that characterize the way that people agree to do things. Norms, values, and culture help determine what is and is not acceptable behavior (Johnson, 2001, 2003; Johnson and Cox, 2004/2005). The societal culture helps to shape the organizational culture (Shafritz and Ott, 1992, p. 482; Johnson, 2001, 2003; Johnson and Cox, 2004/2005). When the term culture is paired with the term organization, conceptual and semantic confusion results (Shafritz and Ott, 1992, p. 492; Johnson, 2001, 2003; Johnson and Cox, 2004/2005). Organizational culture contains groups that are socially distinct from each other (Becker, 1992; Johnson, 2001, 2003; Johnson and Cox, 2004/2005). However, organizational culture is the "programming of the mind that distinguishes the members of one organization from another" (Hofstede, 1991, p. 262). Organizational culture, therefore, resides in the minds of all organization members (Hofstede, 1998, p. 2). Various cultures may be embedded in the groups that make up an organization (Schein and Ott, 1962; Smircich, 1983; Schein, 1984, 1985; Johnson, 2001, 2003; Johnson and Cox, 2005). Smircich (1983) therefore notes that in an evolving police culture, the likelihood of the existence of multiple organizational subcultures or even counter cultures must not be overlooked. Organizations are usually composed of subcultures, which are mutually antagonistic as they compete (overtly and covertly) as different groups of organizational members seek to establish or impose their distinctive systems and definitions of reality (Johnson and Gill, 1993; Johnson, 2001, 2003; Johnson and Cox, 2004/2005).

A Control Culture Mechanism

The oldest concepts of organizations (and the most discredited) assert that the proper way to manage is through control mechanisms (rules and structures), thus regulating behavior and introducing predictability (Van Maanen, 1978; Johnson, 2001, 2003; Johnson and Cox, 2004/2005). Control seemingly offers the ability to determine events or predict or anticipate outcomes (Umiker, 1999; Johnson, 2001, 2003; Johnson and Cox, 2004/2005). The image is of the organization as a machine (Cox, 2000a); the opposite would be uncertainty, confusion, and system breakdowns (Johnson, 2001, 2003; Johnson and Cox, 2004/2005). Organizations instill notions of acceptable behavior into the minds of employees through training or learning processes (particularly with in-group sessions) from the very beginning of employment. The main focus has been to control law enforcement agencies and their officers through the use of a paramilitary system with a bureaucratic hierarchical structure (Wilson, 1989; Zapan, 1991; Johnson, 2001, 2003; Johnson and Cox, 2004/2005). The cadet is enculturated into this hierarchy through the training provided at police academies (West, 1998; Johnson, 2001, 2003; Johnson and Cox, 2004/2005). Such academies have far more in common with military boot camps than the classroom. The lessons are about physicality and esprit (Cox, 2000b).

Changing Culture

The notion of shifting the organization's culture to create a new method of carrying out objectives is itself not new (Johnson, 2001, 2003; Johnson and Cox, 2004/2005). For years there has been a debate over making departments more open by encouraging employees to participate in policymaking (Girodo, 1998). This includes involving the employees through input analysis of ideas (Katz and Kahn, 1978). Transformational leadership theory has been proposed as a way to implement change within an organization. Transformational leadership has all the ingredients of a participatory system because it encourages stakeholder input and consent before change is started. Although leadership allows all stakeholders to speak and vote, in any organization change must include those at the top (Burns, 1978; Johnson, 2001, 2003; Johnson and Cox, 2004/2005). The foundation of change is in the choice of persons to work together for a common goal. This is different than the older transactional style of leadership (Bass, 1994), which is predicated upon a quid pro quo exchange (Johnson, 2001). Transactional relationships are defined and controlled by the leader. Transformational leadership requires all levels be engaged and actively participating in change processes (Keller, 1992; Johnson, 2001). This is not a top–down approach but it requires a strong commitment from the top precisely because the direction of change is not controlled (Johnson, 2001; Johnson and Cox, 2004/2005).

Toward an Ideal Homeland Security Structure

This chapter began with the understanding that the federal government has always responded to public safety concerns for the common good. The country has allowed the feds to intercede in their lives for public safety purposes incrementally each time the country has faced a new crisis. September 11, 2001, has been seen as a day that the United States lost her innocence, raped of her purity, and thrust into the unbalance sea of liberty and freedom over peace. Before America dares to ask why and how, it must struggle with the fact it has known for a while that such an attack was imminent. In the days that followed the attacks, a mass media cable outlet (*CNN/Time Warner*) revealed just how much the FBI knew or should have known about the terrorists and their activities. Moreover, America has begun to refocus and to view homeland security through a wider lens that allows her to see how the federal, state, and local governments and the private sector play an important role (Cohen et al., 2002; Comfort, 2002; Donley and Pollard, 2002; Glendening, 2002; Kirlin and Kirlin, 2002; Walker, 2002; Wise and Nader, 2002). This is a necessary action that should be undertaken by the federal government (Posner, 2002) and is driven by a new broader definition of homeland security: a reorganization of government and private sector resources and their allocation through a unified management system driven by a strategic plan (Cohen et al., 2002; Comfort,

2002; Donley and Pollard, 2002; Glendening, 2002; Kirlin and Kirlin, 2002; Walker, 2002; Wise and Nader, 2002). These steps should allow the new concept of homeland safety to capture all the relevant goals and objectives, missions, methods, variables, and risks that threaten the continued health and welfare of the United States (Donley and Pollard, 2002).

To achieve complete homeland security, there may need to be a reconsideration of what absolute public safety means and how those resources are properly managed. If homeland security is more than policing and law enforcement and, in addition to the coordination of those resources includes those agencies handling natural disasters (wild fires, floods, hurricanes, and volcanoes) and the protection of natural and man-made energy resources and emergency preparedness, then the bureau (along with most other policing or law enforcement agencies) is incapable of taking on home-land security responsibilities. Policing by its very nature is reactionary; something must happen for the police to respond (Crank, 1998; Johnson, 2001; Gaines and Kappeler, 2003). The Constitution provides protection against the actions of the police that would amount to a police state (Johnson and Cox, 2001). Emergency preparedness measures would require the FBI (or other law enforcement commu-nities) to change its mindset from reactionary to proactive. Although it is quite possible in theory for the FBI to change its behavior through a cultural transform-ation, the literature on this subject notes that the leader must successfully marshal the support for the change from the entire organization, which is done under auspices of a long and drawn out process (Burns, 1978; Johnson, 2001; Stewart and Kringas, 2002; Johnson and Cox, 2004/2005).

DHS has all the aspects of a standard police department. A police department operates as a unified organization in theory and in practice because it has one culture. However, DHS has multiple cultures because of how it has been created. It is really a collection of agencies taken from other departments through legal authority. Although each agency (individually as well as a collective whole) is their ultimate responsibility of the secretary, in a practical term, they operate as their own entity driven by the original cultural identity that has been born at their former organization. Ervin (2006) echoes these sentiments as he explains that at the time of the merger of agencies and bureaus to construct DHS, the pervasive cultures and subcultures have long created an atmosphere of dysfunction for the agencies and bureaus. There are present-day examples of this type of cultural emancipation. The creation of DHS is the biggest reorganization of the federal government since the creation of the Department of Defense in which its Army, Air Force, Marines, and Navy operate under the same theoretical approach to unification. In actuality, they operate as individual subdivisions to meet the organization's overall mission.

Organization theory states that an organization has its own unique culture and subcultures. These cultures and subcultures reinforce the mission of the organization and the method in which it is to be carried out (Hofstede, 1991, 1998; Becker, 1992; Argyris, 1999; Johnson, 2001, 2003; Johnson and Cox, 2004/2005; Shafritz and Ott, 1992). Therefore, the consolidation of organizational units from several departments or agencies may seemingly create efficiency, effectiveness, and control, but it also gives rise to a hodge-podge (Cox, 2002) of conflicting cultures and subcultures born from the departments from which the agencies originated. Additionally, the culture may be embedded in the individual members of the old organizations (Schein and Ott, 1962; Schein, 1984, 1985; Johnson, 2001, 2003; Johnson and Cox, 2004/2005). In essence, a variety of law enforcement organizations, all with competing and conflicting cultures and subcultures are trying to carry out the same mission under one crown. For example, although never formally merged into one organization, the attorney general installed two senior FBI agents as the DEA administrator and deputy administrator during the middle 1980s. They directed the FBI Special Agents-In-Charge (SACs) to oversee the activities of the DEA SACs, and transferred the training for DEA agents from FLETC in Glynco, Georgia, to the FBI Academy in Quantico, Virginia. Although both organizations remain as part of the Department of Justice umbrella, throughout this forced relationship, the FBI treated the DEA as second-class law enforcement officials.

Wilson argues that the DEA/FBI marriage has produced some good outcomes for both agencies because of initiatives. The DEA taught the FBI how to conduct proper deep cover investigations. The FBI taught the DEA how to be more effective in its bureaucratic management style. There have been several national initiatives such as communism, the anti-Americanism, the antiwar movement, and the war on drugs and terror that have not pushed federal agencies toward a positive interagency relationship. If the DHS experiences the same hodge-podge problem as the FBI and DEA, a result, perhaps, is a less effective organization than the several agencies and bureaus under the old departments, or independent agencies (Cohen et al., 2002; Comfort, 2002; Donley and Pollard, 2002; Glendening, 2002; Kirlin and Kirlin, 2002; Walker, 2002; Wise and Nader, 2002).

Conclusion

The Founding Fathers constructed a decentralized federal government because they believed that if men were given absolute power, they eventually would act in their own self-interest. Although the colonists were not abused by the English crown, their imaginary fear reminded them of the original sin in which Eve coaxed Adam into sampling the fruit from the forbidden tree and therefore, damning all human souls. Under the Judeo–Christian ethic, this had been the basis for the mistrust of men, especially those in a position of authority (Stillman, 1991, 1999; Mansfield, 2004).

The concept of government at different levels instead of one at the national level has resulted in an intended consequence: no one agency will do the people's business. Federalism allowed the dissemination of authority and power among different levels of government. Specific powers were given to the federal government, the states, and even individuals. The states shared their police powers with local governments (Gaines and Kappeler, 2003). The law enforcement society has been a main fixture in government operations. Therefore, it is likely that policing systems have reflected the government under which they have been created (Gaines and Kappeler, 2003).

Will the fears of some Americans be realized concerning the government going too far to prevent further terrorism? Specifically, is Dubnick (2002) and Gould's (2002) concern about the racial profiling of Arabs and Arab-Americans at the forefront of this issue? What about terrorist acts committed by nonminority Americans? Although by definition, the Oklahoma City bombing qualifies as the first major domestic terrorist attack in the United States, many in mainstream America have problems labeling Americans (especially blue-eyed white men, who are the true fabric of Americanism) as terrorists (Hale, 1998). America used old images of the South to portray whites as being socially better than blacks (Hale, 1998). The Civil War was the "White man's fight" that developed the "national norm [on race equality in this country]" (Grant, 1998, p. 2).

The *Dred Scott v. Sanford*, 60 US 393 (1856) case gave legitimacy for how Americans viewed race. The Supreme Court said that African-Americans were not equal to whites. Specifically, Chief Justice Taney wrote that when the Founding Fathers crafted the Constitution, black people were labeled significantly inferior to whites and as such, did not enjoy the same rights (Yoder, 1995). These negative beliefs about Black Americans were very easily transferred to other people of color. During World War II, Japanese Americans were placed in holding camps because they were perceived as being a threat to the country. We must be wary that in our efforts to defend our country from terrorists, we do not reinstitutionalize prejudice in the name of the cause.

References

Advancing the Management of Homeland Security: Managing Intergovernmental Relations for Homeland Security. 2004. A National Academy of Public Administration Forum on Homeland Security Summary Report. (2004, February). Government Printing Office: Washington, DC.

Argyris, C. (1999). *On Organizational Learning* (2nd ed.). Malden, MA: Blackwell Publishers, Inc.

Barry, J., Hastings, M. and Thomas, E. (2006, March). News Week International.

Bass, F.N. 1994. *Improving Organizational Effectiveness through Transformational Leadership*. Thousand Oaks: Sage Publication.

Becker, G. 1992. Investments in human capital: A theoretical analysis. *Journal of Political Economy, 70*, 1–49.

Boston Globe. 2001. Beyond the FBI. June 1st, A14.

Burns, J.M. 1978. *Leadership*. New York: HarperCollins.

Cohen, S., Eimicke, W., and Horan, J. 2002. Catastrophe and the public service: A case study of the government response to the destruction of the world trade center. *Public Administration Review, 62(Special Issue)*, 24–32.

Comfort, L.K. 2002. Rethinking security: Organizational fragility in extreme events. *Public Administration, Review, 62(Special Issue)*, 98–107.

Cox III, R.W. 2000. Creating a Decision Architecture. *Global Virtue Ethics Review, 2(1)*.

Cox III, R.W. 2000a. Doctoral Seminar on Leadership at Nova Southeastern University, July 2000. Fort Lauderdale.

Cox, R.W. 2004. Perspectives on Bringing Multiple Agency Cultures and Subcultures Under One Organizational Roof. The University of Akron: Akron.

Crank, J.P. 1998. *Understanding Police Cultures*. Cincinnati, Ohio: Anderson Publishing Co.

Denver Post. 2002. The FBI Makeover. June 1st, B7.

de Ruby, V. 2006. What does Homeland Security Spending By? *American Enterprise Institute for Public Policy Research*.

Donley, M.B. and Pollard, N.A. 2002. Homeland security: The difference between a vision and a wish. *Public Administration, Review, 62(Special Issue)*, 138–144.

Dowling, L. (Ed.), *Encyclopedia of Police Science*. New York: Garland.

Dred Scott v. Sanford, 60 U.S. 393, 1856.

Dubnick, M.J. 2002. Postscripts for a "State of War": Public administration and civil liberties after September 11th. *Public Administration, Review, 62(Special Issue)*, 86–91.

Ervin, C.K. 2006. *Open Target Where America Is Vulnerable to Attack*. New York: Palgrave Macmillan.

Frederickson, H.G. and LaPorte, T.R. 2002. Airport security, high reliability, and the problem of rationality. *Public Administration, Review, 62(Special Issue)*, 33–43.

Freedberg, S.J. 2001. Homeland defense effort breaks down walls of government. GovExec.com, October 19. Available at www.Govexec.com/dailyfed/0302202njla. htm. Accessed March 11, 2004.

Gaines, L.K. and Kappeler, V.E. 2003. *Policing in America* (4th ed.) Cincinnati, Ohio: Anderson Publishing Co.

Girods, M. 1998. Machiavellian, Bureaucratic and Transformational Leadership Styles in Police Managers: Preliminary Findings of Interpersonal Ethics. *Perceptual and Motor Skills, 86*, 419–427.

Glenndening, P.N. 2002. Governing after September 11th. *Public Administration Review, 62 (Special Issue)*, 21–23.

Gould, J.B. 2002. Playing with fire: The civil liberties implications of September 11th. *Public Administration, Review, 62(Special Issue)*, 74–79.

Grant, S.M. 1998. Pride and prejudice in the American Civil War. *History Today, 48(9)*, 41–48.

Hale, G.E. 1998. *Making Whiteness: The Culture of Segregation, 1890–1940*. New York: Pantheon Books.

Hofstede, G. 1991. *Cultures and Organizations: Software of the Mind*. London: McGraw-Hill.

Hofstede, G. 1998. Identifying organizational subcultures: An empirical approach. *Journal of Management Studies, 35(1)*, 12.

Johnson, T.A. 2001. An investigation to determine if the culture and subculture of policing stymie the profession's attempt to reform. Unpublished Dissertation. The Wayne Huizuenga Graduate School at Nova Southeastern University, Fort Lauderdale, Florida.

Johnson, T.A. 2003, May/June. The good and bad factors of police culture and subculture. *ACJS Today, 26(2)*, 7–10.

Johnson, T.A. and Cox, III, R.W. 2001. Justifying miranda one last time. *The Justice Professional, 14(1)*, 113–123.

Johnson, T.A. and Cox, III, R.W. 2004/2005. Police ethics: Organizational Implication. *Public Integrity*, 67–69.

Johnson, P. and Gill, J. 1993. *Management Control and Organizational Behavior*. London: Paul Chapman Publishing Ltd.

Katz, D. and Kahn R.L. 1978. *The Social Psychology of Organizations*. New York: John Wiley & Sons.

Keller, R.T. 1992. Transformational Leadership and the Performance of Research and Development Project Groups. *Journal of Management, 18*, 489–551.

Kirlin, J.J. and Kirlin, M.K. 2002. Strengthening effective government-citizen connections through greater civic engagement. *Public Administration, Review, 62(Special Issue)*, 80–85.

Mansfield, H.C. and Winthrop, D. 2004, *Democracy In America:* The University of Chicago Press: Pantheon Books.

McGee, J. 2001. An intelligence giant in the making: Anti-terrorism law likely to bring domestic apparatus to unprecedented scope. *Washington Post*, November 4, A4.

Newmann, W.W. 2002. Reorganizing for national security and homeland Security. *Public Administration, Review, 62(Special Issue)*, 126–136.

Omnibus Crime Bill of 1994, 18 U.S.C.A. § 1033(e).

PATRIOT ACT, P.L. 107–56, 115 Stat. 272, 2001.

Peak, K.J. 2005. *Policing America: Methods, Issues, Challenges* (5th ed.). Upper Saddle River, New Jersey: Prentice Hall.

Posner, P.L. 2002. Combating Terrorism: Intergovernmental Partnership in a National Strategy to Enhance Stat and Local Preparedness. Testimony before the U.S. House Committee on Government Reform, Subcommittee on Government Efficiency, Financial Management, and Intergovernmental Relations. March 22. Washington, DC: General Accounting Office. GAO-02-547T.

Rehnquist, W. 1998. *All the Laws but One: Civil Liberties in Wartime*. New York: Knopf.

San Francisco Chronicle. 2002. A 'New FBI' Is Born. May 31, A28.

Schein, E.H. 1984. Coming to a new awareness of organization culture. *Sloan Management Review, 25*, 3–14.

Schein, E.H. 1985. *Organizational Culture and Leadership: A Dynamic View*. San Francisco, California: Jossey-Bass.

Schein, E.H. and Ott, J.S. 1962. The legitimacy of the organizational influences. *The American Journal of Sociology, 67*, 682–689.

Shafritz, E.H. and Ott, J.S. 1991. *Classics of Organization Theory* (3rd ed.). Belmont, California: Wadsworth Publishing Company.

Shafritz, E.H. and Ott, J.S. 1992. *Organizational Culture and Leadership: A Dynamic View*. San Francisco, California: Jossey-Bass.

Smircich, L. 1983. Concept of culture and organizational analysis. *Administrative Science Quarterly, 28(3)*, 339–359.

Stewart, J. and Kringas, P. 2002. Change management—Strategy and values in six agencies from the Australian public service. *Public Administration, Review, 63(6)*, 675–688.

Stillman, R.J. 1999. *Preface to Public Administration: A Search for Themes and Direction* (2nd ed.). Burke, Virginia: Chatelaine.

Stillman, R.J. 1991. *Preface to Public Administration: A Search for Themes and Direction.* New York: St. Martin's Press.

The Homeland Security Act of 2002, P.L. 107–296.

The Houston Chronicle. FBI Changes/Proposed Reforms Bear Close Constitutional Scrutiny. June 2, A2.

The United States Commission on the Advancement of Federal Law Enforcement.

The U.S. Commission on National Security/21st Century (The Phrase III Report). 2001, February. Government Printing Office: Washington, DC.

Umiker, W. 1999. Organizational culture: The role of management and supervisors. *The Health Care Supervisor, 17*(4), 22–27.

Van Maanen, J. 1978. People processing: Strategies of organizational socialization. *Organizational Dynamics, 7*(1), 18–36.

Vise, D.A. and Adams, L. 2000, February. US: Webster urges streamlining federal law enforcement. *The Washington Post Company*, Washington, DC.

Walker, D.M. 2002. 9/11: The implications for public sector management. *Public Administration, Review, 62*(Special Issue), 94–97.

West, J. 1998. Frontiers in ethics training. *Public Management, 80*(6), 4–9.

Whitehouse Government News, visited on May 13, 2003. http://www.whitehouse.gov/news/releases/2001/10print/20011008.html.

Wilson, J.Q. 1968. *Varieties of Police Behavior: The Management of Law and Society in Eight Communities.* Cambridge, Massachusetts: Harvard University Press.

Wise, C.R. 1990. Public service configurations and public organizations: Public organization design in the post privatization. *Public Administration, Review, 50*(6), 141–155.

Wise, C.R. and Nader, R. 2002. Organizing the federal system for homeland security: Problems, issues, and dilemmas. *Public Administration, Review, 62*(Special Issue), 44–57.

Zupan, M. 1991. Bureaucracy: What Government Agencies Do and Why They Do It. Journal of Economic Literature, *29*(2), 606–607.

URL Web Sites

PA Office of Homeland Security Web site (visited on March 11, 2004) (http://www.homelandsecurity.state.pa.us/homelandsecurity/cwp/view.asp?a=445&q=168038&homelandsecurityNav=|7312|)

State Homeland Security Directors' Web site (visited on March 11, 2004) (http://www.iacsp.com/homelandinfo.html)

PA Office of Homeland Security Website/Responsibilities (visited on March 11, 2004) (http://www.pacode.com/secure/data/004/chapter6/s6.43.html)

PA Homeland Security Web site (visited on March 11, 2004) (http://www.pacode.com/secure/data/004/chapter6/s6.45.html)

Department of Homeland Security Web site (visited on May 13, 2003) (http://www.dhs.gov/dhspublic/display?theme=10&content=11)

Business Executives for National Security (visited on May 13, 2003) (http://www.bens.org?HSDSynthh.html)

Department of Homeland Security Web site (visited on May 13, 2003) (http://www.dhs. gov/dhspublic/display?theme=10&content=429)

Department of Homeland Security Web site (visited on May 13, 2003) (http://www.dhs. gov/dhspublic/theme_home1.jsp)

Monterey Institute of International Studies: Chemical & Biological Weapons Resource Page (visited on May 13, 2003) (http://cns.miis.edu/research/cbw/domestiic.htm)

Chapter 4

Securing Homeland Security: Immigrant Responses to State and Citizenship

Kalu N. Kalu

CONTENTS

Introduction

In a fast changing global environment, the modern state is seriously challenged by the complexity of issues it has to face and the absence of a historical precedent associated with them. None of these poses as much a challenge to the nation-state and its traditional identity than the issue of transnational immigration. Although it can be acknowledged that transnational immigration has been encouraged by an increasingly and cheaper modes of transportation, communications, and commerce; it offers enormous prospects but at the same time portends serious consequences. But the most critical issue facing liberal democracies today "concerns the integration of immigrant minorities as citizens of pluralistic democracies" (Fukuyama 2006, 6), particularly those from traditionally illiberal societies. This problem seems more stacked-up for many European countries. "Even with no new net immigration—which most European countries by now have cut off—higher birth rates among minority immigrant communities will increase their overall proportion in the population in the next generation" (Fukuyama 2006, 6).

For the past few decades, there has been an increasing level of immigration from Asia and the Middle East to Western and Eastern Europe, and from Central and South America to the United States and Canada. Because modern immigrants seek to define and maintain their cultural identities in their host countries, they seek adaptation rather than assimilation. As new immigrants refuse to completely abandon their heritage to the attraction of Western civilization, their insistence on remaining true to their faith and tradition will emerge as the new source of intrastate conflict, which by extension could provide an ideological basis for the kind of self-justification and radical fundamentalism needed to undermine American national security interests.

Competing Issues of Immigration and Identity in the Liberal State

It has been argued that the United States is a nation of immigrants, hence policy makers and, in fact, the public should be more receptive to issues concerning the contemporary surge of immigration from other countries. This argument is nothing new and could well be a genuine statement of fact. Human migration between countries has been with us over the course of thousands of years. Many of the conventional reasons cited as to why most people decide to leave their states of origin range from economic, political, religious, and cultural reasons. But what distinguishes this era of increasing desire to emigrate from earlier ones is that the international environment (mostly among liberal democracies) that had viewed immigration as a matter of right and as partly a humanitarian issue has changed. The immigration of earlier era was mostly legal and officially documented, but today's immigration comes with it a sizeable proportion that is illegal. While earlier immigrants arrived with a genuine sense of purpose and a renewed dedication to their new country, the potential for illegal immigration to offer a conduit for terrorist elements to move across international borders with the intent to harm has increased over the years. Suffice it to say that more than a majority of illegal immigrants really mean well and only seek economic betterment for themselves and their families, but the unfortunate event of September 11 has spoiled the "soup" for everyone and, thus, has created a less than tolerant attitude toward legal and illegal immigration.

Hence "given the ingenuity and perseverance of people desperate to migrate, something resembling a contest has developed between people prepared to adopt unorthodox and illegal methods of entry into desired states of resettlement, and the governments of those states equally determined to prevent unwanted migrants from achieving this goal" (Dirks 1998, 378). The ethnic makeup of the United States is changing very rapidly, as all the recent migrants have come from Asia, Mexico, Middle East, Central America, and the Caribbean, as a result of the lowering of immigration barriers since the 1960s, and especially since the mid-1980s (Shain 1999, 4). While many have argued that immigrant identification with their native homelands would have serious consequences for America's national cohesion and civic culture, such critics of the rising tide of ethnic identification are often rearticulating an old American fear that the devotion to ancestral homelands further exacerbates domestic ethnic strains and endangers the fabric of American society. Rising unemployment in many industrial countries has also led to resentment against immigrant populations who flock to these countries for employment and other economic and welfare opportunities. To the extent that the word globalization could offer a normative argument for unrestrained immigration, it may, in fact, lead to more conflicts among and within societies.

But of equal importance is the issue of identity, and how the state can be more receptive to alien cultures in the search for a reasonable pathway to national integration. Unfortunately, rather than fostering practical propositions on the issue of identity, the debate has been reduced to a level of ideological romanticism bereft of appropriate solutions to dealing with the problem of cultural assimilation and citizenship. As Francis Fukuyama (2006, 18) argues, "the problem of immigration and identity ultimately converges with the larger problem of the valueless-ness of postmodernity, which in itself, has made it impossible for them to assert the kinds of shared beliefs for which they demand as a condition for citizenship." "Multiculturalism, understood not just as tolerance of cultural diversity in de facto multicultural societies but as the demand for legal recognition of the rights of ethnic, racial, religious, or cultural groups, has now become established in virtually all modern liberal democracies" (Fukuyama 2006, 9). Not only does multiculturalism require a noticeable rearrangement in the traditional institutions of sociopolitical relations but it also requires an equivalent reorientation and change in the essential foundations of national identity. But the question remains as to whether multiculturalism can create the kind of high citizenship in the interest of the polis as required in the Aristotelian tradition, or whether it simply shifts hitherto existent political and economic competition into the cultural arena.

Ironically, while liberal societies seek the integration and assimilation of immigrant cultures into the larger national framework of citizenship, its parallel pursuit and emphasis on multiculturalism reinforces specific cultural identities that take away from the very focus on national integration. Multiculturalism recognizes differences in the makeup of the national community whereas integration seeks to subsume such differences in the quest for a universal identity. "By celebrating 'difference,' identity politics raises questions about what defines us as a nation" (Citrin et al. 2007, 31). For most new immigrants, it portends a rather painful experience to abandon the culture and customs they have grown up in for many years; although for the native citizens, continued emphasis on multiculturalism and its reference to diversity raises more questions about identity. What does this mean for my own native culture? What does it mean for identity, and do I have to learn the culture of the other to retain portions of mine? These are both vexing questions that in many practical ways have remained the bane of multiculturalism. When new immigrants seek to retain their cultural identifications and to move into areas more popularly inhabited by some of their own, it becomes one of many coping mechanisms employed in dealing with problems of adaptation and assimilation.

Immigration: Reform without Consensus

It has become obvious that "by stimulating a steady influx of immigrants from Latin America and Asia, the Immigration and Nationality Act of 1965 ended up transforming the ethnic composition of the United States" (Citrin et al. 2007, 31). But increased assertiveness about group identities in the aftermath of the civil rights movement and increased immigration has crushed the liberal expectancy that modernization would overcome the divisiveness of ethnic ties (Glazer and Moynihan 1975). "Instead, the best estimates suggest that since then, the number of illegal immigrants has more than tripled; and local governments are staggering under the cost of dealing with the inflow. Since 9/11, controlling who comes into the country has become a serious security issue" (Tumulty 2006, 32). The difficult nature of immigration reform became more obvious in 2006 when Congress decided to take up the issue as well as the porous nature of America's southern border. As protests erupted in many parts of the country, the debate revealed deep-seated tensions on a partisan level as well as in a country severely dependent on cheap immigrant labor but equally concerned about border security, economic prosperity, and national identity. The issue became how to reconcile the increasing appetite of the business interests for cheap labor and the nation's quest to maintain control of its borders as well as protect the public from harm. But the demonstrations were also sparking other reactions, especially as some of the protesters waved Mexican flags instead of the American flag, which as suggestive as it may seem, resonates an ingrained cultural attachment to the country of origin as opposed to the host country. This is the enduring quality that Samuel Huntington refers to as the kin-country syndrome.

Concern about the country's national identity—and fear that terrorists may cross the border as easily as immigrants—have made border security a hot-button topic. "While the Republicans were locked in a bitter debate over whether a generous program for foreign workers and amnesty are the solution to the problem" (Mascolo 2006, 3), others called for a mixed program of guest-worker permits and the construction of security fence to safeguard critical nodes (passage ways) along the 3141 km (1952 mile) United States–Mexican border. Even though Americans strongly believe that the government should do more to keep new illegal immigrants from entering the country, a majority (82 percent) felt that the United States was not doing enough to protect its borders from entry by illegal immigrants (Figure 4.1). Another side of this is the inherent ambivalence of large sections of the American public on matters of immigration policy. But how much should public opinion drive government's response to illegal immigration that has become a crucial element in the nation's inchoate homeland security policy?

According to Susan Page and Kathy Kiel (2006, 1), while Americans endorse the most controversial proposals of both those who want to penalize illegal immigrants and those who want to let them stay, the seemingly contradictory public attitude about immigration reflects the same problems that bedevil Congress in trying to figure out how to handle immigration. The inherent disconnect between public opinion and the pragmatism of congressional politics is one among many other factors undermining an effective immigration reform and border security.

Much of the central issues in congressional deliberations tend to deal more with immigration-related issues such as guest-worker program, amnesty, cheap labor, jobs that Americans do not want, and earned citizenship. "Every proposal

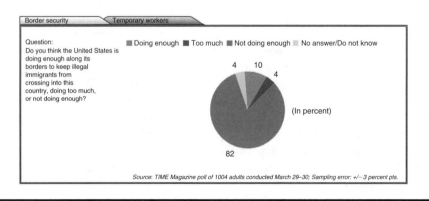

Figure 4.1   Respondents' views on border security (2006).

before Congress calls for more border-patrol agents, more jails and detention centers for captured illegal immigrants, and new technology to enable employers to screen employees to ensure that they are lawfully in the country" (Tumulty 2006, 39). Even though the Immigration Reform and Control Act of 1986 "made it illegal for employers to 'knowingly' hire undocumented workers and imposed penalties of up to $11,000 for each violation, lawbreakers are rarely punished, and on those few occasions when employers are punished, the penalties are so small that they amount to little more than a cost of doing business" (Tumulty 2006, 39). A major security problem posed by immigration into the United States is that lawmakers have not yet internalized it as a central element in national security policy; and that is why the debate has generally been drawn to issues concerning how immigration affects the economy, labor supply, social services, and public opinion. While those who advocate amnesty see it as a recognition of human dignity, those who oppose it see it as an awkward way of rewarding lawbreaking, as an invitation to more illegal immigration, and as fostering a climate that undermines efforts to strengthen homeland security.

The point is that immigration policy should not be driven by a litmus test as to one's ideological leaning or as a moral imperative in the absolute sense of the term. The illegality of an act essentially undermines the legitimacy of any moral consideration used in passing judgment on it. When some people defend illegal immigration as beneficial to the American economy because it adds billions of dollars to the country's gross domestic product (GDP), they also forget (or refuse) to acknowledge how many potential terrorists may have already used the same approach to sneak through the border into the country. And if that is also a cost of doing business, then who knows how much spillover effect it would have on the country's security and what price society would be willing to pay for negating the security risks posed by illegal immigration. It has become a common metaphor to say that there are jobs that Americans will not do, but that is rarely true. There are three explanations that could justify this kind of thinking. Firstly, the increasing application of technology in the work environment, especially those that were hitherto driven by manual labor has reduced the inclination and drive of the average American worker to seek jobs that currently require extensive application of manual/physical labor. Secondly, the cumulative effect of increasing levels of educational advancement and literacy rates has made it possible for more people to seek upwardly mobile and higher paying jobs than the relatively low-paying occupations that require manual labor. Thirdly, the earlier dependence of American agriculture on cheap slave labor left an economic legacy to the effect that to sustain profitability, the agricultural sector would need to be anchored on a regular availability of low-wage labor. In the absence of any other attractive alternative to slave labor, illegal immigration has thus by default become an attractive option.

Salient Boundaries of Homeland Security

The idea of homeland security in its contemporary application was born out of the traumatic experience of September 11, 2001. Since then, it has generated a systemic and institutional transformation in the way we address eminent and potential sources of threat to public safety. Reflecting on America's historical experience, from the first surprise attack on the nation's soil—"the occupation of Washington by the British in August 1814 and the subsequent burning of the Capitol and the White House; the later surprise attack at Pearl Harbor on December 7, 1941—we have become accustomed to the fact that surprise attacks tend to sweep away old conceptions of national security and what it takes to achieve them. They bring new and sometimes radically different assessments of vital interests and available capabilities" (Gaddis 2004, 37). But when we see homeland security as simply a tool for coordinating the nation's response and preempting potential terrorist threats, we unfortunately miss the real point. There was a time when we looked exclusively outside of the nation's borders as the primary source of threats, but today, a new thinking has arisen to the effect that potential threats can also emanate from inside the country.

We oftentimes refer to such term as "the enemy within" as a potential source of threat to the security of this country. But what we seem to have missed is to ask the question as to what could make the enemy within possible? The point is that immigration (most importantly illegal immigration) and its corollary to eventual citizenship in this country has become one of the tools as well as a potential enabler of the enemy within. For those who may wish the United States harm, all they need to do is to emigrate to the United States one way or the other and use many of the different routes available to obtain residency or citizenship. If they are lucky, Congress will pass an amnesty bill that automatically narrows their waiting time for obtaining citizenship and the applicable rights and requisite constitutional protections. With the law on their side (civil liberties protections) and the general availability of potentially harmful materials in the market system, terrorists now have a source and the opportunity to acquire the resources needed to concoct a witches brew of death and devastation. This will not be difficult for the simple fact that new technologies, the Internet, and communications systems have opened new avenues to terrorists to do harm. At a time when "a miniature nuclear bomb can fit within a suit case, microscopic bits of anthrax could kill hundreds, and radioactive and biological materials could injure thousands" (Kettl 2007, 9), terrorists do not need to search too far for opportunities. "Such an assault could be carried out by indigenous or foreign groups, and all it takes is sufficient intelligence gathering and reconnaissance measures" (Combs 2006, 142).

Consider the economic and financial consequences of a simple situation where terrorists would explode in front of Wall Street a few quarts of chlorine laced with radioactive materials or spent plutonium shells that has been smuggled into the country. Certainly, most of the materials are already available in this country in many of the stores or through the Internet and are not considered illegal. "No matter how good a homeland security system the nation builds, it cannot be fool-proof, and terrorists can find a way to exploit any vulnerability" (Kettl 2007, 15). Immigration (legal and illegal) as well as the long-stretch of undefended border territory that the United States maintains with Mexico and Canada pose serious vulnerabilities to the nation's security. While analysts have warned of the need for "tighter control of the nation's borders and ports, they have come to a simple realization that this is a job that requires strong coordination among local governments (which operate ports); state governments (which provide security); and the federal government, which operates the Coast Guard, the Bureau of Citizenship and immigration Services, and other border and coastal defense agencies" (Kettl 2007, 14).

Cultural Enclaves as a Coping Mechanism

As can be observed in the United States, many immigrant populations have been quite successful in carving out for themselves their own territory from the larger American real estate pie. Once in the country, they naturally gravitate to areas where there already exist specific cultural enclaves similar to theirs. They surround themselves with traditional and cultural artifacts from their home countries as a symbol of identity as well as affinity. The tendency to cover up for and to protect one another when in trouble becomes supreme. The Chinatowns, the barrios, and various ethnic enclaves in many urban centers are good examples of resilient subcultures within the larger American cultural domain. Many have argued that immigrant identification with their native homelands would have serious consequences for America's national cohesion and civic culture; and that "even when those newcomers become citizens, group-oriented policies like the amended Voting Rights Act and bilingual education encourage them to identify as members of racial and ethnic groups rather than as members of the entire American people" (Shain 1999, 5). It is also true that certain countries in the world have been (for national security reasons) denied the opportunity to compete in the government's DV-Lottery program, but there is nothing that prevents terrorist elements from obtaining the citizenship of another country and using that as a conduit to enter into the United States. Once in the country, they could start laying the infrastructure for terror within the United States.

As new immigrants refuse to completely abandon their heritage to the attraction of Western civilization, their insistence on remaining true to their faith and tradition will emerge as the new source of global conflict—but this time not between states but within states. As their population increase, they will over time acquire enough voting power to reshape the political fate of their host countries in fundamental ways that can only provoke greater resistance and a sense of cultural ambiguity and loss in the host populations. The choice for governments is to device methods for managing the assimilation or coexistence of immigrant cultures into their societies or to seek their integration in such a way that inherent tensions are not manifested in overt backlash and cultural conflict between native and foreigner. There are also further issues of divided loyalty pertaining to U.S. citizens who hold dual citizenship (one in the United States and the other in their native countries). Regardless of whether immigrants take citizenship or choose to avoid it, proponents of immigration reform claim that "transnational immigration threatens a singular vision of the 'nation' because they seek to bring 'multiculturalism' and not assimilation" (Chavez 1996, 62). In addition to being perceived as a threat to the cultural coherence of the United States, transnationalism is also viewed as a challenge to the sovereignty of the country, and its security. Not only can foreign elements use such a means to enter into the United States but also, once they are in, can quickly disappear into the huge melting pot of American urban population. With the scope of technology, communication, and civil liberties offered by advance liberal democracies (even to noncitizens), potential terrorist enclaves can operate within the country undetected until they unleash their violent activities.

Unfettered Immigration: Restructuring the State of the Union?

The idea of a transnationalist threat to American unity has also received renewed interest from the writings of Samuel Huntington concerning the persistence of kin-country syndrome and diaspora loyalties among new immigrant populations. "In the post-cold war era, diasporic communities which are intensely involved in prolonged conflicts of their kin countries or communities muster considerable political influence over their host governments, redefine their national interest, and affect perceptions of identity in both their old and new countries of residence" (Huntington 1996, 272–291). "Massive immigration (legal and illegal) from Mexico and the new trend toward rapprochement and reconciliation between the Mexican government and Mexican-Americans have also raised some anxiety over Mexican political separatism in America" (Tololyan 1991, 36). Mexican-Americans make up the majority of the U.S. Hispanic community, which has now become the largest ethnic minority in the country. "In Houston, the nation's fourth largest city, Hispanics have overtaken 'Anglo-Americans' as the city's largest ethnic group, largely because of immigration from Mexico" (*Washington Post* 1998). To the extent that this level of immigration benefits Mexico by allowing it to export is own domestic problems (including unemployment) elsewhere, transnationalism has important political implications for both countries. It not only contributes to domestic electoral opportunities in the United States when candidates appeal to new demographic trends within their constituency but also serves as source of indirect influence on U.S. foreign policy and international relations.

Given that by 2050 white America is expected to lose its majority to Hispanics, Asians, and blacks, Huntington wonders whether the trend toward "the de-Westernization of the United States—means its de-Americanization in the democratic sense." He warns that, if the pillars of American identity—the democratic liberal principle and its European heritage—are further eroded, the United States might find itself, like the former Soviet Union, falling "onto the ash heap of history" (Huntington 1993, 180). With an ever increasing birthrate including legal and illegal immigration, the new immigrant population is poised to shape not only the demographic characteristics of the United States but also its national identity and politics. The enormous constitutional protections offered by liberal free societies provide a legal basis for new immigrants to challenge and in most cases reverse the existent state of affairs in their host countries. A case in point would be the State of Texas where it has been noted that Hispanics make up more than a majority of students in its public school system. In June 2005, and to much public dismay, the Dallas (Texas) public school system made a proposal that all principals of its public schools must learn to speak Spanish (perhaps as a first language), so as to be able to communicate more effectively with a majority of its students and their parents. Although the proposal is yet to be voted on, it is one of many incremental but seemingly mundane changes that will visit many parts of the United States as immigrant populations acquire demographic and political majorities at different governmental levels.

The real issue in the American context is the inability to reconcile the increasing appetite of the private sector for cheap labor offered by the immigrant population, and the government's desire to maintain control of its sovereignty and territorial integrity. Recent public opinion surveys of Americans by *Time* magazine in 2006 on the issue of illegal immigration shows a marked public sensitivity to its economic and security implications. While 60 percent held the view that its costs American taxpayers too much money to provide illegal immigrants with social and welfare services, about 45 percent were of the opinion that it would increase the likelihood of terrorism (Figure 4.2). This observation is consistent with a *CNN/USA Today/* Gallup poll (2006, Figure 4.3), in which a majority of respondents (60 percent) felt that illegal immigration hurts the economy by driving down wages for many Americans. Notwithstanding the fact that as some have argued elsewhere, and perhaps correctly, that illegal immigrants contribute to the nation's GDP and tax revenues more than it takes away, but on the contrary it is also important to note that its relative downward impact on wage rates would be highly consequential for unemployment and demand for goods and services, which all things being equal, could have an adverse effect on the rate of GDP. The market failure argument that seems to extol the underground economy that drives illegal immigration would also need to be balanced with the long-term distortions it creates in the normal operation of the market system.

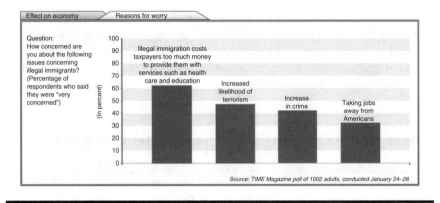

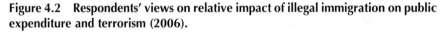

Figure 4.2   Respondents' views on relative impact of illegal immigration on public expenditure and terrorism (2006).

There is also another issue related to illegal immigration that seems to be given little or no attention. It is the health and food security problem it could pose. Normally, when legal immigrants or visitors enter into the country through any of the international airports, they and their belongings are screened by customs agents. Prohibited crops, seedlings, fresh fruits, and vegetables are confiscated to prevent the possible introduction of pests, bugs, worms, or other alien crops/vegetation into the country that could harm the nation's agriculture. Most people who seek to bring prohibited and illicit drugs through the airports are also apprehended. But illegal immigrants circumvent this very important process. At a time when the world is witnessing dramatic increases in the spread of diseases like tuberculosis, cholera, hepatitis, HIV-AIDS, and other pathogens, and when these ailments are potentially

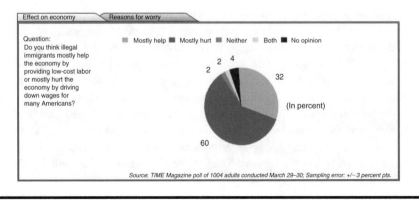

Figure 4.3   Respondents' views on relative impact of illegal immigration on wage rates (2006).

carried into the country without detection, diagnosis, or treatment, they represent a serious and continuing threat to public health. And because of the peculiar status of an illegal immigrant, the fear of being caught and deported would prevent those who may need serious medical treatment from doing so, hence posing an even greater risk to themselves and to public safety.

Power Politics, Control, and Territorial Conquest

In his much acclaimed work titled *Sorrows of Empire*, Chalmers Johnson (2004) decried the impending demise of American global hegemony by recollecting a trail of foreign policy and grand strategic blunders the United States has made over the years and how the cumulative effect has already set the stage for America's decline. It was an apocalyptic assessment of an impending disintegration of the American empire such that even "if the likelihood of perpetual war hangs over the world, the situation in the United States hardly seems any better" (Johnson 2004, 291). By referencing the demise of six earlier empires—Nazi Germany, Imperial Japan, Great Britain, France, the Netherlands, and the Soviet Union—Johnson (2004, 310) denotes that while "empires do not last, their ends are usually unpleasant." And the reason for their collapse can be tied to a combination of imperial overstretch, rigid economic institutions, and an inability to reform which left them vulnerable in the face of disastrous wars. Johnson (2004, 310) therefore concludes that "there is no reason to think that an American empire will not go the same way—and for the same reasons."

One should not be particularly bothered by the historical relativism inherent in Johnson's predictions, but instead, I argue that the impending demise of the American state is less likely to be the result of its "militarism and imperialism which threatens democratic government at home just as they menace the independence and sovereignty of other countries" (Johnson 2004, 291). If the mighty Soviet Union could collapse so inexorably in 1991 without a single shot being fired by either of the cold war adversaries, the predicted collapse of the American empire should not seem so earth-shattering. After all, there was a Roman Empire, and years after that the British Empire. That was a time when kings and monarchs ruled many regions of the world by a combination of imperial majesty laced with brute subjugation. But what will eventually undermine and (even if slowly) set the stage for the eventual demise of the American empire, its national identity and, in fact, its sovereignty will be unchecked illegal immigration. As specious as it may seem, at least in the early stages, its long-term implication for the extant social and political structure, power relations, national interest, and domestic policy will be highly consequential.

While it remains difficult to accurately estimate the number of illegal immigrants in the United States, most data locate them at 11 million the greater majority of whom are Mexicans. Compared to the general American population, "illegal immigrants are less educated, more likely to work in agriculture, construction, and other low-wage jobs, more likely to speak Spanish, and more likely to live in ethnic enclaves. Hence, they are less likely than other immigrants or native-born Hispanics to become integrated into mainstream society or to view themselves as members of the American political community" (Citrin et al. 2007, 46). Statistics show that "about 6.3 million illegal immigrants from Mexico live in the United States, and an average of 485,000 more arrive each year. In response, state legislatures considered nearly 300 bills on immigration policy in the first half of 2005 alone, but passed only 47" (Thornburgh 2006, 38), thus pointing to the political nature and difficulty of making immigration policy even at a time when homeland security has remained the centerpiece of the national security strategy.

Evidence points to the fact that most of the illegal immigrants who come into the United States have settled in the border states of Texas, Arizona, California, and in other states such as New Mexico, Florida, and Colorado. In a few years, a combination of legal and illegal immigration and high birth rates among these populations will grant them enough votes to elect representatives from their own communities into positions of political power. And the figures are indeed rather impressive. "Not only are 11 million people living in the United States illegally but also the 41 million Hispanics living in the country, legally or not, are the nation's largest majority. Former Caucasian majorities in Miami and Los Angeles have become minorities; and in another ten years, the same will likely be true of New York and Washington" (Mascolo 2006, 3). Over time, they would be able to acquire enough numbers to become the majority and to reshape the political, economic, and cultural landscape in these states and communities. The cultural attachment (kin-country syndrome) will continue to strengthen the bond of fellowship between immigrants and their native country. As the political interests of these communities slowly diverge from that of the national government (or the dominant political culture), the momentum to seek a kind of political separation (or political identity) from the national government will start to build up. They can then use their electoral votes to affect the kinds of structural changes they seek. Even if this does not become possible, then there is that other greater (and perhaps more realistic) possibility that border states like Texas, California, Arizona, and even New Mexico will eventually become part of a Greater Mexico, perhaps within the next 25–50 years. If and when a democratic and free-market regime emerges in Cuba in the next couple of years, there is as much certainty that Florida would have become part of a Greater Cuba. If this sociopolitical engineering is repeated in many other states and regions in the United States, that then begins a process in which the body politic starts to disintegrate and the American national identity and character (as we know it) could become irrecoverable. Only then can we begin to envision not only the end of the American empire but also most likely its character and collective identity as a people and as a nation.

The fault lines are already evident in many other ways such as the move by some states to require English as the official language (a reaction to bilingual education), the singing of the national anthem in Spanish without the words as they are in the original version, printing public documents or signposts in many other languages besides English, mandating employees to learn to speak the language of their benefactors, and other incremental changes. As this phenomenon plays itself out over the next few decades, it will become a deciding factor in the evolving battle of identity, cultural dominance, and territorial and political control. The irony is that even if illegal immigration is completely brought to a halt today, the dynamic enunciated above has already become inevitable and would simply be reinforced by a high birth rate and changing residential patterns.

Conclusion

While the current global war on terrorism is focused on seeking out and destroying terrorists and their overseas sanctuaries, American's most daunting domestic challenge is posed by the open nature of its borders. "With some 90,000 miles of coastline, 5,000 miles of intercoastal waterways, and 9,000 miles of land borders, access into America is limitless. The more than 360 ports and major points of entry for international travelers have stretched the capacity of the federal government to maintain even an appearance of control (Hoffman 2006, 143). "Military forces, and the nation's homeland defense can be excellent; but 99.9 percent protection is not enough when terrorists can slip through tiny cracks in the system and inflict massive damage" (Kettl 2007, 9). These cracks are getting wider and wider everyday as a result of lack of political will to deal decisively with illegal immigration. Although the debate has more often than not moved away from the practical realities of transnational immigration into the realm of domestic electoral politics, there is a sense of resigned indignation that any final agreement on the issue would be highly consequential. Uncontrolled immigration (legal or illegal) can enable potential terrorists to enter into the country, set up "shop," incubate, and develop the critical infrastructure and network for terror. And, above all, would still be protected by the liberties and opportunities offered in a liberal society.

Nonetheless, there are practical approaches that could be taken even if some deviates from the current norm. Congress must face up to the danger posed to this country and should see illegal immigration (in particular) as a potential source of security risk. The nation's borders need to be secured by passing a robust immigration policy, hiring more personnel, and providing them with the equipment they need to do the job. Require proof of residency and citizenship status to obtain official documents such as driver's licenses, social security cards, as well as government services (social welfare programs). Hiring illegal immigrants who do not have the proper documentation should earn stiff fines for employers. The reason why this specific provision has generally been ignored is because by inserting the word "knowingly" in the current language, it offers employers an easy means of escape.

They could always claim that they did not know that a potential employee did not have the required documentation. But this defense can always be avoided by requiring employers to verify the documents of potential employees before they offer a job. The burden of negligence should be on the employer, not the government. Government should establish a robust guest-worker program that requires benefactors to renew their permits annually. A time limit should be imposed for each benefactor and renewal would be automatic as long as the job is available and if there is no criminal record.

Another loophole in the nation's security wire is visitors who come into the country with proper immigration papers and visas. It is true that in order "to improve security and screening of travelers, the Department of Homeland Security has implemented the U.S. Visitor and Immigrant Status Indicator Technology (VISIT) program, by which visitors have their photographs and fingerprints taken to confirm their identity and validate their entry into, and exit from, the United States" (Hoffman 2006, 149). This procedure is a post 9/11 development and is available in almost all the major international airports and seaports in the country. Still there are loopholes in the program. Firstly, "few resources are in place to go after those who do not leave at the expiration of their visa, and instead join the millions of illegal aliens loose inside the country. Secondly, since visitors from 27 allied countries are exempt from participation in the VISIT program, many prospective terrorists have traveled to the United States (either by obtaining residency or by establishing citizenship of those countries) via these countries" (Hoffman 2006, 149).

What would need to be done in this regard is to require visitors coming into the United States to sign a consent form at the port of entry agreeing to leave at the end of their officially allowed stay, or to notify authorities of the need for extension if such is allowable under the conditions of entry. Such requests for extension cannot be guaranteed but should depend on the outcome of the review process. If a visitor refuses to sign the consent form, that in itself should provide a legitimate cause for denial of entry. But for visitors who refuse to leave at the expiration of their stay, the person's status would automatically revert to that of an illegal immigrant and would be subject to all applicable statutes, plus would be categorized as a criminal offense. As in all other crimes, the person should be declared wanted and subject to arrest by law enforcement in any of the 50 states. Because the fingerprints were already obtained at the port of entry, what could be done would be to require official providers of such documents as social security card, driver's licenses, passports, etc., to run applicant information through the VISIT system of the DHS. In most cases, pictures and information on these persons could be forwarded to law enforcement agencies. All the same, marrying a U.S. citizen or permanent resident as means of avoiding compliance to the conditions of entry would be nullified by the original consent form signed during entry. In addition, it would also be illegal to register or open up a business or to obtain employment, all of which would be subject to applicable legal penalties both for the individual as well as the employer. Although it may not be humanly possible to provide bulletproof protection of the nation's borders, there are certainly several structural and administrative changes that could make a difference in the long run. The effort made so far to secure homeland security must be driven by a sincere willingness to adapt current operational protocols in such a way that they help to eliminate, or at best, reduce the level of exposure and vulnerability to external and internal threats to the nation's security.

References

Chavez, L.R. 1996. Immigration reform and nativism: The nationalist response to the transanationalist challenge. In *Immigrants Out! The New Nativism and the Anti-Immigrant Response in the United States*, edited by Juan F. Pereas, pp. 61–77. New York: New York University Press.

Citrin, J., A. Lerman, M. Murakami, and K. Pearson. 2007. Testing Huntington: Is hispanic immigration a threat to American identity? *Perspectives on Politics*, 5(1): 31–48, American Political Science Association.

Combs, C.C. 2006. *Terrorism in the Twenty-First Century* (4th Ed.). Upper Saddle River, New Jersey: Pearson-Prentice Hall.

Dirks, G.E. 1998. Factors underlying migration and refugee issues: Responses and cooperation among OECD member states, *Citizenship Studies*, 2(3): 377–395.

Fukuyama, F. 2006. Identity, immigration, and liberal democracy. *Journal of Democracy*, 17(2): 5–20.

Gaddis, J.L. 2004. *Surprise, Security, and the American Experience*. Cambridge, Massachusetts: Harvard University Press.

Glazer, N. and D.P. Moynihan. 1975. *Ethnicity: Theory and Experience*. Cambridge, Massachusetts: Harvard University Press.

Hoffman, F. 2006. Border security: Closing the ingenuity gap. In *Homeland Security and Terrorism: Readings and Interpretations*, edited by Russell D. Howard., James J.F. Forest., and Joanne C. Moore, pp. 143–166. New York: McGraw-Hill.

Huntington, S.P. 1993. If not civilizations, what? Paradigms of the post-cold war world, *Foreign Affairs*, 72(5), November/December, pp. 186–194.

Huntington, S.P. 1996. *The Clash of Civilizations and the Remaking of World Order*. New York: Simon & Schuster, pp. 272–291.

Johnson, C. 2004. *The Sorrows of Empire: Militarism, Secrecy, and the End of the Republic*. New York: Henry Holt & Company.

Kettl, D.F. 2007. *System under Stress: Homeland Security and American Politics* (2nd Ed.). Washington DC: CQ Press.

Mascolo, G. 2006. America's illegals: A nation of immigrants clashes over the future, *Spiegel Magazine Online* (International). http://service.spiegel.de/cache/international/spiegel/0,1518,409683,00.html. Accessed on April 6, 2006, pp. 1–9.

Page, S. and K. Kiely. 2006. Public divided over how to treat illegals, *USA Today*, April 11, 2006. Or http://www.redorbit.com/news/politics/465595/public_divided_over_ how_ to_treat_illegals/index.html#. Accessed on April 7, 2007.

Shain, Y. 1999. *Marketing the American Creed Abroad: Diasporas in the U.S. and Their Homelands*. New York: Cambridge University Press.

Thornburgh, N. 2006. Shadow workers, *Time*, 167(6): 34–45, February 6.

Tololyan, K. 1991. Uprooted peoples enter a new age of migration, *Newsday*, September 8, p. 36.

Tumulty, K. 2006. Who gets to be an American? Inside the immigration debate that is driving the nation, *Time*, 167(15): 30–40, April 10.

Washington Post. 1998. New Law in Mexico, May 31.

Chapter 5

Homeland Security Agencies in Selected Southern States: Case Studies in Politics, Organizations, and Policies

Robert W. Smith

CONTENTS

77

Introduction

Soon after the terrorist attacks of September 11, 2001, federal, state, and local governments mobilized support and resources to (1) establish new organizations or (2) expand current departments, agencies, or offices to coordinate, direct, or administer statewide homeland security efforts. The organizational processes and structures that resulted continue to receive inadequate treatment in the academic literature. Because of the relative newness of homeland security institutions in state government, perhaps this is to be expected. Although there has been some literature on this topic in recent years, it has not been focused on a synthesis of the organizational, policy, and political roles of homeland security agencies within state government. This chapter represents an exploratory effort to determine how best to study homeland security as an organizational phenomenon, and how to better understand the organizational and political attributes that shape state homeland security policies and outcomes.

For example, a state emergency preparedness office will likely approach terrorist threats from a different focus (first responder focus), from that of a law enforcement agency (investigative focus), from that of a state militia/national guard command (mobilization focus), and from that of an office/council of homeland security (a planning focus). This chapter posits that the organizational structures, processes, and politics of these homeland security agencies will be the primary determinants of how homeland security policies are developed, funded, and implemented. The implications of these institutional forces and dynamics will also be examined.

As many scholars and citizens have realized since September 11, 2001, and the aftermath of Hurricane Katrina in August of 2005, terrorism and most natural disasters are, in the final analysis, localized events. Despite efforts to organize and develop federal policies on terrorism (or other emergency situations for that matter), they will always be operationalized in the context of a local or regional event. This de facto places state and local government agencies at the forefront of the "war on terrorism."

Homeland Security in the States

On October 25, 2001, the 107th Congress of the United States passed the USA PATRIOT Act which was subsequently signed into law by President Bush (107-56). The law was designed to provide deterrence to terrorists, and bolster the ability of law enforcement to prevent terrorist attacks. A new federal agency was created one year later when President Bush signed into law the Homeland Security Act of 2002 (PL 107-296). Led by former Pennsylvania Governor, Tom Ridge, the newly formed Department of Homeland Security (DHS) sought to find ways to combine the efforts of state, local, federal government, the private sector (and the entire world community) to protect the United States and other democracies from terrorism.

The PATRIOT Act marked a new effort to make sure federal, state, and local government entities were all on the same page. The efforts were in the form of federal mandates and were thrust upon states. With the introduction of the new DHS came innumerable questions from governors and mayors asking two questions: (1) How should we best protect our local jurisdictions? (2) How are we going to pay for it?

In fact, testimony delivered by Mitt Romney, Governor, State of Massachusetts, to the Senate Governmental Affairs Committee, outlined three areas that governors believe are keys to ensuring that they invest homeland security dollars and resources wisely: investing resources based on comprehensive and integrated statewide plans; maximizing the investment in intelligence gathering and analysis; and, providing a multiyear framework for homeland security (Romney, May 15, 2003). Romney's observations will likely characterize the states homeland security environment for the balance of the twenty-first century.

Legislatures across the nation have subsequently criticized the federal government for not funding its homeland security mandates. In March 2003, state and local government organizations wrote leaders of the U.S. House of Representatives saying the $2 billion appropriated to the states in the fiscal 2004 budget was "only a beginning" (Associated Press State & Local Wire. August 2, 2003). The federal money would not cover the full cost of preventive equipment for local law enforcement nor provide enough dollars to set up a statewide communications network that connects law enforcement, firefighters, and other emergency responders.

These issues remain. In a resolution passed by the National League of Cities (NLC) in 2005, emphasizes the primacy of state and local governments as first responders and stress regional funding scenarios to replace reduced federal funding in critical need areas like first responders and interoperable communications (NLC, Advocacy Priority, 2005). Moreover, the decline of federal funding was also addressed by the NLC's report which called for (1) increased funding for Urban Area Security Grants and State Homeland Security Grants, (2) preservation of funding for homeland security and first responder management programs (pre-9/11), (3) use of homeland security funds to offset overtime expenditures during emergencies, and (4) creation of a Web-based clearinghouse of best practices for homeland security and the waiver of cost-sharing requirements for local governments (NLC, Advocacy Priority, 2005). In a report prepared for the 109th Congress, the Congressional Research Service recommended addressing emergency responder needs, hiring and retention of emergency response personnel, interoperable communications, implications of reductions in federal homeland security funding, cataloging of state and local risk assessments, and state homeland security strategies (http://www.fas.org/sgp/crs/homesec/RL32941.pdf).

The frustration of state officials is equally demonstrated by the recent emergency declarations made by governors' in the states of Arizona and Nevada over acute levels of illegal immigration in these states (Associated Press State & Local Wire. March 29, 2006). The debate over illegal immigration continued in 2006 with a variety of federal proposals to better coordinate state and local efforts (see: http://www.dhs.gov/xnews/releases/press_release_0938.shtm).

In fiscal year (FY) 2006 federal budget, the House of Representatives approved a $1.4 billion increase in homeland security appropriations but reduced funding for state and local first responders by more than $281 million from FY 2005 (http://www.naco.org/CountyNewsTemplate.cfm?template=/Content Management/ContentDisplay.cfm&ContentID=16658). Other shortfalls are not directly related to funding, but can be found in federal requirements in the Homeland Security Grants Program that mandates states that participate in the program plan for 15 specific disaster scenarios, but do so without sufficient oversight and training from the federal government (Caruson and MacManus, 2005). Related to the issue of mandates, a recent study by the State of Florida, which surveyed more than 1000 city and county officials, found that 47 percent of the county government respondents indicated that mandates had the greatest negative impact on their programs and another 40 percent identified financial mandates as a major problem. Moreover, 52 percent of local officials cited the financial burden of federal mandates as a major problem and 31 percent identified management and administrative responsibilities as hindrances (Caruson and MacManus, 2005).

This is not to say that there have not been problems associated with local and state governments using money for homeland security for other than emergency purposes. However, these reports are largely anecdotal and do not indicate a major trend of abuse in these programs; there is simply not enough funds to carry out the homeland security mandates (Caruson and MacManus, 2005). The subsequent round of federal grants awarded in 2006 has been equally criticized as inadequate and misdirected (see http://www.firstresponsecoalition.org/FRCFederal%20Budget-Report.pdf).

In an initial attempt to ascertain whether the nation's capacity to protect itself has improved, the Century Foundation commissioned reports focusing on the ways in which four different states—Pennsylvania, Texas, Washington, and Wisconsin—have attempted to respond to these new threats. This paper utilizes this framework for an analysis of selected state governments in the South. The main theme that emerged from the four reports was business as usual. Either because of budget constraints, institutional inertia, insufficient support and incentive from the federal government, or basic shortsightedness, the reports found little evidence that states and localities have significantly improved protection for their residents (Kettl, 2003). There is nothing to indicate that this trend has been reversed or has been significantly improved.

The task is daunting. Preparing state and local governments to handle the variety of terrorist threats is nearly impossible. Threats could take many forms: nuclear, improvised explosive devices (IEDs), or biochemical threats (anthrax or other airborne illnesses, poisoned water, and food supplies). Each threat requires a different piece of equipment, personnel, or training and at this point, funding does not meet the demand. After the September 11th attacks, states were promised $3.5 billion to fund emergency response activities but received only about $570 million (Brogan, March 26, 2003). In March 2003, the U.S. Conference of Mayors released a study saying American cities are spending an additional $70 million a week to increase security because of the heightened national threat alert from the war in Iraq (Torpy, April 6, 2003).

Indeed, overall federal funding has increased but has been inconsistent. Table 5.1 shows homeland security spending since 2001. But in some respects this was to be expected. Former Secretary Ridge told state security chiefs that, beginning in FY 2004, they would have to provide 25 percent matching funds to be eligible for federal homeland security money (Brogan, March 26, 2003). States do have the broad authority to disperse monies that they receive from the federal government for homeland security measures, but if you are from a jurisdiction mentioned on the departments list of priorities then states must use those funds specifically to protect those locations. DHS listed seven cities as prime targets: New York, Los Angeles, Seattle, Chicago, San Francisco, Houston, and Washington, DC (Scardaville, 2003). To fill some of the funding void, a number of supplemental federal grants were

Table 5.1   Total Federal Resources Allocated for Homeland Security, 2001–2006 (Budget Authority in Billions of Dollars)

Discretionary Budget Authority	*2001 ($)*	*2002 ($)*	*2003 ($)*	*2004 ($)*	*Estimated 2005 ($)*	*Requested 2006 ($)*
Regular appropriations	15.0	17.1	32.2	36.5	43.0	42.2
Supplemental appropriations	3.6	12.3	5.9	0.1	0.6	0
Fee-funded activities	0.7	2.0	2.6	3.2	3.3	5.4
Mandatory spending	1.5	1.7	1.8	1.9	2.2	2.2
Gross budget authority	20.7	33.0	42.5	41.7	49.1	49.7

Note: Components may not sum to totals because of rounding. All years referred to as fiscal years (FYs).

1. The figures in this brief differ slightly from those published by the Office of Management and budget as part of the Administration's 2006 budget request CBO used different estimates of spending for mandatory and fee-funded activities.
2. Excludes offsetting collections and receipts, which are recorded as negative budget authority. (For 2004, those totaled $5.0 billion. For 2005, according to CBO's estimates, they will total $5.3 billion.)

Sources: Adopted from the Congressional Budget Office, 2005. Federal Funding for Homeland Security: An Update. Washington, DC: Congressional Budget Office (CBO).

developed for state and local governments. However, funding for these supplemental programs has been inconsistent. These shortcomings were somewhat addressed in a subsequent rounds of federal funding to major terrorist threat cities. However, although Congress approved the FY 2007 DHS appropriations, of $34.8 billion (an increase of $2.3 billion over FY 2006), funding for state and local first responder assistance programs have decreased from a total of $3.7 billion in FY 2005 to about $2.7 billion in FY 2007 (http://www.naco.org/CountyNewsTemplate.cfm?template=/ContentManagement/ContentDisplay.cfm&ContentID=21763).

But to say there has not been any improvements in the abilities of state and local government to plan and mobilize for terrorist or other homeland security threats would not be accurate. In a report prepared by the National Governor's Association, there is some evidence to suggest that homeland security capacity has improved at the state level (NGA, 2005). In August 2004, 38 of 50 states had homeland security directors. All respondents reported that they had statewide emergency operation centers. The ongoing needs the respondents identifies had to do with training exercises for first responders, bioterrorism preparedness, mutual assistance agreements with neighboring states, coordination among state National Guards, interoperability of communication systems, and protection of critical infrastructure (NGA, 2005). It is interesting to note that some of the early deficiencies cited in tragedy of Hurricane Katrina were problems identified a year earlier.

As a constitutional issue, it is still unclear whether homeland security—a concept unheard of until 2002—is a federal or state responsibility. Asked about the burden on states and cities, DHS Spokesperson Gordon Johndroe said the Bush administration "believes this is a shared responsibility, and we're going to help do much of it." However, he acknowledged that the administration has not figured out what share of the responsibility the federal governing is paying, or should pay (Russakoff and Sanchez, 2003).

In a first of its kind survey of state homeland security offices, Sharkey and Stewart (2002) observed that the ongoing decentralization of federal authority back to state government was clearly evident in the federal strategy on homeland security (see Table 5.2). Even DHS admitted that states must assume a major role. Local governments necessarily retain their first responder role during terror attacks, but state governments needed to develop statewide security plans consistent with federal intent.

The Sharkey and Stewart survey revealed that the majority of the states had homeland security coordinators who report to the governor. At the time of their survey, only two states took action to make the positions permanent. The authors also pointed out that 20 of the 36 functioning homeland security directors were political appointees and thus subject to the vagaries of the election process. Their study noted "the majority of states have responded with task forces, councils, or blue ribbon commissions or councils to study, recommend, or advise the governor on homeland security issues" (Sharkey and Stewart, 2002). Most of the states were working within their existing organizations and budgets with little new funding or personnel provided. In addition, the authors found state homeland security functions

Table 5.2 Homeland Security Organizations (Type and Role)

State	Office of Homeland Security	Department of Emergency Management	Department of Law Enforcement	Health/Public Safety	Role
Alabama	X	—	—	—	A
Arkansas	—	X	—	—	—
Florida	—	—	X	—	DCAF
Georgia	X	—	—	—	DCAF
Kentucky	X	—	—	—	C
Louisiana	—	—	X	—	—
Maryland	—	X	—	—	DCA
Mississippi	—	X	—	—	—
Missouri	—	X	—	—	—
North Carolina	—	—	X	—	—
Oklahoma	—	—	—	X	—
South Carolina	—	—	X	—	—
Tennessee	X	—	—	—	—
Texas	—	X	—	—	—
Virginia	—	X	—	—	DC
West Virginia	—	—	X	—	—

Note: D, directing; C, coordinating; A, advisory; F, funding.

Source: Adapted from Sharkey, E.R. and Stewart, K.B. 2002. Terrorism, Security, and Civil Liberties: The States Respond, Unpublished Manuscript.

were categorized as training of first responders, strategic planning, assessing potential targets, improving modes of communication, evaluating recovery capabilities, coordinating efforts of federal, state, and local agencies, and examining infrastructure, health, and agricultural areas of concern.

They concluded "…the response of the states to the terrorist attacks was limited. Any expectations involving sweeping programmatic attempts to enhance homeland security have largely gone unmet" (Sharkey and Stewart, 2002). With respect to budgets, they noted that of the $6.1 billion available to state and local governments for homeland security, only $1.3 billion came from the state and local jurisdictions (only one-tenth of 1 percent of state and local expenditures for that year). They found that 80 percent of the homeland security offices felt their ability to respond was limited due to monetary constraints. Their survey also revealed a lack of coordination/direction from the federal government, national standards, and personnel with relevant expertise (Sharkey and Stewart, 2002). In a subsequent ICMA study conducted in 2004, state and local governments identified specific need areas in risk assessment, comprehensive planning, and collaboration with other governments (http://icma.org/main/ns_search.asp?Nsid=1886). In addition, many localities reported concerns over the rural versus urban split in funding and emphasis for homeland security (Wodele, 2005). Rural public health capabilities, rural hospital readiness, agricultural industry protection, and funding for primarily urban centers were cited as major concerns. It is also interesting to note in a report by the Council of State Governments that a preliminary analysis of the local, state, and federal coordinated response for Hurricane Katrina highlighted some of these very limitations in terms of planning, evacuations, and significant communication difficulties (http://csg-web.csg.org/pubs/Documents/Brief0410-HomelandSecRural.pdf).

Homeland Security as an Organizational Response

When considering institutional arrangements organized under the guise of homeland security, it becomes clear that in most respects the function is unique and complicated arrangement for state governments to undertake. It is not that states have difficulty with new organizational forms or have trepidations about reorganizations. New agencies, temporary or permanent, are created all the time by state governments and looking over the administrative histories of the states for most of the nineteenth and twentieth centuries can be characterized by one form of reorganization or another. Therefore, why is homeland security different from any other reorganization?

The answer to this question lies in the magnitude of the charge conveyed by homeland security and the multifaceted nature of the goals and objectives of homeland security entities. In essence, the mission of homeland security agencies is to take the disaggregated missions charged to multiple other agencies, coordinate efforts with other jurisdictions in the state, function at some level both as a supra-agency and as a paramilitary organization, coordinate and discharge responsibilities passed down from the federal government, meet the political expectations of citizens and law makers, develop consistent policy, and at the same time carry out its responsibilities as any other agency of state government (with budgetary and resource issues). No other agencies in the history of state government have carried so much responsibility on their shoulders.

As discussed earlier, many states have either created new offices or have simply folded responsibilities into existing agencies. This may or may not be the most effective organizational approach. Despite the passage of PL 107-296, which has created the DHS at the federal level, the ensuing debate over whether or not this was the most appropriate organizational approach is still being continued at numerous levels (Brookings Institution, 2002a). Despite the ongoing debate, the federal DHS offers an appropriate model for understanding the organizations created by state government to implement homeland security policies.

The seminal literature to date suggests that there are two preferred models for the organization of homeland security at the federal, state, and local levels: (1) the Single Agency Model which takes an existing agency or a new agency designated to take the lead in security threats or (2) Interagency/Intergovernmental Model which focuses on coordinating the duties and responsibilities of a variety of agencies working together as a team (Brookings Institution, 2002b). Initially, the federal government functioned in the latter model while evolving to the former and now constitutes the federal DHS.

Each form of organization has its strength and weakness. The creation of a cabinet-level department like DHS results in strong accountability relationships with a single agency responsible for the array of programs and polices of homeland security. This understandably facilitates implementation of policies that cut across many other organizations, functions, roles, and responsibilities. This agency becomes a line agency of government and therefore is assigned personnel and budget authority. This further enhances the ability of an organization to function independently and implement its programs. The agency typically functions with set objectives and missions under its originating legislation, but has a great deal of flexibility in terms of how the originating legislation is actually operationalized. As a cabinet agency the reporting lines of authority flow through the president, governor, or chief executive officer and extend throughout the agency presumably enhancing elements of accountability and efficiency in delivery of services or programs. This equally places the agency under the political responsibility of the chief policy maker.

At the same time, one centralized agency cannot accommodate all related functions of government. Other agencies will still operate as independent components of the larger agency and some will remain largely outside of the sphere of influence of the homeland security agency. For example, at the federal level, the FBI and the CIA must still operate in areas of drug enforcement and intelligence gathering; and at the state level, a Division of State Police or a state health department must still enforce criminal statutes and provide health inspection services in addition to their role in homeland security. Coordination of agencies is complicated by component agency communication systems, political agendas (e.g., turf wars), and even agency cultures. Several times, all these add to a complicated picture of coordinated activity and policy making, as administrative history shows, reverts to a system of rigid rules and monolithic thinking to simplify and make sense of complicated organizations and structures.

On the other end of the spectrum are interagency arrangements that have a czar or central figure heading an office or a task force. The head of this agency is appointed by the chief executive officer, who is likely responsible for crafting homeland security policies, tracks other agency coordination and performance, has some budgetary responsibility of other agencies, and convenes meetings for all relevant agencies. The limitations of this approach suggest that any central figure would unlikely be able to completely control other agencies to craft coherent policies. A derivative of this effort would be a coordinating council similar to the National Security Council or the forerunner to DHS, the Homeland Security Council, at the federal level. The strength would be the ability to pull all agencies under one umbrella for coordination purposes and retain an ability to mobilize those agencies to handle specific problems or policy issues as needed. This was achieved by the creation of the post of an "intelligence czar" or National Intelligence Director (Eisenberg et al., 2005).

Is there a generic or common set of functions associated with both of these models? Literature suggests organizations must coordinate agencies in the homeland security system, prepare strategic plans as the basis for policies on homeland security, budget for all of the component agencies and the ability to direct resources to priority areas as needed, respond and manage crises effectively at the site or sites of terrorist incidents, and possess statutory and regulatory authority to propose legislation or engage in rulemaking such that the agency can effectively respond (Brookings Institution, 2002a).

In the context of optimal organizational arrangements, it is clear that more research needs to be done to examine the proper organization structure to facilitate homeland security. Proposals in Congress have stressed the need for FEMA to be a separate organization from homeland security to ensure better and more focused attention on natural disaster responses (Wittenauer, September 26, 2005).

Developing Homeland Security Policy in the States

The statute creating DHS specifically focuses on a role to be played by state and localities in the delivery of homeland security. In many respects, the federal mandate is that states and localities own the homeland security problem (Brookings Institution, 2002a). In large measure, this is a function of the fact that federal government personnel available to combat terrorism is estimated at 75,000 law enforcement personnel versus approximately 748,000 state and local police force personnel (Kincaid and Cole, 2002).

Hence, the question that state homeland security offices confront is whether or not their states do in fact have a homeland security policy. It is evident states have well-developed protocols and policy initiatives in a variety of areas related to homeland security. For example, all states have a disaster preparedness office and statewide mechanisms and policies to guide law enforcement activities. Moreover, the states have a well-defined National Guard structure, and command and control processes. Each of these component agencies has developed policies that constitute an umbrella of homeland security policies. As Sharkey and Stewart (2002) have confirmed, states have new offices or passed legislation charging specific agencies with new homeland security roles and responsibilities. However, the data available suggests that homeland security policy is largely a matter for the federal government. The state roles seem more to be implementers of component national policies rather than state homeland security policy.

If we apply the organizational prerequisites to the existing structures for homeland security in the states, it is clear that most of the agencies created at the state level fail to meet all the stated criteria for a fully functional agency. This is not to suggest that states are ill prepared to handle the next round of terrorist threats. By necessity, states and particularly local governments are the first responders to any terror threat or action. They have years of experience and in concert with federal entities like FEMA, the organization processes and mechanisms are in place to allow for a coordinated response and for natural disasters (albeit with a mixed record of success). To the extent, National Guard elements are also mobilized in such national disaster scenarios, the potential for states to respond effectively does exist.

Yet the role and issue for state homeland security offices is their ability to predict and collect intelligence and be prepared to respond to the variety of possible terror threats that may be brought to bear in any one state. As experts in counter terrorism remind us, surprise is the hallmark of a terrorist attack and until that point of attack, it is difficult to determine when, if, how, and where such attacks will occur (Comfort, 2002). This is an important role in the context of state homeland security policy and therefore, the question becomes, are the states positioned to perform this intelligence role?

To a degree the answer is evident in the structure of the offices. Of the 16 southern states included in this review, 25 percent of the states have created formal offices of homeland security, 38 percent have homeland security responsibilities within state emergency management offices, 31 percent are located in law enforcement agencies, and 6 percent have states placing responsibility in the health and public safety offices.

Many states have chosen to create separate offices, whose heads are appointed by governors and are at minimum subject to the reality of political appointees serving at the pleasure of the governor given the vagaries of electoral outcomes. Hence, many agency heads and their offices are viewed as temporary arrangements. Second, none of the states meet all the criteria established for determining an effective functioning homeland security organization as outlined in the Century Foundation reports. Table 5.3 shows a selective sample of homeland security offices and whether or not they meet the idealized functional roles.

Another element to consider is the normative pressures applied from professionals that seek to standardize processes and procedures in homeland security. One of the professional pressure points comes from first responders, emergency management,

Table 5.3 Organizational Assessment State Homeland Security Offices

State	Coordinate	Strategic Plan	Budget	Crisis Management	Legal Authority
Alabama	X	—	X	—	X
Georgia	X	—	—	—	X
Kentucky	X	—	—	—	X
Tennessee	X	X	—	—	X

Note: From southern states with formal homeland security offices. Responsibilities were derived from legislation, executive orders, or mission statements available on state home pages.

and law enforcement professionals while the other pressure emanates from military or National Guard elements. These sets of professionals know their business, be that responding to emergencies or securing crucial infrastructure. By looking at the overall appointments to head homeland security institutions many of these professions are represented in the leadership roles. What this has tended to do is to favor mechanisms that are command and control dominated by these professionals. This is clearly acceptable during a crisis, but may not be the best organizational response for proactive efforts or when homeland security requires extensive interactions between traditional line-based civilian agencies (e.g., transportation, health agencies).

Because state and federal institutions are often seen as durable and unchanging, many scholars believe that it takes a dramatic external shock to create significant change. September 11, 2001, an example of such an event, indeed produced an extreme change in government organization, most notable in the creation of the Federal DHS.

Because political decision-making systems and institutional structures shape political outcomes, it is important to understand their effect on the manner in which DHS and state and local agencies were created. Another element to consider is the stability of institutions themselves. U.S. institutions are resilient to change as a result of legislative rules that eliminate instability and minimize the possibility of change at the hand of individual decision makers. Because homeland security agencies were created aftermath the terrorist attacks of September 11, 2001, questions concerning the precision of legislative rules governing both federal and state offices arise. In the event that such rules are not as well formulated, homeland security agencies may be less stable than their executive cabinet-level department counterparts.

Another element to be considered is that many government institutions in place today are not there as a result of conscious design strategy. Although the initial formulation of the DHS was the result of an explicit governmental decision, the operational mandates associated with the organization in the future were not necessarily planned and may arise as a result of the continual functioning of the institution itself. As a result, the role that DHS and related state agencies will play in the management of homeland security is still unfolding, but will become more defined with time and the refinement of standard operating procedures and protocols. Where each state government chooses to locate its homeland security agency (state emergency preparedness office, state law enforcement division, or an individual DHS agency) will also have an affect on the procedures, rules, and protocols that the institution itself develops. As a result, these organizational processes will impact the way that the agency functions, determine the power it maintains, and color the way that it is perceived in its jurisdiction.

The formation of state agencies can be argued to be the result of either conscious or unconscious policy design. On one hand, state decision makers made a distinct decision to incorporate into their governments some form of a domestic security program. Conversely, state agencies were essentially forced to follow the federal precedent. Many of those agencies created were in actuality just piggybacked on another existing agency, leading to the possibility that they were in fact neither consciously nor strategically created.

One final element to consider is that "Institutions do not just constrain options: They establish the very criteria by which people discover their preferences" (Powell and DiMaggio, 1991, p. 28). The creation of an organization such as the federal DHS will undoubtedly affect the relationships between the various organizations within the agency, as well as the dynamic of each part of the agency individually. On a state level, the type of organization that each state government creates to make security policy will affect the policies that are made. As a result, the way constituents of that state view homeland security and respond to homeland security initiatives will vary. Similarly, many scholars reject intentionality; they claim that institutions affect the routine nature of human behavior without individuals even realizing such a change has occurred. The effect that homeland security agencies may have on individuals and policies, therefore, may be a latent effect of which policy makers are unaware. This does not bode well for strategic or proactive policy making for homeland security at the state level.

Although institutions are more than the sum of their parts and have a dramatic effect on individuals, initially, they are products of human action, and the rules behind their initial implementation are constructed amidst conflict between individuals. Major political struggles oftentimes revolve around reformulations of government. Such conflict could be seen in the formulation of the federal DHS, as the formulators of the agency struggled to create, and American citizens struggled to understand, a new government entity. This process is mirrored in the states. However, because state government changes were made following the restructuring of the federal government, they did not receive as much political opposition.

Another element concerns tightly coupled institutions that may be unstable in the face of external shocks. Such assertions indicate that in the event of another occurrence similar to the September 11, 2001, there is uncertainty as to whether or not state departments of homeland security will be able to adequately respond to the crisis. Many observers believe the response is dependent upon the strength of the federal agency's response. If the federal DHS were ill equipped or ill managed to handle the crisis, local and state security entities would likely falter as well.

What these cumulative institutionalist frames point toward is that homeland security policies emanating from the state level will largely mimic that of the federal government and therefore, there will be minimal expectations of variance or innovation in approaches for homeland security. This is confirmed by John Nagy (2002), who writes that "state budget constraints, the slow pace of the federal government in providing funds and guidance along with agency turf battles and neglected public health systems have left little room for creative thinking and cutting edge initiatives in this area" (Nagy, September 11, 2002). He points out that this does not mean that states are not getting things done, but that the name of the game is keeping up, rather than getting ahead. This is in contrast to other areas, such as the welfare to workfare transition, and in any other policy areas, where flexibility is retained by states in terms of how they develop statewide policies and implement programs.

Regardless of the placement of domestic homeland security agencies, it should be noted that the agency websites accessible through the aforementioned link all clearly convey their relationship to the federal DHS. Such similarities attempt to gloss over the differences between agencies and relate them to the institutional framework of the federal model for such a department. Many homeland security home pages contain very little information of their own, and instead serve merely as a location for links to various state organizations that appear to actually have distinct roles in the area of state security.

For example, the Sharkey and Stewart (2002) survey revealed that there is little interaction between southern states over homeland security. In fact, it may be more desirable to develop coherent and regional-based homeland security zones that transcend state boundaries but there has been little movement in this area. What we see at the state level is a redundancy factor across state governments. Redundancy is a tried and true component of a well-functioning bureaucratic environment, but it equally implies a command and control structure approach which may not be the best type of structure to ensure open communications, proactive thinking, and positive interrelationships that must be developed as part of a comprehensive system of homeland security across the states.

Linkages between Politics and Policy

This chapter does not seek to negate the important roles of the states in the homeland security process, but by extension readers can see that the conceptual arguments advanced to this point suggest that, similar to the IRS, FBI, EPA, or even the National Park System, there might be a rationale for a federal DHS office in each state where the responsibility for homeland security is a straightforward matter of federal jurisdiction. Each state office of DHS would then simply develop relationships and networks with first responders and other emergency personnel and law enforcement as necessary.

Why has this form of arrangement been not suggested or adopted? This is precisely where considerations of politics come to bear on homeland security in organization structure and in policy making. Historically, the federal government has been responsible for military action and the states have been responsible for law enforcement activity. The federal government has organized agencies like FEMA to handle large-scale (typically natural) disasters and has developed a system of cooperation with state agencies. Federal law enforcement cooperates with local law enforcement and vice versa (for the most part). First responders have always been a local government concern but with some coordination and funding from the states. The various iterations of long-standing federal–state–local relationships could go on, but the point is that homeland security is a unique policy arena and an even more unique organizational challenge. It confronts traditional federalism that has one level of government responsible for certain sets of responsibilities, but with a mix of interlocking responsibilities. Since the 1980s there has been a steady devolution of federal responsibility back to the states, which desired more local control over their policy choices. But is this devolution conducive to the development of accountable, comprehensive, and responsive homeland security policies in the states?

At the heart of all these activities have been politics and the million dollar question about the proper role of the federal government versus state governments. States have long debated the proper role for government in society (ranging from transportation to education to law enforcement to social services). In this sense, homeland security is another card on the political playing table. However, unlike the political trade-offs in some other policy arenas (e.g., education versus social service funding), everyone in state politics is in favor of homeland security. Although there has been some partisan political squabbles over resources, scope of authority and whether political appointees should hold positions of homeland security (more a political dynamic between governors and the legislature); the politics that is evident in the states in the south and across the nation is largely a form of bureaucratic politics where one institution is pitted against another for primacy in the arena of homeland security. Should the emergency management office play the primary role? should the health department have a substantial say? or is homeland security still primarily a law enforcement responsibility?

While this level of political interplay is dynamic and instructive, a new institutionalist paradigm allows for a keen analysis of the political dynamic as it relates to the development of homeland security policy. The politics of homeland security tends to be the politics of establishing policy priorities. Where can some guidance be found to understand the interplay of politics of homeland security and its implications for homeland security policy? Although not developed in this chapter, some scholars have attempted to advocate and integrate a network theory of public policy

(Blom-Hansen, 1997). This is a fruitful line of inquiry and an appropriate place to close this discussion.

The red flag in this descriptive analysis is that the haste of the response creating homeland security agencies and the seeming disaggregated nature of state homeland security systems (e.g., emergency management versus law enforcement) has given rise to institutions and institutional relationships that may supersede any political imperative. Now that we have these institutions in place, the political sense making will occur in the context of these organizations and may not necessarily produce the most accountable, comprehensive, or responsive homeland security policies in the foreseeable future. However, if political leaders and policy makers understand these institutional influences today, then perhaps there may be the opportunity to craft responsive homeland security policies that will balance the best of what a democratic society has to offer with permanent security arrangements to protect citizens from future terrorist threats. In its simplest form, homeland security policies in the states may be the result of placing the cart before the horse.

References

Associated Press State & Local Wire. August 2, 2003. Experts Say State Needs More Security Funding. LexisNexis Academic.

Associated Press State & Local Wire. March 29, 2006. New Mexico Governor Says He'll Renew Border Emergency Declaration. LexisNexis Academic.

Blom-Hansen, J. 1997. A new institutional perspective on policy networks, *Public Administration*. 75(4), 669–694.

Brogan, P. March 26, 2003. Mo. Homeland Security Chief Says Federal Government Shortchanging States. *Gannett News Service*. LexisNexis Academic.

Brookings Institution. 2002a. *Assessing the Department of Homeland Security*. Washington, DC: The Brookings Institution.

Brookings Institution. 2002b. *Protecting the American Homeland*. Washington, DC: The Brookings Institution. Available at: http://www.brookings-institution.com/dybdocroot/fp/projects/homeland/report.htm

Caruson, K. and MacManus, S.A. 2005. Homeland security preparedness: Federal and state mandates and local government, *Spectrum: The Journal of State Government* (Spring 2005), 78(2), 25–28.

Comfort, L.K. 2002. Rethinking security: Organizational fragility in extreme events, *Public Administration Review*. 62 (September), 98–107.

Congressional Budget Office. 2005. Federal Funding for Homeland Security: An Update. Washington, DC: Congressional Budget Office (CBO).

Eisenberg, D., Burger, T.J., Calabresi, M., Cooper, M., Shannon, E., Waller, D., Ghosh, A., Crain, C., and Michaels, M. 2005. Bush's new intelligence czar, *Time Magazine*. 165(9), February 28, 32–35.

Kettl, D.F. 2003. *The States and Homeland Security—Building the Missing Link*. New York: The Century Foundation.

Kincaid, J. and Cole, R.L. 2002. Issues of federalism in response to terrorism, *Public Administration Review*. 62 (September), 181–192.

Nagy, J. September 11, 2002. State Anti-Terrorism Chiefs Play Unclear Role, *Stateline.org*.

NGA (National Governor's Association), 2005. Issue Brief—Homeland Security in the States: Much Progress, More Work. Washington, DC.

NLC (National League of Cities), 2005. 2005 Advocacy Priority—Homeland and Hometown Security. Washington, DC.

Powell, W.W. and DiMaggio, P.J. (Eds.) 1991. *The New Institutionalism in Organizational Analysis*. Chicago, Illinois: University of Chicago Press.

Romney, M. May 15, 2003. Homeland Security. Capitol Hill Hearing Testimony. LexisNexis Academic.

Russakoff, D. and Sanchez, R. April 1, 2003. Begging, Borrowing for Security; Homeland Burden Grows for Cash-Strapped States, Cities. *The Washington Post*. LexisNexis Academic.

Scardaville, M. May 6, 2003. Adding Flexibility and Purpose to Domestic Preparedness Grant Programs. *Heritage Foundation Papers*. LexisNexis Academic.

Sharkey, E.R. and Stewart, K.B. 2002. Terrorism, Security, and Civil Liberties: The States Respond, Unpublished Manuscript.

Torpy, B. April 6, 2003. Georgia Awaits Security Funding. *Atlanta Journal and Constitution*. LexisNexis Academic.

Wittenauer, C. September 26, 2005. Months before Hurricane, A Warning, *AOL News*. LexisNexis Academic.

Wodele, G. 2005. Rural Lawmakers Fending Off Bid to Alter Security Grants, *Congressional Daily*. (July 12, 2005), 5–6.

Chapter 6

Homeland Security: Emerging Discipline, Challenges, and Research

Dale Jones

CONTENTS

A new period in American history started on September 11, 2001, when the United States was attacked from within its own borders. That event, referred to as "9/11," thrust homeland security to the top of the national agenda. America is experiencing a transformation as a result. Homeland security is a reality, challenge, and necessity. Soon, a decade will have passed since 9/11. Even then, the nation will still be in the initial stage of a long endeavor. America will be concerned with homeland security affairs for many years to come. As expected, homeland security is an emerging discipline of study and practice. The early years are characterized as being dynamic and full of change. This chapter provides an overview of the emerging discipline of homeland security and focuses on its components, challenges, and areas for public administration and public management research.

Understanding Homeland Security

In the American system of government, homeland security is now firmly a primary domestic public policy area just like education, healthcare, environment, national defense, and others (Dye, 2005). The subject of homeland security is quite broad. Although just about every citizen knows homeland security has to do with protecting the nation from harm, many do not truly understand what homeland security is. Thus, an important and necessary starting place is to understand what we mean by homeland security. This section addresses how homeland security was established as a public policy arena, presents definitions of homeland security and homeland defense, introduces the homeland security spectrum, and discusses homeland security as an emerging academic discipline.

The Establishment of Homeland Security

The Cold War era in United States history lasted for 45 years. The dismantling of the Berlin Wall in 1989, reunification of Germany in 1990, and dissolution of the Soviet Union in 1991 marked the end of the Cold War. The United States spent the majority of the 1990s examining threats to America, trying to define the new world order, and projecting America's role in it. Throughout the decade, numerous studies, panels, task forces, and commissions warned of forthcoming dangers for the nation and the need for greater homeland defense as part of national security. The U.S. Commission on National Security/21st Century, known also as the Hart–Rudman Commission, was particularly prescient in its initial report published in September 1999. The first conclusion of the report stated that "America will become increasingly vulnerable to hostile attack on our homeland, and our military superiority will not entirely protect us" (Hart–Rudman Commission, 1999: 4). National security policy makers knew that a high potential existed for attacks against American citizens on U.S. continental territory.

According to the Department of Defense (DOD), the U.S. homeland is "The physical region that includes the continental United States, Alaska, Hawaii, United States territories and possessions, and surrounding territorial waters and airspace" (Department of Defense, 2005a: GL-8). For the first time since the surprise attack on Pearl Harbor in 1941, the United States suffered a serious, direct attack on its homeland on September 11, 2001, when terrorists flew commercial airliners into New York City's World Trade Center towers, the Pentagon, and a field in Shanksville, Pennsylvania. Terrorism acts began more than 100 years before 9/11 with 1968 being the advent of modern, international terrorism (Hoffman, 2002). Furthermore, terrorism evolved during the decade of the 1990s into "a core threat to international security" (Cronin and Ludes, 2004: 1). Some of the most devastating assaults against the United States were terrorist bombings of Khobar Towers in Saudi Arabia in 1996, American embassies in Kenya and Tanzania in 1998, and of the *U.S.S. Cole* in Yemen in 2000. Then, on September 11, America absorbed the culmination of terrorist attacks which "eclipsed anything previously seen in terrorism" and were "unparalleled in their severity and lethal ambitions" (Hoffman, 2002: 303–304).

The national response to the 9/11 attacks resulted in the most sweeping changes to federal government organization since the National Security Act of 1947. The Act and amendments to it created the National Security Council, formed the Central Intelligence Agency (CIA), and combined the military services into a newly named Department of Defense. The national security policymaking structure and processes generated from the law served the nation well during the Cold War. However, new legislation and executive branch actions after 9/11 brought significant changes for the first time in over half a century.

In 2001, President George W. Bush issued Executive Order 13228, which established the Office of Homeland Security and the Homeland Security Council within the Executive Office of the President. That same year, Congress passed the USA Patriot Act of 2001, officially the Uniting and Strengthening America by Providing Appropriate Tools Required to Intercept and Obstruct Terrorism Act, which created new crimes, new penalties, and new powers for searches, seizures, surveillance, and detention of terrorist suspects. A year later, Congress passed the Homeland Security Act of 2002 which created the cabinet-level Department of Homeland Security (DHS). In the largest federal government reorganization since the beginning of the Cold War, the DHS was activated on March 1, 2003, with nearly 180,000 personnel from 22 federal organizations. The mission of the department is to prevent terrorist attacks within the United States, reduce America's vulnerability to terrorism, and minimize the damage and recover from attacks that do occur. Another significant action was the formation of United States Northern Command, known as "USNORTHCOM." With the responsibility for protecting the homeland, U.S. Northern Command was established on October 1, 2002, and reached full operational capability on September 11, 2003. Another key law was the passage of the Intelligence Reform and Terrorism Prevention Act of 2004, which created the position of Director of National Intelligence and reformed the U.S. intelligence enterprise to be more unified.

Together, the magnitude of the actions after 9/11 clearly establishes homeland security as a permanent fixture in American government and society, at least for the foreseeable future. The first secretary of homeland security, Tom Ridge, and his department leadership team emphasized "the new norm" as a broad national mentality and culture for defending the homeland (American University Forum, 2005: 17, 23). They sought to create awareness of the new norm and argued that it should be embraced by all citizens who accept the responsibility to protect America's way of life. Since 9/11, the Bush administration continuously reminds Americans— for example, in the *National Security Strategy of the United States of America* (White House, 2006b)—that the United States is engaged in a global war on terrorism.

Additionally, after the attacks on America, the federal government published numerous strategies and supporting plans to protect the nation from terrorism threats. The White House, DHS, DOD, and other agencies issued or updated key strategy documents and plans beginning in 2002. Since then, at least 21 major strategies and plans related to homeland security are guiding the national effort. The most significant strategies and plans are listed in Table 6.1. Federal, state, and local governments continue to produce additional strategies and implementation plans.

The *National Strategy for Homeland Security* (White House, 2002) recognizes that the nation's strength in science and technology is a key factor to securing the homeland. Advancing scientific knowledge and technological expertise to protect America and our way of life from any threats is a priority. The DHS science and technology directorate through its Office of University Programs oversees Homeland Security Centers of Excellence at major research universities around the nation. The Centers of Excellence are partnerships conducting multidisciplinary research in areas critical to homeland security. Centers are led by a university in collaboration with partners from other academic institutions, agencies, laboratories, think tanks, and the private sector. The foci of research include risk and economic analysis, zoonotic disease defense, terrorism and counterterrorism behavior, and others. Table 6.2 identifies the eight centers of excellence awarded through 2006, lead universities for the centers, and award dates. Thus, the nation is making significant investments in research aimed at securing the homeland.

Definitions of Homeland Security and Homeland Defense

There is a distinction between the roles of the DHS in homeland security and the DOD in homeland defense (Goss, 2006). To protect and defend the United States and preserve the freedoms guaranteed by the Constitution, the nation must secure its homeland from threats and violence, including terrorism. Homeland security is the first priority of the nation and it requires a national effort. According to the

Table 6.1 Homeland Security–Related Strategies and Plans

Strategy or Plan	Office of Primary Responsibility	Date Published
National Strategy for Homeland Security	White House Office of Homeland Security	July 2002
National Security Strategy of the United States of America	The White House	September 2002 and March 2006
National Strategy to Combat Weapons of Mass Destruction	The White House	December 2002
National Strategy for Combating Terrorism	The White House	February 2003
National Strategy for the Physical Protection of Critical Infrastructure and Key Assets	The White House	February 2003
National Strategy to Secure Cyberspace	The White House	February 2003
National Military Strategy of the United States of America	Department of Defense	2004
National Incident Management System	Department of Homeland Security	March 1, 2004
National Response Plan	Department of Homeland Security	November 2004
Interim National Infrastructure Protection Plan	Department of Homeland Security	February 2005
National Counterintelligence Strategy of the United States	Office of the National Counterintelligence Executive	March 2005
National Defense Strategy of the United States of America	Department of Defense	March 2005
National Plan for Research and Development in Support of Critical Infrastructure Protection	Department of Homeland Security	2004 (Signed April 8, 2005)

(*continued*)

Table 6.1 (continued) **Homeland Security–Related Strategies and Plans**

Strategy or Plan	Office of Primary Responsibility	Date Published
Strategy for Homeland Defense and Civil Support	Department of Defense	June 2005
State and Urban Area Homeland Security Strategy: Guidance on Aligning Strategies with the National Preparedness Goal	Department of Homeland Security	July 22, 2005
Joint Publication 3–26, *Homeland Security*	Department of Defense	August 2, 2005
National Strategy for Maritime Security and the following supporting plans: Domestic Outreach Plan Global Maritime Intelligence Integration Plan Interim Maritime Operational Threat Response Plan International Outreach and Coordination Strategy Maritime Commerce Security Plan Maritime Infrastructure Recovery Plan Maritime Transportation System Security Plan National Plan to Achieve Domain Awareness	Department of Defense Department of Homeland Security	September 2005
National Intelligence Strategy of the United States of America: Transformation through Integration and Innovation	Office of the Director of National Intelligence	October 2005
National Strategy for Pandemic Influenza	Homeland Security Council	November 2005
National Infrastructure Protection Plan	Department of Homeland Security	2006
Quadrennial Defense Review	Department of Defense	February 6, 2006

Table 6.2 Homeland Security Centers of Excellence

Center	Lead Universities	Date Awarded
Center for Risk and Economic Analysis of Terrorism Events (CREATE)	University of Southern California	November 2003
National Center for Food Protection and Defense (NCFPD)	University of Minnesota	April 2004
National Center for Foreign Animal and Zoonotic Disease Defense (FAZD)	Texas A&M University	April 2004
National Consortium for the Study of Terrorism and Responses to Terrorism (START)	University of Maryland	January 2005
Center for Advancing Microbial Risk Assessment (CAMRA)	Michigan State University	October 2005
National Center for the Study of Preparedness and Catastrophic Event Response (PACER)	Johns Hopkins University	December 2005
Regional Visualization and Analytics Centers (RVACs)	Georgia Institute of Technology, Pennsylvania State University, Purdue University, Stanford University, University of North Carolina at Charlotte, and University of Washington	February 2005 and January 2006
University Affiliate Centers to the Institute for Discrete Sciences (IDS-UACs)	Rutgers University	July 2006

National Strategy for Homeland Security, homeland security is "a concerted national effort to prevent terrorist attacks within the United States, reduce America's vulnerability to terrorism, and minimize the damage and recover from attacks that do occur" (White House, 2002: 2). The DHS is the lead federal agency for the homeland security mission. The department organizes and leads the homeland security efforts of all levels of government—federal, state, local, and tribal—as well as private and nonprofit sector organizations. Additionally, the department's responsibilities extend beyond terrorism to preventing, preparing for, responding to, and recovering from a wide range of major domestic incidents, natural disasters, and other emergencies.

The DOD has a key role in homeland security. However, its role does not include preventing terrorists from entering the United States and apprehending and arresting terrorists within the nation's borders. These responsibilities belong to the DHS and the Department of Justice (DOJ), respectively. The DOD supports homeland security through homeland defense and defense support of civil authorities (also referred to as civil support), which are two distinct but interrelated mission areas. These missions are the responsibility of U.S. Northern Command. According to the DOD, homeland defense is "The protection of United States sovereignty, territory, domestic population, and critical infrastructure against external threats and aggression or other threats as directed by the President" (Department of Defense, 2005a: GL-9). The DOD is responsible for homeland defense which includes protection against "external threats" that may be planned and executed internally. For homeland defense missions, the DOD is the lead or primary agency. Defense support of civil authorities or civil support is "DOD support, including Federal military forces, the Department's career civilian and contractor personnel, and DOD agency and component assets, for domestic emergencies and for designated law enforcement and other activities" (Department of Defense, 2005b: 5–6). The DOD provides defense support of civil authorities when directed by the president or secretary of defense in response to state governor requests for assistance for domestic incidents to include terrorist threats or attacks, major disasters, designated law enforcement, civil disturbances, and other emergencies.

Throughout the nation's history, U.S. law and policy have limited the military's role in domestic affairs. The Posse Comitatus Act of 1878 generally prohibits the U.S. military from direct participation in civilian law enforcement activities. However, Congress has enacted exceptions to the Posse Comitatus Act that allow the armed forces, in certain situations, to assist civilian law enforcement agencies in enforcing the laws of the United States. Some examples are counterdrug activities, assistance with crimes involving nuclear materials, emergency situations involving chemical or biological weapons of mass destruction, and use of the Insurrection Act to suppress insurrections. The use of military personnel in law enforcement roles is conducted within strict compliance with the constitution and laws and only under the direction of the president and secretary of defense.

The Homeland Security Spectrum

Homeland security as a national effort to prevent terrorist attacks, reduce vulnerability to terrorism, and minimize the damage and recover from attacks that do occur is an extraordinary undertaking. Success in assuring homeland security requires the employment of all instruments of U.S. national power: diplomatic, intelligence, military, economic, financial, law enforcement, and information. Therefore, homeland security consists of a wide range of resources and activities that emanate from all sectors of U.S. society. Understanding terrorism, reducing susceptibilities targeted by terrorists, stopping terrorist attacks, mitigating damages from terrorist actions, and recovering from terrorist hits are achieved by significant contributions from numerous disciplines and fields.

The homeland security spectrum encompasses many academic disciplines and fields that make up homeland security. Figure 6.1 shows the breadth of the spectrum that includes the 14 disciplines of international relations, law, history, political science, public administration, criminal justice, sociology, psychology, economics, geography, urban planning, science, medicine, and engineering. Each discipline includes fields of study related to homeland security. Thirty-four fields are listed in Figure 6.1. The spectrum starts on the left end with understanding the root causes of terrorism through fields such as international security, Islamic studies, and terrorism studies. Next, international law, world history, and American government comprise important fields. A significant portion of the middle of the spectrum includes the role of government in the fight against terrorism through the fields of public policy, public administration, public bureaucracy, public management, and federalism and intergovernmental relations. Social science fields such as psychology of terror and physical geography among others are highly relevant. Another key part of the spectrum focuses on the sciences—chemistry, biology, and physics—and medicine that are indispensable components. Finally, the far right end of the spectrum is comprised of engineering fields such as civil, computer, electrical, mechanical, and software engineering. Additionally, systems engineering is related to the design of secure systems for all critical infrastructure sectors and key assets identified in the *National Strategy for the Physical Protection of Critical Infrastructures and Key Assets* (White House, 2003).

Homeland Security as an Emerging Discipline

According to a report by the National Research Council, "the academic context of homeland security could be stretched to include almost every discipline and topic area imaginable, with 'homeland security' serving more as a target for the application of such studies, rather than as a descriptor of the studies themselves" (National Research Council, 2005: 4). Clearly, a multidisciplinary approach to homeland security education has significant merit. The National Research Council report further finds that colleges and universities have roles in support of homeland security higher education. These roles are to prepare students for homeland security–related careers, provide knowledge concerning homeland security issues to the broad community, educate citizens about the nature of threats and about core democratic

Virginia Commonwealth University

VCU National Homeland Security Project

L. Douglas Wilder School of Government and Public Affairs

Homeland Security Spectrum
Disciplines Related to Homeland Security*

International Relations 1 2 3 4 5 6	Law 7 8	History 9	Political Science 10 11	Public Administration 12 13 14	Criminal Justice 15	Sociology 16	Psychology 17	Economics 18 19	Geography 20 21	Urban Planning 22	Science 23 24 25 26 27 28 29 30	Medicine 31 32	Engineering 33 34

Fields of Study Related to Homeland Security**

1) International security, security studies, and peace studies
2) Comparative politics and foreign area studies
3) Islamic studies
4) Foreign policy and diplomacy
5) Terrorism studies
6) Intelligence studies
7) International law (law of war and maritime law)
8) Constitutional law
9) History (world, Middle East, and military)
10) Political science (American government)
11) Public policy (defense policy, environmental policy, health policy, national security policy, and science and technology policy)
12) Public administration, bureaucracy, and management
13) Organizational theory and organizational behavior
14) Federalism and intergovernmental relations
15) Crime, public safety, law enforcement, and judicial and correctional systems
16) Sociology (of terrorists and their networks)
17) Psychology (of terror and fear)
18) Business economics and finance
19) Agricultural economics
20) Physical and environmental geography
21) Settlement and land use
22) Land use planning and development
23) Environmental sciences
24) Chemistry (chemical weapons)
25) Biology (biological weapons)
26) Physics (radiological weapons, nuclear devices, and explosives)
27) Bioterrorism agents and diseases
28) Emergency management and preparedness
29) Mathematics and operations research
30) Science and technology for information, surveillance, sensing, detection, and warning systems
31) Medicine (antibiotics, drugs, vaccines, and treatment) and public health
32) Emergency medical services
33) Civil, computer, electrical, mechanical, and software engineering
34) Systems engineering for the design of critical infrastructure sectors and key assets

* A discipline is defined as a branch of instruction or learning.
** A field is defined as an area of academic interest or specialization within a discipline.

"Research and Education for Homeland Security"
© National Homeland Security Project
Virginia Commonwealth University

Version 1.0, October 2006

Figure 6.1 Homeland security spectrum.

values to consider in responding to those threats, and serve as a forum for public debate on critical homeland security issues.

Since the 9/11 attacks, academic institutions across the nation responded by offering courses, concentrations, continuing education modules, certificates, bachelor's degrees, master's degrees, and professional master's degrees in homeland security. Concomitantly, textbooks are appearing for use in these programs (Sauter and Carafano, 2005; Purpura, 2007). Program offerings are wide and range from the causes and nature of terrorism to government strategies and policies for addressing the new threats, to interagency relationships for enabling effective government activities, to critical infrastructure protection, and to enhanced practical training for professional first responders. Increased interest is spawning courses, programs, and degrees without national-level consensus, direction, or guidance. The proliferation of programs reflects a high degree of content and quality variation. Homeland security programs are often oriented around preexisting courses and strengths. For example, some programs emphasize terrorism, criminal justice, aviation security, biological and chemical threats, or emergency management. Emergency management curricula and degree programs were well established prior to 9/11 and benefit from association with the Federal Emergency Management Agency (FEMA). Emergency management programs focus on comprehensive emergency management which includes the phases of mitigation, preparedness, response, and recovery. But, as explained above, homeland security higher education consists of many fields and is, therefore, much more than emergency management.

Efforts are underway to address issues associated with higher education for homeland security (U.S. Coast Guard Academy, 2005). The Homeland Security and Defense Education Consortium, founded by U.S. Northern Command in collaboration with the University of Colorado at Colorado Springs Center for Homeland Security, the University of Denver Graduate School of International Studies, and the Naval Postgraduate School Center for Homeland Defense and Security, advances homeland security education programs. Additionally, the National Academic Consortium for Homeland Security, under the leadership of the Ohio State University, is dedicated to homeland security studies. Both consortia include hundreds of university members and promote, support, and enhance education, research, technology development, collaboration, and information sharing among academic institutions, researchers, and scholars. Furthermore, national conferences bring together homeland security faculty interested in improving homeland security education. For example, in 2007, Virginia Commonwealth University hosted the Undergraduate Homeland Security Curriculum Development Conference and Texas A&M University hosted the Graduate Homeland Security Curriculum Development Workshop. Participating universities discussed the process of curriculum development; challenges associated with obtaining program approval; issues associated with program implementation; lessons learned; and recommendations for curriculum guidelines, options, and minimum core courses and contents. Outcomes were recommendations for homeland security curricula and proposals for future actions.

Additionally, the DHS has a strong interest in promoting and supporting homeland security higher education. The DHS chief learning officer is responsible for homeland security education affairs and is organizationally located in the Office of the Chief Human Capital Officer. The consortia and the DHS are committed to assisting the development of the evolving discipline of homeland security. They continue to address issues related to core knowledge requirements, standards, and accreditation to serve as a foundation for consideration by academic institutions and future accrediting bodies.

Public Administration and Public Management in Homeland Security

Public administration and public management are at the core of the emerging discipline of homeland security. The reaction of the nation to the terrorist attacks on September 11, 2001, is primarily a response of government organizations and their activities. Federal, state, and local government organizations and their personnel are on the front lines performing critical actions daily to protect the American people. The roles of public sector employees and agencies are essential to the welfare of citizens in many policy areas such as education, health, environment, economy, international trade, and national defense. Without any doubt, the 9/11 and subsequent events reinforced to the public in a much more visible way how critical and effective public administration and public management are to our way of life (Goodsell, 2002; Rosenthal, 2003). According to Hal Rainey, distinguished professor of public administration and policy of the school of public and international affairs at the University of Georgia, "As Congress, the president, the media, experts, and interest groups deliberated over how to design the new Department of Homeland Security, they debated many questions long familiar to public administration scholars and practitioners... The debate over these questions illustrated the issues and values that infuse the processes of organizing and managing in government" (Rainey, 2003: 4). Thus, high-performing government organization, administration, and management are vital to homeland security.

This section discusses 5 fields of study related to homeland security activity, 11 major homeland security challenges, and 15 prominent areas in need of research. The objective is to inform how public administration and public management scholarship can be applied to the developing discipline of homeland security.

Fields of Study

Several fields of study are relevant to public sector organizations and management. These fields are organizational theory, organizational behavior, public administration, public bureaucracy, and public management, which are discussed below. In the early post-9/11 era, the majority of the attention given to government organizations and their activities and performance is focused on the homeland security policy arena.

Organizational theory. Organizations are "(1) social entities that (2) are goal-directed, (3) are designed as deliberately structured and coordinated activity systems, and (4) are linked to the external environment" (Daft, 2004: 11). In other words, an organization exists when people interact with one another to perform essential functions that help attain goals. Organizational theory is "the study of how organizations function and how they affect and are affected by the environment in which they operate" (Jones, 2004: 8). The primary dimensions of organizations that are studied are organizational change, communication, culture, decision making, design, effectiveness, environment, innovation, politics, and structure.

Organizational behavior. Organizational behavior is defined as "the actions and attitudes of people in organizations" (Gordon, 1999: 11). Organizational behavior theories and principles about individual and group behaviors are fundamental to helping public sector managers understand complexities and problems within their organizations. Through an understanding of organizational behavior, public managers can better assess and increase organizational efficiency and effectiveness, which are at the heart of public management.

Public administration. Public administration at its core is government in action and "can be defined from political, legal, managerial, and occupation perspectives" (Shafritz and Russell, 2005: 34). Furthermore, "the provision of public services... remains the very essence of public administration" (Shafritz and Russell, 2005: 35). Public administration is a combination of theory and practice to advance the understanding of government, improve public management actions, and enhance public policy implementation.

Public bureaucracy. Public bureaucracy is defined as "the structure and personnel of organizations, rooted in formal laws and informal processes, that collectively function as the core system of U.S. government and that both determine and carry out public policies using a high degree of specialized expertise and technologies" (Stillman, 2004: 3). Public bureaucracy can be viewed as the central operating system of the U.S. government. For anyone interested in how well government organizations carry out their missions and functions, public management activities within the public bureaucracy should be the focus.

Public management. Public management is "the development or application of methodical and systematic techniques, often employing comparison, quantification, and measurement, that are designed to make the operations of public organizations more efficient, effective, and increasingly, responsive" (Henry, 2004: 147). Public management is part of the larger field of public administration and consists of the art and science of applied methodologies for public sector organizations. Furthermore, it is a combination of the planning, organizing, and controlling functions of management and human resources management, budgetary and financial management, information technology management, and asset management. Techniques of performance measurement, public program evaluation, and productivity improvement are applied in all areas of public management to increase efficiency and effectiveness of government programs.

It is unambiguous that the fields of public administration and public management have much to contribute by examining, increasing the understanding of, and improving homeland security. Public administration and public management scholars have an important role in homeland security by conducting research in this emerging discipline.

Homeland Security Challenges

Notable challenges confront the homeland security community. To achieve a secure homeland, federal, state, local, and tribal governments; nongovernmental organizations; the private sector; communities; and individual citizens will have to remain engaged and work together to achieve common goals. Table 6.3 identifies the 23

Table 6.3 Homeland Security Agencies and Offices

Agency or Office	Federal Department or State and Local Government Level	Primary Mission
Animal and Plant Health Inspection Service (APHIS)	Agriculture	Protect U.S. agriculture by ensuring the health and care of animals and plants
Centers for Disease Control and Prevention (CDC)	Health and Human Services	Promote health and quality of life by preventing and controlling diseases, injuries, and disabilities
Central Intelligence Agency (CIA)	Independent Agency	Collect intelligence, provide all-source analysis, and conduct covert action to preempt threats to the United States
Counterterrorism Office	State	Develop, coordinate, and implement U.S. counterterrorism policy and improve counterterrorism cooperation with foreign governments
Customs and Border Protection (CBP)	Homeland Security	Protect the sovereign borders of the United States, at and between the official ports of entry

Table 6.3 (continued)   Homeland Security Agencies and Offices

Agency or Office	Federal Department or State and Local Government Level	Primary Mission
Defense Intelligence Agency (DIA)	Defense	Provide timely, objective, and cogent military intelligence to warfighters, defense planners, and defense and national security policymakers
Department of Emergency Management[a]	States and Counties	Ensure the state/county is able to mitigate against, prepare for, respond to, and recover from effects of emergencies such as disasters and acts of terrorism
Domestic Nuclear Detection Office (DNDO)	Homeland Security	Prevent nuclear or radiological terrorism through detection and reporting of unauthorized attempts to import, possess, store, develop, or transport nuclear or radiological material
Federal Bureau of Investigation (FBI)	Justice	Protect and defend United States against terrorist and foreign intelligence threats and enforce criminal laws of the United States
Federal Emergency Management Agency (FEMA)	Homeland Security	Manage and coordinate the federal response to all major domestic disasters and emergencies
Immigration and Customs Enforcement (ICE)	Homeland Security	Through enforcement of immigration and customs laws, detect vulnerabilities and prevent violations that threaten national security. Also, protect federal government facilities
Missile Defense Agency (MDA)	Defense	Develop, test, and prepare for deployment of a missile defense system capable of providing a layered defense against ballistic missiles
National Geospatial-Intelligence Agency (NGA)	Defense	Provide timely, relevant, and accurate geospatial intelligence in support of national security objectives

(continued)

Table 6.3 (continued)   Homeland Security Agencies and Offices

Agency or Office	Federal Department or State and Local Government Level	Primary Mission
National Guard Bureau (NGB)	Defense	As the organized militia of the states, provide security to states for natural disasters and man-made emergencies and, when mobilized by the federal government, deploy for combat or combat support to defend the nation
National Nuclear Security Administration (NNSA)	Energy	Enhance U.S. national security through military application of nuclear energy, maintain security of U.S. nuclear weapons stockpile, and reduce global danger from weapons of mass destruction
National Reconnaissance Office (NRO)	Defense	Develop and operate unique and innovative space reconnaissance systems and conduct intelligence-related activities essential for U.S. national security
National Security Agency (NSA)	Independent Agency	As the U.S. cryptologic organization coordinate, direct, and perform specialized activities to protect government information systems and produce foreign signals intelligence information
Office of Emergency Management[b]	Cities	Ensure the city is able to mitigate against, prepare for, respond to, and recover from effects of emergencies such as disasters and acts of terrorism
Office of the Director of National Intelligence (ODNI)	Independent Office	Build a more unified, coordinated, and effective U.S. intelligence community
Transportation Security Administration (TSA)	Homeland Security	Protect the transportation system and ensure the freedom of movement for people and commerce

Table 6.3 (continued)   Homeland Security Agencies and Offices

Agency or Office	Federal Department or State and Local Government Level	Primary Mission
U.S. Coast Guard (USCG)	Homeland Security	Through humanitarian, law enforcement, regulatory, diplomatic, and military capabilities, provide maritime security, maritime safety, protection of natural resources, maritime mobility, and national defense services
U.S. Citizenship and Immigration Services (USCIS)	Homeland Security	Grant or deny immigration benefits to individuals seeking to enter, reside, or work in the United States
U.S. Maritime Administration (MARAD)	Transportation	Improve and strengthen the U.S. marine transportation system, including infrastructure, industry, and labor, to meet the economic and security needs of the nation
U.S. Northern Command (USNORTHCOM)	Defense	Conduct operations to deter, prevent, and defeat threats and aggression aimed at the United States and provide defense support of civil authorities
U.S. Secret Service (USSS)	Homeland Security	Protect the president and vice president, investigate financial crimes, and implement operational security plans for national special security events

[a] Names of state and county departments of emergency management vary. For example: California Governor's Office of Emergency Services, Colorado and Florida Division of Emergency Management, Louisiana Office of Homeland Security and Emergency Preparedness, and Virginia Department of Emergency Management; Fulton County (Georgia) Emergency Management Agency and Maricopa County (Arizona) Department of Emergency Management.

[b] Names of city offices of emergency management vary. For example: Chicago Office of Emergency Management and Communications, Los Angeles Emergency Preparedness Department, and New York City Office of Emergency Management.

Table 6.4   Homeland Security Challenges

Understanding and communicating threats
Integrating security into society
Balancing trade-offs between security and liberties
Sharing information and intelligence
Strengthening border security
Achieving transportation security
Protecting critical infrastructure
Establishing maritime security
Researching, developing, and using technology
Improving emergency preparedness and response
Operating with enhanced interagency relationships and intergovernmental relations

primary homeland security agencies and offices at the federal government level, as well as emergency management departments at the state, county, and city government levels. The 11 principal homeland security challenges are listed in Table 6.4 and described below. Government homeland security agencies and offices contend with the challenges on a daily basis.

1. Understanding and communicating threats. The events of 9/11 were a wake-up call that the United States is a target for those who wish to harm the nation. Terrorism is a serious threat with the potential for mass casualties, economic damage, and alteration of our way of life. The nation must gain a deeper understanding of the threats we face. Furthermore, it is essential that the threats be communicated to citizens, the private sector, and the nonprofit sector to engage them in homeland security efforts.

2. Integrating security into society. Integrating security into all aspects of American society will take time. It is crucial to prevent attacks and minimize effects of any attacks that do occur. Richard Falkenrath, former deputy homeland security advisor to the president stated that "the most important challenge for the Department of Homeland Security is to weave ever greater levels of security into the fabric of American society" (Falkenrath, 2005: 9). Some believe that Americans need to view security the same way they view safety, "not as a government-imposed burden but as a valued necessity" (Flynn, 2004: 61). America faces the challenge of improving security the same way

it improved safety by incorporating it into the normal course of business and personal lives.

3. Balancing trade-offs between security and liberties. American people are most concerned about striking a proper balance between measures that achieve security against new, uncertain threats and the preservation of civil rights and individual liberties. Don Kettl, in *System under Stress: Homeland Security and American Politics* (Kettl, 2007), addresses how the American political system is undergoing a stress test of its processes, agencies, programs, and officials as they respond to the shock of 9/11. The stress test necessitates a rethinking by citizens about our values. Homeland Security Secretary Michael Chertoff reflected the views of most Americans when he stated, "Our goal is to maximize our security, but not security at any price. Our security regime must promote Americans' freedom, prosperity, mobility, and individual privacy" (Department of Homeland Security, 2005a).

4. Sharing information and intelligence. After 9/11, a major focus of governments at all levels is information sharing. Furthermore, there is an increase in the exchange of intelligence information among federal agencies and in the transfer of intelligence information from the federal government to state and local law enforcement (Betts, 2002; Drake et al., 2004; Hitz and Weiss, 2004; Johnson and Wirtz, 2004; 9/11 Commission, 2004; White, 2004; Waterman, 2005; Zegart, 2005). The Intelligence Reform and Terrorism Protection Act of 2004, known as the 9/11 Reform Bill, mandated the establishment of an information-sharing environment (ISE) to distribute intelligence regarding terrorism to appropriate federal, state, local, and private entities (Russack, 2005). National intelligence is codified by the Intelligence Reform and Terrorism Prevention Act of 2004 as the U.S. intelligence enterprise that is more unified, coordinated, and effective (Office of the Director of National Intelligence, 2005). However, barriers remain that must be overcome for an ISE that is truly effective.

5. Strengthening border security. Homeland security begins with securing the U.S. border. A comprehensive strategy to control the border for cargo and human entry and enforce immigration laws is a high priority for the nation. The challenge is to prevent terrorists from entering while still allowing the efficient entry of legal commerce and travel. There are significant diplomatic, political, organizational, economic, and societal implications to be considered.

6. Achieving transportation security. Protecting the nation's transportation system and ensuring freedom of movement for people and commerce is central to our economy and way of life. The goal is to move people and cargo more securely and efficiently. Included are aviation, rail, mass transit, trucking, and cargo security. Critical locations are airports, seaports, rail yards, and mass transit stations. Moreover, it is imperative to secure multimodal transportation systems and nodes. Container security is especially of concern. Many issues exist such as passenger and cargo identity screening. Achieving transportation security has numerous inherent challenges.

7. Protecting critical infrastructure. All critical infrastructure sectors and key assets are potential targets that require protection. According to the USA Patriot Act of 2001, critical infrastructure means "systems and assets, whether physical or virtual, so vital to the United States that the incapacity or destruction of such systems and assets would have a debilitating impact on security, national economic security, national public health or safety, or any combination of those matters." The sectors are agriculture and food, water, public health, emergency services, defense industrial base, telecommunications, energy, transportation, banking and finance, chemical industry and hazardous materials, and postal and shipping. According to the Homeland Security Act of 2002, key resources are "publicly or privately controlled resources essential to the minimal operations of the economy and government." Finally, key assets (a subset of key resources) are "individual targets whose attack—in the worst-case scenarios—could result in not only large-scale human casualties and property destruction, but also profound damage to our national prestige, morale, and confidence" (White House, 2003: viii). Examples are symbols, historical attractions, national monuments and icons, government or local facilities, nuclear power plants, dams, high-profile events, and commercial key assets. Characteristics of the sectors are that they produce and deliver essential goods and services that contribute to a strong national defense and thriving economy; ensure security, safety, freedom, and governance; are highly sophisticated and complex; consist of human capital and physical and cyber systems; have a series of key nodes; interconnect and are mutually dependent; are reliable, robust, and resilient; and create public confidence. Protection requires a risk-based management approach with consideration of threats, vulnerabilities, and consequences.

8. Establishing maritime security. The nation's safety and economic security depends upon secure use of the world's oceans and an absence of threats to the maritime environment. According to the *National Strategy for Maritime Security*, the maritime domain is defined as "all areas and things of, on, under, relating to, adjacent to, or bordering on a sea, ocean, or other navigable waterway, including all maritime-related activities, infrastructure, people, cargo, and vessels and other conveyances" (Department of Defense and Department of Homeland Security, 2005: 1). Broad principles include preserving freedom of the seas, facilitating and defending commerce, and exercising secure border management.

9. Researching, developing, and using technology. Science and technology is one of four foundations of homeland security described as unique American strengths (the others are law, information sharing and systems, and international cooperation) that will help the United States win the war against terrorism. Thus, science advancements and research and develop programs are pivotal to producing new technologies for use against threats to the nation. Examples of technologies for use in homeland security are sensor

and detection technologies such as biosensors and explosive detection equipment; next generation systems to detect and intercept various types of threats; advanced technologies to detect chemical, biological, and radiological attacks; secure identification that incorporates biometric technology; screening technology; and "smart" surveillance equipment.

10. Improving emergency preparedness and response. The national preparedness system is designed to provide capabilities to prevent, protect against, respond to, and recover from all hazards (major natural disasters, terrorist incidents, and other emergencies). The *National Response Plan* (NRP) is an all-hazards plan that establishes a single, comprehensive framework for managing domestic incidents across all levels of government and across a spectrum of activities that include prevention, preparedness, response, and recovery. The NRP using the *National Incident Management System* (NIMS) provides the structure and mechanisms for national-level policy and operational direction for federal support to state and local domestic incident managers (Department of Homeland Security, 2004b). The NIMS establishes standardized incident management protocols and procedures that all responders (federal, state, and local) should use to conduct and coordinate response actions. It sets forth a "core set of doctrine, concepts, principles, terminology, and organizational processes to enable effective, efficient, and collaborative incident management at all levels" of government and "provides a consistent, flexible, and adjustable national framework within which government and private entities at all levels can work together to manage domestic incidents" of any magnitude (Department of Homeland Security, 2004a: ix, 2). The incident command system (ICS) is the central component of NIMS and provides a means—through a command system ensuring a unified command—to coordinate the efforts of individual responders and agencies as they respond to and help manage an incident. The ICS clarifies reporting relationships and eliminates confusion. Close coordination among federal, state, and local governments is required. Additionally, comprehensive collaborative arrangements are necessary. Also, best practices and lessons learned should be shared. Issues relate to the roles, authorities, and procedures for the federal government and state governments in incident preparedness, response, and recovery efforts. Other issues relate to the roles of FEMA and the DOD in incident preparedness, response, and recovery efforts.

11. Operating with enhanced interagency relationships and intergovernmental relations. Interagency relationships, intergovernmental relations, and collaboration can foster improved organizational performance (Page, 2003; National Academy of Public Administration, 2004; Stever, 2005). Interestingly, interagency relationships is not defined in the Homeland Security Act of 2002, the *National Strategy for Homeland Security* (White House, 2002), the *National Response Plan* (Department of Homeland Security, 2004b), or the *Strategy for Homeland Defense and Civil Support* (Department of Defense, 2005b).

Therefore, the term interagency relationships is defined here as interrelationships, processes, and interdependencies among two or more government agencies and departments within one level of government or between more than one level of government. Interagency activities are sometimes defined as cooperation, coordination, integration, and networking (U.S. Government Accountability Office, 2005b). Interagency relationships refer to agency-to-agency such as among Customs and Border Protection (CBP), Immigration and Customs Enforcement (ICE), and the U.S. Coast Guard (USCG), all within the DHS; department-to-department such as among the DHS, DOD, and DOJ; and federal-to-state such as between the Federal Bureau of Investigation (FBI) and local law enforcement. Intergovernmental relations refers to federalism. Federalism is a system of governance in which a national, overarching government shares power with subnational or state governments. Intergovernmental relations can be viewed as federalism in action. It is the complex network of day-to-day interrelationships among the governments within a federal system (Shafritz and Russell, 2005). The bottom line is that due to the enormity of homeland security, governments at all levels are compelled to operate with enhanced interagency relationships and intergovernmental relations.

Homeland Security Areas for Research

The homeland security challenges are indeed far reaching for the nation. University research is fundamental in addressing the challenges. All of the fields of study on the homeland security spectrum (see Figure 6.1) can make research contributions toward overcoming the challenges. Because public administration and public management are integral to homeland security, scholars in these fields are able to conduct research with great relevancy to the challenges confronting homeland security. Research is needed to help organizations responsible for homeland security to be more efficient and effective in carrying out their operations and accomplishing their missions. Fifteen significant areas for research by public administration and public management scholars are discussed next and contained in Table 6.5.

1. Leadership. High-quality leadership is a prerequisite for successful homeland security organizations. When addressing leadership in large-scale organized systems, John Gardner states, "The first thing that strikes one as characteristic of contemporary leadership is the necessity for the leader to work with and through extremely complex organizations and institutions" (Gardner, 1990: 298). Homeland security is an obviously complex enterprise requiring strong leadership. Primary leadership functions are establishing direction for organizations, aligning people within organizations, and motivating and inspiring people to move in the established direction (Kotter, 1990). The following are

Table 6.5   Homeland Security Public Administration and Public Management Areas for Research

Leadership
Organizational structure and alignment
Organizational culture
Strategic planning
Legal and managerial authorities
Risk management approach to decision making
Organizational learning, innovation, and change
Consolidation and integration of information technology and administrative systems
Organizational roles and missions
Disaster response and emergency recovery operations
Collaborative relationships through partnerships and networks
Information and intelligence sharing
Performance measurement
Public service
Recruitment, training, and retention of employees

the key questions for research: What leadership qualities and skills are especially required for homeland security organizations? How can future leaders of homeland security best prepare themselves?

2. Organizational structure and alignment. The new DHS was established in March 2003 and then reorganized in July 2005. Much has been written about how to organize the department, internal organizational challenges faced by the department during its first two years, and how to best remedy those early challenges (Hillyard, 2002; Waugh and Sylves, 2002; Wise and Nader, 2002; National Academy of Public Administration, 2003; Scardaville, 2003; Carafano and Heyman, 2004; Haynes, 2004; Kettl, 2004; Lehrer, 2004; Carafano, 2005a,b; Falkenrath, 2005; Mintz, 2005; Peters, 2005; Priest, 2005; Wermuth, 2005). A long list of issues could benefit from research: mergers and difficulties associated with them; actions and time frames necessary to successfully integrate organizations; bureaucratic challenges; operational agencies

versus support agencies; organizational change, reorganization, and redesign; dual accountability reporting (Carafano, 2005a: 3); span-of-control and length of operational chains of command; functionally integrated and aligned organizations; functional versus geographical/regional structures; organizational alignment to maximize mission performance; roles and missions; organizational "turf"; and overlapping jurisdictions.

3. Organizational culture. Organizational culture is defined as the set of values, norms, guiding beliefs, and understandings that is shared by members of an organization and taught to new members as correct (Daft, 2004). Furthermore, organizational culture controls organizational members' interactions with each other and with suppliers, customers, and other people outside the organization (Jones, 2004). Of all organizational activity dimensions, organizational culture is perhaps cited the most as being problematic for some of the agencies in the DHS and in the homeland security community of organizations. The first secretary of homeland security, Tom Ridge, stated, "From day one this leadership team took on the responsibility of creating a new 21st century department with a culture of integration, communication, and information sharing" (American University Forum, 2005). Stephen Flynn, an expert on homeland security issues, notes that "The secretive, top-down, us-versus-them culture that is pervasive in government security circles must give way to more inclusive processes" (Flynn, 2004: 166). Many scholars of organizational culture believe it will take a generation for significant culture change to occur. Principal questions for research are the following: How can homeland security organizations with different organizational cultures best cooperate, communicate, coordinate, share, integrate, and network? What actions are necessary to change the culture of organizations to enable them to place a higher priority on homeland security missions? What can be done to speed up the transition in the FBI and the CIA from a need-to-know culture to a need-to-share culture?

4. Strategic planning. Homeland security agencies must have capabilities for long-range strategic thinking, strategies, policies, and plans. Moreover, strategies, policies, and plans should be cohesive and well integrated. During its initial years of operations, the DHS was criticized for lacking robust strategic planning and analysis capabilities. An important question for research is: How can strategic planning be better developed and coordinated for homeland security?

5. Legal and managerial authorities. In order for homeland security agencies to operate as intended, legal and managerial authorities must be clearly understood. Homeland security leaders and managers are able to act more decisively and appropriately if they have the necessary authorities and know the extent of authorities. A key question for research is: What are some ways for homeland security professionals to exercise managerial flexibility within the limits of authorities?

6. Risk management approach to decision making. The DHS is in the risk-management business. The United States cannot achieve 100 percent protection against 100 percent of the potential threats and vulnerabilities. Therefore, our goal should be to manage the risk of acts of terrorism. This means basing security efforts on priorities driven by risk. Risk analysis is based on the three variables of threats, vulnerabilities, and consequences of attacks. Therefore, distribution of homeland security funds should be determined by a comprehensive risk assessment or risk-based approach. A fundamental question for research is: How can risk assessment models for homeland security be improved?

7. Organizational learning, innovation, and change. A learning organization is one in which its members are engaged in identifying and solving problems, thus enabling the organization to continuously experiment, change, and improve. If the DHS practices organizational learning, it will increase its capacity to fulfill its mission. Additionally, agencies with homeland security missions will be more successful if they have characteristics of flexibility, alertness, agility, urgency, innovativeness, adaptability, and alignment (Light, 2005; Light and Hamilton, 2005). Secretary of Homeland Security Michael Chertoff recognized the power of these characteristics by stating, "My job—and the job of the leadership team at the Department—is to provide the strategic direction, tools, and aggressive support needed by our colleagues who carry out the vital mission of protecting America. We must continue to build effectiveness, agility, and capacity in this effort every day" (Department of Homeland Security, 2005b: 1). Chief questions for research are: How can innovation be fostered by homeland security organizations? How can bureaucratization be overcome to result in agencies with greater flexibility, alertness, agility, urgency, innovativeness, adaptability, and alignment?

8. Consolidation and integration of information technology and administrative systems. The 22 agencies that were merged into the DHS had widely varying administrative systems. To achieve operating and cost efficiencies, they needed to be consolidated and integrated. Thus, a massive process is underway to consolidate and integrate financial management (budget, accounting and reporting, cost management, and asset management), human resources management, payroll, procurement, grant management, service center, and information technology systems. Goals include improving financial controls and systems, strengthening human capital policies, and operating well-integrated information technology systems. Research into effective principles and methods for consolidating and integrating diverse administrative systems will go a long way toward achieving the desired operating and cost efficiencies.

9. Organizational roles and missions. With so many organizations involved in homeland security from all sectors and at all levels of government (see Table 6.3), understanding and executing roles and missions are paramount. The organizations include federal civilian agencies; DOD agencies; state, local, and

tribal governments and agencies; nongovernmental organizations; and private sector entities. Leading questions for research are: How can organizations and agencies work jointly to accomplish their missions and the overall mission of homeland security? How can role and mission redundancy be minimized when appropriate? What is the proper role of the DOD in homeland security and homeland defense?

10. Disaster response and emergency recovery operations. Hurricane Katrina put a spotlight on emergency management, disaster response, and emergency recovery operations (U.S. Government Accountability Office, 2005a, 2006; U.S. Congress, 2006; U.S. Senate, 2006; White House, 2006a). The National Preparedness System is designed to provide capabilities to prevent, protect against, respond to, and recover from all hazards, including major natural disasters, terrorist incidents, and other emergencies. Numerous topics and issues could benefit from research: statutes, local response, first responders, declarations of emergencies, requests for assistance to the federal government, use of the National Guard, communications, interoperability, procedures, and others. Material questions for research are: How should the NRP and the NIMS be modified? What are best practices for disaster relief and emergency recovery operations? What lessons learned from Hurricane Katrina and other incidents should be emphasized and shared?

11. Collaborative relationships through partnerships and networks. Federal, state, and local governments are increasingly relying on collaborative public management as a process of facilitating and operating in multiorganizational arrangements to solve problems that cannot be solved or easily solved by single organizations (O'Leary et al., 2006). Collaboration is about co-labor and joint effort and ownership. Collaboration occurs when people from different organizations (or units within one organization) produce something together through joint effort, resources, and decision making, and share ownership of the final product or service (Linden, 2002). For homeland security, governments at all levels are using multiagency, cross-jurisdictional networks and collaborative relationships to solve their complex challenges. There is strong recognition that homeland security agencies need to work together more effectively and improve interagency cooperation, coordination, communication, collaboration, integration, and networking (Bardach, 1998; Mandell, 2001; Rockefeller Institute of Government, 2003; Agranoff, 2004, 2006; Kamarck, 2004; Kamensky et al., 2004; Klitgaard and Treverton, 2004; National Academy of Public Administration, 2004; U.S. Government Accountability Office, 2005b; Abramson et al., 2006; Kiefer and Montjoy, 2006; Milward and Provan, 2006). Secretary of Homeland Security Michael Chertoff made the following statement when he announced the reorganization of the DHS on July 13, 2005: "[O]ur work must be guided by the understanding that effective security is built upon a network of systems that span all levels of government and the private sector" (Department of Homeland

Security, 2005b: 2). Post-Hurricane Katrina analysis and criticism points at federal, state, and local government emergency management efforts that suffered due to insufficient collaborative structures and working relationships before the disaster and a lack of coordination during the disaster (Waugh and Streib, 2006). Federal government agencies can improve their ability to accomplish their missions through collaborative management processes and practices with state and local emergency management agencies. Federal government agencies do understand the critical importance of and are committed to stronger interagency cooperation, interagency ties and capabilities, unity of effort, and communication and collaboration in emergency operations. But, much more work remains to be done in these areas. Aviation, border, maritime, and port security operations are examples of multiple complex security networks based on collaborative relationships. There is a need for extensive research in the following areas associated with collaborative management processes and practices: communication, cooperation, coordination, consensus-seeking behavior, relationship building, capacity building, joint operations, interoperability, trust, and listening to external partners.

12. Information and intelligence sharing. The sharing of information, in particular intelligence information, is a cornerstone of homeland security processes and procedures. Issues for research include accelerating the sharing of intelligence information vertically and horizontally within and among agencies; determining what information should be shared between the federal level and the state and local levels; ascertaining what information should be shared among governments, the private sector, law enforcement, and first responders; improving information exchange protocols; moving from a need-to-know to a need-to-share orientation; fusing intelligence information; promoting greater situational awareness; identifying types of support for regional and state data fusion centers; refining the homeland security threat advisory system; and providing the public with more information.

13. Performance measurement. The Government Performance and Results Act (GPRA) of 1993 requires federal agencies to define long-term goals, complete strategic plans, set annual performance targets as part of performance plans, and annually report actual performance compared to the targets. Measuring performance and progress of national efforts against terrorism are essential to prioritizing and allocating scarce resources (Perl, 2005). Homeland security agencies are not exempt from these requirements. Basic questions for research are: How should the performance of homeland security agencies be measured and reported? What should the performance metrics be for homeland security activities?

14. Public service. Homeland security is the ultimate public service to America. There are a multitude of career opportunities for those who wish to make a career in homeland security. Vital questions for research are: How can homeland

security employees and agencies be effective stewards of public resources? How can homeland security employees and agencies be responsible stewards of the public trust? How can homeland security employees and agencies act in the public interest?

15. Recruitment, training, and retention of employees. Threats to the United States and the global war on terrorism are expected to persist for decades to come. Homeland security agencies, like agencies in other policy arenas, will compete to recruit, train, and retain employees. Homeland security agencies must make investments in their people. Primary questions for research are: How will homeland security agencies best recruit, train, and retain employees? What professional career training, education, and development programs should be implemented for homeland security agencies?

Conclusion

The event of 9/11 ushered in a new era for the United States. Homeland security is a national effort to protect the nation from the harms of terrorism. This chapter presented the homeland security spectrum consisting of a wide range of academic disciplines and fields and explained how homeland security is an emerging discipline. The fields of public administration and public management are at the core of homeland security studies. Very importantly, 11 serious homeland security challenges confront America. Fortunately, university research can help to address these challenges. For public administration and public management scholars, 15 primary homeland security areas for research are identified. Scholars of public administration and public management can make valuable contributions to their fields and homeland security studies by conducting needed research in the areas discussed.

References

Abramson, M.A., Breul, J.D., and Kamensky, J.M. 2006. *Six Trends Transforming Government.* IBM Center for the Business of Government. Washington, DC: IBM Center for the Business of Government.

Agranoff, R. 2004. Leveraging networks: A guide for public managers working across organizations. In *Collaboration: Using Networks and Partnerships*, edited by John M. Kamensky and Thomas J. Burlin, pp. 61–102. Lanham, Maryland: Rowman & Littlefield Publishers, Inc.

Agranoff, R. 2006. Inside collaborative networks: Ten lessons for public managers. *Public Administration Review.* Supplement to Volume 66 (December), 56–65.

American University Forum. 2005. Reflections from the Nation's First Homeland Security Team. School of Public Affairs Forum, May 10. Washington, DC: Transcript by Federal News Service.

Bardach, E. 1998. *Getting Agencies to Work Together: The Practice and Theory of Managerial Craftsmanship*. Washington, DC: Brookings Institution Press.

Betts, R.K. 2002. Fixing intelligence. *Foreign Affairs* 81(1): 43–59.

Carafano, J.J. 2005a. Testimony before the Senate Committee on Homeland Security and Governmental Affairs, January 25. http://www.heritage.org/Research/HomelandDefense/tst012604a.cfm.

Carafano, J.J. 2005b. Testimony before the Subcommittee on Management, Integration, and Oversight, House Committee on Homeland Security, March 10. http://www.heritage.org/Research/HomelandDefense/tst031005a.cfm.

Carafano, J.J. and Heyman, D. 2004. DHS 2.0: Rethinking the Department of Homeland Security. The Heritage Foundation Special Report No. SR-02, December 13. Washington, DC: The Heritage Foundation.

Cronin, A.K. and Ludes, J.M., Eds. 2004. *Attacking Terrorism: Elements of a Grand Strategy*. Washington, DC: Georgetown University Press.

Daft, R.L. 2004. *Organization Theory and Design*, 8th ed. Mason, Ohio: Thomson South-Western.

Department of Defense. 2005a. *Homeland Security*. Joint Publication 3–26. August 2. Washington, DC: Department of Defense.

Department of Defense. 2005b. *Strategy for Homeland Defense and Civil Support*. June. Washington, DC: Department of Defense.

Department of Defense and Department of Homeland Security. 2005. National Strategy for Maritime Security. September. Washington, DC: Department of Defense and Department of Homeland Security.

Department of Homeland Security. 2004a. *National Incident Management System*. March 1. Washington, DC: Department of Homeland Security.

Department of Homeland Security. 2004b. *National Response Plan*. November. Washington, DC: Department of Homeland Security.

Department of Homeland Security. 2005a. Homeland Security Secretary Michael Chertoff Announces Six-Point Agenda for Department of Homeland Security. Press Release, July 13.

Department of Homeland Security. 2005b. Secretary Michael Chertoff U.S. Department of Homeland Security Second Stage Review Remarks. July 13.

Drake, D.B., Steckler, N.A., and Koch, M.J. 2004. Information sharing in and across government agencies: The role and influence of scientist, politician, and bureaucrat subcultures. *Social Science Computer Review* 22(1): 67–84.

Dye, T.R. 2005. *Understanding Public Policy*, 11th ed. Upper Saddle River, New Jersey: Pearson Prentice Hall.

Falkenrath, R.A. 2005. Present and Future Challenges Facing the Department of Homeland Security. Testimony before the Senate Committee on Homeland Security and Governmental Affairs, January 26. http://www.brookings.edu/views/testimony/fellows/falkenrath20050126.htm.

Flynn, S. 2004. *America the Vulnerable: How Our Government Is Failing to Protect Us from Terrorism*. New York: HarperCollins Publishers.

Gardner, J.W. 1990. Leadership in large-scale organized systems. In *The Leader's Companion*, edited by J. Thomas Wren, Chapter 40, pp. 297–302. New York: The Free Press. Reprinted from *On Leadership* by John W. Gardner. New York: The Free Press, 1990.

Goodsell, C.T. 2002. Insights for public administration from the terrorist attacks. *Administration and Society* 34(3): 255–260.

Gordon, J.R. 1999. *Organizational Behavior: A Diagnostic Approach*, 6th ed. Upper Saddle River, New Jersey: Prentice-Hall, Inc.

Goss, T. 2006. Who's in charge? New challenges in homeland defense and homeland security. *Homeland Security Affairs* II(1): Article 2.

Hart–Rudman Commission. 1999. New World Coming: American Security in the 21st Century, Major Themes and Implications. Phase I Report on the Emerging Global Security Environment for the First Quarter of the 21st Century, September 15. Washington, DC: U.S. Commission on National Security/21st Century.

Haynes, W. 2004. Seeing around corners: Crafting the new department of homeland security. *Review of Policy Research* 21(3): 369–395.

Henry, N. 2004. *Public Administration and Public Affairs*, 9th ed. Upper Saddle River, New Jersey: Pearson Prentice Hall.

Hillyard, M.J. 2002. Organizing for homeland security. *Parameters: U.S. Army War College Quarterly* 32(1): 75–85.

Hitz, F.P. and Weiss, B.J. 2004. Helping the CIA and FBI connect the dots in the war on terror. *International Journal of Intelligence and CounterIntelligence* 17(1): 1–41.

Hoffman, B. 2002. Rethinking terrorism and counterterrorism since 9/11. *Studies in Conflict and Terrorism* 25(5): 303–316.

Johnson, L.K. and Wirtz, J.J. 2004. *Strategic Intelligence: Windows into a Secret World, An Anthology.* Los Angeles: Roxbury Publishing Company.

Jones, G.R. 2004. *Organizational Theory, Design, and Change: Text and Cases*, 4th ed. Upper Saddle River, New Jersey: Pearson Prentice Hall.

Kamarck, E.C. 2004. Applying 21st-century government to the challenge of homeland security. In *Collaboration: Using Networks and Partnerships*, edited by John M. Kamensky and Thomas J. Burlin, pp. 103–146. Lanham, Maryland: Rowman & Littlefield Publishers, Inc.

Kamensky, J.M., Burlin, T.J., and Abramson, M.A. 2004. Networks and partnerships: Collaborating to achieve results no one can achieve alone. In *Collaboration: Using Networks and Partnerships*, edited by John M. Kamensky and Thomas J. Burlin, pp. 3–20. Lanham, Maryland: Rowman & Littlefield Publishers, Inc.

Kettl, D.F., Ed. 2004. *The Department of Homeland Security's First Year: A Report Card.* New York: The Century Foundation Press.

Kettl, D.F. 2007. *System under Stress: Homeland Security and American Politics*, 2nd ed. Washington, DC: CQ Press.

Kiefer, J.J. and Montjoy, R.S. 2006. Incrementalism before the storm: Network performance for the evacuation of New Orleans. *Public Administration Review*. Supplement to Volume 66 (December), 122–130.

Klitgaard, R. and Treverton, G.F. 2004. Assessing partnerships: New forms of collaboration. In *Collaboration: Using Networks and Partnerships*, edited by John M. Kamensky and Thomas J. Burlin, pp. 21–59. Lanham, Maryland: Rowman & Littlefield Publishers, Inc.

Kotter, J.P. 1990. *A Force for Change: How Leadership Differs from Management.* New York: The Free Press.

Lehrer, E. 2004. The homeland security bureaucracy. *The Public Interest* 156: 71–85.

Light, P.C. 2005. *The Four Pillars of High Performance: How Robust Organizations Achieve Extraordinary Results*. New York: The McGraw-Hill, Inc.

Light, P.C. and Hamilton, L.H. 2005. Rumsfeld's Revolution at Defense. Brookings Institution Briefing Transcript Prepared from a Tape Recording, July 19. Washington, DC: Miller Reporting Company, Inc.

Linden, R.M. 2002. *Working across Boundaries: Making Collaboration Work in Government and Nonprofit Organizations*. San Francisco, California: Jossey-Bass.

Mandell, M.P., Ed. 2001. *Getting Results through Collaboration: Networks and Network Structures for Public Policy and Management*. Westport, Connecticut: Quorum Books.

Milward, H.B. and Provan, K.P. 2006. *A Manager's Guide to Choosing and Using Collaborative Networks*. IBM Center for the Business of Government. Washington, DC: IBM Center for the Business of Government.

Mintz, J. 2005. Infighting cited at homeland security. *The Washington Post*, February 2.

National Academy of Public Administration. 2003. Advancing the Management of Homeland Security: Protecting the Homeland: Lessons from Prior Government Reorganizations. A National Academy of Public Administration Forum on Homeland Security Summary Report, Summer. Washington, DC: National Academy of Public Administration.

National Academy of Public Administration. 2004. Advancing the Management of Homeland Security: Managing Intergovernmental Relations for Homeland Security. A National Academy of Public Administration Forum on Homeland Security Summary Report, February. Washington, DC: National Academy of Public Administration.

National Research Council. 2005. Frameworks for Higher Education in Homeland Security. Committee on Educational Paradigms for Homeland Security. National Academy of Sciences. Washington, DC: The National Academies Press.

9/11 Commission. 2004. National Commission on Terrorist Attacks upon the United States. *The 9/11 Commission Report: Final Report of the National Commission on Terrorist Attacks Upon the United States*. Washington, DC: U.S. Government Printing Office.

Office of the Director of National Intelligence. 2005. *The National Intelligence Strategy of the United States of America*. Washington, DC: Department of Defense.

O'Leary, R., Gerard, C., and Bingham, L.B. 2006. Introduction to the symposium on collaborative public management. *Public Administration Review*. Supplement to Volume 66 (December), 6–9.

Page, S. 2003. Entrepreneurial strategies for managing interagency collaboration. *Journal of Public Administration Research and Theory* 13(3): 311–339.

Perl, R. 2005. Combating Terrorism: The Challenge of Measuring Effectiveness. Congressional Research Service Report #RL33160, November 23. Washington, DC: The Library of Congress.

Peters, K.M. 2005. Round 2. *Government Executive* 37(3): 37–48.

Priest, D. 2005. Panel warns of headstrong agencies. *The Washington Post*, April 1.

Purpura, P.P. 2007. *Terrorism and Homeland Security: An Introduction with Applications*. Burlington, Massachusetts: Elsevier, Inc.

Rainey, H.G. 2003. *Understanding and Managing Public Organizations*, 3rd ed. San Francisco, California: Jossey-Bass.

Rockefeller Institute of Government. 2003. *The Role of "Home" in Homeland Security: The Federalism Challenge: The Challenge for State and Local Government.* Albany, New York: The Nelson A. Rockefeller Institute of Government.

Rosenthal, U. 2003. September 11: Public administration and the study of crises and crisis management. *Administration and Society* 35(2): 129–143.

Russack, J.A. 2005. Information Sharing Environment. Testimony before the Senate Committee on the Judiciary, July 27.

Sauter, M.A. and Carafano, J.J. 2005. *Homeland Security: A Complete Guide to Understanding, Preventing, and Surviving Terrorism.* New York: The McGraw-Hill Companies, Inc.

Scardaville, M. 2003. Principles the Department of Homeland Security Must Follow for an Effective Transition. The Heritage Foundation Backgrounder No. 1630, February 28. Washington, DC: The Heritage Foundation.

Shafritz, J.M. and Russell, E.W. 2005. *Introducing Public Administration*, 4th ed. New York: Pearson Longman.

Stever, J.A. 2005. Adapting intergovernmental management to the new age of terrorism. *Administration and Society* 37(4): 379–403.

Stillman, R., II. 2004. *The American Bureaucracy: The Core of Modern Government*, 3rd ed. Belmont, California: Wadsworth/Thomson Learning, Inc.

U.S. Coast Guard Academy. 2005. *Multiple Fairways: Developing a Strategic Studies Program for the Department of Homeland Security.* A Report on Charting a Course for Homeland Security Strategic Studies. New London, Connecticut: U.S. Coast Guard Academy.

U.S. Congress. 2006. *A Failure of Initiative. House Select Bipartisan Committee to Investigate the Preparation for and Response to Hurricane Katrina.* Washington, DC: U.S. Government Printing Office.

U.S. Government Accountability Office. 2005a. *Hurricane Katrina: Providing Oversight of the Nation's Preparedness, Response, and Recovery Activities.* Report GAO-05-1053T, September 28. Washington, DC: U.S. Government Accountability Office.

U.S. Government Accountability Office. 2005b. *Results-Oriented Government: Practices That Can Help Enhance and Sustain Collaboration among Federal Agencies.* Report GAO-06-15, October. Washington, DC: U.S. Government Accountability Office.

U.S. Government Accountability Office. 2006. *Catastrophic Disasters: Enhanced Leadership, Capabilities, and Accountability Controls Will Improve the Effectiveness of the Nation's Preparedness, Response, and Recovery System.* Report GAO-06-618, September. Washington, DC: U.S. Government Accountability Office.

U.S. Senate. 2006. *Hurricane Katrina: A Nation Still Unprepared. Committee on Homeland Security and Governmental Affairs.* Washington, DC: U.S. Government Printing Office.

Waterman, S. 2005. U.S. info sharing effort off to slow start. United Press International, July 28.

Waugh, W.L., Jr. and Streib, G. 2006. Collaboration and leadership for effective emergency management. *Public Administration Review.* Supplement to Volume 66 (December), 131–140.

Waugh, W.L., Jr. and Sylves, R.T. 2002. Organizing the war on terrorism. *Public Administration Review* 62: 145–153.

Wermuth, M.A. 2005. The Department of Homeland Security: The Road Ahead. Testimony before the Senate Committee on Homeland Security and Governmental Affairs, January 26. http://www.rand.org/publications/CT/CT233/.

White House. 2002. *National Strategy for Homeland Security*. July. Washington, DC: The White House.

White House. 2003. *National Strategy for the Physical Protection of Critical Infrastructures and Key Assets*. February. Washington, DC: The White House.

White House. 2006a. *The Federal Response to Hurricane Katrina: Lessons Learned*. February. Washington, DC: The White House.

White House. 2006b. *The National Security Strategy of the United States of America*. March. Washington, DC: The White House.

White, J.R. 2004. *Defending the Homeland: Domestic Intelligence, Law Enforcement, and Security*. Belmont, California: Wadsworth/Thomson Learning, Inc.

Wise, C.R. and Nader, R. 2002. Organizing the federal system for homeland security: Problems, issues, and dilemmas. *Public Administration Review* 62: 44–57.

Zegart, A.B. 2005. September 11 and the adaptation failure of U.S. intelligence agencies. *International Security* 29(4): 78–111.

TERRORISM, EXTREMIST MOVEMENTS, AND WEAPONS OF MASS DESTRUCTION

II

Chapter 7

Understanding New Global Multicellular Terrorism

Tatah Mentan and Moye Bongyu

CONTENTS

Introduction

On 11 September 2001, 19 young men, mostly Saudi Arabian nationals, commandeered four passenger airplanes and rammed three of them into critical U.S. targets, the World Trade Center and the Pentagon. The resulting social and economic impact—some 3000 lives lost and billions of dollars in economic damage—catapulted terrorism onto an entirely new level of strategic importance. Catastrophic or mass-casualty terrorism, once a theory, had now become a reality.[1] But the larger issue revolved around the nature of terrorism itself and its emerging modus operandi. Whether the September 11 attacks in the United States were the delayed manifestation of Oplan Bojinka, as some believe, or whether they were an isolated plan, it is clear that terrorism—and particularly that form of terrorism practiced by al-Qaeda—has fundamentally changed.[2]

The September 11 attacks on the United States were a bold, calculated transnational attack by an organization that has established and maintained a multinational presence in more than 50 countries, directed by a base located—at least until recently—in Afghanistan. Like many multinational corporations, al-Qaeda is both the product and beneficiary of globalization. The organization took advantage of the fruits of globalization and modernization—including satellite technology, accessible air travel, fax machines, the Internet, and other modern conveniences—to advance its political agenda. No longer geographically constrained within a particular territory, or financially tied to a particular state, al-Qaeda emerged as the ultimate transnational terror organization, relying on an array of legitimate and illicit sources of cash, including international charities that were often based in the West.

In the weeks following the attacks, many politicians, journalists, and pundits pointed to a massive intelligence failure that facilitated or allowed the attacks.[3] Some attributed this failure to the lack of human intelligence operations within Afghanistan. However, some experts have argued that the greatest intelligence failure of the September 11 attacks was the inability on the part of intelligence and law-enforcement agencies to grasp and understand that al-Qaeda represented a different type of terrorism, one less anchored to specific geographic locations or political constituencies and one capable of achieving transglobal strategic reach in its operations.[4]

Terrorism is not new in world politics. Indeed, it is a method of violence with ancient historical roots. For instance, terrorist methods were used by anarchists and other revolutionaries in the nineteenth century. In fact, the First World War was triggered partly by an act of terror, the assassination of Franz Ferdinand. However, at this time, terrorism was driven largely by ideology, nationalism, or homegrown cults.

Implications of September 11 Attacks

Firstly, it was the worst crime in American history; and it has triggered the greatest dragnet ever known. The investigation into the atrocities of September 11 has involved police forces across the United States and around the world. From Michigan to Malaysia, from San Diego to Ciudad del Este, Paraguay, law-enforcement agencies have been trying to figure out how the terrorists carried out their attacks, who helped them, and what they might do next. Along the way, the American public has been introduced to a confusing mass of names and faces and has learned of more links between them than any but the most nimble fingered could ever untangle. After more than a year, there is much that we know about the global terrorist network that goes by the name of al-Qaeda. But there is an awful lot that is still a hunch. Any simple investigation into al-Qaeda's structure reveals that it is as global in its range as it is ruthless in its ideology.

Secondly, September 11 rendered the conception of geographical space thoroughly obsolete. Of course, geographical space was already anachronistic with respect to thermonuclear war. It had already been called to question by earlier acts of transnational informal violence like piracy. But this globalized informal violence or transnational terrorism carried out by nonstate actors has altered the assumptions of foreign policy in a fundamental way.[5] For example, Afghanistan was never a foreign policy concern in the United States until the Soviet invasion in 1979 and the Union's collapse in 1991. On traditional grounds of U.S. national interest, Afghanistan became critical after September 11 and eventually a theatre of war—a demonstration which shows that threats to U.S. homeland security can come from anywhere in the global era.

Thirdly, the transnationalization of informal violence defined by commitments rather than by territory brought to the fore the fact that all mainstream theories of world politics have been basically secular with respect to motivation. They ignore religion despite the fact that many earth-shaking movements have often been motivated by religious fervor. Although human desires either to dominate or hate have been very strong in human history as well as in classical realist thought, most theoreticians erroneously assume that the world is run by rational and unheroic members of the bourgeoisie.[6]

Fourthly, September 11 took terrorism to entirely new levels of destructiveness. It was not the terrorism of the powerful against the weak, as in the case of the Ku Klux Klan violence against underprivileged Blacks. The event of September 11, 2001, was terrorism against the most powerful in the world. The Pentagon is the symbol of America's military might. And the World Trade Center its economic might. Criminal and cruel as the action stands, the accused al-Qaeda cave-dwellers picked on the superrich and the mightiest military power in the world to challenge.

Finally, after September 11, belief as a motivation for terrorism must be taken seriously into account. Religious motivations in world politics are rarely highlighted in theoretical considerations. But, when Osama bin Laden declares that terrorism against infidels will assure one "a supreme place in heaven,"[7] the politics should neither be ignored nor given casual attention.

These historical and theoretical landmarks can be ignored only at man's peril. After all, are human activities across regions and continents not being increasingly linked together through technological and social change? And, has globalism as a state of affairs not been defined as "a state of the world involving networks of interdependence at multicontinental distances, linked through flows of capital and goods, information and ideas, people and force, as well as environmentally relevant substances"?[8]

Technological and social change have dwarfed distances as well as rendered mankind very vulnerable. The World Trade Center bombing of the early 1990s and the Oklahoma bombing that followed some years later had already brought the United States within the circle of vulnerable states. The Middle East, Europe, Asia, and Latin America were already at the center of the waves of terrorist attacks from the late 1960s onward. Africa, potentially the most vulnerable part of the globe, did not however see the international character and the destructive power of terrorism until the bombings of the U.S. embassies in Kenya and Tanzania in August 1998.

Distinctiveness of Modern Terrorism

What is new about terrorism in the twentieth and twenty-first centuries is that technology has been put into the hands of destructive groups and individuals. First, the destructive capabilities of technology, once reserved for governments, are now at the reach of many, even the most elusive enemies of humankind. Thus, technology has rendered modern societies very vulnerable to large-scale attacks. And, this vulnerability of modern society accounts for why transnational terrorism has become very important today. The September 11, 2001, terrorist attack on the United States and the global reverberations it triggered made it categorically clear that even America is not safe anymore.

A second difference between new and old terrorism is that new terrorism tends to adopt a networked and less-hierarchical form. Both the anticapitalist and the national liberation terrorist groups of the 1970s and 1980s mostly had hierarchical forms and chains of command. Some even had identifiable operational leaders (e.g., Andreas Baader and Ulrike Meinhof of the German extreme left Rote Armed Fraction; Ahmed Jibril of the Popular Front for the Liberation of Palestine—General Command; Abimael Guzman of the Peruvian Sendero Luminoso). Moreover, new terrorism tends to be diffused. In defining "leaderless resistance," Louis Beam, suggested that hierarchy be downplayed in favor of a network of elusive or "phantom cells." These cells would communicate covertly. But there must be allowance for offensive flexibility while protecting the security of the organization as a whole. In fact,

> Utilizing the leaderless resistance concept, all individuals in groups operate independently of each other, and never report to a central headquarters or single leader for directional instruction... participants in a program of leaderless resistance through phantom cell or individual action, must know exactly what they are doing and exactly how to do it... all members of phantom cells or individuals, will tend to react to objective events in the same way through usual tactics of resistance.

Organs of information distribution, such as newspapers, leaflets, computers, etc which are widely available to all, keep each person informed of events allowing for a planned response that will take many variations. No one need issue an order to anyone.[9]

The far right *Free Militia Manual* puts it thus:

The fundamental rule guiding the organization of the Free Militia is generalized principles and planning but decentralized tactics and action . . . What is meant by this key statement is that the whole Militia must be committed to the same cause and coordinated in their joint defense of a community. Thus, there must be allegiance to a higher command. But specific tactics should be left up to the individual elements so that compromise of the part does not compromise the whole. Furthermore, all training and combat actions should be up to the smaller elements, again so that isolation or decapitation does not render the smaller units inept.[10]

In his second fictitious work *Hunter*, Pierce describes the mission white supremacist Oscar Yeager set himself in murdering mixed racial couples. *Hunter* served as a model for recent acts of terrorism in the United States and the United Kingdom to a greater extent than has the more generously quoted *The Turner Diaries*. Yeager is described as a man compelled to fight the alleged evil that afflicted America in the 1990s, and who declares war on "race-mixers," homosexuals, drug-pushers, and adherents of pluralism.[11]

Eric Robert Rudolph, Bufford Furrow, and James Kopp all acted out the scenarios described in *Hunter*. For example, Bufford Furrow, a former member of the Aryan Nations, was sentenced to life imprisonment in March 2001 for a shooting attack on a Jewish community centre in Los Angeles in August 1999; James Kopp was arrested in March 2001 in France and has since been charged with the assassination of Dr. Barnett Slepian in New York in October 1998. They sought no formal ties with organized far right groups. However, all were influenced by them. More recently in the United Kingdom, David Copeland was sentenced in June 2000 to four life terms for the London nail bombings in April 1999; he acted alone but under the complete influence of Pierce's writings and various National Alliance postings he had downloaded from the Internet, which were found in his possession. Likewise, Cameron Martin Dudley, a former Ku Klux Klan supporter living in Grimsby, Lincolnshire, planned to murder blacks on the streets of his town and was in touch, via the Internet, with the National Alliance in the United States. He had attempted to buy a handgun from an American far right Web site, but his postings were intercepted by U.S. law-enforcement officials and resulted in his arrest by the British police and subsequent trial and conviction.[12]

In a recent examination of far right terrorism in the United States, Gregory Walker states

> A disturbing new offender profile is emerging with every successful terrorist attack within the United States. This profile is unlike the European offender model with its step-by-step progression involving the making of identification of a terrorist. The US model, as represented by bombers Timothy McVeigh, Eric Robert-Rudolf, James Leroy Moody and alleged abortion doctor sniper James Kopp, takes the form of violent actions being perpetrated independently by individuals with little or no ties with one particular group or ideology.

His analysis concludes

> Today's terrorist actors seek no formal ties to any one composer's organization, and indeed the composer may not invite such affiliation. Current FBI thinking concludes it is not possible or effective to attempt to identify the new breed of offender by targeting extremist organizations and their followers. Ongoing case histories show those carrying out terrorist strikes in the US seldom have such traditionalist links, nor are they interested in being so categorized.[13]

Much the same can be said of transnational or international terrorism, which is now dominated by actions inspired by religious fervor. The shift is "from well-organized, localized groups supported by state-sponsors to loosely organized international networks of terrorists... This shift parallels a change from primarily politically motivated terrorism to terrorism that is more religiously or ideologically motivated."[14]

The State Department notes that the greatest terrorist threat comes from the Middle East and South-East Asia (with Afghanistan and Pakistan the primary sources of recruits and hosting). Here terrorism is almost completely Islamist. Islamist terrorists have also adopted the network form, with disparate actors coming together to commit a terrorist act. The GIA bombings in France in the early 1990s were carried out by a networked organization with its command and control center in London, safe-housing in Belgium, and targets in France. Likewise, the American Jihad group of Shaykh Omar Abdurrahman was composed of members from disparate backgrounds, as is the al-Qaeda group of Osama bin Ladin, which was responsible for bombing the U.S. embassies in East Africa in 1998. And the group arrested by police in January 2001 in Germany, Italy, and the United Kingdom alleged to have been plotting to blow up Strasbourg Cathedral also operates as a network.

Islamists have successfully demonstrated that geographical dispersion provides the security that a rigid hierarchy does not. Hamas constitutes yet another example of the network format, compared with, for instance, the hierarchical format of

Arafat's al-Fatah. Hamas has separated its political and military wings, and its leadership is divided between Gaza, Jordan, and Syria. Yet, some of its political direction and most of its fund raising have been carried out in the United States while its publications are partly produced in the United Kingdom. (*Filistin al Muslima*, the main Hamas paper is published in London, as is *Palestine Times*, the editorial line of which is pro-Hamas.)

It is noteworthy that Islamists have been more effective in their coordination and networking than have the far right. The far right, particularly in the United States and Germany, has been unable to follow through with their stated goals, and currently poses no effective terrorist challenge to the state. Because it has been so individualistic and random, it has taken on a self-destructive and nihilistic character.

Islamists, even without state backing, have coordinated terrorism transnationally in pursuit of predetermined goals. Criminal activity by Algerian Islamists in Canada and the United Kingdom to finance terrorism in a second country, while retaining command and control in a third country, indicates a sophisticated level of networking, which the far right has been unable to achieve so far.

Third, the networked form is assisted by the growing use of information and communication technologies (ICTs). ICTs enable extremists to communicate covertly and to bridge distances, and the far right was the first to understand its potential. According to Ken Stern, the use of ICTs was one of the major reasons the militia movement expanded so rapidly.[15] A movement eschewing an organized national center or leadership nevertheless needed to communicate its ideas and plans. The vast size of America represented no communication problem for the new medium and meant that an activist in a remote state in the Pacific northwest could be as involved in the movement as one on the east coast or deep south.

The former "Net Nazi Number One" Milton John Kleim, Jr. described these benefits, thus:

> All my comrades and I, none of whom I have ever met face to face, share a unique camaraderie, feeling as though we have been friends for a long time. Selfless cooperation occurs regularly amongst my comrades for a variety of endeavors. This feeling of comradeship is irrespective of national identity or state borders.[16]

ICTs allow the publication of material that in hard copy format would be illegal. They also allow encryption, thus frustrating the efforts of law-enforcement agencies to investigate their plans.

Islamists have also seized on the advantages offered by ICTs, which allow advanced communications within the diaspora and between the military and religious leadership and their followers. As Middle East terrorism researcher Yehudit Barsky writes[17]

In contrast to the heavily surveilled, oppressive atmosphere within most Middle Eastern countries, terrorist leaders who have relocated in the West face no difficulties in acquiring state-of-the-art communications technology. They have spread throughout the West to make use of ever more advanced modes of communication – audio tapes, video tapes, fax machines, and now the Internet.[18]

ICTs also allow diffused command and control previously only available within a single-theatre organization. In the early 1990s, Hamas was able to collect and analyze field reports from Gaza in Chicago and send the resultant operational orders back to Gaza.

Fourth, the new terrorist frequently does not claim responsibility for the action and may even deny it. It is the act that is important and not the claim to it, exemplified in the 1998 East African bombings. The terrorism of the 1970s and 1980s was often marked by the issuing of postfactum communiqués. And indeed with the Provisional Irish Republican Army (PIRA) and other terrorist groups, what is en vogue is the issuing of co-warnings beforehand. The new terrorist intends to strike, and to go on striking without publicity for himself or his cause, until he is caught. He does not need to claim responsibility perhaps because he acknowledges only God as his master, and God has seen his action. No one else matters.

> Willie Ray Lampley believes he is a brigadier general in the US militia and a prophet of God. His group was following God's orders when its members assembled a huge fertilizer bomb ... in Oklahoma ... The FBI says Lampley, his wife, Cecilia, 49 and three other men planned to blow up an office of the Anti-Defamation League or the Southern Poverty Law Center.

One of Lampley's coconspirators in 1996 stated

> We were taught by other people involved with the militia that cells are small groups of people who can act independently ... the smaller amount of people that know about what you're doing, the better off you are.[19]

Fifth, many of the new terrorists are amateurs or operate on a part-time basis. The terrorism of the 1970s and 1980s was characterized by professionalism in the sense that many of its actors had dropped out of society to concentrate on this activity. European anticapitalist groups, particularly, were frequently composed of people living in communes. Therefore, law enforcers only had to infiltrate the commune to find out what their plans were. With the lone terrorist or small cell, this is now impossible.

It has been noted that law-enforcement and security agencies now complain that while the new terrorists may have religious or quasi-religious motives they are not linked to any organization, have no base, raise their own funds, and attack soft targets, leaving no trace. This has been described by RAND Corporation Director, Bruce Hoffman as "a more amorphous, enigmatic, form of terrorism."[20]

Sixth, the new terrorism, especially religiously impelled terrorism, does not confine itself to any boundaries and possesses a terrifying lethality. When terrorism was backed by states, there were limits to the extent to which the perpetrators would go. These inhibitions no longer apply. Frequently, the old terrorism sought out representative targets and made its point by one or two surgical strikes. The new terrorism tends to go for the highest possible body count (e.g., the Oklahoma City bombing, 1995; the World Trade Center bombing, 1993; the Tokyo sarin gas attack, 1995; and the World Trade Center bombing, 2001). Exceptions to this pattern do exist such as in recent cases of covert state-sponsored terrorism, for example, the downing of Pan Am 102 over Lockerbie in December 1988, and the UTA flight over Chad in August 1989, both perpetrated by Libya; the bombing of the Argentine Israetine Mutual Association (AMIA) building in Buenos Aires in 1994, where Iran is regarded as culpable.

It is to be understood that Islamists are not the only people driven by religious motives. The influence of Christian Identity ideology is vital to our understanding of modern far right terrorism. Christian Identity adherents believe that the white Anglo-Saxon Protestant is the true descendant of the lost tribes of Israel and that the Jews are impostors. They and the "Mud" people (Blacks and Asians) are polluting America or Europe, and their influence must be stopped. An even more extreme and violent variant of this is also emerging. Evidence suggests that several acts of terrorism in the United States in recent years were committed by the Army of God, or the Phineas Priesthood. The Army of God is violently opposed to abortion, gays and lesbians, and promotes white supremacist teachings. It believes that government (including local government) is the enemy to be attacked. The term Army of God was first coined in 1982 and the group is believed to have been responsible for a series of terrorist acts. Eric Robert Rudolf, for example, still sought in connection with the Olympics Centennial Park bombing (1996), was connected to the Army of God.[21]

The Phineas Priesthood, guided by Richard Kelly Hoskins' book *Vigilantes of Christendom: The Story of the Phineas Priesthood*, perverts the biblical story of Phineas (Numbers, Ch. 25) to promote the idea of violence against Jews, abortion clinics, and banks, *inter alia*. However, the Phineas Priesthood cannot be classified as an extremist organization because it has no organizational system at all. Nevertheless, its adherents, who take it upon themselves to carry out "God's will" are thought to have been responsible for a series of terrorist acts, starting in 1963 with the murder of civil rights leader Medger Evers.[22]

The World Church of the Creator (WCOTC) is yet another white supremacist group that believes itself to be a religion carrying out God's work. Unlike the Phineas Priesthood or the Army of God, the WCOTC now has chapters throughout the world, including Australia and Scandinavia. An attempt to establish a British branch in the early 1990s failed partly as a consequence of police action, but the British National Party (BNP) still advertises its publications.[23]

The threat from the "religiously impelled" American far right and Islamists will continue for as long as its respective leaders make statements such as the following:

> There are Americans who care about these things as much as I do. And by God, we intend to do something about these things, even if we have to do it Timothy McVeigh's way. I hope it doesn't come to that, but we will break the grip of these Jews and their collaborators on our society.[24]

Their only strategic agenda is to wage Jihad to reconstitute the Muslim community (*umma*) beyond the national and ethnic divides; hence their support for the various jihads at the periphery of the Muslim world: Kashmir, the Philippines, Chechnya, Uzbekistan, Bosnia, and so forth. In this sense, they are genuinely global and recruit among uprooted cosmopolite, de-territorialized militants, themselves a sociological product of globalization: many migrated to find employment or education opportunities, they easily travel and change their citizenship. In their use of English, computers, satellite phones, and other technology, they are an authentic product of the modern, globalized world. Their battlefield is the whole world from New Jersey to the Philippines.[25]

Misleading Stereotypes

Therefore, terrorism is disturbing not just emotionally and morally but intellectually, as well. On terrorism, more than on other subjects, commentary seems liable to be swayed by wishful thinking. Or, it may base itself on unwarranted or flawed assumptions. It can also draw from these assumptions muzzily expressed irrational inferences. Here is one example. The following is the conclusion to a recent *Washington Post* editorial, "Nervous Mideast Moment":

> The United States, however, cannot afford to let its struggle against terrorism be overwhelmed by its differences with Libya. That gives the Qaddafis of the world too much importance and draws attention from the requirement to go to the political sources of terrorism. A principal source, unquestionably, is the unresolved Palestinian question. The State Department's man for the Middle East, Richard Murphy, has been on the road again, cautiously exploring whether it is possible in coming months to bring Israel and Jordan closer to a negotiation. This quest would be essential even if terrorism were not the concern it is. It marks the leading way that American policy must go.

This implies clearly that negotiation between Israel and Jordan can dry up "a principal source of terrorism." Now, nobody who has studied that political context at all, and is not blinded by wishful thinking, could possibly believe that. For the Arab terrorists—and most other Arabs—the unresolved Palestinian question and the existence of the state of Israel are one and the same thing. The terrorists could not possibly be appeased, or made to desist, by Jordan's King Hussein's getting back a slice of the West Bank, which is the very most that could come out of a negotiation between Jordan and Israel. The terrorists and their backers would denounce such a deal as treachery and seek to step up their attacks, directing these against Jordan as well as Israel. The case of Egypt is witness to this wishful thinking.

That *Washington Post* editorial exemplifies a dovish, or sentimental, variety of wishful thinking on the subject of terrorism. There is also a hawkish, or hysterical, variety. Each has its own misleading stereotypes of the terrorist. These stereotypes are:

Sentimental stereotype.   According to this stereotype, the terrorist is a misguided idealist, an unsublimated social reformer. He has been driven to violence by political or social injustice or both. What is needed is to identify the measures of reform that will cause him to desist. Once these can be identified and undertaken, the terrorist, having ceased to be driven, stops.

Hysterical stereotype.   Less stable than the sentimental variety, this can be divided into subvarieties:

1. Terrorist is some kind of a nut—a disgruntled abnormal given to mindless violence. Mindless violence may be applicable to the deeds of isolated, maverick assassins. As applied to the planned activities of armed conspiracies, it is itself a mindless expression. This mindless, catastrophic, or mass-casualty violence[26] is real in the suicidal tendencies of transnational terrorism.
2. Terrorist is nothing more than a thug, a goon, or a gangster. His political demands are simply a cover for criminal activity.
3. Terrorist is an agent, or dupe, or cat's-paw of the other superpower. (He might, of course, be a nut or a goon as well as a dupe.)

These stereotypes serve mainly to confuse debate on the subject of terrorism. There is no point in arbitrarily attributing motives, nice or nasty, to the terrorist. It might be more useful to look at the situations in which terrorists find themselves and at how they act, and may be expected to act, given their circumstances.

The Al-Qaeda Multicellular Terror Model

Al-Qaeda (Arabic for "The Base") traces its roots to Afghanistan and the pan-Islamic resistance to the invasion of Afghanistan by the Soviet Union in 1979. In 1982, Osama bin Laden, then a young Saudi Arabian national, joined the anti-Soviet jihad. He traveled to Afghanistan where, after just a few years, he established his own military camps from which anti-Soviet assaults could be launched. In 1988, bin Laden and others established al-Qaeda, not as a terrorist organization, but rather as a reporting infrastructure so that relatives of foreign soldiers who had come to Afghanistan to join the resistance could be properly tracked.[27] Al-Qaeda reportedly had the additional function of funneling money to the Afghan resistance.[28] In 1989, the year the Soviets withdrew their last troops from Afghanistan, bin Laden returned to Saudi Arabia, where he began delivering public lectures about topics that were sensitive to the government—including predictions that Kuwait would soon be invaded by Iraq. When his prediction came true, he became frustrated when the Saudi government ignored his advice (including offers of military assistance), and instead turned to the United States for military help.

Increasingly unhappy with bin Laden's public activities and his militant views, the Saudi government placed him under house arrest. Through his family connections, bin Laden was nevertheless able to secure permission for a business trip to Pakistan. Once in Pakistan, he traveled to Afghanistan and stayed there for a few months. But soon after, he left for Sudan where he was welcomed by National Islamic Front (NIF) leader, Hassan al-Turabi.[29] Bin Laden's time in Sudan is probably the most important in terms of al-Qaeda's development. During this period, al-Qaeda forged alliances with militant groups from Egypt, Pakistan, Algeria, and Tunisia, as well as with Palestinian Jihad and Hamas.[30] Also while in Sudan, al-Qaeda began to develop its signature transnational modus operandi by engaging in a range of international operations, such as deploying fighters to Chechnya and Tajikistan, establishing satellite offices in Baku, Azerbaijan, and funding affiliates based in Jordan and Eritrea.[31] Under American pressure, however, Sudan forced bin Laden to leave in 1996. He and other members of al-Qaeda relocated their operations to Afghanistan where they remained, until recently.

Al-Qaeda has traditionally operated with an informal horizontal structure, comprising more than 24 constituent terrorist organizations, combined with a formal vertical structure. Below Osama bin Laden was the "majlis al shura," a consultative council that directed the four key committees (military, religious, finance, and media), members of which were handpicked by senior leadership. The majlis al shura discussed and approved major operations, including terrorist attacks.[32] Bin Laden and his two cohorts, Ayman al-Zawahiri and Mohammed Atef, set general policies and approved large-scale actions. Until the U.S. intervention in Afghanistan, al-Qaeda acted in a manner somewhat resembling a large charity organization that funded terrorist projects to be conducted by preexisting or affiliate terrorist groups.

The United States emerged as a central enemy to al-Qaeda almost from the beginning of the organization's existence for a variety of reasons, including al-Qaeda's unhappiness with U.S. operations in the 1990–1991 Gulf War and the 1992–1993 Operation Restore Hope in Somalia. Al-Qaeda's overarching complaint against the United States has centered on its continued military presence in Saudi Arabia and throughout the Arabian peninsula. To publicize its disdain for the

United States, al-Qaeda issued various fatwas (verdicts based on Islamic law) urging that U.S. forces should be attacked. In 1992 and 1993, the group issued fatwas urging that American forces in Somalia should be attacked. In 1996, the group issued a "Declaration of Jihad on the Americans Occupying the Country of the Two Sacred Places," which urged the expulsion of American forces from the Arabian Peninsula.[33] This was followed by a media interview in 1997 in which bin Laden called for attacks on U.S. soldiers.[34]

The anti-American rhetoric emanating from al-Qaeda hit a high pitch in 1998 when the organization essentially fused with Egypt's two main terrorist organizations, al Jihad (Islamic Jihad) and al Gamaa al Islamiya (Islamic Group), both of which were linked to the assassination of former Egyptian President Anwar Sadat. The new campaign would be known as the World Islamic Front for Jihad against the Jews and the Crusaders, and would also include cosignatories from Pakistan and Bangladesh. This World Islamic Front calls for attacks not on only U.S. soldiers, but also U.S. civilians. The proclamation demands that Muslims everywhere should "abide by Allah's order by killing Americans and stealing their money anywhere, anytime, and whenever possible."[35]

To understand al-Qaeda's evolution, it is especially important to recognize the importance of the Egyptian influence on bin Laden, which dates back to his time in Afghanistan. Currently most of al-Qaeda's membership is drawn from these two Egyptian groups. Moreover, one Egyptian in particular, Ayman al-Zawahiri—a former key figure in al Jihad—has had a tremendous intellectual influence on Osama bin Laden and is considered by many to be a candidate to succeed him.[36]

As indicated above, al-Qaeda's model has been to establish bases with indigenous groups throughout the world. Early in its existence, al-Qaeda developed the ability to penetrate Islamic nongovernmental organizations (NGOs) to the point that it was "inseparably enmeshed with the religious, social, and economic fabric of Muslim communities worldwide."[37] In some cases, al-Qaeda pursued a virtual hands-off policy with its affiliated group. It may have guided or directed the group's operations, but at the same time required it to raise its own funds. Ahmed Ressam, who was intercepted entering the United States in December 1999 as part of the infamous Millennium Plot, was part of a cell in Montreal, Canada, that survived by engaging in petty theft—including passport theft—and other crimes. However, for certain operations, such as the September 11 attacks in the United States, al-Qaeda was much more willing to provide substantial and direct financial support.

Al-Qaeda's strength lay in its reliance on a multicellular structure, spanning the entire globe, which gave the organization agility and cover. One French terrorism expert recently lamented, "If you have good knowledge of the [al Qaeda] network today, it's not operational tomorrow."[38] He compared its networks to a constantly changing virus that is impossible to totally grasp or destroy. Al-Qaeda's multicellular international structure provided an ironic backdrop to President George Bush's proclamation that the United States would find terrorists wherever they were located and would consider attacking any nation that harbored terrorists. The uncomfortable reality is that many states—including those allied with the United States—harbored al-Qaeda cells, but did nothing to neutralize them, either because they did not know of their presence (or the precise danger they posed) or were unwilling, for political or security reasons, to disrupt their operations. Certain German investigators, for instance, ruefully admit that their lack of aggressive intervention—despite full awareness of al-Qaeda's activities in many of its main cities—probably contributed to the September 11 tragedy.

As a truly transnational terrorist organization, al-Qaeda has sought to expand beyond the traditional venue of the Middle East, Western Europe, North America, and South Asia. Increasingly, the organization has pursued Southeast Asia as a key basing and staging region. Al-Qaeda has long cultivated links with groups such as the Philippine-based Abu Sayyaf and Moro Islamic Liberation Front (MILF) and the Indonesian group Laskar Jihad. Al-Qaeda is also linked to regionwide organizations, such as Jemaah Islamiah, the mastermind of plots against the U.S. Embassy in Singapore and other critical American and Western targets. In late September 2001, the Philippine military's chief of staff confirmed speculation that al-Qaeda was seeking to support the Abu Sayyaf group with "materiel, leadership, and training support."[39]

Similar trends have been detected in Indonesia, where officials suspect growing linkages between al-Qaeda and indigenous groups such as Laskar Jihad. In December 2001, the head of Indonesia's intelligence services, Abdullah Hendropriyono, asserted that al-Qaeda and other international terrorist organizations were attempting to sow unrest on the Indonesian island of Sulawesi by promoting interethnic violence between Muslims and Christians. He also confirmed that al-Qaeda and other international groups had used the territory as a base and training site for international terrorist operations.[40]

Al-Qaeda has also established links in Africa and South America. In South America, the triple border area (where Brazil, Argentina, and Paraguay meet) is viewed as a base for such Middle Eastern terrorist organizations as Hezbollah, al Gamaa al Islamiya, and Hamas, all al-Qaeda constituent or affiliate groups. A 1999 Argentine intelligence report stated that al-Qaeda was operating in the region in an attempt to forge links with Hezbollah supporters.[41] The region, and other locations in Brazil, appears to have played a significant role in the planning of the September 11 attacks.[42] Al-Qaeda also has established links in various African countries, including Somalia, Sudan, and South Africa.[43] Al-Qaeda reportedly has considered moving to Somalia following U.S. military operations in Afghanistan, a possibility that recently prompted a U.S. Naval blockade of the entire Somali coastline.

Al-Qaeda has flourished in an environment of weak or quasi-states that are undergoing disruptive political or social change. Vast swaths of political instability in many parts of the world, and particularly in Africa and Asia, have provided a breeding ground for al-Qaeda and its analogues. As one French analyst stated, wide expanses of anarchic territory "need no longer be considered a regrettable feature of the postmodern world, but rather a strategic challenge that should be addressed urgently."[44] Such areas are not only hospitable to terrorists, but may also attract transnational crime groups, drug traffickers, and maritime pirates. Despite their isolation, paradoxically, these areas constitute an acute threat to global security.

Conclusion

The contemporary terrorism has some peculiarities, which administrators are supposed to know to be better able to tackle it. The modern terrorism, especially as practiced by al-Qaeda, as Senator Richard Shelby rightly puts it, has fundamentally changed its form. According to Tatah Mentan, the reality of transnational terrorism is far from white and black. Terrorism has ultimately worn a new dress, and even if we witness the demise of al-Qaeda, we are not likely to witness the demise of its model. Its operating environment, the nature of terrorism itself, and its modus operandi have drastically changed.

Transnational terrorism is to the twenty-first century is what piracy was to an earlier historical period. All states no matter their strengths are vulnerable to the terrorist attacks. The September 11 attacks exposed fundamental weaknesses of modern Western states, including vulnerable borders, inadequate immigration controls, and insufficient internal antiterrorism surveillance. Indeed, investigations conducted following the U.S. terror attacks would reveal an uncomfortable truth about al-Qaeda and its affiliate groups. Probably their most important bases of operation—from a financial and logistical perspective—were located not in Afghanistan or Sudan, but rather in Western Europe and North America, including in the United States itself.[45]

The core evil of deliberately killing innocent people is broadly condemned by all moral codes of religious groups and international law. Thus, President George Bush is not alone in calling all to unite in "opposing all terrorists, not just some of them. No national aspiration, no remembered wrong can ever justify the deliberate murder of the innocent."

Endnotes

1. Investigations conducted in Southeast Asia after the September 11 attacks in the United States provide linkages between Bojinka and the attacks on New York City and Washington, DC, suggesting that the former was possibly a blueprint for the latter. Specifically, certain key leaders of a newly discovered group, Jemaah Islamiah, have reported links to both plots. See Richard C. Paddock, Southeast Asian Terror Exhibits Al Qaeda Traits, *Los Angeles Times*, 3 March 2002, p. A1.
2. This specific phrase was uttered by U.S. Senator Richard Shelby on the CBS News Show Face the Nation on 16 September 2001 (file accessed through Lexis-Nexis).

3. Ed Blanche, Al-Qaeda Recruitment, *Jane's Intelligence Review*, 14 (January 2002), 27–28.
4. Ed Blanche, What the Investigation Reveals, *Jane's Intelligence Review*, 13 (November 2001), pp. 16–17; see also article by John Mintz and Rom Jackman, Finances Prompted Raids on Muslims, *The Washington Post*, 24 March 2001, p. A01.
5. Keohane, R.O., The Globalization of Informal Violence, Theories of World Politics, and 'the Liberalism of Fear,' in *Understanding September 11*, Craig Calhoun, Paul Price, and Ashley Timmer (Eds.) (New York: The New Press, 2002), p. 80.
6. Joseph Schumpeter, *Capitalism, Socialism, Democracy* (New York: Harper and Row, 1950), p. 137.
7. Statement by Osama bin Laden cited by *New York Times*, October 8, 2001, p. B7.
8. Robert O. Keohane and Joseph S. Nye, *Power and Interdependence*, 3rd Edition (New York: Addison Wesley Longman, 2001), p. 229.
9. Beam, L., Leaderless Resistance, *The Seditionist*, Vol 12, 4, February 1992.
10. Field Manual Section 1: Principles Justifying the Arming and Organizing of A Militia, *The Free Militia*, 1994, Wisconsin, p. 78 (quoted in Tom Burghardt, Militias and LeaderlessResistance, p. 1, 27 April 1995, www.webcom.com/~pinknoiz/right/bacorr7.html).
11. Macdonald, *Hunter*, back cover.
12. Former Klansman's Gun Plan Foiled, *Scunthorpe Evening Telegraph*, 26 June 2000; I'm Just an Internet Loner, Says Man on Gun Charge, *Grimsby Evening Telegraph*, 27 June 2000.
13. Gregory A. Walker, The New Face of Right Wing Terror, *International Police Review*, pp. 10–11, March/April 1999.
14. *Patterns of Global Terrorism 1999*, Introduction, pp. 1–4.
15. Kenneth Stern, *A Force upon the Plain*, University of Oklahoma Press, 1997. pp. 225–227.
16. Milton John Kleim Jr., On Tactics and Strategy for USENET, 1955, bb748 Free Net, Carlton, California.
17. Yehudit Barsky, Terror by Remote Control, *Middle East Quarterly*, June 1996, pp. 3–9.
18. In the Matter of the Extradition of Moussa Abu Marzuk, U.S. District Court Southern District of New York, Affirmation 95, Cr.Misc 1, Oct. 5, 1995, statement of Bassam Musa, 17 Feb. 1993, p. 12.
19. Bill Morlin, Militias Imprisoned Prophet Says System Is Doomed, *The Spokesman Review*, 30 Dec. 1996 (downloaded from Dan McComb, Long-Term Project: The Radical Right in America, http://www.visnet-contact.com/pages/rightwing.html).
20. Richard Norton-Taylor and Martin Walker, Blast Alerts West to Elusive Threat, *The Guardian*, 21 April 1995.
21. Deputy Larry Richards, Domestic Terrorism: Army of God, http://eob.org/terror/html/army_of_god.html.
22. Deputy Larry Richards, Domestic Terrorism: Phineas Priests, P1, http://eob.org/terror/html/phineas_prieshood.html.
23. In *Spearhead*, the monthly journal published by John Tyndall in support of the BNP.
24. William Pierce, The Evil among Us, *American Dissident Voices* broadcast, 1 July 2000.

25. Olivier Roy, Islam, Iran and the New Terrorism, published in a Response to America and the New Terrorism: An exchange, p. 160, *Survival*, International Institute for Strategic Studies Vol. 42 No. 2, Summer 2000.

26. Regarding warnings about the rise of "catastrophic terrorism," see Ashton Carter et al., Catastrophic terrorism: Tacking the new danger, *Foreign Affairs*, 77 (November/December 1998), p. 80.

27. Osama bin Laden: A Chronology of His Political Life, background article for PBS documentary series Frontline, internet, www.pbs.org/wgbh/pages/frontline/shows/binladen/etc/cron.html, accessed 24 March 2002.

28. Peter L. Bergen, *Holy War: Inside the Secret World of Osama Bin Laden* (New York: Free Press, 2001), p. 79.

29. Ibid., p. 85.

30. Ibid., p. 86.

31. Indictment of Zacarias Moussaoui, U.S. District Court for the Eastern District of Virginia, Alexandria Division (December 2001).

32. Bergen, P.L., 2001, Holy War: Inside The Secret World of Osama bin Laden, (New York: Free Press, 2001), 93.

33. Ibid., p. 94.

34. Ibid., p. 95.

35. Ibid., p. 96.

36. Ed Blanche, The Egyptians around Bin Laden, *Jane's Intelligence Review*, 13 (December 2001), pp. 19–21.

37. Phil Hirschkorn, et al., Blowback, *Jane's Intelligence Review*, 13 (August 2001), pp. 42–45.

38. Steven Erlanger and Chris Hedges, Terror Cells Slip Through Europe's Grasp, *The New York Times*, 28 December 2001, p. 1.

39. Abu Sayyaf Gets Arms, Training from Bin Laden: Philippine Military, *Agence France Presse*, 28 September 2001.

40. Fabiola Desy Unidjaja, International Terrorists Train in Poso, *Jakarta Post*, 13 December 2001.

41. Mario Daniel Montoya, War on Terrorism Reaches Paraguay's Triple Border, *Jane's Intelligence Review*, 13 (December 2001), pp. 12–15.

42. John, C.K. Daly, Moroccan Has 'Much to Tell,' *Jane's Intelligence Review*, 13 (December 2001), p. 13.

43. See testimony of Dr. J. Stephen Morrison before the House International Relations Committee, Subcommittee on Africa, Hearing on Africa and the War on Global Terrorism Federal Document Clearing House Congressional Testimony, 15 November 2001.

44. Therese Delpech, The Imbalance of Terror, *Washington Quarterly*, 25 (Winter 2002), p. 31.

45. A Biography of Osama bin Laden, background article for PBS documentary series Frontline, Internet, www.pbs.org/wgbh/pages/frontline/shows/binladen/who/bio.html, accessed 24 March 2002.

Chapter 8

The Abu Sayyaf Group and Maritime Terrorism

Eric D. Johnson

CONTENTS

The Abu Sayyaf Group and Maritime Terrorism

The phenomenon of international maritime terrorism has been somewhat neglected during the recent increase in antiterrorism awareness. This is a wrong-headed approach to combating terror; in that all possible scenarios should be investigated to ensure as complete a body of knowledge on the subject exists as is possible. Recent large-scale terrorist attacks, such as the Tokyo subway attack carried out by the Aum Shinriko cult in 1995, as well as the attacks of September 11, 2001, have proven that modern transportation systems are viable as weapons systems for both sophisticated and unsophisticated terrorist organizations. Arguably, there are inherent tactical and logistical challenges involved in conducting terrorism in the maritime environment as opposed to on land. Even attacks via or against aircraft are comparably simpler. Aside from the inherent security screening process, the logistics of accessing an aircraft are exponentially simpler and safer than boarding a ship at sea.

As terrorist organizations become more sophisticated and well funded, however, their ability to board, commandeer, or hijack vessels at sea or in port increases proportionally. In fact, an extremely well-funded terrorist organization could certainly find itself in a position to simply purchase a ship or even obtain one from a rogue state willing to sponsor the organization. In such a scenario, the organization can bypass the force, planning, and potential risk of casualties, while still obtaining a capable vessel that provides them the flexibility and capabilities required to carry out the organization's goals and missions.

One method of strategic planning against terrorism involves the examination of threats by assessing the capabilities of individual terrorist organizations to carry out possible terrorist stratagems and tactics to determine of these options are the most plausible or likely. This chapter adheres to this methodology by examining the possible employment of piracy by the Abu Sayyaf Group (ASG). The chapter also provides some possible scenarios for acts of piracy by the ASG, with evaluations of complexity and likelihood of occurrence.

As an additional note, this chapter addresses the debate over consolidation of the terms maritime terrorism and piracy. Currently, much discussion surrounds the interchangeability of these terms when one refers to acts committed against shipping and in the maritime environment. An attempt will be made not to belabor the point, although a thorough discussion of the topic requires that the semantics of the issue be touched upon. The importance of the acts being viewed similarly is that independent strategies need not be developed for two distinct threats. Rather a single, comprehensive strategy may be formulated and adapted as needed. Currently, little agreement exists as to the compatibility of the two acts, nor as to the accepted independent definitions of either piracy or maritime terrorism. Indeed, there is still disagreement within the international community regarding the correct comprehensive definition of terrorism itself, let alone maritime terrorism.

Why Differentiate?

Piracy has arguably existed for as long as the seas have been traveled. The historical record of ancient piracy is incomplete. However, it is believed that the Greeks, Phoenicians, and Romans (among others) engaged in the act of piracy in conjunction with maritime trade in the Mediterranean region. One of the earliest recorded incidents of piracy occurred in AD 793, when Norse raiders landed on the Holy Island of Lindisfarne and sacked the church and township. These Viking pillagers virtually destroyed the city, leveling the church and laying ruin to religious symbols and icons, and completely looting the island. Piracy continued throughout the centuries, reaching a height of activity during the eighteenth and nineteenth centuries, when pirates, privateers (some of whom were pirates at one time or returned to this vocation), and other bandits, roamed many of the world's seas and oceans.

In the modern era, the international community has undertaken the task of attempting to formally define piracy. What once was a fairly obvious categorization of violent behavior on the seas as piracy has now become the subject of much debate. Various definitions of modern maritime piracy exist. Two important maritime organizations define the act quite differently. Article 101 of the United Nations Conference on the Laws of the Sea (UNCLOS) defines piracy as

> Any illegal acts of violence or detention, or any act of depredation, committed for private ends by the crew or the passengers of a private ship or a private aircraft, and directed:
> (a) On the high seas, against another ship or aircraft, or against persons or private property on board such ship or aircraft
> (b) Against a ship, aircraft, persons or property in a place outside the jurisdiction of any State (United Nations, 2001, Part VII)

The International Maritime Bureau (IMB) defines the act of piracy somewhat differently. In a recent report on piracy statistics published by the IMB, which is a component of the International Chamber of Commerce (ICC), piracy is defined as "an act of boarding any vessel with the intent to commit theft or any other crime and with the intent or capability to use force in the furtherance of that act" (Ong, 2004, p. 16).

A precise and generally acceptable definition of terrorism similarly eludes the modern international community. Jonathan Weinberger provides an in-depth historical study of the attempts to define the term, as well as the act of terrorism itself. Weinberger provides an excerpted definition of terrorism from the 1795 Dictionnaire Supplement of the Academie Francaise and cites it as the first attempt to define terrorism by the French government (Weinberger, 2003, p. 66). This definition was crafted during a time of intense political and cultural upheaval in France, and attempts to be inclusive of all possible perpetrators, victims, and causes of terrorism.

Notable within the definition, aside from its inclusiveness, the definition clearly asserts that terrorism revolves around politics and political agendas. Further, the act of terrorism can be perpetrated by those in positions of legitimate power (e.g., governmental authorities, etc.) or those lacking legitimacy, but still attempting to influence change in the political landscape. This is certainly important, as the theme of the definition illustrates that acts of terrorism are committed to achieve a desired outcome and, more importantly, the commitment of those perpetrating the acts is clearly linked to their commitment to fulfilling their objectives.

Although the basic tenets of the definition of terrorism (i.e., actions to gain political ends, etc.) have survived, the definition itself has evolved significantly. One of the most significant evolutions involves the addition of a distinct definition of international terrorism to cope with the ease of transnational travel in the modern world. Certainly, the French in 1795, still recovering from the revolution, were not envisioning outsiders as terrorists when they crafted their definition. However, the modernization of travel and the shrinking of the world have increased the ease with which terrorists may engage in operations around the world. In April 2001, the Department of State, Office for the Coordinator for Counterterrorism, in a document concerning the trends in terrorism, released the following statement:

> "No one definition of terrorism has gained universal acceptance. For the purposes of this report, however, we have chosen the definition of terrorism contained in Title 22 of the United States Code, Section 2656 f (d). That statute contains the following definitions:

> ■ The term "terrorism" means premeditated, politically motivated violence perpetrated against noncombatant targets by subnational groups or clandestine agents, usually intended to influence an audience.
> ■ The term "international terrorism" means terrorism involving citizens or the territory of more than one country.
> ■ The term "terrorist group" means any group practicing, or that has significant subgroups that practice, international terrorism.

> The U.S. government has employed this definition of terrorism for statistical and analytical purposes since 1983 (Department of State (DOS), 2001, Definitions)."

The above definition, while maintaining the core theme of terrorism (politics), diverges from the French definition by appearing to make exceptions for acts committed by legitimate bodies, such as governments, armies, militias, etc. Although this is certainly a vital issue in itself, it cannot be fully discussed in this chapter. The point of this discourse is that the ambiguity of the various definitions of terrorism resembles the difficulty of the United States to precisely identify pornography. Justice Stewart (in *Jacobellis v. Ohio* 378 US 184 (1964)) famously stated that, regarding his ability to define pornography that "perhaps I could never succeed in intelligibly doing so. But I know it when I see it" (FINDLAW, 2005, Mr. Justice Stewart, concurring). This statement exemplifies the dilemma facing those involved in stanching the flow of terrorist activities worldwide. These individuals are charged with combating an activity that cannot be precisely identified, which inhibits the effective development of comprehensive strategies, because not all activities which could or should be included in prevention planning can be anticipated.

Maritime terrorism, on the other hand, has been loosely defined by combining several general definitions of terrorism, and adding the caveat that these activities occur in the maritime environment. The inherent problem with this approach to defining maritime terrorism is that, as stated above, there is no universally accepted definition for terrorism. Ong (2004, p. 16) notes that, "like piracy, maritime terrorism has no internationally accepted definition to date." Therefore, those involved in combating or preventing the issue are left to attempt to identify the individual occurrences of the activity themselves with little or no legal support for their efforts.

There are glaring differences between the two definitions. These differences have been illustrated and expounded upon by experts in the field, such as Ong and others, and have provided the basis for much debate within the international community. One of the glaring differences between the definition of piracy and terrorism involves the reasons that an individual or organization engages in the activity. As defined above, terrorism involves political motivations, whereas piracy is more generally accepted as a crime for profit. However, it could certainly become somewhat cumbersome to attempt to identify the particular reasons for each and every incident of piracy or maritime terrorism to properly classify the event. Further, there is no reason to assume that the activities are mutually exclusive. A terrorist group may spontaneously engage in piracy simply for financial support, to gain supplies, or for other reasons. The simple fact that the activity engaged in was not specifically contained within the politically themed genre of terrorist-related activities must not be allowed to abrogate the terrorist status of the group.

Examining the motivations of the offenders in an attempt to categorize them as either pirates or terrorists serves little constructive purpose. Although the single act of piracy may not fit neatly under the definition of international terrorism, it would almost assuredly be committed in furtherance of the terrorist agenda if committed by a designated terrorist organization. There is little or no chance that a known terrorist organization would simply shift gears and begin engaging in other illegal activity for unrelated motives. Simply put, terrorists are terrorists.

Some believe that the discrepancies between the definitions of international maritime terrorism and piracy are merely semantic, and both should be considered synonymous, while allowing for minor differences (see Ong, 2004). Although this approach is certainly meritorious, the attempt to link the two terms by illustrating the commonalities between the activities involves taking the "long way around the barn" so to speak. Instead, perhaps one should focus on the fact that terrorism lacks any officially accepted definition. As there is no such definition, which could very easily be crafted in such a way as to exclude piracy or similar acts, we can then assume piracy does qualify as terrorism, especially when committed by a terrorist group. More simply stated, in much the same way one does not attempt to limit what another considers as offensive, we must not pigeonhole terrorism into a restrictive definition, which excludes other heinous acts simply because they are not explicitly included in the definition. Further, does one realize any benefit by excluding piracy from the definition of international maritime terrorism? Surely, the offenders themselves do not worry about being categorized as pirates or terrorists.

The Philippines

To fully comprehend the motivations that drive the ASG, one must examine the history; specifically the religious history, of the Philippines and South Eastern Asia. "Islam was introduced in the Philippines in 1210 by Arab merchants and Islamic missionaries, preceding the introduction of Catholicism via Spanish colonialism in 1521" (Gershman, 2002). Although various scholars including Mujar and Jubair, among others, debate the exact date of the introduction of Islam to the region, it is believed that the introduction of Islam to the Philippines simultaneously introduced monotheism to the country (Jubair, 2004, Arrival of Islam). The religion quickly took hold and spread north throughout the country. However, subsequent colonization and association with Spain and America provided the impetus for a continuing shift in the religious demographics of the country, resulting in the Philippines finally becoming the only predominantly Christian country in Asia.

Western influence first reached the shores of the country with Ferdinand Magellan in 1521 and the colonization of the island nation by the Spanish empire. Spain brought with it Christianity. Christianity, in the form of Roman Catholicism, had established a strong foothold in the country by the time the Philippines became a protectorate of the United States in 1897. Islam retreated to the western and southern coastal regions of the country's Mindanao region where its stronghold remains to this day. Currently, more than 80 percent of the country's total population observes Roman Catholicism as their religion, while approximately 5 percent of the population is Muslim. As noted above, the Islamic adherents mainly reside in the southwest provinces of Mindanao, or along the Sulu Archipelago (see Figure 8.1). In the specific region of Mindanao, the percentage of Muslims is significantly more concentrated, being calculated at approximately 19 percent (Gershman, 2002). The portion of the Filipino population which is neither Roman Catholic nor Muslim observes other forms of religion including Iglesia ni Cristo, which was founded in the Philippines in 1914.

The Muslim population of the Philippines has found itself in unenviable positions during the Westernization, and corresponding modernization, of the country. Historically, Muslims have either found themselves "on the outside looking in" or subjected to outright hostility and persecution. Either way, the Muslim population has consistently been alienated from the progress of the nation. The attempt to Christianize the Philippines brought with it, necessarily, an agenda involving ridding the country of Muslims. The Spaniards first coined the term "Moro" to refer to any of the broad range of ethnic groups in the Philippines adhering to the Muslim faith. The term is derived from the hated Turkish Moors, whom the Spanish had defeated before Spain's colonization of the Philippines. The term was

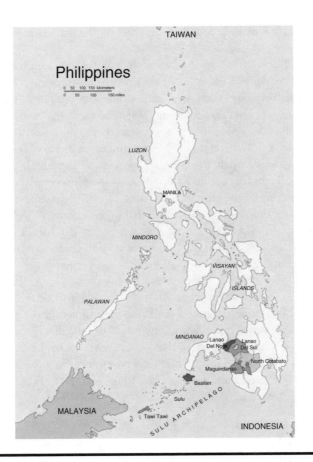

Figure 8.1   Map depicting areas of Muslim concentrations in the Philippines, as of 2001. (From Foreign Policy in Focus. 2001. Moros in the Philippines (Self-Determination Conflict Profile). John Gershman. Retrieved November 3, 2005, from: http://www.fpif.org/selfdetermination/conflicts/philippines_body.html. Reprinted with permission.)

certainly not used by the Spaniards as a sign of endearment to the Muslim inhabitants of the country. To the Spaniards, the Moro was always seen as "a cunning, ruthless, cruel, treacherous savage; a pirate; a raider; a slaver" (Gowing, 1979, p. 41).

The Moros presented a formidable adversary for the Spanish, who never fully resolved the issue before the ceding of the Philippines to the United States. The American forces that were then faced with the issue of dealing with the Moro rebels quickly learned to respect the tough fighters. The difficulty in dealing with the Moro fighters resulted, finally, in the development of the .45 caliber ACP (automatic colt pistol). The .38 caliber sidearm carried before the advent of the .45 ACP was virtually ineffective against the Moros, who would sometimes endure several hits with the .38 and still manage to inflict casualties on the soldiers before falling (The Great War Society).

Many islands comprise the Mindanao region of the southern Philippines. Additionally, all regions of the country are divided into provinces based on many factors including language, ethnicity, culture, and others. The Mindanao region consists of several provinces, including Magindanao, Sulu, and Baslian. Most Muslims in Mindanao reside in the southwestern provincial districts, and along the Sulu Archipelago. These areas of the Philippines are those closest to Indonesia and Malaysia, separated by merely 50 miles of ocean in some locations.

Throughout the history of the Philippines, the Muslim population has pursued the idea of independency and self-determination. The largest and most well-organized group to lobby for the autonomy of Muslims in the country is the Moro National Liberation Front (MNLF). One may also assert that the MNLF was the most successful of the groups, in that the achievement of the Tripoli Agreement, which resulted in the granting of autonomy to 13 provinces. Ironically, although the advent of the Tripoli Agreement may be viewed as a significant achievement by the MNLF, it may also be viewed as a significant failure of the group (Donnelly, 2004, p. 3). The backlash of infighting resulting from those factions within the MNLF desiring full independence, versus mere autonomy, resulted initially in the founding of the Moro Islamic Liberation Front (MILF), and eventually in the emergence of the ASG. A full cease-fire between the Philippine government and the MNLF was not initiated until 1985, after President Corazon Aquino came to power.

ASG History

"The Abu Sayyaf Group (ASG) first emerged in 1989 under the leadership of Abdurajak Janjalani" (Manalo, 2004, p. 31) as a more radical and violent group of skirmishers than the parent organization, the MNLF. Although Manalo cites the date as 1989, various sources provide conflicting information as to the exact date the organization formally emerged. However, the first known attributable operational action of the ASG (claimed by the group) was conducted in Zamboanga City in August of 1991. The attack, interestingly enough, was against a floating missionary ship, the *M/V Doulous*. During this attack, the ASG killed two individuals and wounded approximately 40 others in the crowd, who were listening to a Christian missionary presentation.

A survey of the available literature on the ASG indicates that the general consensus of the time frame for the evolution of the ASG is somewhere between 1989 and 1992. Additionally, there exists some degree of agreement that the ASG formed in direct response to the Tripoli Agreement, signed by the MNLF and the Philippine government in 1976. Notwithstanding the ambiguity regarding the exact chronological history of the ASG, the impetus for the emergence of the group is generally attributed to dissention within the ranks of the MNLF over the Tripoli Agreement (Niksch,

2002, CRS-3). The more radical members of the MNLF felt the leadership had betrayed them by ratifying the agreement, causing a schism, resulting in the formation of the ASG. The stated goal of the ASG has remained constant; the formation of an independent Islamic state in the southwest region of the Philippines.

Of interest, these factional shifts seem to occur somewhat predictably within the Philippine terrorist networks, as the ASG itself spawned a splinter faction in 1997, after the death of Janjalani. After his death in December, 1997 at the hands of Philippine policemen, the Abdurajak Janjalani Brigade (AJB) was formed as a reflex action to seek revenge for his death. Although the members of the AJB appear to have receded back into the arms of the ASG, future significant events regarding the Muslim community in the Philippines may lead to further excursions by radical splinter cells.

Although most security experts originally viewed the ASG simply as a criminal organization, time has caused this view to change. Currently, the U.S. Secretary of State classifies the ASG as one of 36 foreign terrorist organizations (Department of State, 2005). Additionally, documented ties to the Al Qaeda organization, discussed later in this chapter, indicate that the maturation of the group from criminal organization to full-fledged terrorist group has been achieved. Further, the employment of the Armed Forces of the Philippines (AFP) against the ASG indicates that the status of the group has been elevated from mere bandits to terrorists.

The ASG persists as the most violent and unpredictable of the terrorist groups inhabiting the southern Philippine islands. The ASG has become known for especially violent behavior that includes, but is not limited to: kidnappings for ransom, beheadings, bombings, and armed assault. Current estimates of the strength of the ASG conflict, attesting to the fact that the organization is quite secretive and difficult to locate. Further, there may be a constant state of flux in the ASG, with members moving in and out of the organization infrequently. The U.S. Department of State currently puts the estimated strength of the ASG at well below 1000 members (Department of State, 2005). However, other sources place the strength at more than this number (see Figure 8.2).

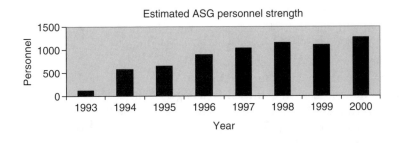

Figure 8.2 Estimated Abu Sayyaf Group (ASG) personnel strength, as of 2001. (From Filler, A.L., *Terrorism and Political Violence,* 14, 131, 2002. Reprinted with permission.)

Contrary to the personnel strength, the ambitions of the group are anything but small. Of perhaps greater significance, the international terrorist community seems to recognize the potential of the group, as the ASG has not only attracted assistance from terrorist celebrities, such as Ramsi Yousef, but also has been involved in planning high-visibility operations. In 1995, the ASG was central in the planning and would have played a leading role in Oplan Bojinka, which was a sophisticated plot involving several ambitious goals, including the assassination of the Pope and simultaneously detonating bombs on several airliners while transiting from Asia to the United States. Oplan Bojinka's other goals included a planned kamikaze attack by a commandeered airliner against CIA headquarters in Langley, Virginia (Smith, 2002, p. 48).

Although direct organizational connections between the ASG and Al Qaeda remain debatable, there is a familial connection, typical in many terrorist organizations: "one of Abu Sayyaf's founders, Mohammad Jamal Khalifah, is Osama Bin Ladin's brother-in-law" (Smith, 2002, p. 48). Additionally, many members of the ASG either served with the mujahideens in Afghanistan, have trained in the Middle East, or have previous combat experience with terrorist organizations (e.g., fighting in Chad, Somalia, etc.). A modern common career path is for a new recruit to train in the Middle East, and then be exported to one of Southern Asia's terrorist cells to obtain practical experience before returning to the Middle East. Thus, the interconnection of terrorists links the organizations together. Of course, this fluidity of the organizations also precludes accurate assessments of strengths, personnel locations, and other valuable information.

The name "Abu Sayyaf" has been translated variously as either "bearer of the sword" or "father of the swordsman." However, when several translators were consulted via an interactive web translation site, the consensus drawn was that the most literal interpretation is "father of the swordsman," with the word swordsman specifically relating to an individual who executes others with a sword. Although the precise meaning of the name may be ambiguous, the reason for employing the name is not. The name was adopted by the acknowledged founder of the group, Abdurajak Abubakar Janjalani, as an honor to Abdul Rasul Sayyaf, a resistance leader Janjalani served with in Afghanistan (Manalo, 2004). This type of idolatry is consistent with the "cult of personality" trait inherent in many terrorist organizations. The strength of the personality of the leader, founder, etc., acts as a catalyst to keep the group focused on goals and objectives.

The area of operations for the ASG encompasses the southern region of the country, with the majority of the activity along the Sulu Archipelago (see Figure 8.3). Additionally, the ASG has been known to operate in the Basilan region and Tawi-Tawi, among others. The ASG operates in a maritime environment, and many members of the group have maritime ties or backgrounds. As stated previously, early on, the Spaniards identified Moros as sea raiders and pirates, alluding to their historically maritime society and culture. Many Moros are fishers, come from fishing

Figure 8.3   Map depicting the Philippines, including major population centers and bodies of water. (From International Crisis Group. 2005. Detailed Map of the Philippines. Retrieved November 9, 2005, from: http://www.crisisgroup.org/home/index.cfm?id=2861&1=1. With permission.)

backgrounds, or have other ties to the maritime environment, thus making them natural seamen and comfortable in the maritime environment. Most importantly perhaps, their consistent exposure to the waters and land masses around the region provides them with exceptional local area knowledge.

Why Piracy?

The main topic of this chapter deals with the employment of piracy by the ASG. Thus far, the discourse has covered the historical issues surrounding the country, the nexus for the emergence of the ASG, and its goals. Additionally, the categorization of acts upon the sea as either piracy or international maritime terrorism has been discussed. Now, one must examine why the ASG would, or perhaps more importantly, how the ASG could engage in these activities. Further, solutions to preventing these activities by the ASG must be developed and evaluated.

The littoral region surrounding the ASG's area of operations, including the Sulu Archipelago, lends itself to acts of piracy. To the south of the Sulu Archipelago, the Celebes Sea, with an area of approximately 110,000 square miles, is a throughway for almost all maritime traffic in the region of Southern Asia. To the north of the Sulu Archipelago, land surrounds the considerably smaller Sulu Sea on all sides. The numerous small islands provide a plethora of possible staging areas for raiding parties, and the regions of Tawi-Tawi and Basilan (all components of the negotiated Autonomous Region of Muslim Mindanao) effectively bracket the Sulu Sea, forming choke points for shipping in the region. Depending upon the size or class of vessel involved, transiting between the island of Luzon and points south (e.g., Cebu, Mindanao, etc.), may necessitate entering the Sulu Sea.

Of course, it would be nearly impossible to obtain any inventory of maritime assets available to the ASG without infiltrating the organization. However, the nature of the composition of the ASG (mainly persons native to the region) would indicate, at the very least, that they possess the nautical heritage and competencies necessary to operate in the maritime environment. As previously stated, many members of the organization are believed to be fishers, relatives of fishermen, or have similar maritime exposure. A comparable demographic would be New Bedford, Massachusetts or Dutch Harbor, Alaska, in the United States, where a large portion of the community has had some exposure to the maritime environment. However, one must also consider that the ASG has proven especially difficult to exterminate due, in part, to the sympathy and support for the organization by some within the region. This means that, although the members of the group may not possess a required skill set or equipment, there may be means of obtaining support (e.g., logistics, supplies, or personnel) from the local community.

Additionally, one must consider that the ASG has known ties to Tehran, possible ties to Al Qaeda, and Janjalani was "connected with a Muslim fundamentalist movement, Al Islamic Tabligh... That organization received financial support from Saudi Arabia and Pakistan" (Niksch, 2002, CRS-2). While Janjalani has gone to his final reward, so to speak, one may assume that others within the ASG may have developed similar ties to the organization, providing fiscal support to the ASG. Of course, both countries have been supportive of the current war on terror, and no recent report of such funneling of money to the ASG could be located. Funding, in the guise of donations to religious charities, flows between Iran and the ASG. Of course, this manner of funneling fiscal support for terrorist organizations through apparently legitimate religious charities is not endemic to the Philippines. These types of activities have been uncovered in many parts of the world, including the United States.

Considering the various sources for logistical, financial, and personnel support available to the ASG, coupled with the maritime environment in which the organization exists, one may easily come to the conclusion that the ASG does possess the competencies and ability to engage in acts of piracy. Further, the historical record of the ASG indicates that the organization does engage in activities not only as a means of furthering their political goals, but also as a means of financing future activity. The ASG is known for kidnapping for ransom, with many of their initial activities being of this type, leading to the group originally being classified as merely a group of bandits (Bandow, in Manalo, 2004, p. 32). Arguably, however, there are additional motives for these kidnappings, including the release of other imprisoned terrorists, as Manalo (2004, p. 32) states when citing Ressa (2003, p. 111).

Lastly, dependent upon the definition of piracy one applies, it can be asserted that the ASG has already engaged in piracy. The attack against the *M/V Duolos,* and the kidnapping of 21 vacationers from the Sipadan Island resort in Malaysia (Filler, 2002, p. 162) via heavily armed speedboats, could qualify as acts of piracy. Certainly, the claim of responsibility by the ASG for the February, 2004, bombing of the SuperFerry 14, which killed 116 passengers, would qualify as an act of piracy. Although the Philippine government initially disputed the claim of responsibility, President Macapagal-Arroyo later released a statement indicating the Philippine government believed the group was, indeed, responsible (*World's News*, 2005). Of note, bombings of ferries have occurred several times within the past several years, similar to the SuperFerry 14 incident, with no claims of responsibility. These certainly could have been the work of the ASG, as there are similarities between the acts.

Southeast Asia is one of the most prevalent areas of the world for maritime piracy events (see Figure 8.4). As indicated by the diagram, four incidents of piracy occurred in 2004 specifically within the region of the Philippines. This is a decrease from highs of 12 in 2000 and 2002 (Maritime Security Organization, 2005, Overall Report). The geography of the region makes the use of quick, high speed, small vessels as platforms for piracy acts quite logical and easy. Adding to this the remote nature of some of the land masses, along with the natural choke points, and the conditions are right for piracy. Therefore, the task becomes how to best defend the maritime community from piracy attack from groups such as the ASG.

Recommendations

The issue of differentiating between piracy and maritime terrorism is complex, and not the subject of this chapter. However, it was discussed in depth in an attempt to illustrate the complexity of the issue, as well as explain how a group, such as the ASG

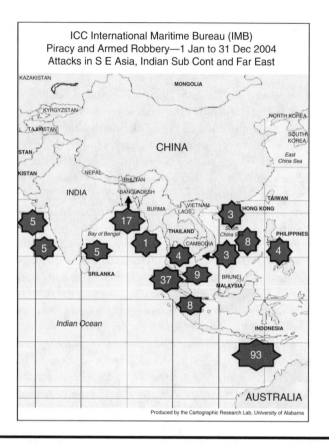

Figure 8.4 Map of reported piracy acts. (From International Maritime Bureau, Piracy Reporting Center. 2005. Piracy and Armed Robbery 1 January–31 December 2004. Retrieved November 12, 2005, from: http://www.icc-ccs.org/prc/piracy_ maps_2004.php. With permission.)

may very well engage in both activities. A terrorist group certainly possesses the capability to engage in piracy simply to fill its coffers for future activities. Conversely, a well-organized and capable pirate organization may very well evolve into a terrorist organization with a strong maritime operating sphere. Simply put, an organization with maritime capabilities may easily move between the realms of piracy and maritime terrorism, thus making effective combating of the organization difficult.

Successful combating of piracy involves meeting the threat at the point of origin. The AFP, the Philippine National Police (PNP), and the United States have been working together since the early part of the decade to combat the terrorist threat in the Philippines. As outlined in Section 25 of Article 18, the Philippine Constitution prevents the U.S. military from participating in any way other than an advisory capacity in the prosecution of operations within the

Philippines, unless the previous treaty is negotiated (Philippine Constitution). This would also, one assumes, apply to antipiracy efforts within the territorial and claimed seas of the Philippines as described in Article 1 of the Philippine Constitution (ibid., Article I).

Although Section 15 of Article 10 of the 1987 Constitution of the Republic of the Philippines establishes the Autonomous Region of Muslim Mindanao (ARMM) (ibid., Article X), these regions are still protected by the AFP and PNP. Therefore, any recommendation involving the assistance of any armed force, navy, coast guard, etc., for assisting the Philippine government in combating acts of piracy must include the negotiation of a specific treaty between the concerned bodies to allow joint military operations to be conducted. This must occur, if the issue is to be effectively addressed, as the Philippine Coast Guard and Navy has limited infrastructure to cope with the threat. However, an effective campaign by any outside force is even more impotent, as the ability to effectively gather intelligence, local knowledge, and other necessary facets of conducting a successful operation are impossible without local assistance.

The institution of routine naval and coast guard patrols through the region of the Sulu and Celeb Seas, coupled with a structured program of professional exchange between the navies and coast guards of both countries would significantly enhance the effectiveness. Currently, there is limited professional exchange, but it mostly exists in one direction, with AFP officers attending training in the United States and U.S. personnel stationed in limited numbers in the Philippines. Reciprocity in this area would not only enhance the relationship between the nations, but also increase the cultural and historical understanding of American officers working within the region. Additionally, continuation of the annual Balikatan exercises, expanded southward and including naval interdiction exercises, would greatly aid in the efforts.

Further, implementation of deck plate training in littoral warfare, either locally or in the United States, coupled with the continuation of the significant increases in military aid during the past four years (Berrigan, Hartung, and Heffel, 2005, Philippines section), will shore up the AFP and PNP efforts. Lastly, the continuing recognition of the Republic of the Philippines as a "major non-NATO ally" (ibid.), by both the American President and the American people, can only serve to bolster the resolve to eliminate the ASG.

Conclusion

Notwithstanding the difficulties experienced during the fledgling years of the American association with the Philippines, the United States and the Republic of the Philippines have shared a robust, respectful, and lengthy history. These two great nations are both dedicated to the extermination of the terrorist threat, and have worked together consistently to address the issue in various theatres. The Republic of the Philippines has been a vital partner in the current Global War on Terror, and has deployed troops in support of the effort, even as they have faced internal terrorist threats and activity.

If any two countries are jointly capable of exterminating a terrorist threat of less than 1500 individuals, surely these two countries must be the Philippines and the United States. Filipinos and Americans have shed blood and suffered together for years in the pursuit of freedom, mutual advancement, and independence. Certainly, as in any relationship, there have been difficulties and problems. However, one must only read and compare the preambles to the constitutions of the two countries to discover the evidence of the goals of democracy, independence, and liberty that are shared by the peoples of both nations.

References

Berrigan, F., Hartung, W.D., and Heffel, L., 2005, June. U.S. Weapons at War 2005: Promoting Freedom or Fueling Conflict? U.S. Military Aid and Arms Transfers since September 11. Retrieved November 15, 2005, from: http://www.worldpolicy.org/projects/arms/reports/wawjune2005.html#10.

Department of State. Retrieved 2005, from: http://www.state.gov/s/ct/rls/fs/37191.htm.

Donnelly, C., 2004, June. Terrorism in the Southern Philippines: Contextualising the Abu Sayyaf Group as an Islamist Secessionist Organization. Paper presented to the 15th Biennial Conference of the Asian Studies Association of Australia, Canberra, Australia. Retrieved October 10, 2005, from: http://coombs.anu.edu.au/ASAA/conference/proceedings/Donnelly-C-ASAA2004.pdf.

Filler, A.L., 2002. The Abu Sayyaf Group: A growing menace to civil society. *Terrorism and Political Violence, 14*(4), 131–162.

Foreign Policy in Focus. 2001. Moros in the Philippines (Self-Determination Conflict Profile). John Gershman. Retrieved November 3, 2005, from: http://www.fpif.org/selfdetermination/conflicts/philippines_body.html.

Gowing, P.G., 1979. *Muslim Filipinos—Heritage and Horizon.* Quezon City, RP: New Day.

Institute of Southeast Asian Studies. 2004. Ships can be Dangerous too: Coupling Piracy and Maritime Terrorism in Southeast Asia's Maritime Security Framework (International Policies & Securities Issues Series, No. 1). Keng Terrace, Singapore: Ong, G.G. Retrieved September 29, 2005, from: http://www.iseas.edu.sg/ipsi12004.pdf.

International Crisis Group. 2005. Detailed Map of the Philippines. Retrieved November 9, 2005, from: http://www.crisisgroup.org/home/index.cfm?id=2861&1=1.

International Maritime Bureau, Piracy Reporting Center. 2005. Piracy and Armed Robbery 1 January–31 December 2004. Retrieved November 12, 2005, from: http://www.icc-ccs.org/prc/piracy_maps_2004.php.

Johnson, D. and Pladdet, E., 2003. An Overview of Current Concerns in Piracy Studies and New Directions for Research. Position paper for the Piracy Panels and Rountable at the People and the Sea II: Conflicts, Threats, and Opportunities, Amsterdam, The Netherlands. Retrieved September 26, 2005, from: http://www.marecentre.nl/people_and_the_sea_2/documents/piracy.pdf.

Manalo, E.P., 2004. The Philippine response to terrorism: The Abu Sayyaf Group. Unpublished master's thesis, Naval Postgraduate School, Monterey, California. Retrieved September 20, 2005, from: http://www.fas.org/irp/world/para/manalo.pdf.

Maritime Security Organization. 2005. Reported Attacks on Vessels: 1998, 1999, 2000, and 2001. Retrieved November 15, 2005, from: http://www.marisec.org/piracy/reported%20attacks.htm.

Niksch, L., 2002, January 25. *Abu Sayyaf: Target of Philippine–U.S. Anti-Terrorism Cooperation.* Washington, DC: Congressional Research Service, the Library of Congress.

Patterns of Global Terrorism—2000, 2001. Retrieved November 11, 2005, from: http://www.state.gov/s/ct/rls/pgtrpt/2000/2419.htm.

Ressa, M., 2003. *Seeds of Terror: An Eyewitness Account of Al Qaeda's Newest Center of Operations in Southeast Asia.* New York: Simon & Schuster.

Smith, P.J., 2002. Terrorism in Asia: Confronting an emerging challenge. *Harvard Asia Pacific Review* 6(1), 44–50. Retrieved September 29, 2005, from: http://web.mit.edu/lipoff/www/hapr/spring02_wto/terrorism.pdf.

The Great War Society. (n.d.). The Automatic Pistol Caliber .45, Model 1911. Retrieved November 14, 2005, from: http://www.worldwar1.com/dbc/colt45.htm.

United Nations. 2001. International Convention on the Law of the Sea. Retrieved November 11, 2005, from: http://www.un.org/Depts/los/convention_agreement/texts/unclos/part7.htm.

United States Supreme Court. 1964. *Jacobellis v. Ohio, 378 U.S. 184 (1964).* Retrieved November 13, 2005, from: http://caselaw.lp.findlaw.com/scripts/getcase.pl?court=US&vol=378&invol=184.

Weinberger, J., 2003, Winter/Spring. Defining terror. *Seton Hall Journal of Diplomacy and International Relations*, 63–81.

World's News. (n.d.). Retrieved November 17, 2005, from: http://www.internationalheralddailynews.org/world5.htm.

Chapter 9

Promise and Perils of Politicized Islam in Africa

Tatah Mentan and Moye Bongyu

CONTENTS

Introduction

The *coup d'état* in Pakistan in 1977, the Islamic Revolution in Iran in 1979, the seizure of the Grand Mosque in Mecca in 1979, the assassination of President Anwar El Sadat of Egypt in 1981, and the bloody 1982 suppression of the Muslim brotherhood in the Syrian city of Hama, brought political Islam on the agenda. These acts of political activism have been branded political Islam. Political Islam is the adversary of democratic empowerment in the sense that it advocates submission, not emancipation. It is obviously far from liberation theology inspired by the Qur'an. It has no bearing on secularism because it advocates theocracy.

No development of the last decade of the twentieth century has caused as much confusion in the West as the emergence of political Islam. Political Islam has become even very resilient with Saudi support for innumerable madrassas (Islamic schools) that are proving to be what an Ethiopian journalist deemed jihad factories nurturing potential bin Ladens (Alem-Zelalem, 2003). These schools make political Islam sustainable. This sustainability compels us to argue in this chapter that political Islam of the Wahhabi ideology and massive infusions of Saudi cash are rapidly transforming the once peaceful Sufi-inspired sub-Saharan Islam into politicized Islam. The likely result would be unmanageable intercommunal strife between Muslims and non-Muslims and a hospitable environment for terrorists with an international agenda on African soil.

Just what does political Islam portend? Is it against modernity, or is it an effect of modernity? Is it against nationalism, or is it a form of nationalism? Is it a striving for freedom, or a revolt against freedom?

One would think that these are difficult questions to answer. And that they would inspire deep debates. Yet over the past couple of years, a surprisingly broad consensus has emerged within academe about the way political Islam should be measured. This consensus has begun to spread into parts of government as well, especially in the United States and Europe. A paradigm has been built, and its builders claim that its reliability and validity are beyond question (Kepel, 2004; Roy, 2004).

This currently dominant paradigm runs as follows. The Arab Middle East and North Africa are stirring. The people in these lands are still under varieties of authoritarian or despotic rule. But they are moved by the same universal yearning for democracy that transformed Eastern Europe and Latin America. True, there are no movements we would easily recognize as democracy movements. But for historical and cultural reasons, this universal yearning has taken the form of Islamist protest movements. If these do not look like democracy movements, it is only a consequence of Western age-old bias against Islam. When the veil of prejudice is lifted, one will see Islamist movements for what they are the functional equivalents of democratic reform movements.

True, on the edges of these movements are groups that are atavistic and authoritarian. Some of their members are prone to violence. These are the extremists.

But the mainstream movements are essentially open, pluralistic, and nonviolent, led by moderates or reformists. These moderates can be strengthened if they are made partners in the political process, and an initial step must be dialogue. But ultimately the most effective way to domesticate the Islamists is to permit them to share or possess power. There is no threat here unless the West creates it, by supporting acts of state repression that would deny Islamists access to participation or power.

There are several hidden assumptions beneath this paradigm:

■ First, the yearning for democracy is today universal, and stands behind the mass Islamist movements.

■ Second, there are extremists and moderates in Islamist movements, and that they can be reliably identified, classified, and separated, both for analytical and policy purposes.

■ Third, power has a moderating effect upon those who share or exercise it, and would have such an effect upon Islamists as well.

■ Fourth, because Islamism represents the populist will, its triumph is inevitable.

These assumptions form the four legs of the paradigmatic table. Take one out, and the paradigm collapses. Do any of these legs wobble? Perhaps all four do. For instance, when one looks at the autocratic state of governments across the expanse of Islam, many observers tend to conclude that all broad-based opposition can have only one purpose: democratic reform. One political scientist (Norton, 1992: 41) assures us that "the Islamist movements are basically social reform movements," another expert (Esposito, 1992: 12–13) tells us these are "political reform movements." Still another political scientist (Hudson, 1992: 36), a bit more cautious, tells a congressional committee that "whatever the ultimate intent of Islamist movements, their current function is a liberalizing one." The dominant but faulty analogy is to the parties of reform in the former Eastern bloc.

Armed with such faulty analogical thinking, Americans were shocked when they saw the demonstrations going on after the attack on the World Trade Center and the Pentagon on 9/11. People were dancing in the streets in Jakarta, way out in Indonesia, Palestinians, people in northern Nigeria jubilating, and people in Jordan rejoicing. There was the feeling, it's their turn now.

And this is important to remember. It was not that they approved the taking of the lives of innocent people. But it was the act of hitting America hard that was very important. And do not let your mind focus only on the 19 people, who were in the plane. Who paid for them? Important businessmen in the Arab Emirates and elsewhere paid for them. The critical question here is why should people pay for those who want to hijack planes and kill innocent people? As we are going to talk about the roots of Islamism in Africa and terrorism, we have to ask, what is Islamic terrorism?

Historical Overview of Islam and Terrorism

The Oxford Dictionary defines a terrorist as a person who uses or favors violent and intimidating methods of coercing a government or a community. Others might say it's harming innocent civilians in a cause. Would that make Hiroshima a terrorist act? Osama Bin Laden has mentioned that in one of his bills of particular. Or, was Hiroshima an act of declared war, and perhaps what governments do does not count as terrorism?

Maybe terrorism is like pornography: hard to define, but you know it when you see it. No one would doubt that the bombing of a discotheque in Tel Aviv was a terrorist act. But what would you say about innocent Palestinian civilians who were killed in retaliation by Israel?

Obviously, the people who are threatening America are Islamic at this point. But terrorism goes far beyond that. There have been many explanations why Muslims turn to terrorism, or why they turn to fundamentalism. We have heard that the U.S. troops on Saudi Arabian soil are a reason, that America's support for Israel is a reason. Osama Bin Laden talks about the legacy of colonial domination. And there is also the fear of change, and westernization. And I do not believe myself that all Islamic fundamentalism is violent or evil. But it clearly presents a danger when the fanatical fringe leaps forth and takes Islamic fundamentalism to mean that they can attack people.

So Arabs look around, and they see a series of failed states, and few of them can be said to represent the will of the government. And they see that westernization, attempts at westernization have failed them. Marxism has failed them. Pan-Arab nationalism has failed them. And in fact, Islam, violent Islam has failed them, as the revolution in Iran has not improved the standards of living.

Is transnational Islamic terrorism the answer to these failures? Is transnational Islamic terrorism even new? With the birth of Islam in the seventh century came its steadfast dissemination, often through violence and jihad, or holy war. Over centuries, millions of people have converted to Islam through good faith while others have done so through subjugation and force under the ultimatum of the medieval sword. On Western soil, this form of terror is largely a new reality to cope with and is now even deemed a threat to the very existence of civilization.

The first people in the modern era to collectively fall victim to Islamic terror were the Armenians of the Islamic Ottoman Empire. What is today the eastern portion of the Republic of Turkey was for three millennia the homeland of the Armenians. This land that had nurtured generations of these people 2000 years before the Turkic invasions of the eleventh century became a distant land for them almost overnight in 1915. The outcome was one of the worst quantitative measures of terror and genocide in human history, resulting in the massacre of 1.5 million people and the destruction of an astounding 4000 Christian churches and monasteries. The entire people were systematically targeted and annihilated on the grounds of their religion and what it represented in the confines of the Islamic empire.

Although this forgotten genocide, long ignored by the West, was a calculated result of Turkish nationalism and racist policies of Turkification, Islam was the ideological weapon for mass annihilation and slaughter. "Whoever kills seven Christians will go to heaven," Islamic clerics and town criers would call out. For backward, rural Kurdish and Turkish religious communities, killing *gavour* (infidel) Armenians was an opportunity for salvation, while for the Turkish government it was the ultimate weapon for genocide.

This is the same logic and method recently employed by al-Qaeda, the Taliban and other deadly Islamic terror groups to incite their people against peaceful populations. Religion is a powerful ideology, and ideology has proven to be the single most destructive element in history. Today's Turkey—a member of NATO—is considered a strategic U.S. ally in the Middle East. It is in this very context of alliance that the United States should expose this dark chapter in world history and require Turkey to own up to its Ottoman past, and hence secure a more reliable and responsible partner in the region. This is particularly important if this partner is said to be committed to fighting extremism and terrorist-prone elements within its own borders and in surrounding regions.

In Israel today, Islamic terror against the Jewish infidels, as Islamists have long labeled them, has claimed the lives of hundreds of innocent civilians. Afghan mujahideen, the Islamic world's favored religious fighters, have long been known to assist the struggles of Islamic countries and regimes. Recently, Azerbaijan hired hundreds of such mercenaries to fight the Armenians in the Nagorno-Karabakh conflict. These very mercenaries were later exported to Chechnya to fight against Russians in the name of Islam. In Africa, the Islamic *Janjaweed* militias of Sudan are annihilating millions of indigenous Sudanese in Darfur.

Islam has given the world a tremendous amount of knowledge, piousness, and wisdom. Meantime, however, exploiters of the religion have unleashed an incredible degree of havoc on peaceful populations in the name of their faith. What we have witnessed among certain Muslim regimes over the past century is nothing more than an abuse of Islam for reasons of expedience and convenience. Their actions have been atrocious, immoral, and bellicose acts of desperation to dominate and dictate.

The war that rages today within our own borders is a new, globalized variant of international terrorism. This latest extent of Islamic terror, quite ironically, has been advanced by modern, Western technology. This is a clear contradiction of the terrorists' struggle against modernization, and hence a clear sign of convenience of choice by the fighters as well as an indication of the incoherence of their jihad.

Understanding Political Islamism

Reacting to the spectacular and violent events of September 11, 2001, many Western observers and policy-makers have tended to lump all forms of Islamism together, brand them as radical and treat them as hostile. That approach is fundamentally misconceived. Islamism—or Islamic activism (we treat these terms as synonymous)—has a number of very different streams, only a few of them violent and only a small minority justifying a confrontational response. The West needs a discriminating strategy that takes account of the diversity of outlooks within political Islamism that accepts that even the most modernist of Islamists are deeply opposed to current U.S. policies and committed to renegotiating their relations with the West, and that understands that the festering Israeli-Palestinian conflict, the war of occupation of Iraq, and the way in which the war against terrorism is being waged all significantly strengthen the appeal of the most virulent and dangerous jihadi tendencies.

What then is political Islam? Some Western scholars have compared political Islam with Western-style concepts and simply concluded that it is the opposite of democracy, personal freedom, equality, human rights, and liberalism (Eickelman, 1997: 18). Others have said that although the West is based on secular materialism, scientific reason, and lacks moral philosophy, Islam is based on faith, patience, pace, and equilibrium (Moussalli, 1999: 71–73). Such views make the conflict with the West potent, and the former mentioned clash-theory is thereby strengthened. One scholar observed that political Islam is increasingly, and needlessly, being seen as a major threat to the West. The two cultures are obviously different. They are products of two unique historical experiences. However, this ought to be recognized in terms of diversity and not enmity (Shahin, 997: 3). His point is that different traditions and experiences do not necessarily lead to conflict. Therefore, to avoid conflicts, one has to understand the phenomenon of political Islam in its historical, political, and social context.

Political Islam is part of a broad intellectual, cultural, social, and political movement throughout the Islamic world. The movement is often referred to and called Islamic resurgence or Islamic revival, and political Islam are only one component of the greater resurgence and revival of Islamic ideas, practices, and rhetoric (Huntington, 1993: 22–49). The term political Islam is used throughout this chapter because the following analysis is limited to a study of the political elements of the Islamic revival/resurgence.

The terminology is nevertheless confusing. Islamic resurgence and revival is often used interchangeably with concepts like Islamism, fundamentalism, neo-fundamentalism, integrism, Khomeinism, traditionalism, Arabism, Puritanism, rebirth, reassertion, awakening, reformism, renewal, renaissance, revitalization, militancy, activism, millenarianism, messianism, return to Islam, upsurge, and reassertion (Burgat and Dowell 1997: 2,8; Dekmejian, 1995: 4; Dessouki, 1982: 4; Voll, 1982: 283). Proponents of Islam itself often use the following expressions: *al-ba'th al-islami* (Islamic resurrection), *al-sahwah al-islamiyyah* (Islamic awakening), *ihya' al-din* (religious revival), *al-usuliyyah al-islamiyyah* (Islamic fundamentalism), *al-harakah al-islamiyyah* (Islamic movement), *al-tayyar al-islami* (Islamic current), *al-ittijah al-islami* (Islamic tendency). The Islamic resurgence is both complex and multifaceted, and this variety of concepts illustrates the difficulty of coming to terms with this diversity. As pointed out by Ali E. Hillal Dessouki, the Islamic resurgence is "not a monolithic phenomenon but, rather, socially and historically conditioned."

Nevertheless, all of the concepts and terms mentioned above describe the Islamic resurgence in one way or another. It is thus difficult to find a common definition of Islamic resurgence, but the moderate Dessouki offers a good description when he writes that Islamic resurgence refers to the increasing prominence and politicization of Islamic ideologies and symbols in Muslim societies and in the public life of Muslim individuals. Another scholar, the right-wing Daniel Pipes, states that Islamic resurgence is understood to mean an increase in Islamic activism and that it involves working for the goals of the shari'a, the sacred law of Islam (Pipes, 1982: 35,36). Other manifestations of the Islamic resurgence are increased use of religious and social symbols and the emergence of sociopolitical opposition groups (Dessouki, 1982: 10–12).

In understanding the different streams of Islamic activism, the starting point is to distinguish between Shiite and Sunni Islamism (see Middle East/North Africa Report N°37, March 2, 2005). The concept of political Islam first appeared in the wake of the 1979 Iranian revolution, with Shiite activism then viewed as the most worrying threat. In fact, however, because Shiism is the minority variant of Islam (Sunnis constitute over 80 percent of Muslims) and because Shiites, typically, are minorities in the states in which they find themselves, the most widespread and natural form of Shiite activism has been communal—defending the interests of the Shiite community in relation to other populations and to the state itself. For this reason, and also because of the leading political role played by scholars and religious authorities, (ulema) Shiite Islamism has remained unified to a remarkable degree and has not fragmented into conflicting forms of activism as has Sunni Islamism.

Sunni Islamism—on which most Western emphasis is today placed, and about which most fears are held—is widely viewed as uniformly fundamentalist, radical, and threatening to Western interests. Yet it is not at all monolithic. On the contrary, it has crystallized into three main distinctive types, each with its own worldview, modus operandi and characteristic actors:

- *Political*: The Islamic political movements (*al-harakât al-islamiyya al-siyassiyya*), exemplified by the Society of the Muslim brothers in Egypt and its offshoots elsewhere (including Algeria, Jordan, Kuwait, Palestine, Sudan, and Syria) and by locally rooted movements such as the Justice and Development Party (*Adalet ve Kalkinma Partisi, AKP*) in Turkey, and the Party for Justice and Development (*Parti pour la Justice et le Développement, PJD*) in Morocco, whose purpose is to attain political power at the national level. These now generally accept the nation-state, operate within its constitutional framework, eschew violence (except under conditions of foreign occupation), articulate a reformist rather than revolutionary vision, and invoke universal democratic norms. The characteristic actor is the party-political militant.
- *Missionary*: The Islamic missions of conversion (*al-da'wa*), which exists in two main variants exemplified by the highly structured Tablighi movement on one

hand and the highly diffuse Salafiyya on the other. In both cases political power is not an objective; the overriding purpose is the preservation of the Muslim identity and the Islamic faith and moral order against the forces of unbelief, and the characteristic actors are missionaries (*du'ah*), and the 'ulama.

■ *Jihadi*: The Islamic armed struggle (*al-jihad*), which exists in three main variants: internal (combating nominally Muslim regimes considered impious); irredentist (fighting to redeem land ruled by non-Muslims or under occupation); and global (combating the West). The characteristic actor is, of course, the fighter (*al-mujahid*).

All these varieties of Sunni activism are attempts to reconcile tradition and modernity, to preserve those aspects of tradition considered to be essential by adapting in various ways to modern conditions; all select from tradition, borrow selectively from the West, and adopt aspects of modernity. Where they differ is in how they conceive the principal problem facing the Muslim world, and what they believe is necessary, possible, and advisable to do about it.

Political Islamists make an issue of Muslim misgovernment and social injustice and give priority to political reform to be achieved by political action (advocating new policies, contesting elections, etc.). Missionary Islamists make an issue of the corruption of Islamic values (*al-qiyam al-islamiyya*) and the weakening of faith (*al-iman*) and give priority to a form of moral and spiritual rearmament that champions individual virtue as the condition of good government as well as of collective salvation. Jihadi Islamists make an issue of the oppressive weight of non-Muslim political and military power in the Islamic world and give priority to armed resistance.

Which of these three main outlooks will prevail in the medium and longer term is of great importance to the Muslim world and to the West. Although the West in general and the United States in particular ought to be modest about their ability to shape the debate among Islamists, they also should be aware of how their policies affect it. By adopting a sledgehammer approach which refuses to differentiate between modernist and fundamentalist varieties of Islamism, American, and European policy-makers risk provoking one of two equally undesirable outcomes: either inducing the different strands of Islamic activism to band together in reaction, attenuating differences that might otherwise be fruitfully developed, or causing the nonviolent and modernist tendencies to be eclipsed by the jihadis.

■ Wahhabi Theology—*Force Motrice* of Politicized Islam in Africa Today?

In traditional Islamic political theory the state rests on three pillars: the *Ummah* (the community of Muslim believers), the Caliphate, and the *Shari'ah* (Islamic law). Except perhaps in the early decades of Islam, this theory, however, did not always conform to what happened in real life. The *Ummah* embodied an ideal which could not be realized in full even in the early period of Islam. As long as Islam was confined to the Arabian Peninsula, the *Ummah* was a homogeneous community held together by the bonds of Islam. Today the *Ummah* has gone beyond Saudi Arabia and has been confronted with many daunting tasks like adjusting to the invading forces of globalization.

The political and cultural environment of contemporary Saudi Arabia and beyond has been influenced by a religious movement that began in central Arabia in the mid-eighteenth century. This movement, commonly known as the Wahhabi movement, grew out of the scholarship and preaching of Muhammad ibn Abd al Wahhab, a scholar of Islamic jurisprudence who had studied in Mesopotamia and the Hijaz before returning to his native Najd to preach his message of Islamic reform.

Muhammad ibn Abd al Wahhab (Algar, 2002) was concerned with the way the people of Najd engaged in practices he considered polytheistic, such as praying to saints; making pilgrimages to tombs and special mosques; venerating trees, caves, and stones; and using votive and sacrificial offerings. He was also concerned by what he viewed as a laxity in adhering to Islamic law and in performing religious devotions, such as indifference to the plight of widows and orphans, adultery, lack of attention to obligatory prayers, and failure to allocate shares of inheritance fairly to women.

When Muhammad ibn Abd al Wahhab began to preach against these breaches of Islamic laws, he characterized customary practices as jahiliya, the same term used to describe the ignorance of Arabians before the Prophet. Initially, his preaching encountered opposition, but he eventually came under the protection of a local chieftain named Muhammad ibn Saud, with whom he formed an alliance. The endurance of the Wahhabi movement's influence may be attributed to the close association between the founder of the movement and the politically powerful Al Saud in southern Najd.

This association between the Al Saud and the Al ash Shaykh, as Muhammad ibn Abd al Wahhab and his descendants came to be known, effectively converted political loyalty into a religious obligation. According to Muhammad ibn Abd al Wahhab's teachings, a Muslim must present a *bayah*, or oath of allegiance, to a Muslim ruler during his lifetime to ensure his redemption after death. The ruler, conversely, is owed unquestioned allegiance from his people so long as he leads the community according to the laws of God. The whole purpose of the Muslim community is to become the living embodiment of God's laws, and it is the responsibility of the legitimate ruler to ensure that people know God's laws and live in conformity to them.

Muhammad ibn Saud turned his capital, Ad Diriyah, into a center for the study of religion under the guidance of Muhammad ibn Abd al Wahhab and sent missionaries to teach the reformed religion throughout the peninsula, the gulf, and into Syria and Mesopotamia. Together they began a jihad against the backsliding Muslims of the peninsula. Under the banner of religion and preaching the unity of God and obedience to the just Muslim ruler, the Al Saud by 1803 had expanded their dominion across the peninsula from Mecca to Bahrain, installing teachers, schools, and the apparatus of state power. So successful was the alliance between the Al ash Shaykh and the Al Saud that even after the Ottoman sultan had crushed Wahhabi political authority and had destroyed the Wahhabi capital of Ad Diriyah in 1818; the reformed religion remained firmly planted in the settled districts of southern Najd and of Jabal Shammar in the north. It would become the unifying ideology in the peninsula when the Al Saud rose to power again in the next century.

Central to Muhammad ibn Abd al Wahhab's message was the essential oneness of God (tawhid). The movement is therefore known by its adherents as *ad dawa lil tawhid* (the call to unity), and those who follow the call are known as *ahl at tawhid* (the people of unity) or *muwahhidun* (unitarians). The word Wahhabi was originally used derogatorily by opponents, but has today become commonplace and is even used by some Najdi scholars of the movement.

Muhammad ibn Abd al Wahhab's emphasis on the oneness of God was asserted in contradistinction to shirk, or polytheism, defined as the act of associating any person or object with powers that should be attributed only to God. He condemned specific acts that he viewed as leading to shirk, such as votive offerings, praying at saints' tombs and at graves, and any prayer ritual in which the suppliant appeals to a third party for intercession with God. Particularly, objectionable were certain religious festivals, including celebrations of the Prophet's birthday, Shia mourning ceremonies, and Sufi mysticism. Consequently, the Wahhabis forbid grave markers or tombs in burial sites and the building of any shrines that could become a locus of shirk.

The extensive condemnation of shirk is seen in the movement's iconoclasm, which persisted into the twentieth century, most notably with the conquest of At Taif in the Hijaz. A century earlier, in 1802, Wahhabi fighters raided and damaged one of the most sacred Shia shrines, the tomb of Husayn, the son of Imam Ali and grandson of the Prophet, at Karbala in Iraq. In 1804, the Wahhabis destroyed tombs in the cemetery of the holy men in Medina, which was a locus for votive offerings and prayers to the saints.

Following the legal school of Ahmad ibn Hanbal, Wahhabi ulama accept the authority only of the Quran and sunna. The Wahhabi ulama reject reinterpretation of Quran and sunna in regard to issues clearly settled by the early jurists. By rejecting the validity of reinterpretation, Wahhabi doctrine is at odds with the Muslim reformation movement of the late nineteenth and twentieth centuries. This movement seeks to reinterpret parts of the Qur'an and sunna to conform with standards set by the West, most notably standards relating to gender relations, family law, and participatory democracy. However, ample scope for reinterpretation remains for Wahhabi jurists in areas not decided by the early jurists. King Fahd ibn Abd al Aziz Al Saud has repeatedly called for scholars to engage in ijtihad to deal with new situations confronting the modernizing kingdom.

The Wahhabi movement in Najd was unique in two respects: first, the ulama of Najd interpreted the Qur'an and sunna very literally and often with a view toward reinforcing parochial Najdi practices; second, the political and religious leadership exercised its collective political will to enforce conformity in behavior. Muhammad ibn Abd al Wahhab asserted that there were three objectives for Islamic government and society; these objectives have been reaffirmed over the succeeding two centuries in missionary literature, sermons, fatwa or rulings, and in Wahhabi explications of religious doctrine. According to Muhammad ibn Abd al Wahhab the objectives were to believe in Allah, enjoin good behavior, and forbid wrongdoing.

Under Al Saud rule, governments, especially during the Wahhabi revival in the 1920s, have shown their capacity and readiness to enforce compliance with Islamic laws and interpretations of Islamic values on themselves and others. The literal interpretations of what constitutes right behavior according to the Qur'an and hadith have given the Wahhabis the sobriquet of Muslim Calvinists. To the Wahhabis, for example, performance of prayer that is punctual, ritually correct, and communally performed not only is urged but also publicly required of men. Consumption of wine is forbidden to the believer because wine is literally forbidden in the Qur'an. Under the Wahhabis, however, the ban extended to all intoxicating drinks and other stimulants, including tobacco. Modest dress is prescribed for both men and women in accordance with the Qur'an, but the Wahhabis specify the type of clothing that should be worn, especially by women, and forbid the wearing of silk and gold, although the latter ban has been enforced only sporadically. Music and dancing have also been forbidden by the Wahhabis at times, as have loud laughter and demonstrative weeping, particularly at funerals.

The Wahhabi emphasis on conformity makes of external appearance and behavior a visible expression of inward faith. Therefore, whether one conforms in dress, in prayer, or in a host of other activities becomes a public statement of whether one is a true Muslim. Because adherence to the true faith is demonstrable in tangible ways, the Muslim community can visibly judge the quality of a person's faith by observing that person's actions. In this sense, public opinion becomes a regulator of individual behavior. Therefore, within the Wahhabi community, which is striving to be the collective embodiment of God's laws, it is the responsibility of each Muslim to look after the behavior of his neighbor and to admonish him if he goes astray.

To ensure that the community of the faithful will enjoin what is right and forbid what is wrong, morals enforcers known as mutawwiin (literally, those who volunteer or obey) have been integral to the Wahhabi movement since its inception. Mutawwiin have served as missionaries, as enforcers of public morals, and as public ministers of the religion who preach in the Friday mosque. Pursuing their duties in Jiddah in 1806, the mutawwiin were observed to be constables for the punctuality of prayers ... with an enormous staff in their hand, who were ordered to shout, to scold, and to drag people by the shoulders to force them to take part in public prayers, five times a day. In addition to enforcing male attendance at public prayer, the mutawwiin also have been responsible for supervising the closing of shops at prayer time, for looking out for infractions of public morality, such as playing music, smoking, drinking alcohol, having hair that is too long (men) or uncovered (women), and dressing immodestly.

In the first quarter of the century, promoting Wahhabism was an asset to Abd al Aziz in forging cohesion among the tribal peoples and districts of the peninsula. By reviving the notion of a community of believers, united by their submission to God, Wahhabism helped to forge a sense of common identity that was to supersede parochial loyalties. By abolishing the tribute paid by inferior tribes to militarily superior tribes, Abd al Aziz undercut traditional hierarchies of power and made devotion to Islam and to himself as the rightly guided Islamic ruler the glue that would hold his kingdom together. In the early 1990s, unity in Islam of the Muslim umma (community) under Al Saud leadership was the basis for the legitimacy of the Saudi state.

The promotion of Islam as embracing every aspect of life accounted in large measures for the success of Wahhabi ideology in inspiring the zealotry of the Ikhwan movement. Beginning in 1912, agricultural communities called *hujra* (collective pl.) were settled by *Bedouin* who came to believe that in settling on the land they were fulfilling the prerequisite for leading Muslim lives; they were making a *hijra*, the journey from the land of unbelief to the land of belief. It is still unclear whether the Ikhwan settlements were initiated by Abd al Aziz or whether he co-opted the movement once it had begun, but the settlements became military cantonments in the service of Abd al Aziz's consolidation of power. Although the Ikhwan had very limited success in agriculture, they could rely on a variety of subsidies derived from raids under the aegis of Abd al Aziz and provisions disbursed directly from his storehouses in Riyadh.

In the 1990s, Saudi leadership did not emphasize its identity as inheritor of the Wahhabi legacy as such, nor did the descendants of Muhammad ibn Abd al Wahhab, the Al ash Shaykh, continue to hold the highest posts in the religious bureaucracy. Wahhabi influence in Saudi Arabia, however, remained tangible in the physical conformity in dress, in public deportment, and in public prayer. Most significantly, the Wahhabi legacy was manifest in the social ethos that presumed government responsibility for the collective moral ordering of society, from the behavior of individuals, to institutions, to businesses, to the government itself.

The export of Wahhabist theology carries along these principles peacefully or violently as recent history has shown us. In the case of African Muslims and foreigners from the Arab(oil-rich) countries, Eva Evers Rosander (1997: 21) notes, "those who have the financial means dictate the Islamic discourse." But, the common goal expressed succinctly by Moammar Qaddafi is "to make Islam triumph in Africa" (Marshall, 2003).

Rise of Politicized Islamism in Africa

Sub-Saharan Africa has what it takes to become a breeding ground for transnational terrorism. The continent has a lot of oppressive governments, a sprinkling of chaotic failed states and millions of Muslims, many of whom resent the West's military, economic, and cultural hegemony. But can you name a single black African terrorist? Probably not yet! However, no region is as vulnerable as Africa and its 400 million Muslims (see Table A9.1 on Growth of Islam in Africa).

The differences between the Saudi ruling family and bin Laden are not so much about goals as about methods. The Saudis were furious over the 1998 embassy bombings in Nairobi and Dar es Salaam not because of the viciousness of the acts, but because the attacks threatened to call the West's attention to quiet subversion by fundamentalist Wahhabis in the region.

An understanding of the multifaceted nature of political Islam on the African subcontinent would place it in a historical and contemporary context. In East Africa, discrimination against Muslims began in colonial mission schools and continued in education and employment following independence. This discrimination played an important role in the development of political Islam.

The impact of Saudi-sponsored Wahabism on the radicalization of Muslims in the Horn of Africa has been mixed. Its potential impact is most acute in Ethiopia, although the radicalization of Islam in Sudan has followed its own independent path. Islamic fundamentalism in Nigeria acquired a more pronounced political edge as the national fortunes of the governing Muslim national elite declined dramatically with the election of Olusegun Obasanjo, a born-again Christian, to the presidency in 1999.

This brand of political Islam was manifested in the adoption of Islamic law in one-third of Nigeria's states and sporadic communal violence between Muslims and Christians. Senegal stands as an illustration of the reality that political Islam can be a constructive and regime-stabilizing force. Senegal has found a balance between a modernizing, secular state and the Muslim tradition. Democracy co-exists with a religiously encouraged grassroots social conservatism.

In fact, Islam is the fastest growing religion on the African sub-continent and has a significant presence in an array of states. Although mystical and often syncretic variants of Sufi Islam are evident in much of East and West Africa, the austere, illiberal Wahabi sect, coming out of Saudi Arabia, has found a growing audience in these regions and in the Horn. The consequent battle for the heart of African Islam constitutes an important part of the African religious landscape, with implications for internal African politics, peace, stability, and security.

According to Arab oral tradition, Islam first came to Africa with Muslim refugees fleeing persecution in the Arab peninsula. This was followed by a military invasion, some seven years after the death of the prophet Mohammed in 639, under the command of the Muslim Arab General, Amr ibn al-Asi. It quickly spread West from Alexandria in North Africa (the Maghreb), reducing the Christians to pockets in Egypt, Nubia, and Ethiopia.

Islam came to root along the East African coast some time in the eighth century, as part of a continuing dialogue between the people on the East coast and traders from the Persian Gulf and Oman. Like early Christianity, Islam was monotheistic, that is, Muslims worship only one God. Islam was a modernizing influence, imposing a consistent order among different societies, strengthening powers of government and breaking down ethnic loyalties.

Unlike Christianity, Islam tolerated traditional values, allowing a man to have more than one wife. For many, this made conversion to Islam easier and less upsetting than conversion to Christianity. In the early centuries of its existence, Islam in Africa had a dynamic and turbulent history, with reforming movements and dynasties clashing and succeeding each other. Gaining power depended on securing trade routes into gold-producing areas in sub-Saharan Africa. Islamic rulers expanded north as well as south. In the last quarter of the eleventh century, Islam dominated the Mediterranean world.

In the fourteenth century, the Black Death came from Europe and seriously undermined the social and economic life of North Africa, or the Maghreb, as it is known. However, Islam remained the dominant religion. From the sixteenth to the nineteenth century, much of the Maghreb was under Ottoman rule. By the 1880s, Islam had taken root in one-third of the continent.

Encounters between Sufis and Islamists have been persistent in Africa. The rise of Islamism in sub-Saharan Africa is remarkable. Islamists accept the new interpretations of Qur'an and Sunna and also maintain their anti-Sufi stance. The stance prevails in most of the Muslim areas in Africa. The rise of Islamism has dual origins, that is, it arose due to socioeconomic and psychological factors as well as perceived and real Western dominance. He argues that Islamism has the potential of bringing better moral and material life to the people. For example, Islamism has its own version of modernity which is embraced by women, with education open to all playing an important factor.

Sufi orders or brotherhood have had great political and religious impact in Africa over the centuries. Apart from benefiting from the British colonial rule in Tanganyika, Sufi orders gained considerable political influence in the eighteenth and nineteenth centuries while at the same time collaborated with the French colonialists in North and West Africa at the expense of the non-Muslims.

There is some correlation between Islam and cultures of the Sahelian peoples. Cultural diversity which prevails in societies need not be a hindrance to the growth and legitimacy of international law, particularly in relation to human rights. This view is in conformity with what is prevailing in a number of countries in Sahel except Sudan. Sudanese leadership does not recognize human rights because they equate human rights regime with Western values and norms. Islamization which is taking place in the Sahel region is not unique, but similar to what prevailed in the eighteenth and the nineteenth centuries, with jihad playing important role. Islamic views of human rights are different from international human rights norms in that non-Muslims and women are seen to be unequal and inferior.

For many centuries there has been intense interaction between Muslims in sub-Saharan Africa and the Arabo-Islamic world. These include travel by African Muslim scholars to the Arabo-Islamic world, the inflow of visitors to sub-Saharan Africa, the formation of pan-African Islamic organizations and networks as well as membership in international Islamic associations are some of the contributing factors to the linkage between Muslims in Africa and those in other parts of the world. Because of these continued contacts with the Arabo-Muslim world sub-Saharan Africa is increasingly being integrated into the Muslim world at the expense of the West.

There is an eternal dichotomy between Sufis, rural, and popular religious practices and the learned, urban, and elitist Islam in the Maghrib region of North Africa. Irrespective of the fact that the two Islamic orientations do not intermingle, they form part of a dynamic complementary and dialectical social process. This has been the long standing tradition in the Maghrib religious culture. Islamic radicalism has a negative impact in popular forms of Islam, comparing it to what prevailed in the area during the colonial period.

The impact of Islamic radicalism in the societies in the Maghrib region varied from country to country. In Tunisia, for example, the Hizb Nahda, the Harakat al-Islami (aka the 15–21 Movement) and the Hizb al-Tahri-ral-Islami which had influence in the 1970s and 1980s had virtually been eliminated. Similarly, the al-Adl wa'l-Ahsan and al-Shabiba al-Islamiyya committed to the violent overthrow of the monarchy in Morocco have either been successfully repressed or co-opted into the government. However, the Algerian case differs in that the Islamic radicalism, notably led by the Front Islamique du Salut (FIS), the Groupe Islamique Armé (GIA), and the Armee Islamique du Salut (AJS), have destabilized the country for a number of years.

In Algeria, Islamists embarked on a campaign of killing intellectuals, blowing up journalists, and slitting the throats of unveiled women. Whole segments of society learned to fear the Islamists more than the regime. If the government has an upper hand today, this is largely because of the egregious mistakes of the Islamists in reading the response of the Algerian people. The same occurred also in Egypt, where the Islamist targeting of tourism undermined the millions of individual Egyptian households that depend on tourism for their livelihoods. It was the broader Egyptian society, which was harmed by the Islamist violence—and was turned against the Islamists.

The controversial and contentious issue of translation of the Qur'an into other languages is becoming a serious one. In West Africa, the *arabisants* have a strong view that Qur'an was originally given by God in Arabic and as such cannot be distorted by way of translations. They condemn the practice where, for example, the Mouride women in Senegal sing religious songs in Wolof, their founder's language. The same negative views about the translation of the Qur'an prevail in Nigeria. The main disagreement about the authenticity of the translation of the Qur'an in East Africa is mainly due to the existing translations which were done by a Christian and others by a member of the Ahmadiyya movement, regarded as non-Muslim.

The idea of establishing an Islamic state in Sudan has historical roots dating back to the unification of Sufism and Islamism by the Mahdis in the nineteenth century. There is the Yan Izala movement in Nigeria led by Abubakar Gumi (Hunwick, 1997). The conflicts arise not only as a result of internal Islamic reform and rejuvenation (tajdid) but also because of the perceived threat by the Christians. This latter form of threat also functions as a unifying factor to the Sufis and Islamist religious movements in Nigeria. The Yan Izala is opposed to some traditional beliefs and customs of the Sufi. For example, the Yan Izala established a constitution which rejected, among other things, *bida* (evil or sinful innovation), popular religious pilgrimages to the tombs of saints and the recitation of songs for praising the Prophet, practiced by the Sufi brotherhoods. Conflicts which have occurred between the Sufi and the reformists are politically motivated.

When one reads Hasan al-Turabi of the Sudan, the Sorbonne-schooled ideologue of Islamism, one becomes aware of the political or liberationist motivations of political Islamism. In his own words "You talk about freedom, so that the people can express its will. Profess freedom without national liberation and the imperialist will intervene and falsify your will. Elections will express *his* will, the political party will be *his* agent, and the newspaper will be *his* mouthpiece." (Turabi, 1991).

This is a classic nationalist argument, with a slight fascist overtone that has become the stock-in-trade of the Sudanese oracle. But Turabi puts it precisely: Islamist movements are first of all about national liberation, not individual liberties; they are about power before politics; their populism is a form of mass mobilization, not participation. It is not the yearning for democracy that drives these movements. It is the yearning for authenticity, by people who are aggrieved and angry, and vulnerable to Islamist promises of power and revenge.

There is a debate among Islamists about democracy, and it is useful to follow it. But it is a circular debate over whether democracy is or is not authentically Islamic. By Islamist consensus, however, democracy is not a value in its own right; and the very fact that a democratic outcome is debated, and not assumed, is the sign of a profound ambivalence.

Political Islamism in North Africa

Islamism, terrorism, and reform—the triangle formed by these three concepts and the complex and changeable realities to which they refer is at the centre of political debate in and about North Africa today. The role of Egyptian elements in the leadership of Osama bin Laden's al-Qaeda organization is well known, if not necessarily well understood. The involvement of Maghrebis in terrorist networks in Europe—whether linked to al-Qaeda or not—has recently been underlined by the suspected involvement of Moroccans in March 11, 2004 attack in Madrid. Egypt itself has endured years of terrorist violence; few if any countries have suffered as much from terrorism as Algeria has over the last 12 years; and the bombings in Casablanca on May 16, 2003 suggest that Morocco is not immune.

At the same time, Egypt, Algeria, and Morocco have all been sites of important attempts at pluralist political reform. Morocco's political system has exhibited a measure of party-political pluralism since the early years of independence. Egypt experienced political pluralism before 1952, and under both Anwar Sadat and Hosni Mubarak, a degree of pluralism has been allowed at some periods only to be stifled at others. In Algeria, formal party pluralism was introduced in 1989 and has survived although it has fallen far short of substantive democracy.

Yet, debate over these issues has become bogged down in a welter of fixed but erroneous ideas. One is the notion that posits a simple chain of cause and effect: absence of political reform generates Islamism which in turn generates terrorism. This simplistic analysis ignores the considerable diversity within contemporary Islamic activism, the greater part of which has been consistently nonviolent. It also overlooks the fact that the rise of Islamist movements in North Africa has not been predicated on the absence of reform, but has generally occurred in conjunction with ambitious government reform projects. The expansion of Islamic political activism in Egypt occurred in the context of President Sadat's audacious economic and political opening—*infitah*—in the 1970s; the spectacular rise of the Islamic Salvation Front (FIS) in Algeria in 1989–1991 occurred in the context of the government's liberalization of the political system and its pursuit of radical economic reform.

The problem of reform, therefore, has not been its absence so much as the particular character of the reform projects that have been adopted by North African governments, the political alliances, and manoeuvres in which they have engaged in the process, and their complex, unforeseen and sometimes disastrous consequences. The problem of Islamism has not been its doctrinal outlook—this has been varied and variable—so much as the difficulty the Egyptian, Algerian, and Moroccan states have had in accommodating the more dynamic forms of nonviolent activism and, in particular, their inability to integrate a major Islamic movement into the formal political system. Egypt has refused to legalize the Muslim brothers. Algeria, having legalized the FIS and allowed it to contest and win two elections, then decided it could not cope with the consequences and took the fateful decision to dissolve the party. Morocco has consistently refused to legalize the Justice and Charity movement led by Sheikh Abdesselam Yacine. Whatever justifications have been advanced for these decisions, it is likely that a major element of the rationale has been the essentially pragmatic concern that their special resonance and dynamism rendered these movements so indigestible that their legalization threatened to destabilize the political system.

This consideration should not be dismissed. Although arguments about stability can be overstated and abused, how democratic reform in North Africa can be achieved without destabilizing the region's political systems is a fundamental and entirely valid question which has received far too little attention. A striking feature of the debates in the West and the region alike has been the prevalence of ideological as opposed to political arguments.

The various actors have been preoccupied with questions of legitimacy—who are the real democrats? Who has the right to participate in the political game?—rather than policy—how should the form of government be changed? What specific reforms are desirable and feasible? A new approach is required in both Western and North African discussions of political reform and the place and potential role of Islamist movements, not least because of the following changes in the outlook and behavior of Islamic political activists in the region over the last decade.

Political Islamism in Sub-Saharan Africa

Political Islam, by definition, is neutral. It is any variant of Islam inspiring or serving as a vehicle for political mobilization or activity. Productive scholarship and policy-making must reject definitions that categorically treat political Islam as either a malevolent or benevolent force. Political Islam in Africa can indeed be manifested in al-Qaeda-type terrorism as tragically illustrated by the horrific loss of life in the 1998 simultaneous bombings of the U.S. embassies in Kenya and Tanzania or the 2002 attack on an Israeli-owned hotel in Mombasa, Kenya.

Another face of political Islam, however, can be found in Senegal, where the Sufi brotherhoods—religious and social networks with deep historical roots—have bolstered a democratic and secular government. The ideological preconceptions of conservative traditionalists and liberal revisionists must be cast aside in achieving an understanding of political Islam in its many incarnations on a continent where challenges defy easy solutions.

East Africa

Poverty may not create international terrorists, but poverty, social turmoil, starvation, lack of infrastructure, and weak political systems attract them. East Africa and the Horn suffer from all of these afflictions. Transnational terrorism demonstrated its ferocity via al-Qaeda's coordinated bombings of the U.S. embassies in Nairobi, Kenya and Dar el Salaam, Tanzania on August 7, 1998. Two hundred and twenty-four lives were stolen and more than 5000 people were injured. The United States ineffectually responded with missile attacks on an alleged al-Qaeda chemical weapons factory in Sudan and a training camp in Afghanistan. These attacks only served to obscure pertinent issues.

East Africa—specifically Kenya, Tanzania, and Uganda—is an appropriate starting point for a survey of the nature of political Islam in Africa. Among the pertinent issues obscured by the attacks were the emergence and evolution of political Islam in East Africa and across the continent.

Muslims were deeply involved in the anticolonial nationalist movements in Kenya, Tanzania, and Uganda. For instance, Julius Nyerere of Tanzania collaborated with Muslims in the early days of the independence movement. On the East African coast, you find groups that clearly identify themselves with Islam, many of whom define themselves in terms of their Arab heritage. This, in turn, influences how they respond to political Islam.

Politicization of Muslims in East Africa must also be seen in terms of their status relative to the political governing elite, Malik Chaka believes. Muslims were often discriminated against in the mission schools that educated people for clerical, civil service, and teaching positions and produced the core of the emerging African middle class during the colonial period. Educational and employment discrimination continued after independence. Africans with Arabic, and usually Qur'an, education were marginalized by Westernized political elites. Whether trained abroad or in Wahabi-financed schools at home, many Muslims followed a distinctive path and increasingly assumed the role of a regional underclass.

The spiritual and mystical Sufism that Muslims in the region embraced often gave way to Wahabism, especially as seeds were sown for growing tensions with the prevailing power structure. Chaka explained that political Islam became linked to the agitation of those Africans who felt victimized by the beneficiaries of Western education. In Uganda, a pernicious variant of political Islam emerged, supported by the Sudanese, attracting remnants of deposed tyrant Idi Amin's forces. Tanzanian Muslims charged that the ostensibly secular national unity projects of the country's Catholic founding father, Julius Nyerere, were really designed to constrain Muslims.

In such a changing politico-religious environment, al-Qaeda found it relatively easy to build an infrastructure in the outskirts of Nairobi, Kenya and along the coast—a situation that seems to have been replicated in Zanzibar, the Comoros Islands, and along the Tanzanian coast (Lyman and Morrison, 2004: 77). Deadly results were realized in the 1998 East African embassy attacks and, later, in assaults on an Israeli-owned hotel and a passenger plane in Mombasa, Kenya in 2002.

Economic, governance, and security challenges in East Africa provide fertile ground for the expansion of al-Qaeda and its ideological allies. What is to be done? First and most fundamentally, engaging Africans and formulating policy attuned to indigenous realities. Mombasa, Kenya, and Zanzibar, Tanzania are crucial examples. Active outreach to Muslim communities must replace the fatalistic acceptance of the deepening radicalization of Africans in the region.

Second, one cannot win hearts and minds simply on the basis of sophisticated public diplomacy. Economic and resource commitments are crucial to this effort. The African Growth and Opportunity Act, with its promise of job creation; the Millennium Challenge Account, and AIDS funding are a start. In addition, active Wahabi educational programs must be offset by support for educational programs fostering tolerance. Job opportunities must be promoted for Muslims and non-Muslims alike. The continued socioeconomic marginalization of Muslims can, in some circumstances, contribute to extremism. Economic assistance packages should address this.

Third, even earnest economic efforts will come to naught without encouraging and ultimately institutionalizing good governance in East Africa. African states should practice good governance and have policies which are inclusive rather than exclusive because divisions based on religion are ultimately not in the American interest. There are dark forces which will use them and mobilize forces against the United States. The Tanzanian elections scheduled for late 2005 are a prime opportunity. Special attention should be paid to electoral developments in heavily Muslim Zanzibar, where elections in 1995 and 2000 lacked credibility. Diplomatic, economic, and political initiatives of governments in East Africa must be coordinated to avert instability and the growth of terrorist cells in the region.

The Horn of Africa

In strict geographic terms, the Horn of Africa is defined as Djibouti, Eritrea, Ethiopia, Somalia, and Sudan. In mainstream political science terms, the Horn is also defined by the disorder and state breakdown that provide fuel for the most virulent forms of political Islamic radicalism and terrorist activity. A survey of Islam in the Horn illustrates that Somalia and Djibouti are overwhelmingly Muslim, whereas a little less than three-quarters of the Sudan and roughly half of Ethiopia and Eritrea are Muslim. Islamic movements challenged Ethiopian Christian hegemony in the fourteenth and sixteenth centuries and created obstacles to British rule in Somaliland in the early twentieth century. The Muslim League in Eritrea, following World War II, and the Muslim–dominated Eritrean Liberation Front, in the early 1960s, both agitated against Ethiopian rule.

Wahabism has had mixed success in radicalizing Muslims in the Horn. In Ethiopia, Wahabis have been connected to reported mosque burnings, thereby introducing intra-Islamic divisions into an already volatile ethno-religious mix. In Somalia, the fundamentalist Al Ittihad al Islami evolved from Wahabi roots. Al Ittihad is a self-described *Salafist* group; however, *Salafists* seek a return to Muslim orthodoxy of yore. Although Somalia has served as a transit route for terrorists—most visibly al-Qaeda—the depth of its involvement with terrorists is ironically constrained by the very disorder seen as a classical setting for terrorism; it has almost no legitimate terrorist targets, and terrorists themselves can be subject to extortion in a largely lawless setting (Menkhaus, 2004: 66–75). Hostility from indigenous religious authorities has impeded the growth of Wahabism in Djibouti.

Political Islam—independent of Wahabism—has deep historical roots in Sudan. In line with this long tradition, Hassan al-Turabi created the National Islamic Front in 1985. It was transformed later into the Popular National Congress, but al-Turabi's political maneuverings, ultimately culminated in his assumption of the role of speaker of the National Assembly and power broker in an Islamic fundamentalist government. Later, al-Turabi would fall from political grace.

Throughout much of the 1990s, the Sudanese Military Industrial Corporation (MIC) and Sudanese intelligence were virtually inseparable from al-Qaeda. If the Iraqis were providing WMD technology to these elements of the corrupt Sudanese regime—led by Hasan al Turabi, who was openly sympathetic to Osama bin Laden—they were effectively providing it to al-Qaeda. Meanwhile, Sudan served as a base for Osama bin Laden from 1991 to 1996, and in the eyes of some, as an epicenter for international terrorism. Sudan publicly renounced terrorism against the backdrop of a long-running civil war and engaged in revitalized efforts to normalize relations with the West beginning in 2000 and accelerating after September 11, 2001. These developments should not hide a complicating factor. Radical Islam, as exhibited in the Popular National Congress, remains a potent force in the Sudan (Hayes and Joscelyn, 2005).

Writing in *The London Free Press* of August 30, 2004, Salim Mansur, pointed out that Darfur, in the arid deserts of the eastern Sahara, where living is a bitter daily struggle against sand and sun, a genocide is unfolding, with nary a whimper from the folks at the UN and sophisticates in cosmopolitan centers. Within 18 months, nearly 50,000 Darfurians were killed and more than a million made refugees by Arab *Janjaweed* militias, supplied with military support by the Sudanese government of strongman General Omar al-Bashir in Khartoum. For more than two decades, Sudan, with an estimated population of 35 million, has been torn apart in a bitter civil war between a predominantly Arab-Muslim north, and a Christian-black south. This conflict resulted in an estimated two million dead and another four million made homeless in their own country.

Darfur, however, exposes another dimension of the internal conflict in Sudan. Here, the victims are Muslim, black, and non-Arab. Those perpetrating the brutalities are Muslims of Arab origin. Under the prodding of U.S. Secretary of State Colin Powell and UN Secretary-General Kofi Annan—both of whom visited Darfur—the UN Security Council produced a resolution demanding the Sudanese government, within a month, to disarm the militias and restore security in Darfur, or be faced with sanctions.

But Sudan is a member of the Arab League, an organization representing 22 Arab countries of the Middle East and North Africa. Hence, the Arab League immediately rallied around Sudan at the UN to ease pressures being placed on Bashir's regime. The diplomatic maneuvers of the Arab League are predictable. It exists to defend the interests of Arab states—meaning regimes in power—and not the Arab people.

The one constant in the history of Arab states over the past five decades is the abuse of people by power-holders in a part of the world—between the Atlantic Ocean and the Persian Gulf—where regimes rule without popular legitimacy. It is understandable, though inexcusable, that there are no demonstrations in the streets of Cairo, Damascus, Beirut, Tunis, Algiers, or elsewhere in the wider Arab-Muslim world, denouncing the Khartoum regime for its crimes in Darfur.

This silence among the Arab League members is also revealing of culturally entrenched bigotry among Arabs, and Muslims from adjoining areas of the Middle East. Blacks are viewed by Arabs as racially inferior, and Arab violence against blacks has a long, turbulent record. The Arabic word for blacks (*abed*) is a derivative of the word slave (*abd*), and the role of Arabs in the history of slavery is a subject rarely discussed publicly. Here, the contrast between the Arab treatment of blacks, irrespective of whether they are Muslims or not, and the Israeli assimilation of black Jews of Ethiopia, known as Falashas, cannot go unnoticed. The tragedy of Darfurians ironically has exposed to the world the racial dimension of Arab-Muslim culture and the hollowness of rhetoric proclaiming the brotherhood of Muslims.

The multifarious problems of the Horn defy easy solutions. There are promising measures to address the growth of the most insidious variants of radical political Islam, while also bettering the lives of the Horn's people. First, a serious effort should be made to train officers with Arabic and Islamic training to serve Africa. This move can generate a change in the culture and incentive system.

Second, military and antiterrorist assistance should continue to patrol the Horn, combined with a consciousness of human rights realities. It is naive to foreswear military assistance to countries in the Horn that must battle terrorism, whereas transnational groups such as al-Qaeda use military means. However, such assistance must be linked to sound human rights practices and the protection of marginalized groups. Since 2002, the United States has deployed 1800 troops to Djibouti as part of the Combined Joint Task Force–Horn of Africa, designed to thwart terrorists in Somalia, Kenya, Yemen, and elsewhere in the region. In mid-2003 the Bush administration committed itself to an additional $100 million to address terrorism in the Horn and East Africa; two-thirds of these funds are marked for military support (Lyman et al. op.cit.: 77).

To achieve tangible long-term success in the Horn and reduce the ranks of terror recruits, Western countries must reach ordinary Muslims and non-Muslims by improving health care systems, combating HIV-AIDS, financing secular schools, and boosting agriculture. "It would be particularly helpful," argued Shinn, "if wealthy Arab countries joined development efforts in the Horn and Africa at large without linking their aid to support for a fundamentalist philosophy. This will require some very frank talk with the Saudis and others."

The United States will need a carefully considered re-engagement plan to build a new relationship with strategically located Somalia once a central government emerges with at least rudimentary influence in most parts of the country. The formal emergence of a largely impotent central government in the latter part of 2004 following clan-based negotiations does not yet appear to meet this criterion (*Washington Post*, October 10, A17). Before an effective national government emerges, informal contacts can and should be cultivated with local authorities, including clan leaders and both religious and secular leaders in the larger civil society (Menkhaus, op.cit.: 83–84). Such contacts provide insight into political patterns and lay the groundwork for more extensive and formal contacts in the future.

The consummation of a peace deal in January 2005 between the central government and the Sudan People's Liberation Army inspires hope for improved relations. The agreement will open the door for an accommodation with rebels in the troubled Darfur region, where government complicity in genocide is alleged (Kanina, 2005: A1; Kessler and Lynch, 2004: A1; Lynch, 2004: A11; Lynch, 2005:

A11). A comprehensive peace throughout Sudan will accelerate Sudan's reintegration into the mainstream international community.

Nigeria

Nigeria is currently experiencing increasingly volatile relations between its Islamic and Christian communities. Destabilization of this strategically crucial West African state would ripple through the region and beyond if precipitated by new confrontations among politicized Muslims and Christians. Economic distress only exacerbates the danger.

Paul Marshall, *National Review Online*, May 5, 2004, examined the outside encouragement of Muslim extremism in Nigeria. Since the governor of Zamfara State, Alhaji Ahmed Sani, introduced a draconian version of *sharia* in 1999, 11 of Nigeria's 36 states have followed suit. Five women have been sentenced to death by stoning for adultery, though no punishment has yet been carried out. Thieves have had their hands amputated by court order. One man had his eye removed after accidentally blinding a friend (he could have escaped this by paying 60 camels, but the injured party was not interested in the camels).

Under these sharia dictates, women are harshly subjugated. In northern Nigeria, they have been forbidden to rent houses and barred from riding motorbikes or traveling in the same vehicles as men. Taxi drivers have been caned for carrying female passengers in violation of the law in Zamfara State. Zamfara requires all high school girls to wear a hijab and bars them from wearing skirts and other Western forms of dress. State officials have advocated public flogging of those violating an Islamic dress code. Prostitution charges have been leveled at women merely for the crime of being unmarried after the age of 13. Judges in Bauchi State have told women to get married immediately or be sent to prison. A judge ordered four of them to pick out husbands from among the men in the court. Women are at a particular disadvantage in these criminal prosecutions because their testimony usually counts for only half that of a man.

Non-Muslims, usually Christians, have become second-class citizens. Their taxes pay for Islamic preachers, although hundreds of churches have been closed by government order. Recently, Sani announced that all unauthorized places of worship in Zamfara State would be demolished. Those who exercise their right under the Nigerian constitution to change their religion from Islam are threatened with death, a punishment for apostasy under sharia law. The Catholic and Anglican churches have had to set up protected centers for converts.

This spread of radical Islam has also led to riots, mob attacks, and vigilantes, producing the largest death toll in Nigeria since the civil war over Biafra in the 1960s. Over 10,000 people have died in the last four years in sharia-related violence— perhaps over 1000 in the central states this year alone. Recent months have seen the emergence of more organized militias. In early January, in Yobe State, there was an uprising by a group calling itself the Taliban, led by a Mullah Omar, and demanding an Islamic state. It took several hundred troops two weeks to put it down.

Foreign groups have been aiding the institutionalization of Islamic law. Saudi, Sudanese, Syrian, and Palestinian representatives appeared with Governor Sani in the days before he announced his plans for sharia. The Jigawa State government has sent Islamic judges for training in Malaysia and Sudan. The government of Katsina State has sent a delegation to Sudan to study its laws. Other states have been offered assistance from some of these same countries as well as from Iran and Libya.

In January, the Saudi religious and cultural attaché in Nigeria, Sheik Abdul-Aziz, said that his government had been monitoring the implementation of sharia in Nigeria and noted the results with delight. There is also evidence of infiltration by foreign Islamic radicals. According to some reports, extremists from neighboring Chad were involved in the July 2001 violence in Bauchi State. In November 2001, Nigerian police arrested six Pakistani preachers, accusing them of inciting religious violence in Ogun State. The police have announced that scores of Pakistanis have been arrested in different parts of the country for allegedly fomenting religious trouble since 9/11. Last month, church spokesmen in Plateau State said that local Muslim extremists have brought in thousands of mercenaries from Niger and Chad to invade Christian towns and villages.

However, despite repeated rumors, there has until this year been little evidence of organized foreign support for violence and domestic terrorism. Now such evidence is appearing. On February 3, the Nigerian government announced that an unnamed Iranian diplomat was arrested on January 23 in Nigeria's capital, Abuja, after he was found taking photographs of Churches, a presidential villa, the defense headquarters, and the Israeli, British, and American embassies.

The usually reliable news service Compass Direct reports that one of January's Taliban raiders, Muslim cleric Alhaji Sharu, confessed to police that he was a middleman between Nigerian extremists and the Al-Muntada Al-Islami Trust, a Saudi funded charity headquartered in Britain. Sharu said that the trust's money had been used to propagate a Wahabist version of Islam in Nigeria and fund religious violence. Subsequent investigation by Nigeria's police led to the discovery of financial transactions running into millions of dollars between Sharu and the Trust's local head, a Sudanese businessman named Muhiddeen Abdullahi. Authorities arrested Abdullahi on February 20, accusing him and the Trust of financing attacks on Christians, including the January Taliban uprising. When authorities released Abdullahi ten days after his arrest, more than 5000 Qadiriyya Sufi Muslims, the largest tradition within Nigerian Islam, mounted a protest march. Chanting Allahu Akbar (God is great), demanded that Wahabis be banned from the country.

Nigeria must be seen in the regional context of the West Africa region, where roughly 140 million Muslims live. West Africa is home to three pro-Western democracies: Senegal, Mali, and Niger. Further, the region could account for up to a quarter of U.S. oil imports by 2015. Although there are only small pockets of support for terrorism regionally, al-Qaeda has taken advantage of the region's interlocking conflicts and cases of state breakdown to acquire funds through local diamond purchases (Lyman et al., op.cit.: 83–84).

Nigeria has the largest population in Africa and is the seventh largest oil producer in the world. Nigeria has maintained a reputation as a regional peacekeeper in Liberia, Sierra Leone, and elsewhere. Yet it has a fragile internal political order. Nigeria's population is almost evenly split between predominately northern Muslims and predominately southern Christians. Religious and ethnic divisions raise the prospect of further conflict. Before the emergence of a legitimate democratic government at the end of the 1990s, Nigeria had experienced ethnic tension, civil war, and frequent military coups. Its oil wealth was mismanaged, leading to a precipitous decline in living standards for the average Nigerian.

Expectations rose with President Olusegun Obasanjo's election in 1999, but subsequent ethnic unrest in Nigeria's oil-producing Niger Delta region, rising religious tensions, and a lack of discernible improvement in the economy soon cast a cloud over the democratic experiment. More than 10,000 deaths were recorded from ethnic and religious conflicts since the election. Yet even this high number does not adequately describe the tenuous nature of the country's governing institutions.

Political Islam has played an important role in the evolution of Nigeria's polity, but it must be assessed in terms of the daunting political and economic challenges facing the country. Northern Nigeria's largely Muslim Hausa–Fulani people have long-standing transnational connections to Middle Eastern centers of learning and West African Sufi brotherhoods. British colonialism bolstered northern Nigeria's control by political Islamists. In exchange for support of British rule, Ahmadu Bello was able to insist on the teaching and practice of Islam in this region. Traditional Islamic clans coalesced into a northern party that effectively excluded Westernized intellectuals and secularized non-Muslims.

The resurgence of Islamic fundamentalism in Nigeria following independence was influenced by an infusion of Saudi-educated religious scholars who challenged less austere versions of Islam. That Islamic fundamentalism acquired a more pronounced political edge as the national fortunes of the governing Muslim national elite declined dramatically with the election of President Obasanjo, a born-again Christian from the south. After playing a major, often dominant, role in the government and military for almost 40 years, northern Muslims felt sidelined. Among the reasons for these feelings was Obasanjo's removal of politicized military officers, who were disproportionately Muslim (Ibid.: 79).

In the context of a northern Muslim political decline, a gubernatorial candidate in Zamfara State, running on a platform of restoring sharia, or Islamic law, won a resounding victory. Very quickly, sharia was introduced in an additional 11 of Nigeria's 36 states. Sharia offers the prospect of law-and-order to the Muslim masses outraged at how their children were being seduced by siren calls of easy money and lax morals. To the governing elite, however, the spread of sharia was also a by-product of Nigerian Muslims' desire to reassert their political prerogative in response to what they feared was a newfound southern Christian political hegemony. In contrast, many Christians in predominately Muslim and mixed religious states view sharia as an alien religious and cultural imposition designed to delegitimize both their religion and political standing.

The Nigerian electoral process, with its mandated requirement for cross-religious and cross-regional alliances, prevented sharia from achieving a formal national platform; yet it remains a potential source of religious and cultural tension and is symptomatic of the depth of national religious divisions. Fears of looming communal religious violence in Nigeria became a reality in February and May of 2000 in Kaduna City, with at least 2000 deaths, and again in Kaduna in 2002, when a newspaper printed a story deemed an affront to the Prophet Mohammed. The states of Kano and Sokoto, and the cities of Jos, Bauchi, and Yelwa, have similarly experienced religious violence.

It may be premature to characterize clashes between Nigerian police and religious students in Yobe State in early 2003 and between security forces and Islamic militants in September 2004 as opening skirmishes in a battle with transnational Islamic-inspired terrorism, but the conditions for just such a battle may develop (*Washington Post*, September 25, 2004: A18). Growing economic and political marginalization, political mobilization of alienated youth and the intelligentsia, and the injection of extremist Islamic ideologies into the body politic are ingredients in a volatile recipe.

Nigerian history is littered with precedents for the use of violence to settle political scores, and those with an interest in Nigeria's success cannot remain sanguine about recent examples and potential hot spots of violence in the country. State failure in Nigeria will reverberate well beyond Nigeria's borders. Second, there should be support for inter-religious dialogue.

Third, the world can best assist Nigeria economically—via debt relief, for example—through its influence in international financial institutions. This assistance is imperative in light of the magnitude of the Nigeria's economic crisis, a state of affairs reinforcing ethnic and religious divisions. Strengthening the Nigerian educational system should also be a priority, acknowledging the potential destabilization of a surge of undereducated and disenfranchised young people. Fourth, let Nigerian local communities have more of a stake in the mediation of disputes and economic development.

Senegal

Senegal is a vivid illustration that political Islam can be a constructive and regime-stabilizing force in a country of almost 11 million people, 94 percent are Muslim. The cordiality between the Senegalese state and Muslim leaders is rooted in the colonial period. The French, fearing jihad, deferred to these leaders on religious affairs in exchange for acceptance of French control of administrative matters, such as taxation.

In the post independence period and beyond, Senegal's Sufi groups became pillars for the governing authorities, turning out the vote and extending religious sanction to secular heads of state. Governing leaders, in turn, paid allegiance to groups within the Sufi brotherhoods. Creevey added that President Abdoulaye Wade, for instance, has declared himself a Mouride, a politically active reform group within the Hizbut Tarquiyyah brotherhood; he expresses his loyalty to the Mouride leader. The Sufi brotherhoods have become less overt in their expression of political sympathies over the years, yet they maintain an instrumental role by encouraging popular support for the government.

Senegal is home to a minority of radical Islamist groups and militants who were inspired by the 1979 Iranian Revolution. The leaders of these groups are mostly individuals schooled in Arab countries and critical of Westernization. Although they remain a minority, their opposition to U.S. policy in the Middle East and to the secularization of the country's family code is shared by the Sufi brotherhoods. Only 40 percent of Muslim leaders believe that Senegal should be governed by sharia; this is a small number relative to many other Muslim states. Moderation within the Senegalese polity and balance between traditional Islam and secularism remains the norm.

Senegal may be a model for political modernity on the continent, but in a state proud of its Islamic traditions it is best that this model not be trumpeted by an American whose standing is low in the Islamic world. The Senegalese model should remain a quiet testimony to the potential for states willing to reconcile the best in the Islamic tradition with the requirements of modern state building. Its merits must be identified, weighed, and selectively adopted by states on their own volition based on their peculiar historical and contemporary circumstances.

Conclusion, Research, and Policy Strategies

Islam was traditionally conceived as being in a class with Judaism and Christianity. But, Islamism today is a response to ideologies that emerged in the modern West— communism, socialism, or capitalism. Islamism is largely synonymous with political Islam—an effort to draw meaning out of Islam applicable to problems of contemporary governance, society, and politics.

Contemporary political Islam developed as a response to problems created by colonialism. Colonialism posed a double challenge, that of foreign (Western) domination and of the need for internal reform to address weaknesses exposed by external aggression. Early political Islam grappled with such questions in an attempt to modernize and reform Islamic societies. The Pakistani thinker, Abu ala Mawdudi, placed political violence at the centre of political action, and an Egyptian thinker, Sayyed Qutb, argued that it was necessary to distinguish between friends and enemies, for with friends you use reason and persuasion, but with enemies you use force.

There is no gainsaying that there are current tensions, suspicions, confrontations, and enmities that characterize the relationship of Islam to the West compelling the use of these ideas in the Islamized world. These are certainly not purely affairs of the spirit, or simply clashes of religious ideas or theological interpretations, or merely matters of beliefs, values, images, and perceptions. They are the normal affairs of history, power politics, international relations, and the pursuit of vital interests.

There can be no illusion that Western, particularly U.S., policy on the African subcontinent can be dramatically and quickly altered. Nor can the damage rendered by the pervasive perception that the West led by the United States is hostile toward global Islamic interests be erased in the near term. However, steps can be taken to incrementally establish the foundation for a more constructive and beneficial relationship between the West and members of the Muslim and non-Muslim communities in Africa.

A more sophisticated understanding of political Islam by the West should be a precondition for policy formulation. In this spirit, certain policy and conceptual questions surface and beg further analysis and answers:

- What are the politically active sectors of the Muslim population on the African subcontinent? How is their activity manifested?
- What is the nexus between Islam, ethnicity, and class in selective African cases?
- Is the conventional dichotomy between moderate and radical Islamists on the subcontinent appropriate? If not, what categorization should be substituted?
- To what extent are radical transnational Islamic movements influencing indigenous variants of African Islam? To what extent are they operating independently on the subcontinent?
- How can dialogue and understanding be fostered between the United States and representatives of Islam on the subcontinent in both government and in the broader civil society?

It is imperative that we understand why and how this phenomenon called political Islamism comes about, why a great deal of Islamist thinking is not some exotic belief that could only come from a strange reason, but in many ways is reflective of the anxieties, concerns, and problems of the entire African continent. It perhaps has a different garb in the Middle East, some of it not fully familiar. But at a closer look, one can see elements that resemble Chinese angers and frustrations at their former eclipsed greatness; one can see it reflected in India or Latin America or Africa. It has local characteristics; but it also has some very broad, general characteristics.

When some people talk about political Islam or Islamism, they have bin Laden or the Taliban in mind. Both of those are part—but on the fringes—of what is a very broad movement of political Islam. They cannot be excluded, but they are simply violent and extremist parts of the spectrum. This viral spectrum is growing and diversifying all the time. Political Islam may be attributed to anyone who believes that the Qur'an and the Traditions of the Prophet—what the Prophet said and did during his lifetime in an effort to apply his best understanding of the Qur'an—have something important to say about the way politics and society should operate in the Middle East.

On this spectrum we have, on the one hand, violent radicals or nonviolent radicals or moderates. We have rather totalitarian-minded individuals, but a much greater number of Islamists who increasingly see benefits of democratic process. We see traditionalists who believe that somehow the old, glorious days of the golden age of the Islamic world is the goal to return to. The greater majority would say, "No, we are moving on into a new world" and would be more modernist in their interpretation. So you can be traditionalist, you can be modernist, you can be anywhere along the spectrum which is broadening as any number of people consider themselves driven in one way or another by their concern with linking Islam and politics.

There are several reasons why political Islam today is very successful, particularly in opposition in many parts of Africa. First, saying in opposition is an important statement in itself, because it is much easier to be in opposition than it is to be in power anywhere. We can criticize what is wrong with any number of governments and regimes, but to say what we would do if we were in power and had to assume those problems is rather different. So right away Muslim Islamists, like any other opposition group, have that advantage.

Secondly, most regimes in the continent help the Islamists, wittingly or unwittingly, by eliminating most other political opposition. So you can take the socialist party and close it down, or the nationalist party, or the communist party, or the liberal party. But with Islamists it is much harder, because they are operating out of mosques and neighborhoods. Islamist movements have deep grassroots, much more than any other movement. It is regrettable to say that because one's bias would be to see reforming liberal movements as dominant. But the reality is that one can get a mass of crowds into Liberation Square in any Arab or Muslim city in the world and you could not fill up any square in any part of the Muslim world with liberal democrats. It is simply not a vibrant tradition, at least so far in Africa.

So with legal or illegal elimination of other rivals, Islamists win by default, or they gain by default, in this position, including both the extremists and the others. Extreme conditions generally produce extremist results. Many of the situations now in so much of the Arab and African world are negative conditions: oppressive governments, incompetent governance; unelected, and hence you might say illegitimate, governance in many cases; violent governance; brutal and destructive governance, of which the former president of Iraq and unlamented Saddam Hussein was the supreme example. These regimes produce the frustration and anger that ultimately pushes people towards political Islam and infect other corners of the world where Islam has a toehold.

However, protection of the rights and freedoms of citizens around the world is the duty of every state. Chief of them is the right to life. But it is the life of the common man that is threatened by terrorists. The world community is obliged to ensure for its citizens the right to safe protection against terrorism. The solution is possible if an effective code of protecting human rights against terrorism is developed under the UN aegis, a code aimed at

- Preventing and stopping acts of terrorism
- Opposing the funding of terrorism
- Prosecution of the people who have perpetrated acts of terrorism or are complicit in them in other ways
- Ensuring that such persons should not escape from responsibility and punishment
- Assistance to persons who have suffered from terrorism, including financial assistance, social, and psychological rehabilitation and reintegration into society
- Effective international cooperation towards achieving the above goals

References

Alem-Zelalem. 2003. Saudi Arabia's Wahhabism and the threat to Ethiopia's national security, Ethiomedia.com, http://ethiomedia.com/press/wahabism_threat_to_ethiopia. html, 26 September 2003.

Algar, H. 2002. *Wahhabism: A Critical Essay*. New York: Islamic Publications International.

Burgat, F. and Dowell, W. 1997. *The Islamic Movement in North Africa*, Austin, Texas: Center for Middle Eastern Studies, University of Texas, pp. 2, 8.

Dekmejian, R.H. 1995. *Islam in Revolution—Fundamentalism in the Arab World*, 2nd edn., New York: Syracuse University Press, p. 4.

Dessouki, A.E.H. 1982. The islamic resurgence: sources, dynamics, and implications, in Hillal Dessouki, A.E.H (Ed.), *Islamic Resurgence in the Arab World*, New York: Praeger Publishers, 1982, p. 4.

Eickelman, D. 1997. Muslim politics: The prospects for democracy in North Africa and the Middle East, in John P. Entelis (Ed.), *Islam, Democracy, and the State in North Africa*, Bloomington/Indianapolis, Indiana: Indiana University Press.

Esposito, J. 1992. In Timothy D. Sisk (Ed.), *Quoted in Islam and Democracy: Religion, Politics, and Power in the Middle East*, Washington DC: United States Institute of Peace.

Hayes, S.F. and Joscelyn, T. *Weekly Standard*, 27 July 2005.

Hudson, M.C. 1992. Statement to the House Committee on Foreign Affairs, Subcommittee on Europe and the Middle East, Promoting Pluralism and Democracy in the Middle East, 102d Congress, 2d sess., 11 August 1992.

Huntington, S. 1993. The clash of civilizations. *Foreign Affairs*, 72(3).

Hunwick, J. 1997. In Rosander, E.E. and Westerlund, D. (Eds.) *Sub-Saharan Africa and the Wider World of Islam*, op.cit.: 42–43.

Kanina, W. 2005. Sudanese Leaders, Southern Rebels Finish Peace Deal, *Washington Post*, January 1, A1.

Kepel, G. 2004. *The War for Muslim Minds: Islam and the West*, Cambridge: Belknap.

Kessler, G. and Lynch, C. 2004. U.S. Calls Killings in Sudan Genocide, *Washington Post*, September 10, A1.

Lyman, P. and Morrison, J.S. 2004. The Terrorist Threat in Africa, *Foreign Affairs,* January/February.

Lynch, C. 2004. UN Official Blames Sudan for Violence, *Washington Post,* May 8, A11.

Lynch, C. 2005. U.S. Europe Debate Venue for Darfur Trials, *Washington Post,* January 21, A11.

Marshall, P. 2003. Radical Islam's Move on Africa, *Washington Post,* October 16.

Menkhaus, K. 2004. *Somalia: State Collapse and the Threat of Terrorism. Adelphi Paper* 364. New York: Oxford University Press.

Middle East/North Africa Report N°37, March 2, 2005.

Moussalli, A.S. 1999. *Moderate and Radical Islamic Fundamentalism,* Gainesville, Florida: University Press of Florida.

Norton, A.R. 1992. Breaking through the Wall of Fear in the Arab World, *Current History,* January.

Pipes, D. 1982. Oil wealth and Islamic resurgence. In Dessouki (Ed.). *Islamic Resurgence in the Arab World,* New York: Praeger Publishers.

Rosander, E.E. 1997. Introduction: The Islamization of 'tradition' and modernity. In Rosander, E.E and Westerlund, D. (Eds.) *African Islam and Islam in Africa: Encounters between Sufis and Islamists,* Athens, Ohio: Ohio University Press.

Roy, O. 2004. *Globalized Islam: The Search for a New Ummah.* New York: Columbia University Press.

Shahin, E.E. 1997. *Political Ascent—Contemporary Islamic Movements in North Africa,* Boulder, Colorado: Westview Press.

Turabi, H. 1991. Speech to the Popular Arab-Islamic Conference, Al-Islam wa-Filastin, Nicosia, May–June 1991.

U.S. State Department's International Religious Freedom Report 2004.

Voll, J.O. 1982. *Islam: Continuity and Change in the Modern World,* Boulder, Colorado: Westview Press, p. 283.

Appendix

Table A9.1 Growth of Islam in Africa

Islam in Africa				
Region	Total Population	Muslims	Muslim (Percent)	Total Muslim (Percent)
Central Africa	83,121,055	12,582,592	15.138	0.852
East Africa	193,741,900	66,381,242	34.263	4.497
North Africa	202,151,323	180,082,076	89.083	12.199
Southern Africa	137,092,019	8,935,043	6.518	0.605
West Africa	268,997,245	133,994,675	49.813	9.077
Total	885,103,542	401,975,628	45.416	27.23

Source: U.S. State Department's International Religious Freedom
Report 2004.

Chapter 10

Environmental Terrorism: A Weapon of Mass Destruction for the Future

DeMond S. Miller, Joel C. Yelin, and Jason D. Rivera

CONTENTS

Introduction

To combat and prevent terrorism, an understanding of what constitutes terrorism in its many forms and how it manifests in those forms is needed. Understanding the etiology of terrorism can be difficult because people in power perceive the concept of terrorism in different ways. Terrorist activities and ideologies have symbolic meanings that establish points of view that differ from those held by radical extremist groups.

The symbolic meaning of the physical target is used to inspire fear and caution within nations. For example, the terrorists behind the attacks on September 11, 2006, targeted the World Trade Towers, symbols of the United States' economic power, the Pentagon, the symbol of its military force, and the White House, the symbol of its political force. Attacks such as these were designed to change the policies of the target nation.

Along with this comes the continuing trend of violence inherent in activities deemed terroristic. As Waugh (1990, p. 51) stated, "Intent is crucial to the definition of terrorism which suggests a conscious and premeditated application of violence to achieve a state of terror." However, when violence couples with symbolism and declarative statements, terrorism can be more accurately defined. A true act of terrorism goes beyond the immediate victims to impact an entire society. It is the destruction of a symbol that underlies the actions of every terrorist. It might also be within the destruction itself that the symbolism lies. Regardless of the combination of terms, symbolism and destruction are inherent in any working definition of terrorism.

Among the many targets of terrorism, such as an economy or innocent civilians, the environment may also become a target of attack because it is a symbol of social and economic balance. Furthermore, the natural environment serves as a way to connect the people to the land and culture. When the natural environment is damaged in an attack, it is either a victim or a casualty. If the environment is damaged as a byproduct of a terrorist attack, the environment is only a casualty of the attack. When the environment is the clear target of an act of terrorism, the act becomes known as environmental terrorism.

Overall, it is the symbolism of the target or the violence against the target that separates terrorism from all other acts of violence. "By its very nature, the destruction of lives and property by terrorists has symbolic meaning in an attempt to render a psychic blow and spark fear" (Miller and Rivera, 2007). Moreover, during a time of peace, a terrorist attack can be construed as a radical expression; therefore, during wartime, terrorist attacks can be construed as military strategy. The differences between warfare and terrorism are their goals and methods. Where the strategy of warfare is to determine how to obtain and maintain an advantage over the opponent and, when possible, avoid involving civilians, the strategy of terrorism seeks to directly involve the civilians by instigating mass panic and hysteria. Within warfare the targeting of noncombatants is not permitted. However, it is the very heart of terrorism to target noncombatants for the purpose of inflicting a psychological effect on the target population (Chalecki, 2001, p. 5). One exception to this can be observed in Saddam Hussein's burning of the Kuwaiti oil fields during the first Gulf War. When discussing the Gulf War, McClain (2001) asserted

> After his forces invaded Kuwait in August 1990, and coalition forces were massing together to force them out, Hussein said if he had to be evicted from Kuwait by force, then Kuwait would be burned. Just as promised, Iraqi troops set fire to more than 700 oil wells in several Kuwaiti oil fields as they were evacuating the country. Officials from the Kuwait Oil Company indicated that all of Kuwait's oil fields had been damaged or destroyed by the Iraqis. (p. 1)

Although Hussein ignited the oil fields during a time of war, he garnered attention by destroying the Kuwaiti symbol of environmental and economic security through an act of terrorism. With a flagrant disregard for the environment, he ignited every oil field in Kuwait. Even before the fires, Hussein ordered approximately "... 11 million barrels of oil into the Arabian Gulf from January to May 1991, oiling more than 800 miles of Kuwaiti and Saudi Arabian coastline" (McClain, 2001 p. 1). This act of environmental terrorism not only destroyed the chief source of finance for the region but it also caused substantial harm to the environment. This act illustrated Saddam Hussein's defiance for Kuwaiti natural sovereignty and the international community.

Terrorists use the destruction of the environment as a means to force governments and nations to adhere to their demands.

> In essence, environmental terrorists—individuals or groups—commit acts so that natural resources can not be used by overall populations symbolizing a commitment to political or ideological beliefs, which they hope force authorities to adhere.   (Miller and Rivera, 2007)

Natural resources are targeted because they form the basis of national economic trade. Hence, if natural resources are disrupted, international trade can be disrupted and thereby adversely affect the economic stability of other nations or regions (Chalecki, 2001; Le Billon, 2005). When natural resources become the immediate victims of environmental sabotages, humans, economies, and the communities that rely on those natural resources may not have the resiliency to rebound quickly. Therefore, the destruction of the environment and the potential to induce great havoc garners more attention from the terrorists. As Chalecki (2001) states, "[t]he destruction of a natural resource can now cause more deaths, property damage, political chaos, and other adverse effects than it would have in any previous decade" (Chalecki, 2001, p. 2).

The most commonly employed tool terrorists use is fear. Environmental terrorists use environmental destruction to inspire fear among civilians and civic leaders. Such destruction forces civilians to live in newly configured landscapes that are ever changing and unfamiliar to the victims. In the case of the first Gulf War, in which the desert was covered in oil, images of a black desert-wasteland of oil sparked concerns, fears, and uncertainties about the futures of many Kuwaiti citizens. It is with fear that terrorists can pursue their short-term and long-term objectives. " . . . [T]errorists pursue their ultimate goal through inculcation of fear and humans do fear damage or destruction of particular nonhuman objects" (Gibbs, 1989, p. 331).

Responses to environmental terrorism cannot wait until an attack occurs and the damage is done; the time and money spent to repair damage that could have been used in mitigation and prevention is wasted. Counter environmental terrorism is difficult because the terrorists aim to attack with a high degree of unpredictability. When preventative strategies are in place well before the attack, sudden ecological destruction becomes less likely. Given the correct measures to raise awareness, many acts of terrorism can be avoided, saving lives and the environment.

Although it is a possibility that a nuclear device might fall into the hands of terrorists, this scenario is somewhat unlikely within the notion of environmental terrorism. A nuclear weapon, or another weapon of mass destruction, can cause much damage over a large area, but the probability of terrorist groups obtaining and using these devices is not high. However, even without the use of weapons of mass destruction, the environment can be damaged in ways that might take years of recovery efforts. "Environmental terrorism has a higher probability than a nuclear attack with the effects lasting just as long and being just as widespread as a terrorist attack using weapons of mass destruction" (Chalecki, 2001). Saddam Hussein devastated Kuwait without the need to acquire weapons of mass destruction when he burned the oil fields. With conventional explosives, the oil wells and facilities were destroyed. And with no Kuwaiti national environmental protection plan for the oil-rich region, Hussein then placed mines around the wells to slow the firefighters who responded.

Environmental terrorism poses a real threat. Attacks such as the Kuwaiti oil fires have long-lasting effects on the environment and must be avoided. By understanding all its facets, environmental terrorism can be curbed and possible disaster avoided. Schwartz (1998, p. 484) stated, "Environmental terrorism should be reserved for incidents in which the environment itself is disrupted or threatened by the perpetrator as a symbol that elicits trepidation in the larger population over the ecological consequences of the act." By raising awareness and strengthening current antiterrorism policies, acts of terrorism can be more difficult to carry out, possibly dissuading attacks against the environment. The people of the world share the same environment and they must take a stand in defending it. It is the primary concern of this chapter to explain environmental terrorism and its effects on nature, nations, people, and economies using the Kuwaiti illustration while addressing mitigation strategies that can be used to avert disaster in the United States and in other parts of the world.

Environmental Terrorism as an Act against Nature

Environmental terrorism not only damages nature but also holds it hostage to be used against the rest of the world. Damage to the environment not only affects those in the immediate vicinity; the environment is part of the balance of the world and if it is damaged in any way, the rest of the world is affected. The destruction of Kuwait's oil fields caused people and wildlife to suffer. Kellner (1992) stated

> ... reports described the plumes of black acrid smoke filled with sulfur that made day look like night and made it hard to breath in some places in Kuwait and Saudi Arabia. The pollution was already producing acid rain throughout the area, with smoke rising to 10,000 feet, but the real danger would appear if the smoke rose to 30,000 feet, where it could hit the jet stream and travel around the earth.

Did Hussein know the damage he would inflict by ordering the ignition of more than 700 oil fields? Was he aware of the health issues and the corruption of the environment that would ensue? "Although there are some analysts that suspect this attack had some military strategic value, such as using the smoke from the fires as cover from allied bombers, the Allies claim this was not the case" (Schwartz 1998, p. 491). Hussein's intention was to take control of the oil in Kuwait and hoard it for himself. By threatening to ignite the oil fields if he was challenged, Hussein made a statement to the world meant to show he was willing and able to devastate the precious oil supply and disrupt the ecological balance of a region, if challenged.

This disregard for the environment is not new and can be seen throughout history. Even in ancient times, destruction of the environment was observed during times of war. Up until the time of the Mongol invasion, Baghdad was one of the cultural centers of the world, supported by an irrigation complex thousands of years old. The Mongols destroyed the canals and the natural environment and depopulated the country so thoroughly that the canals were never restored (Dutch, 2006). The division between warfare strategy and terrorism is that warfare strategy does not involve attacking civilians and destroying the environment. Environmental terrorism seeks to destroy the environment and natural resources and render them useless to the people.

Although environmental terrorism is a more recent term because of natural resources that were not available in those ancient times, the destruction of the environment beyond that of typical warfare is not a new concept. War today consists of massive explosives, chemical, and nuclear weapons. These tools were not available thousands of years ago, so any damage done to the environment had little to no long-term effects. It was when nations developed these strides in military technology and their dependency on natural resources grew that environmental terrorism was born.

Hussein's attack on the environment was not unprecedented. It was the large-scale damage it did, and is still doing, to the environment of Kuwait that has made the attack so significant. "Even now, more than a decade after the First Gulf War, Kuwait is still dealing with the effects of the attack. Roughly 300 lakes and pools of oil cover the landscape of Kuwait, contaminating around 40 million tons of soil" (McClain, 2001, p. 2). Millions of gallons of oil burned daily, and even after the fires were contained and extinguished, oil continued to pour out of the damaged wells, covering the landscape of Kuwait; this damage to the wildlife had many unforeseeable consequences. For example, the group Earthtrust reported that migrating birds often mistake the oil lakes for water. When the birds attempt to land on or near the water, they face an almost certain death as they come into contact with the oil (Kellner, 1992). Birds died by the thousands due to their exposure to these pools of oil and the polluted waters of the Persian Gulf. Additionally, marine life suffered due to the gallons of oil that Iraqi soldiers dumped into the Gulf. "The endangered species of sea turtles were devastated by the pollution caused by the oil in the Gulf.... In 1999, some 400 to 500 tons of fish died in the Gulf, a problem traced to a lack of oxygen in the water and the growth of phytoplanktons" (McClain, 2001, p. 1). The environment of Kuwait was changed in a way that damaged everything and everyone, regardless of their involvement in the war. Although the immediate damage of the fires had been stopped months after the oil was ignited, the environment had been reshaped in a way that would take years to fully recover.

The importance of oil as a natural resource made it an obvious target for Hussein, and with that opportunity he was able to cause immense damage to Kuwait. Oil is a vital from of energy, thus governments are quick to obtain as much of it as possible, either through trade or through military action, such as those seen by Iraq in the First Gulf War. Chalecki (2001 p. 12) stated, "Sites involving non-renewable resources with high economic value make attractive targets for violence of every kind." Because of their scarcity, natural resources are attractive targets for terrorists. Oil is not abundant in all parts of the world so many countries must depend on trade to obtain oil. Because the goal of terrorism is to broadcast a symbolic message to a larger audience, terrorists try to disrupt this trade to gain the attention of a particular nation or the entire world. By destroying the natural resources that the world depends on, terrorists make their message and demands known. Terrorists realize the severe damage these attacks create and the fear they inspire; however, in some cases the damage can be irreparable.

Terrorists manipulate the environment without regard for the damage their actions cause. With modern weaponry and the emergence of fossil fuels, the destruction of the environment is on a much grander scale than it was in the past. The Kuwaiti oil fires had an effect on the environment that will be experienced for another decade. To respond to this, nations adjusted their policies to counter or prevent such terrorist actions, sometimes even at the expense of civil liberties. The preservation of natural resources is of utmost importance to nations, thus it is an appealing target for terrorists because it offers them yet another target to use to shake the foundations of their target audiences.

Environmental Terrorism against Nations

Nations are forced to change their policies when terrorists strike. Environmental terrorists seek to disrupt the environment to provoke a change or a response on a national level. With a dependency on natural resources and the environment, some nations are forced to yield to the terrorists who destroy the environment, keeping the government and its citizens in a constant state of fear. In response to this, nations must change and create new policies to deter terrorism in the future. In reference to the nation's response, the exact target of the attack is irrelevant. It is the attack itself that forces a nation to create new policies to deter future attacks and, in the case of environmental terrorism, to protect natural resources. These policies vary depending on the type of government indicative to each nation. Each nation has its own obstacles in developing policies regarding environmental terrorism.

Civil liberties are more important in democratic governments than in others, so when creating policies to deter future terrorist attacks, democratic governments must be careful not to sacrifice the civil liberties given to its people.

The need to deter terrorism spawns many different reactions depending on the government in power. For some countries, a complete restriction on the people might be the best course of action and would have little opposition. In the United States, however, the need to prevent and respond to terrorism causes the sacrifice of many civil liberties, most notably the constitutional right to free speech. "In times of crises, statements of defiance may no longer be a constitutionally guaranteed right" (Miller and Rivera, 2007). In an effort to curb terrorism, organized groups that may speak out against the policies set forth by the government are suddenly associated with and labeled as terrorist groups. As the United States wrestled with a newer, more accurate definition of terrorism laws such as the Patriot Act and the Anti-Terrorism Act of 2001, they were more capable of pursuing terrorists. "Specifically the Anti-Terrorism Act of 2001 placed the same penalties on those individuals that attempt or conspire to commit the newer definitions of terrorism. These newer definitions expand the number of people and groups now being labeled and prosecuted as terrorists" (Miller and Rivera, 2007). What was once considered free speech could now be considered a crime. The first amendment is being reworded for the sake of security and protection from terrorists.

After an attack in which a natural resource is damaged, a nation's population and its government are filled with tension and caution. Fear is attributed to the nation's reliance on the natural resource and the government's realization that the damage could be irreparable. "As resources become depleted, prices collapse, or corruption-weary businesses leave, and the legitimacy and capacity of local rulers are further eroded" (Le Billon, 2005, p. 7). Environmental destruction garners the attention of an entire nation and sometimes, in the case of the Kuwaiti oil fires, the attention and concern of the entire world. Terrorists can then state their beliefs and intents to a much wider audience once they have essentially attacked the entire nation. Each nation adapts its policies to this fear in its own way, depending on the government. Each nation has its own obstacles to overcome. Although it is necessary to defend these finite resources that every nation depends on, at what point does a nation go too far in the pursuit of environmental security?

The need for natural resources is a concept that every nation embraces. However, not all natural resources are immediately available so many nations must trade to acquire them. This leads to some nations becoming dependent on trade and they are sometimes taken advantage of because of this dependency. For environmental terrorists, however, this proves to be an enticing opportunity. In a scenario where a nation is dependent on its trade of natural resources with another nation, an environmental attack would be devastating. Should a terrorist attack a facility for this natural resource, not only would the nation exporting it suffer but also the smaller nation that depended on that trade would be devastated as well.

The concept of resource dependency is not new and has been seen throughout history. "Since sea power itself rested on access to timber, naval timber supply became a major preoccupation for major European powers from the seventeenth century onwards" (Le Billon, 2005, p. 3). The importance of natural resources changes with time and with the presence of new natural resources. Just as timber was important for naval strength, oil has become immensely valuable as a source of energy in the twentieth and twenty-first centuries. Because of natural resource dependency, nations place a high priority on the acquisition and maintenance of natural resources. "Of 'strategic' importance to domestic or foreign economic and political concerns, resource access and exploitation can become highly contested issues" (Le Billon, 2005, p. 5). Terrorists take advantage of this dependency and seek to destroy natural resources to gain the attention of these nations. This dependency on natural resources represents vulnerability, which is used to the advantage of terrorists. "As natural resources gain in importance for belligerents . . . the focus of military activities becomes centered on areas of economic significance" (Le Billon, 2005, p. 7). Just as this strategy is adopted in warfare, terrorists view it as a target so their attacks can cause the most damage.

Environmental Terrorism against People

The effect of environmental terrorism on innocent civilians is often overlooked because, unlike other forms of terrorism, civilians are not the victims but rather the casualties. They suffer indirect damage from terrorist attacks on the environment. There are two types of civilian effects, physical and mental. In Kuwait, respiratory problems were a physical effect of the burning oil for not only the soldiers but also the Kuwaiti people. "Breathing, one Kuwaiti described, was 'like taking the exhaust pipe of a diesel truck in your mouth and breathing that'" (McClain, 2001, p. 2). Concerns regarding air quality were not the only dilemma. Once the fires were extinguished, many wells continued to spew oil, creating lakes and rivers of oil. This presented a problem because there was the possibility that the oil could seep through the sand and possibly contaminate the water supply, rendering the groundwater unusable. Fortunately this scenario did not happen, but the fear of the severity of what could have happened still loomed even after Hussein's removal from power as terrorist groups' (such as al-Qaeda) threats emerge.

Moreover, the Kuwaiti people were not the only ones suffering from the smoke from the fires. United States' soldiers stationed during the First Gulf War suffered as well:

> ...270 veterans from the First Gulf War were selected for a survey to analyze their knowledge and preparation for the oil fires. The study showed that troops were generally unaware of the hazards of oil fire exposure. Although they were given measures to combat the threat of chemical/biological weapons, there was no standard operating procedure for the oil fire smoke threat. Other than gas masks the troops were not provided with protective equipment to be used against the smoke and soot that filled the air. (Rostker, 1998)

The U.S. troops felt the effects of the smoke just as the Kuwaiti people did, but they were not properly prepared. The U.S. government had not anticipated the intense oil fires, so it was unable to properly prepare the soldiers for the smoke that covered the landscape. As a result, the soldiers suffered the same effects as the Kuwaiti citizens.

The physical damage that is inflicted on people by an act of environmental terrorist assault is obvious. The psychological and mental impacts of terrorism are not always easily seen. The goal of terrorism is to inspire panic and spread fear throughout the population. After September 11, 2006, American citizens were afraid to fly in airplanes. This widespread fear persists years after the attacks as the threat level is raised and lowered and serves as a constant reminder to remain vigilant against terrorism. Some people elect to stay home or away from the troubled areas where they feel most secure (Starkov, 2001). Disasters inspire a sense of fear, uncertainty, panic, and a sense of "waiting to do something". "Common perception from the media and movies is that when met with disaster people react in a socially disorganized manner, exhibiting panic, shock, and an inability to act. This, however, is not the case" (Perry and Lindell, 2003, pp. 49–50). Additionally, Starkov (2001) contends that the unique mentality and "can do" attitude helped the United States overcome the devastating effects of many natural, political, and economic disasters; such resilience in the aftermath of tragic incidents has had a mobilizing and unifying effect. Such behavior could be seen after September 11, 2006. After the attacks, rather than the city falling into disarray, the people became unified. People helped each other alongside police and firefighters in assisting victims of the World Trade Center buildings when they collapsed. After Saddam Hussein's invasion of Kuwait and the ignition of the oil fields, the coalition forces and the Kuwaiti citizens extinguished the fires and recovered oil that was released into the Persian Gulf. The innocent people of Kuwait suffered the detrimental health effects of the oil fires. They suffered from Hussein's attack and they had no involvement in the First Gulf War. However, the people were not thrown into a state of chaos. The coalition forces pushed the Iraqi soldiers out of Kuwait and took part in the recovery efforts as well. The Kuwaiti people were able to recover from the attack and rebuild. With the goal of terrorism to spread fear and panic in mind, it would seem that, aside from the damage these attacks caused to the environment and the people who were killed, the terrorists failed.

Environmental Terrorism against the Economy

In addition to a loss of resources, environmental terrorism causes a twofold economic effect—paying for cleanup efforts and paying for stronger deterrence. The act of terrorism itself was the cost to the country of Kuwait. "At approximately eleven million barrels a day, Kuwait lost an average of $2,500 a second while the fires burned" (Hawley, 1992, p. 150). Because of these fires, Kuwait lost a vast amount of its supply of oil, the country's main source of income. The money needed later to rebuild the country put Kuwait further into deficit. Although Hussein's true target was not Kuwait itself, the economy was devastated until Kuwait was able to rebuild its petroleum infrastructure.

The cost of repairs and the creation of adequate defenses become a concern after an attack. The costs vary depending on the target. "When greater physical protection is provided for potential targets (target hardening) because of the fear of attacks, costs will increase" (Lutz and Lutz, 2006, p. 3). Oil is such an important resource now and money is needed to increase the security of the petroleum infrastructure. Failure to protect the petroleum infrastructure compromises the political–economic stability of the country and region.

> While the Persian Gulf area has received most attention as a prominent terrain for 'resource wars' due to foreign oil supply interests, tensions and civil unrest in the region also testify in part to the problems of the historical trajectories as well as political economy and governance of resource dependent countries.   (Le Billon, 2005, p. 5)

Kuwait's dependence on oil makes the country an attractive target for environmental terrorism and warfare. However, the goal for a terrorist may not just be Kuwait in general. When Hussein ignited the oil fields, the damage extended beyond that of the systematic destruction of Kuwait's most vital natural resource. Kuwait's economy would obviously suffer but so would the other countries that depend on Kuwait's exportation of oil. "At times adverse economic consequences may be unintentional, but it is also obvious that at least some dissident groups have been quite aware of the potential economic costs of their actions" (Lutz and Lutz, 2006, pp. 2–3).

A wealthy economy is important for a country. Terrorism affects the economy in many different ways. As stated before, the costs of recovery and further deterrence of terrorism rises after an attack, but there is another effect. "Companies operating in the international economy have faced increased costs in their supply chains as a consequence of terrorist attacks, especially September 11 . . ." (Lutz and Lutz, 2006, p. 3). Terrorism can target companies specifically to force them to leave, which means less revenue is being sent to the government. This then frightens away employees from potential opportunities. "Attacks against projects of foreign companies and workers also led to declines in investment by driving away potential investors" (Lutz and Lutz, 2006, p. 7). By driving away potential investors, terrorists are preventing the acquisition of income for the target government. Thus, the government begins to weaken and political stability falls into question. Political stability is important for potential companies and investors and steers economic development.

Environmental terrorism affects the economy because most often vital natural resources are being targeted. "Economic targeting of business interests has been perhaps the most obvious in the case of the oil industry. Disrupting oil flows can also damage the ability of the governments to generate revenue" (Lutz and Lutz, 2006, p. 6). The oil facilities in Kuwait during the first Persian Gulf War were poorly defended and thus were easily taken by Iraqi soldiers. To effectively defend these areas would have required money that Kuwait did not have available. In the recent U.S. occupation of Iraq, there have been reports of terrorist attacks against pipelines and oil fields. The goal is to discourage U.S. involvement and presence in Iraq by attacking a prime source of income for the United States.

> The lack of oil revenue also has increased the cost of maintaining US and other troops in the country, leading to increasing domestic discontent with the continued involvement in that country. The pipeline disruptions along with other types of attacks have also been designed to discourage foreign investment—and foreign involvement—in Iraq. (Lutz and Lutz, 2006, p. 6)

This goal of terrorist groups is effective. Not every country or company could afford the increased costs of security in addition to maintaining their position against terrorists. Even as the United States is able to maintain their position in Iraq, regardless of the increase in costs, as Lutz and Lutz (2006) point out, it leads to discontentment and a lowered opinion of the government on behalf of the civilians.

A strong economy is vital for any country. Once disrupted, countries begin to experience difficulties maintaining their military or, in the case of Kuwait, maintaining a stable exportation of a vital natural resource that not only provides Kuwait with income but also provides fuel for many other countries around the world. "It is clear that terrorists choose targets because of their economic value and the possible costs of disruption have occurred with some regularity" (Lutz and Lutz, 2006, p. 15). Environmental terrorism may not view the disruption of the economy as a primary goal, but it is a side effect that is consistently prevalent in terrorist attacks. Economic disruption is strategically effective for terrorists due to the significant global dependence on financial systems. Protection of global financial institutions and the natural environmental resources that provided the foundation of economic stability is significant. Although full protection from environmental terrorism is extremely difficult to achieve, mitigation and prevention efforts must be put in place to limit the after effects and possibly deter a terrorist attack from occurring.

Environmental Terrorism and Disaster Mitigation

The potential severity of environmental terrorism in reference to national security is extremely significant in relation to other forms of terrorism. As described above, the effects of environmental terrorism have a variety of effects on local and national populations, domestic and international economies, and the overall global availability of scarce natural resources, which makes the mitigation policies dealing with terrorist actions important. Although current disaster mitigation policies mainly attempt to aid localities in disaster mitigation practices and relief in reference to natural and technological disasters (Rivera and Miller, 2006), which are purely accidental in nature, mitigation in reference to disasters caused by terroristic acts is similarly important.

Since the occurrence of Hurricane Katrina and the devastation to the physical, cultural, and political landscapes caused by the storm (Miller and Rivera, 2006), President Bush has attempted to make emergency management and prevention more centralized and militaristic (Office of the Press Secretary, 2005, as cited in Rivera and Miller, 2006). Adhering to a more centralized manner (Schneider, 1990; Schneider, 1992; Rivera and Miller, 2006) of regulation, controlling mitigation and relief efforts, and following a military command style structure of action theoretically has the potential to decrease inefficiencies in response to future disasters. Moreover, the military has had a successful history of protecting the nation's natural resources in the interests of national security (Wheeler, 2006). According to Myers (1993; Wheeler, 2006), protection of the nation's natural resources should fall under the responsibility of the military due to the following reasons:

> security concerns can no longer be confined to traditional ideas of soldiers and tanks, bombs and missiles. Increasingly they include the environmental resources that underpin our material welfare. These

resources include soil, water, forests, and climate, all prime components of a nation's environmental foundations. If these foundations are depleted, the nation's economy will eventually decline, its social fabric will deteriorate, and its political structure will become destabilized (Myers, 1993, as cited in Wheeler, 2006, p. 477).

The potentially detrimental effects of an environmental terrorist attack necessitate clearly guided and efficient manners of response. "The military's hierarchal command structure an aid in streamlining the response".

Even before the passage of Katrina, Congress had passed the Public Health Security and Bioterrorism Preparedness Act of 2002, which delegated the responsibilities of protecting community water systems and the public from international contamination of water supplies to the Environmental Protection Agency (EPA) (Wheeler, 2006; see also 107th Congress, 2002). Although the EPA's policies are implemented on a local level by individual states, the agency's overriding policies are dictated at the federal level, thereby reducing the possibility of variation among environmental standards. Reduction of variations in environmental standards is important because it allows environmental specialists the ability to easily observe abnormal environmental circumstances, allowing responses to environmental contamination to be more time efficient; resulting in lower risk to the public's and environment's health (Wheeler, 2006).

The recent policy responses to environmental terrorism disaster mitigation illustrate the U.S. government's concerns with environmental resource destruction. Although the protection of the nation's environmental resources is a matter of national security, the authors are not proposing that military personnel be assigned to guard all of the country's resources; such a proposal would be impractical from both a personnel and financial perspective. However, an inventory of the nation's environmental resources and their potential risk to terrorist attacks would aid in prioritizing the resources that should be guarded. The potential risk of attack could be evaluated in relation to proximity and direct usage of a resource by a population, the micro- and macroeconomic value of the resource, the resource's possible international usage, the effect a terrorist attack on the resource would have on the broader ecosystem, and the resource's national social worth. By assessing the potential risk in relation to these variables, government officials would be in a better position to prioritize the security of one resource over another. Additionally, deterrence of environmental terrorism may be advanced through the creation of new legislation that expands the definition of terrorism to include damage to the environment (Stuhltrager, 2003) alongside the current definitions of terrorism presented in the Patriot Act and the Anti-Terrorism Act of 2001.

The potential of an environmental terrorist attack in the United States is as conceivable as any other terrorist attack. As explained above, the effects of environmental terrorism reach beyond the short term and, depending on the specific act of terrorism, can have significant long-term effects on economies, entire ecosystems, and social interactions. In the United States, the risk of environmental terrorism is high due the number of unguarded resources, its society's significant economic dependency on natural resources, and the nation's largely porous national borders. Although a high level of risk may be associated with the possibility of an environmental terrorist attack, this does not necessarily mean an attack will occur; however, without mitigation strategies in place in the event of an attack, relief and cleanup efforts will be more complicated than necessary.

References

107th Congress. 2002. *Public Health Security and Bioterrorism Preparedness and Response Act of 2002: Public Law 107–188.* Retrieved November, 25, 2006, from http://frwebgate.access.gpo.gov/cgi-bin/getdoc.cgi?dbname=107_cong_public_laws&docid=f:publ188.107.pdf.

Chalecki, E.L. 2001. *A New Vigilance: Identifying and Reducing the Risks of Environmental Terrorism.* Retrieved October 5, 2006, from http://www.pacinst.org/reports/environment_and_terrorism/environmental_terrorism_final.pdf.

Dutch, S. 2006. *Military Impacts on the Environment.* Retrieved October 19, 2006, from http://www.uwgb.edu/dutchs/EnvirGeol/Military.HTM.

Gibbs, J.P. 1989. Conceptualization of terrorism. *American Sociological Review,* 54(3), 329–340.

Hawley, T.M. 1992. *Against the Fires of Hell: The Environmental Disaster of the Gulf War.* Orlando, Florida: Harcourt.

Kellner, D. 1992. *The Persian Gulf TV War.* Retrieved September 21, 2006, from http://pnews.org/PhpWiki/index.php/EcoTerrorism.

Le Billon, P. 2005. *Geopolitics of Resource Wars: Resource Dependence, Governance and Violence.* London: Frank Cass.

Lutz, J.M. and Lutz, B.J. 2006. Terrorism as economic warfare. *Global Economy Journal,* 6(2), Article 2.

McClain, H.M. 2001. *Environmental Impact: Oil fires and Spills Leave Hazardous Legacy.* Retrieved September 14, 2006, from http://www.cnn.com/SPECIALS/2001/gulf.war/legacy/environment.

Miller, D.S. and Rivera, J.D. (2006). Reconfigured landscapes and Placescapes in the wake of natural disasters: The Indian Ocean; The Great Hanshin Earthquake of Kobe, Japan; and Hurricane Katrina. The 2nd Annual Conference of the International Association for the Study of Environment, Space and Place. (April 28–30, 2006). Towson, Maryland.

Miller, D.S. and Rivera, J.D. (2007). Political expression: Radical environmental groups or eco-terrorists. *Journal for the Study of Radicalism.*

Myers, N. 1993. *Ultimate Security: The Environmental Basis of Political Stability.* New York: W.W. Norton.

Office of the Press Secretary. 2005. *President Discusses Hurricane Relief in Address to the Nation.* Retrieved November 26, 2006, from http://www.whitehouse.gov/news/releases/2005/09/20050915-8.html.

Perry, R.W. and Lindell, M.K. 2003. Understanding citizen response to disasters with implications for terrorism. *Journal of Contingencies and Crisis Management,* 11:49–61.

Rivera, J.D. and Miller, D.S. 2006. A brief history of the evolution of United States' natural disaster policy. *Journal of Public Management and Social Policy,* 12(1), 5–14.

Rostker, B. 1998. *Environmental Exposure Report: Oil Well Fires.* Retrieved November 9, 2006, from http://www.gulflink.osd.mil/oil_well_fires/.

Schwartz, D.M. 1998. Environmental terrorism: Analyzing the concept. *Journal of Peace Research,* 35(4), 483–496.

Schneider, S.K. 1990. FEMA, Federalism, Hugo and Frisco. *Publius: The Journal of Federalism,* 20, 97–116.

Schneider, S.K. 1992. Governmental response to disasters: The conflict between bureaucratic procedures and emergent norms. *Public Administration Review,* 52(2), 135–145.

Starkov, M. 2001. *Terrorism: Impact on Travel and Hospitality.* Retrieved November 9, 2006, from http://www.m-travel.com/news/2001/09/terrorism_impac.html.

Stuhltrager, J.M. 2003. Combating Terrorism in the Environmental Trenches: Responding to Terrorism: Oil Pollution and Environmental Terrorism—An Overview of the Potential Legal Response in the United States. Widener Law Symposium.

Waugh, W.L., Jr. 1990. *Terrorism and Emergency Management: Policy and Administration.* New York: M. Dekker.

Wheeler, K.D. 2006. Homeland security and environmental regulation: Balancing long-term environmental goals with immediate security needs. *Washburn Law Journal,* 45(2), 437–466.

Chapter 11

Pandemics and Biological/Chemical Terrorism Attacks: A New Role for Disaster Mental Health

Thom Curtis

CONTENTS

The threat of an avian influenza pandemic has forced the healthcare system of the United States to reexamine its capability to respond to a sudden, overwhelming demand for services. Researchers have been consistent in their conclusions that most American medical systems do not have sufficient resources to adequately meet the surge in demand expected in the event of a pandemic or bioterrorism attack (AHRQ, 2004 & AHRQ, 2005).

Billions of dollars have been spent preparing for such events in the six years since the attacks of September 11, 2001, and the mailing of letters containing anthrax to politicians and media outlets in Florida, New York, and Washington, DC (Lurie et al., 2004). The Center for Biosecurity at the University of Pittsburgh reported that even with these increased benefits, "hospitals' capacity to absorb an unexpected surge of patients from an attack— or epidemic—has not improved because relatively little money has been spent on that aspect (Mackenzie, 2006, p. 21)."

It is expected that announcement of a pandemic disease or a bioterror attack will overwhelm the health systems' ability to respond to the crush of people seeking medical aid. There are approximately 5,756 hospitals in the United States. Together, they have about 946,997 beds available. On an average day, over two-thirds of those beds are occupied (American Hospital Association, 2005). Epidemiologists predict that during a pandemic outbreak of avian influenza, as many as 5.8 million Americans will require hospitalization. Although the disease is expected to hit in waves and not all those infected will require hospitalization at the same time, one does not need complex mathematics to recognize that there will not be sufficient additional beds in the system to meet even a fraction of the increased demand.

To further compound this problem, previous experience with similar events indicates that those who are truly ill or have been exposed will be greatly outnumbered by multitudes of fearful, unexposed citizens who will unnecessarily seek treatment. A major roadblock to a successful response to either emergency is a lack of trained professionals to deal with the numbers attempting to access medical services unnecessarily.

This chapter describes the prospects of overwhelming demand for services and a proposal that mental health professionals can be cross-trained to assist medical professionals in some phases of the emergency response.

Surge Capacity

The Agency for Healthcare Research and Quality (AHRQ) of the U.S. Department of Health and Human Services (2006) defined surge capacity as "a health care system's ability to expand quickly beyond normal services to meet an increased demand for medical care in the event of bioterrorism or other large-scale public health emergencies (p. 1)." The Nevada Health Association (2006) added detail to the definition:

Hospital surge capacity refers to the ability of a health care system to provide appropriate medical care and treatment for a markedly increased volume of patients based on the situation. This term "capacity" is a metric that specifically measures the volume of patients that can be accommodated, and is not a metric that measures the quality of service, patient care services or medical capabilities (p. 5).

Hospital facilities in the United States have most of their facilities in use most of the time. There are not lots of empty hospital beds or unused emergency capacity anywhere in the country. It will be difficult to suddenly produce additional beds, equipment, or staff if there is a widespread emergency that pushes the system's capacity with sick and dying patients. Tommy Thompson, former secretary of the U.S. Department of Health and Human Services, described one aspect of surge capacity. "The just-in-time economy is really the enemy for getting prepared for a pandemic. We have 100,000 ventilators, and 85,000 are in use daily. What happens if we have a pandemic? You don't just call someone and say deliver another 50,000 (Seeman, 2005)."

A 2004 study (Lurie et al., 2004) of seven healthcare regions in California representing about 39 percent of the state's population, found that only "one jurisdiction had comprehensively assessed surge capacity" and "one jurisdiction had well-developed plans to handle the worried-well" (p. 40). This and other studies indicate that while surge capacity and problems dealing with the worried-well are recognized at a theoretical level, there is still a considerable shortfall in meeting those needs.

The federal government has recognized that the lack of surge capacity is not isolated to California. The Health Resources and Services Administration (HRSA) of the U.S. Department of Health and Human Services (DHHS) is responsible for assisting healthcare systems across the country to prepare for emergencies such as bioterrorism attacks or pandemics. HRSA has taken the lead along with the Center for Disease Control (CDC) in recognizing and defining the need for surge capacity throughout the United States.

Following most natural disasters and terror attacks, impacted communities can expect help from outside the impact area. Depending on the size and type of the catastrophe, help and additional medical resources may take a while to arrive. However, impacted communities can rely on the fact that outside help will eventually come. Woodson (2006b) points out that when an influenza pandemic strikes, the problems of surge capacity will be aggravated by the likelihood that infectious outbreaks will affect many different locations simultaneously. There may not be any outside help available.

A further surge capacity variable contemplated by many emergency planners concerns willingness of healthcare workers to report to work during a pandemic or bioterror incident. Surveys have shown that a portion of workers will not report because of fears of becoming infected themselves or they will be unwilling to take the risk of spreading the infection to their families.

Worried-Well

Research indicates that the surge capacity of health systems will be tested not only by those who are in genuine need of medical treatment during such an event but also by multitudes of worried-well who will be present with or without symptoms at medical facilities. Numerous research papers have been published in medical journals over the past decade addressing the need for healthcare facilities to prepare for surges of demand during catastrophic situations.

During the morning rush hour on March 20, 1995, the Japanese religious sect Aum Shinrikyo released the deadly nerve agent, sarin gas, on five Tokyo commuter trains. Twelve commuters died from exposure to the gas, 54 were seriously injured, and about 980 others were sufficiently exposed to require medical attention. Civil defense and emergency medical professionals around the world have learned many lessons from these attacks and their aftermath.* Among the most significant was that 5500 people rushed to hospitals for treatment. For every one person who was exposed to the gas and required medical attention, four nonexposed citizens arrived at medical facilities and expected treatment. The difficulty sorting out the ill from the simply panicked delayed medical treatment for those who really needed it (Olson, 1999; Beaton et al., 2005; Taneda, 2005).

Similar patterns have been noted following virtually every incident in which some portion of the public has been exposed to toxic or infectious agents (either natural or human induced). The number of people believing they have been exposed and seeking treatment far surpasses those actually at risk. The flood of worried-well overwhelms the ability of the healthcare system to determine who is sick or may have been exposed and would benefit from immediate treatment.

In 2003, hospitals in Toronto, Ontario, Canada, were swarmed by people fearing exposure to the severe acute respiratory syndrome (SARS) virus. Final analysis indicated there were only 438 confirmed cases of SARS in Toronto resulting in 44 deaths. Hospital facilities were barraged by people seeking medical assistance who had not been exposed to someone with an infection. Coming to a hospital that was treating actual SARS patients exposed them to the risk of contacting the

---

* In addition to recognition of the worried-well phenomenon, civil defense and medical professionals took note of public communication difficulties, operational logistics problems such as transportation and surge capacity, and secondary exposure risks of emergency responders and hospital personnel. See Beaton et al. (2005) for details of lessons learned from the Tokyo sarin gas attacks.

disease. It was decided to resort to a telephone hotline system, which handled approximately 300,000 calls during a four month period from March to June 2003 (Bogdan, 2004).

The SARS virus was spread to Canada by people traveling from infected regions of Asia. Hospitals throughout Asia experienced the same panic as those in Toronto. A hotline was established in Taipei, Taiwan, to screen people who feared they were infected. Using body temperatures and other selected symptoms, it was determined that less than 1 percent of those who thought they had SARS exhibited actual symptoms and needed to be further screened by medical professionals (Kaydos-Daniels et al., 2004).

Evans et al. (2002) pointed out that these worried-well consume limited resources and interfere with access to needed assistance by critically-ill patients who were exposed. A number of different plans have been proposed to enable medical facilities to deal with the rush of patients expected. Some of these plans include protocols for determining appropriate treatment for each patient depending on their exposure to the infectious agent or symptoms that are observed. These triage protocols provide excellent outlines for handling each case. The shortcoming recognized in many plans is the lack of trained personnel to both triage the masses of sick or worried-well and at the same time provide the necessary intensive treatment required by those who can be saved.

As healthcare facilities mobilize to meet the medical needs of individuals who have been injured or infected by the event, they will be overwhelmed by a rush of individuals who have heard about the catastrophe and believe that they are also in need of medical attention. Some will present with physical symptoms similar to those of actual victims as described in the media even though they were not someplace impacted by the event. Others who were not in the impact area present with various stress-related symptoms or no symptoms at all, but express fear of exposure and the desire for propylactic treatment just in case they might have been infected.

Under most existing systems, the professionals who are responsible for sorting the genuinely afflicted from those who are experiencing anxiety or nonevent-related symptoms are the same people who are needed to provide desperately needed treatment to the ill or injured. The entire system faces gridlock as the number of people requiring emergency treatment approaches the medical facility's capacity and new casualties continue to arrive mixed among throngs of the worried-well.

To effectively assist in the triage effort, mental health professionals need to understand the worried-well phenomenon. In a publication for military commanders, Fran Pilch (2003) divides the worried-well into three categories:

> The first are those who experience symptoms of the disease in question, or generalized symptoms, but who do not have the disease. These

individuals may not have been exposed in any real way, and yet they are genuinely convinced that they are ill. This group would include those who experience physiological symptoms as a consequence of heightened fear, alertness, or feelings of helplessness. The second group consists of those who are anxious about potentially being or becoming infected, but are not experiencing physical symptoms. In these cases, there may or may not be a rational basis for their anxiety. These may seek health care partly as a preventive measure or due to their uncertainty as to risk. The third category consists of those who experience psychological distress during or after a traumatic event, such as chronic anxiety, depression, fatigue, and despair. These categories may overlap, but all represent unique problems that must be addressed in planning undertaken by disaster response teams and health facilities (p. 8).

Disaster Mental Health Responsibilities

Many protocols for dealing with bioterrorism and pandemics recognize that mental health (sometimes referred to as behavioral health) professionals have an important role to play. Unfortunately, most of those plans do not go far beyond recognizing the roles and some of the tasks of mental health workers but fail to provide much detail regarding their training or treatment protocols.

In its 2004 National Bioterrorism Hospital Preparedness Program, the HRSA outlines ten critical benchmarks for surge capacity preparation: beds, isolation capacity, healthcare personnel, pharmaceutical caches, personal protective equipment, behavioral health, advanced registration, trauma and burn care, communication and information technology, and decontamination.

Advanced registration is defined as a plan to identify volunteers in the community who will be available to reinforce the existing medical staff during a surge in demand. It states, "Initial efforts should be directed toward identification of volunteer Physicians, Registered Nurses and Behavioral Health Professionals (including social workers, psychologists, psychiatrists, and therapists)." (Health Resources and Services Administration, 2004, p. 14.)

The national hospital preparedness program's surge capacity benchmark for behavioral health stipulates that the following points should be included in every plan:

> Enhance the networking capacity and training of healthcare professionals to be able to recognize, treat and coordinate care related to the behavioral health consequences of bioterrorism or other public health emergencies.

...develop behavioral health components of hospital preparedness plans that are integrated with other existing emergency behavioral health plans developed by the state behavioral health authority. These plans should include the following issues:

- Behavioral health issues related to quarantine
- Behavioral health issues related to evacuation
- Addressing anxiety among patients and families
- Addressing need of patients with medically-unexplained physical symptoms
- Family support in hospital settings
- Death notification
- Risk communication in coordination with public health authorities to educate the public on potential risks and whether they should report to hospitals (Health Resources and Services Administration, 2004, p. 21)

Triage

Any time conditions exist that cause more people to seek medical assistance than is available, choices must be made regarding who will receive treatment and who will have to wait. This is true when the first paramedics arrive at a multi-injury motor vehicle accident and on busy weekend evenings in emergency rooms. Medical personnel sort, screen, and prioritize patients based on who is in greatest need. This selection process is called triage. In cases of mass casualties when there are limited resources, it is sometimes necessary to also include survivability into the triage equation. Difficult decisions must sometimes be made to allocate resources to those who are most likely to survive at the expense of those who are least likely.

Woodson (2006a) describes protocols for medical triage during pandemic influenza outbreaks that are adaptable to some types of bioterrorism agents as well. He uses the 1918 worldwide Spanish flu pandemic as a model for what can be expected if the H5N1 Avian Influenza or bird flu mutates so that it is easily transmitted from one human to another. As with most triage plans, he starts with the assumption that individuals presenting at hospitals have actually contracted the disease and describes procedures for treatment depending on the seriousness of the symptoms or likelihood of the patient's recovery.

Frederick "Skip" Burkle is the director of the Asia-Pacific Center for Biosecurity, Disaster and Conflict Research at the University of Hawaii John Burns Medical School. He has written extensively about medical triage following disasters and recommended specific protocols, which clinicians should use to make treatment decisions following bioterror attacks or during pandemics (Burkle, 2002, 2003, 2006). He recognized that a significant resource consuming aspect of triage is dealing with the worried-well.

Perhaps most difficulty will come in distinguishing those individuals actually exposed from those individuals potentially exposed, psychologically impaired casualties, individuals with multiple unexplained physical symptoms (MUPS), and those simply susceptible but concerned that they might have been exposed. This subgroup may well make up most of those seeking care. Triage personnel not accustomed to managing people with anxiety may under-triage these victims as "worried well." System planning must provide predesignated programs for evaluation, education, and reassurance; emotional support can occur separate from but close to any health facility, to ensure ready access, availability, and compliance (p. 424).

Disaster Mental Health Role

When exposed to traumatic or catastrophic events, people exhibit a wide range of emotional responses. Most people have an inherent natural resilience and develop useful mechanisms to cope with the stresses that accompany such experiences. Mental health professionals have observed and studied these reactions. A number of modalities (some controversial) have been developed to assist people who struggle to deal with emotional stresses in the wake of catastrophes.

Most of these interventions propose to offer psychological first aid to victims of disasters or other traumatic stress. Together, the various paradigms fall into a practice field called disaster mental health. Some disaster mental health interventions are provided informally by peers in workplace environments and some more closely resemble formal psychotherapy sessions. Although many of those who provide disaster mental health services in the wake of disasters are licensed professional psychiatrists, psychologists, marriage and family therapists, counselors, social workers, or psychiatric nurses, the services may often more accurately be described as psychoeducational rather than psychotherapeutic.

The purpose of this chapter is not to compare or contrast various paradigms of disaster mental health. Instead, it proposes that the professionals who provide these services are a potential reservoir of talent that should be accessed by the medical community to expand its surge capacity in the event of a bioterrorism attack or pandemic.

The Role of DMH in Pandemic and Bioterrorism Responses

Although public health publications repeatedly recognize the potential for including behavioral health professionals in both hospital and regional response plans to pandemics or bioterrorism, there are few suggestions provided on how these suggestions can be implemented.

Even though the role to be played by disaster mental health specialists is not always clear, researchers have recognized that too few are available to meet the potential needs. The working group on Governance Dilemmas in Bioterrorism Attacks found "few trained disaster mental health professionals, a weak infrastructure for implementing broad mental health protections, little knowledge on effective treatment, and scarce funds for long-term mental health care inhibit U.S. response to terrorism's psychological effects." Butler et al. (2003) detail the need for greater disaster mental health capacity for the public health system to appropriately respond to terrorism.

Disaster mental health professionals are an obvious choice to assist family members of the ill or infected to deal with the stresses of their situations. They can also play a valuable role by assisting emergency services and medical facility employees deal with the emotional challenges presented when these staff members work in an infectious environment while worrying about their own loved ones being at risk of infection.

In recent workshops, Frederick "Skip" Burkle has described how disaster mental health professionals are uniquely qualified to assist the medical community meet the threat of insufficient surge capacity presented by either a pandemic or bioterrorism attack. First, they have professional backgrounds in making differential psychiatric diagnoses that with proper training is transferable to the certain tasks required of a medical triage team. They understand the purposes and processes of diagnosis. His proposal in no way suggests that social workers, psychologists, or marriage and family therapists without medical degrees are to be expected to make medical diagnoses and determine who is ill and who is not. It does propose that these mental health professionals can be trained to assist with non-symptom-related triage activities such as determining whether the individual was likely to have been exposed to the disease or infective agent.

Second, disaster mental health professionals have the professional training to help those who are not symptomatic and not likely to have been exposed deal with the anxiety they are experiencing. They should be equipped with communication skills that will allow them to redirect the worried-well away from medical facilities and provide salient information on how individuals can further protect themselves from exposure or obtain available prophylactic treatment.

In Hawaii and elsewhere, Burkle has conducted workshops to teach mental health professionals basic triage skills, which will enable them to work with and support the existing health services during a pandemic or following a bioterrorism attack. The multiday seminars provide details of the medical, social, and psychological impacts of such events and define ways in which mental health professionals can relieve some of the duties that would otherwise need to be carried out by medical staff. He does not propose that counselors or social workers will make medical diagnoses. Rather, their primary role would be to provide information to individuals regarding the likelihood that they have been infected, symptoms they should watch for and ways they can protect themselves from infection.

The mental health professionals would work in a number of different environments including hospitals, telephone hotlines, and triage centers. Their primary focus would be on relieving medical professionals from the responsibility of dealing with the worried-well.

Burkle recognizes that there is a great deal of work that must be done to clearly establish ways to organize, train, and supervise these efforts. In some areas, local chapters of the American Red Cross have taken the lead in organizing training classes and bringing together representatives of the many different organizations and agencies that will need to work together during a pandemic or following a bioterrorism attack.

One concern voiced by several experienced disaster mental health workers regards liability insurance. Medical triage probably does not fall into the generally recognized scope of practice for most mental health professionals. Some have expressed reluctance to become involved in a program such as this unless there is an umbrella sponsoring agency that can offer liability coverage similar to that offered by the American Red Cross to disaster mental health volunteers.

Conclusion

The American healthcare system does not have sufficient surge capacity to deal with a major pandemic or bioterrorism attack. Although there is a general philosophical recognition of those deficiencies, the task of building a system that will be able to respond is overwhelming. This chapter proposes one possibility for adding additional capacity that may be able to help deal with the panic and crush of the worried-well during one of these eventualities.

Until all of the players in the response system and the citizens for whom they are responsible recognize the dire straits in which they will find themselves during one of the events described in this chapter, there is little hope that the significant resources required to prepare a response will be forthcoming. If such a preparation is postponed for long, a catastrophe that could eclipse the unnecessary consequences of September 11 and Hurricane Katrina may result.

References

Agency for Healthcare Research and Quality (AHRQ). 2004. Optimizing Surge Capacity: Hospital Assessment and Planning. Washington, DC: U.S. Department of Health and Human Services, Public Health Service. Last accessed October 22, 2006: http://www. ahrq.gov/news/ulp/btbriefs/btbrief3.pdf.

Agency for Healthcare Research and Quality (AHRQ). 2006. Addressing Surge Capacity in a Mass Casualty Event Issue Brief #9. Washington, DC: U.S. Department of Health and Human Services, Public Health Service. Last accessed November 2, 2006: http://www.ahrq.gov/news/ulp/btbriefs/btbrief9.pdf.

American Hospital Association. 2005. Fast Facts on US Hospitals. Last accessed October 22, 2006: http://www.aha.org/aha/resource-center/Statistics-and-Studies/fast-facts.html.

Beaton, R., Stergachis, A., Oberle, M., Bridges, E., Nemuth, M., and Thomas, T. 2005. The sarin gas attacks of the Tokyo subway—10 years later/Lessons learned. *Traumatology*, 11 (2), pp. 103–119.

Bogdan, G.M. 2004. Addressing Surge Capacity through Information Exchange. Research Presentation at Colorado's Health Emergency Line for the Public Web Conference. Last accessed October 22, 2006: http://www.ahrq.gov/news/ulp/btsurgemass/bogdantxt.htm.

Burkle, F.M. 2002. Mass casualty management of a large-scale bioterrorist event: An epidemiological approach that shapes triage decisions. *Emergency Medical Clinics of North America*, 20, 409–436.

Burkle, F.M. 2003. Measures of effectiveness in large-scale bioterrorism events. *Prehospital and Disaster Medicine*, 18 (3), 258–262.

Burkle, F.M. 2006. Population-based triage management in response to surge-capacity requirements during a large-scale bioevent disaster. *Academic Emergency Medicine*, 13(11): 1118–1129.

Butler, A.S., Panzer, A.M., and Goldfrank, L.R. 2003. *Preparing for the Psychological Consequences of Terrorism: A Public Health Strategy.* Washington, DC: Institutes of Medicine.

Evans, R.G., Crutcher, J.M., Shadel, B., Clements, B., and Bnonze, M.S. Terrorism from a public health perspective. *Am. J. Med. Sci.* 2002. 323(6): 291–298.

Health Resources and Services Administration. 2004. National Bioterrorism Hospital Preparedness Program. Washington, DC: U.S. Department of Health and Human Services. Last accessed October 22, 2006: http://www.dhs.ca.gov/epo/PDF/HRSAbhppguidance.pdf.

Inglesby, T.V., Nuzzo, J.B., O'Toole, T., and Henderson, D.A. 2006. Disease mitigation measures in the control of pandemic influenza. *Biosecurity and Bioterrorism: Biodefense Strategy, Practice and Science*, 4 (4): 366–375.

Kaydos-Daniels, S.C., Olowokure, B., Chang, H., Barwick, R.S., Deng, J., Lee, M., Kuo, S.H., Su, I., Chen, K., and Maloney, S.A. 2004. Body temperature monitoring and SARS fever hotline, Taiwan. *Emerging Infectious Diseases*, 10 (2), 373–376. Last accessed October 22, 2006: http://www.cdc.gov/ncidod/Eid/vol10no2/pdfs/03-0748.pdf.

Lurie, N., Valdez, R.B., Wasserman, J., Stoto, M., Myers, S., Molander, R., Asch, S., Mussington, B.D., and Solomon, M. 2004. *Public Health Preparedness in California: Lessons Learned from Seven Health Jurisdictions.* Santa Monica, California: The RAND Corporation. Last accessed October 22, 2006: http://www.rand.org/pubs/technical_reports/2005/RAND_TR181.pdf.

Mackenzie, D. 2006. Biodefense special: Fortress America? *New Scientist.* Last accessed September 25, 2007: http://www.newscientist.com/channel/opinion/mg19225725.000-bio defence-special-fortress-america-html.

Nevada Health Association. 2006. Disaster Medical Response: A Model for America. Last accessed November 2, 2006: http://www.nvha.net/bio/postings/2006surgecapq1.pdf.

Olson, K.B. 1999. Aum Shinrikyo: Once and future threat? *Emerging and Infectious Diseases,* 5 (4), 513–516.

Pilch, F. 2003. The Worried Well: Strategies for Installation Commanders. Colorado Springs, Colorado: United States Air Force Academy. Last accessed October 22, 2006: www.usafa.af.mil/inss/OCP/OCP53.pdf.

Seeman, B.T. July 20, 2005. U.S. Ill-prepared for flu pandemic, experts fear. *Newhouse News Service*. Last accessed October 22, 2006 http://www.newhousenews.com/archive/seeman072005.html.

Taneda, K. 2005. The sarin gas attack on the Tokyo subway: Hospital responses to mass casualties and psychological issues in hospital planning. *Traumatology*, 11 (2), 75–85.

Woodson, G. 2006a. Patient triage during a pandemic. *The Bird Flu Manual.com*. Last accessed November 2, 2006: http://www.birdflumanual.com/articles/patTriage.asp.

Woodson, G. 2006b. Pandemic disruption of essential services and supplies. *The Bird Flu Manual.com*. Last accessed November 2, 2006: http://www.birdflumanual.com/articles/panDisrupt.asp.

Chapter 12

Terrorism as Societal Conflict Resulting in Response

John M. House

CONTENTS

Introduction

Terrorism is not a new phenomenon; however, the attacks on September 11, 2001, have resulted in a "new normal" for the United States in the world today. American citizens are not free of the threat of terrorism whether at home or abroad. The complexity of the threat calls for simultaneous development of strategies to safeguard citizens and to defeat terrorists. This chapter briefly describes definitions, the changing nature of terrorism, religious-based terrorism, and responses that may be used to counter terrorism.

Terrorism Definitions

Many authors have provided definitions of terrorism. Elements of each definition may vary, but a political element and violence are generally present. A person's opinion of terrorism also is affected by their opinion of the cause behind the act. The level of violence and motivation for terrorist acts has changed over time. Hoffman (2004) wrote that terrorism is a political act associated with the desire for power. Terrorism is the use of violence or the threat of violence to achieve a political objective. Hoffman considered terrorism to be a "planned, calculated, and indeed systematic act" (p. 4).

Terrorism today is difficult to define because people tend to use the term differently depending on their perspective. Some authors refer to terrorists as freedom fighters due to their revolutionary viewpoint although others view terrorists as criminals. Terrorists generally do not refer to themselves as terrorists. The underlying causes of unrest in a country may result in the belief that violence is the only means to gain attention for a cause or oppose an oppressive regime (Hoffman, 2004, pp. 13–15).

Terrorism has a political aim, is violent, is designed to have far-reaching psychological repercussions beyond the immediate victim or target, is conducted by an organized group, and is the work of a nonstate organization. Therefore, terrorism is the deliberate creation and exploitation of fear through violence or the threat of violence in the pursuit of political change. Terrorism attempts to enhance the power of a group when that group currently has little or no power (Hoffman, 2004, p. 23). Pillar (2004) highlighted that terrorism is always a premeditated act and politically motivated. The targets of terrorisms are noncombatants, and terrorists typically are members of subnational groups or are clandestine agents. The threat of violence can be an act of terrorism as well. Pillar characterized terrorism as a method of action rather than a group of people (pp. 25, 28).

Terrorism has changed over time as political issues have given way in some instances to religious views. Even criminal acts and revenge have motivated violence that is sometimes considered terrorism. The threat of weapons of mass destruction and the beginning of cyber attacks are elements of the terrorists' arsenal today (Maniscalco and Christen, 2002).

Terrorism's Changing Nature

Terrorism is not a concern of any single nation. Its effects are felt globally and must be addressed by the international community. The development of information technologies and the rise of Muslim extremism as espoused by Osama bin Laden have fueled effectiveness and the global reach of terrorism organizations. Terrorism has changed from a description of government abuse of its citizens to that of a protest against a government or society. During the French Revolution, terrorism was a deliberate act by the revolutionary government designed to produce a better society. However, the collapse of the revolution resulted in the evolution of the term's meaning to that of an abuse of power (Hoffman, 2004, p. 5). In the twentieth century, terrorism came to be associated with revolutionary movements. The rise of Fascism, Nazism, and Stalin's repression in Russia again resulted in terrorism being associated with a government abusing its citizenry. Revolutions after World War II again resulted in terrorism being used in a revolutionary sense (Hoffman, 2004, pp. 6–11). Terrorism has become more lethal in recent years. The threat of an attack using weapons of mass destruction has risen a great deal. However, the actual impact of such an attack using chemical, biological, radiological, or nuclear (CBRN) weapons would be more psychological than physical. The fear of CBRN attacks may result in governments focusing on defense to such a threat when other types of attacks are much more likely to occur (Pillar, 2004, p. 31).

Terrorist acts affect the international political environment. Security concerns affect the U.S. government's interactions with other nations. Military deployments may be used to change the security posture in locations around the world. Attempts to broker peace agreements can be affected by terrorist acts. Terrorism against the United States can also destabilize a government that is friendly to the United States (Pillar, 2004, pp. 34–35).

In his State of the Union Address, President Bush (2002, January 29) highlighted the terrorist threat that the United States now faces. The president identified the axis of evil consisting of Iran, Iraq, and North Korea, which threaten the United States and our allies. President Bush made it clear that the war against terrorism has only just begun and that the resources of the nation are focused on winning it. Terrorists today are moving away from a hierarchical structure toward a network design consistent with the new information age. Information-age technology is helping terrorist attack their targets and defend themselves. This new method of operations by terrorists has been referred to as netwar (Arquilla et al., 2004). As information and communication technologies continue to change, terrorists will expand their conduct of netwar. Netwar reflects a focus on conflict with society (pp. 89–90).

The National Commission on Terrorist Attacks upon the United States (2004) reported that Osama bin Laden announced in 1998 that it was the duty of Muslims to kill Americans. Bin Laden has denounced U.S. policies in the Middle East and has stated that America should end its godless behavior and convert to Islam. Bin Laden also blames the United States for conflict in the world that involves Muslims. The inability of Arab national governments to improve the economic conditions of many of their citizens provides fuel to the unrest that causes some Muslims to be receptive to bin Laden's message (pp. 47, 51, 53–54). Bin Laden had four strategic goals. His first goal was to force American troops to leave Saudi Arabia. Bin Laden's second goal was to overthrow those Muslim regimes that he felt were corrupt. The third goal was to destroy Israel. Bin Laden's fourth goal was to punish the United States for its aggression against Islam (Robbins, 2004, pp. 392–393).

Some of the indirect effects of terrorism are of greater concern than the direct physical aspects. The fear resulting from a terrorist attack has a negative social and economic impact. Ethnic groups associated with the perpetrators of a terrorist act may be ostracized from society in general. A terrorist act may make citizens too fearful to travel or patronize certain businesses to avoid a future attack. Counter-measures to fight terrorism divert funds that might otherwise be used elsewhere. These government and business costs are felt at national, state, and local levels (Pillar, 2004, pp. 32–33). Terrorist and transnational criminal organizations may also see benefits by joining forces. Narcotics provide a ready source of funding for terrorist groups in a chaotic environment. The behaviors and aims of criminal narcotics organizations and terrorist groups may converge as both try to foster societal disruption to achieve their respective goals (McCaffrey and Basso, 2004, pp. 250–251).

Religious-Based Terrorism

The changing nature of terrorism has seen the growth of terrorism based on radical Islamic views that are that much more dangerous due to the possibility of the use of weapons of mass destruction. Societal conflict further complicates international response because these entities that are perpetrating violence do not necessarily represent state-based political bodies that form the basis for diplomatic discourse. In his discussion of terrorism, Ahmad (2004) described Osama bin Laden's actions in relation to Islam's concept of jihad, meaning struggle. The big jihad refers to struggle within oneself. Small jihad is the violent struggle against external oppon-ents. Osama bin Laden fought against the Soviet Union's invasion of Afghanistan in the 1980s with U.S. help. Bin Laden's culture is tribal even though he is wealthy, which affects his perception of the world. Bin Laden turned on the United States because the United States retained its military forces in Islam's holy land, Saudi Arabia. From bin Laden's view, the United States betrayed Islam by staying in Saudi Arabia after the 1991 defeat of Saddam Hussein (p. 51).

This new form of terrorism is more violent than terrorism of the past. Terrorists during the Cold War were typically substate actors with a political agenda; however, terrorists today are transnational, nonstate actors whose purpose is to destroy the West and Islamic secular states. Terrorism today is better financed. It is much more difficult for intelligence agencies to penetrate today's religious terrorist organizations. The final difference noted by Howard is that today's terrorists have access to weapons of mass destruction (Howard, 2004, pp. 75–76). Religious terrorists are more prone to attempt to produce large numbers of casualties in an attack than traditional terrorists with a secular orientation are likely to do. Religious terrorists view violence as an end not simply means. Religious terrorists have no external support outside their religious affiliation. Ellis says that religious terrorists target a broader enemy than traditional secular terrorists. Religious terrorists also have a much different view of the world than secular terrorists. For religious terrorists, the conflict between their definition of good and evil characterizes their struggle. There is no room for compromise (Ellis, 2004, p. 112). Ranstorp (2004) concluded that religious terrorists view themselves as being in a crisis due to external factors such as social or political upheaval. Religion provides a refuge from external tumult. Religion may even provide a sanctuary or a means of political action. However, religion alone does not explain the lack of moral constraint in the violence shown by religious terrorists. The use of young, educated recruits who recently became members of urban society is a factor in this new phenomenon. These new recruits bring very radical and intolerant views to the religious movements that they join (pp. 127, 131).

The increased violence associated with religious terrorist groups means that if a CBRN terrorist attack occurs, it will most likely be the act of a religious group. Dolnik also stated that the most important factor in the rise of religious terrorist acts was the end of the Cold War. This loss of an ideological divide resulted in a one-world view arising, which threatens religious views (Dolnik, 2004, pp. 162, 168). Regardless of the motivation for terrorist acts, governments must develop the means to combat terror. Governments must protect their citizens' lives and property. These actions will face scrutiny from a nation's citizens as well as the international community.

Combating Terror

The government must not only respond to terrorism but also respond in such a manner that the response is seen. Donohue (2004) described eight categories of responsive actions due to a terrorist attack including incident management, emergency powers including military operations, managing the consequences of an incident, statements to reassure the public, security actions such as population control and protecting infrastructure and facilities, investigating and prosecuting the perpetrators of an incident, governmental restructuring to address deficiencies, and international actions aimed at enhancing security from terrorist activities (pp. 314–320). The United States' reaction to the attacks on September 11, 2001, has affected the individual rights of citizens and noncitizens. Questioning and detaining individuals of Middle Eastern ethnic backgrounds have increased tension within those cultural communities at home and abroad. The potential use of military tribunals has also raised objections in many areas. Because many nations do not allow capital punishment, the threat of execution for people found guilty of terrorist actions threatens U.S. international relations (Donohue, 2004, pp. 321–325, 331).

Nations may execute military operations against terrorism under the just war theory (Arend, 2004). The president must have greater authority to react to the terrorist threat than he has to conduct conventional war. Self-defense is equated to a just cause in countering terrorist actions as long as the intent is to prevent continued terrorist actions and not simply for revenge and consequently military force would be allowed. However, military operations should not be an automatic reaction without considering some form of diplomatic action first. As long as elimination of the threat defines success, then using military force is within the just war issue of probable success (Arend, 2004, pp. 351–353).

The United States has a stronger case for preemption if the enemy has threatened the use of weapons of mass destruction, the enemy has built the weapons in contradiction to an international agreement, the use of the weapon threatens the security of the nation, Congress has approved the action, and the United Nations Security Council has endorsed the action. There is a moral case for preemption as a means of self-defense (Roberts, 2004, pp. 356, 369–371). A comprehensive approach to combating terror is needed. A focus on one method will provide a terrorist an opportunity to concentrate his efforts to counter government action. Dershowitz (2002) emphasized four techniques for countering terror. The first technique is to deter terrorist acts by making it clear that the perpetrator will not benefit from that act. The second technique is to incapacitate the terrorists by killing or imprisoning them. Persuading the terrorist that the act is wrong is the third method. The fourth technique is proactive prevention. Intelligence operations are emphasized as a means to infiltrate terrorist organizations (Dershowitz, 2002, pp. 16–17).

President Bush (2002, September) has stated that the United States will use its power to champion aspirations for human dignity; strengthen alliances to defeat global terrorism and work to prevent attacks against the United States and its allies; work with others to defuse regional conflicts; prevent our enemies from threatening us, our allies, and our friends with weapons of mass destruction; ignite a new era of global economic growth through free markets and free trade; expand the circle of development by opening societies and building the infrastructure of democracy; develop agendas for cooperative action with other main centers of global power; and transform America's national security institutions to meet the challenges and opportunities of the twenty-first century. The president emphasized that the United States will continue to stand for liberty and justice around the world. Strengthening alliances globally to fight terrorism is important to the security of the United States (pp. 1–2). Some have argued for a broad strategy oriented on identifying intelligence requirements and foreign policy (McCaffrey and Basso, 2004). The United States must focus on terrorist vulnerabilities. A human intelligence capability is needed for operations worldwide. The United States should use Islamic clergy to foster a jihad against narcotics operations. Responses, including preemptive ones, should consider diplomatic, economic, and military options. Before the terrorist attacks on September 11, 2001, terrorism was one of the several national security concerns. Those attacks have now resulted in terrorism becoming the national security priority.

The Department of Defense and ten other federal agencies are spending over $70 billion per year to combat terrorism while receiving aid from 150 countries around the world. However, Conetta (2002) believes that a better explanation of the threat within a political and historical context, critical attention to a range of counterterrorism actions, and a view of counterterrorism within a broad security agenda are needed. A cooperative security agreement with international consensus is also needed to develop global countermeasures. Regardless of the underlying causes for the terrorists' actions, these violent acts constitute a war against the United States and Western society. War-like acts require military action. The nature of war does not change. Only the "superficial manifestations" of war change. War means killing with maneuver and firepower forming a partnership to kill enemy combatants. In particular, the war against terrorists is a war of attrition because the terrorists will not stop attacking until they are dead. Therefore, a war of attrition where the preponderance of casualties is on the other side is in the best interests of the United States. Precision attack against a few targets will not win the war that we are now fighting. Network operations will not win our war on terrorists, but killing terrorists can (Peters, 2004, pp. 24–31).

U.S. global primacy has resulted in it becoming the target of terrorists, and this has affected the tactics used. Deterrence can still work when facing state-sponsored terrorists but not transnational terrorists. Counteroffensive operations are important when fighting terrorists because the terrorists are focused on their own offensive operations. U.S. foreign policy must seek to reduce the conditions of political unrest and imbalances of power that foster terrorism (Betts, 2004, pp. 377, 384–385, 388).

Relieving the underlying causes behind one group's decision to resort to terrorism may very well result in other groups noticing that success and adopting terror as a course of action. Palestinian terrorists have adopted suicide bombings as a tactic because it succeeded in capturing the attention of the international community. Nations must convince terrorists that using terror always hurts their cause rather than helping it. An all-out war against terrorism would require such a loss of individual freedom in the United States that the nation's citizenry would no longer feel free (Dershowitz, 2002, pp. 32, 81, 86, 126). Nations or groups who support terrorism must know that they face collective punishment for doing so. Only a lengthy prison sentence or death will stop the terrorist who has no real political agenda but is instead motivated by religious fervor. The United States must maintain an aggressive posture if it is to defeat terrorist operations (Dershowitz, 2002, pp. 181, 186). Most terrorists do not fully exploit the vulnerabilities of modern industrial societies. Nations must carefully establish priorities in the fight against terrorism because resources are limited. Offensive military action and offensive military capabilities for deterrence should be components of a counter terror strategy. Patience and sustained national will are essential to defeat terrorism (Posen, 2004, pp. 431–435). If terrorism is a political act that employs violence, then impediments to the Defense Department's participation in homeland security must be addressed. Military forces may be the only organization capable of responding to the level of catastrophe that may result from future terror attacks. The Congress and the president must work together to prevent misunderstandings of the limitations of the Posse Comitatus Act from preventing the use of military force in support of law enforcement operations (Norwitz, 2004, pp. 471, 477–478).

Western armies are not prepared to fight counterinsurgency wars due to a failure to prepare for it and this affects the ability of these nations to react to terrorism. Collateral damage concerns, proportionality of response, and combat deaths prevent some Western nations from showing the resolve to press the fight against terrorists. Support of the population where terrorists live and operate is very important for nations to defeat terrorism. Military operations are a necessary evil and should be carried to states where terrorists receive sanctuary. This includes coercive diplomacy against states that support terror and depends on human intelligence to gather information on terror networks. It also requires a campaign to win the hearts and minds of the Islamic people as key elements of a strategy for the United States and its allies to defeat terrorism (De Wijk, 2004, pp. 483, 486, 489, 493). Combating terrorism includes preventing attacks as well as responding to them. Emergency response actions are critical to mitigate the results of a terrorist act. Military forces may be the best means to respond to an attack or to preempt an attack. Intelligence operations are crucial. Foreign policy actions will also affect the justification for terrorism. The underlying causes of terrorism resulting from frustration and anger with the disparity of living conditions can be addressed by government action. However, eliminating all such disparities around the world is unlikely, certainly in the short term. Offensive and defensive actions are necessary to preclude attack and to protect resources from attack.

Summary

Terrorism has been a threat for many years, but the attacks on September 11, 2001, made it clear to all that we must act to defeat this threat. We cannot ignore it and have it go away. Terrorism is a violent political act with domestic and international repercussions. A terrorist act has immediate impact with the creation of casualties, and has social and economic impacts through the fear that it imposes. Terrorists may be motivated by political conflict or religious hatred. The addition of religious extremism as a factor in international terrorism complicates defining and combating terror. The religious intolerance of radical Islamic views is indicative of societal conflict, not simply political conflict. Defeating terrorism requires law enforcement and military style operations combined with the determination of the nation's political leadership and the citizenry to persevere. Terrorism is an evil that we cannot avoid or ignore. We have no choice but to confront it and win.

References

Ahmad, E. 2004. Terrorism: Theirs & ours. In Howard, R.D. and Sawyer, R.L. (Eds.), *Terrorism and Counterterrorism: Understanding the New Security Environment* (pp. 46–52). Guilford, Connecticut: McGraw-Hill/Dushkin.

Arend, A.C. 2004. Terrorism and just war doctrine. In Howard, R.D. and Sawyer, R.L. (Eds.), *Terrorism and Counterterrorism: Understanding the New Security Environment* (pp. 345–355). Guilford, Connecticut: McGraw-Hill/Dushkin.

Arquilla, J., Ronfelt, D., and Zanini, M. 2004. Networks, netwar, and information-age terrorism. In Howard, R.D. and Sawyer, R.L. (Eds.), *Terrorism and Counterterrorism: Understanding the New Security Environment* (pp. 86–108). Guilford, Connecticut: McGraw-Hill/Dushkin.

Betts, R.K. 2004. The soft underbelly of American primacy: Tactical advantages of terror. In Howard, R.D. and Sawyer, R.L. (Eds.), *Terrorism and Counterterrorism: Understanding the New Security Environment* (pp. 376–391). Guilford, Connecticut: McGraw-Hill/Dushkin.

Bush, G.W. 2002, January 29. 2002 State of the Union Address. Retrieved March 16, 2004, from http://www.whitehouse.gov/news/releases/2002/01/20020129–11.html.

Bush, G.W. 2002, September. The National Security Strategy of the United States. Retrieved March 16, 2004 from http://www.whitehouse.gov/nsc/nss.html.

Conetta, C. 2002, September 9. Terrorism, World Order, and Cooperative Security: A Research and Policy Development Agenda. Retrieved July 31, 2003, from the Project on Defense Alternatives The RMA Debate Web site: http://www.comw.org/rma.

De Wijk, R. 2004. The limits of military power. In Howard, R.D. and Sawyer, R.L. (Eds.), *Terrorism and Counterterrorism: Understanding the New Security Environment* (pp. 482–494). Guilford, Connecticut: McGraw-Hill/Dushkin.

Dershowitz, A.M. 2002. *Why Terrorism Works: Understanding the Threat and Responding to the Challenge*. New Haven, Connecticut: Yale University Press.

Dolnik, A. 2004. All God's poisons: Re-evaluating the threat of religious terrorism with respect to non-conventional weapons. In Howard, R.D. and Sawyer, R.L. (Eds.), *Terrorism and Counterterrorism: Understanding the New Security Environment* (pp. 159–179). Guilford, Connecticut: McGraw-Hill/Dushkin.

Donohue, L.K. 2004. Fear itself: Counterterrorism, individual rights, and U.S. foreign relations post 9–11. In Howard, R.D. and Sawyer, R.L. (Eds.), *Terrorism and Counterterrorism: Understanding the New Security Environment* (pp. 313–338). Guilford, Connecticut: McGraw-Hill/Dushkin.

Ellis, B. 2004. Countering complexity: An analytical framework to guide counter-terrorism policy-making. In Howard, R.D. and Sawyer, R.L. (Eds.), *Terrorism and Counterterrorism: Understanding the New Security Environment* (pp. 109–122). Guilford, Connecticut: McGraw-Hill/Dushkin.

Hoffman, B. 2004. Defining terrorism. In Howard, R.D. and Sawyer, R.L. (Eds.), *Terrorism and Counterterrorism: Understanding the New Security Environment* (pp. 3–23). Guilford, Connecticut: McGraw-Hill/Dushkin.

Howard, R.D. 2004. Understanding al Qaeda's application of the new terrorism—The key to victory in the current campaign. In Howard, R.D. and Sawyer, R.L. (Eds.), *Terrorism and Counterterrorism: Understanding the New Security Environment* (pp. 75–85). Guilford, Connecticut: McGraw-Hill/Dushkin.

Maniscalco, P.M. and Christen, H.T. (Eds.) 2002. *Understanding Terrorism and Managing the Consequences*. Upper Saddle River, New Jersey: Prentice Hall.

McCaffrey, B.R. and Basso, J.A. 2004. Narcotics, terrorism, and international crime: The convergence phenomenon. In Howard, R.D. and Sawyer, R.L. (Eds.), *Terrorism and Counterterrorism: Understanding the New Security Environment* (pp. 245–259). Guilford, Connecticut: McGraw-Hill/Dushkin.

National Commission on Terrorist Attacks upon the United States. 2004. The 9/11 Commission Report: Final Report of the National Commission on Terrorist Attacks upon the United States. New York: W.W. Norton & Company.

Norwitz, J.H. 2004. Combating terrorism: With a helmet or a badge. In Howard, R.D. and Sawyer, R.L. (Eds.), *Terrorism and Counterterrorism: Understanding the New Security Environment* (pp. 470–481). Guilford, Connecticut: McGraw-Hill/Dushkin.

Peters, R. 2004, Summer. In praise of attrition. *Parameters, 34*(2), 24–32.

Pillar, P.R. 2004. The dimensions of terrorism and counterterrorism. In Howard, R.D. and Sawyer, R.L. (Eds.), *Terrorism and Counterterrorism: Understanding the New Security Environment* (pp. 24–45). Guilford, Connecticut: McGraw-Hill/Dushkin.

Posen, B.R. 2004. The struggle against terrorism: Grand strategy, strategy, and tactics. In Howard, R.D. and Sawyer, R.L. (Eds.), *Terrorism and Counterterrorism: Understanding the New Security Environment* (pp. 429–441). Guilford, Connecticut: McGraw-Hill/ Dushkin.

Ranstorp, M. 2004. Terrorism in the name of religion. In Howard, R.D. and Sawyer, R.L. (Eds.), *Terrorism and Counterterrorism: Understanding the New Security Environment* (pp. 125–139). Guilford, Connecticut: McGraw-Hill/Dushkin.

Robbins, J.S. 2004. Bin Laden's war. In Howard, R.D. and Sawyer, R.L. (Eds.), *Terrorism and Counterterrorism: Understanding the New Security Environment* (pp. 392–404). Guilford, Connecticut: McGraw-Hill/Dushkin.

Roberts, B. 2004. NBC-armed rogues: Is there a moral case for preemption. In Howard, R.D. and Sawyer, R.L. (Eds.), *Terrorism and Counterterrorism: Understanding the New Security Environment* (pp. 356–373). Guilford, Connecticut: McGraw-Hill/Dushkin.

PLANNING, PREVENTION, PREPAREDNESS, RECOVERY, AND ASSISTANCE

Chapter 13

Profiling

Glenn L. Starks

CONTENTS

Introduction

Profiling is a very complex issue because no standard laws expressly forbid the practice, and its use in law enforcement varies and is not discernable in some cases. Although some officials at the federal, state, and local levels condemn the practice as discriminatory and contra to the principles of the equal rights, others justify it as a viable means to combat specific types of crimes. In the absence of specific laws, the courts have relied upon interpretations of constitutional amendments on a case-by-case basis. To further confuse the issue, policies are being put in place at the federal level that allow security and law enforcement agencies to target specific groups when in the interest of national security. This is a very broad justification that allows for varied interpretations. Demands for laws completely forbidding the practice have been elevated to the national level because of continuing reports of discrimination by law enforcement agents. While each side of the issue postulates the pros and cons of profiling, statistics are becoming more readily available on the use of profiling. These statistics are part of the basis for national reforms to end the practice.

The war on terrorism has refueled the profiling debate and hindered progress to fully end profiling. In response to the events of September 11, 2001, the U.S. federal government established numerous laws and programs to identify accomplices of the suicide pilots that flew commercial airlines into the World Trade Center and the Pentagon, and those that were unsuccessful in reaching their target and crashed in Pennsylvania. The government took these actions to also prevent future acts of terrorism. Although there is generally no public argument that aggressive actions are needed to fight terrorism, there are outcries condemning many of these laws and programs as restrictive and utilizing profiling. National leaders, including the president, quickly denounced hate crimes and discrimination immediately after September 11th, while putting in place efforts to identify people domestically and internationally connected to al-Qaeda. The government detained thousands of people within the United States and at the U.S. Naval Base in Guantanamo Bay, Cuba, and deported others.[1] The Federal Bureau of Investigation interviewed thousands of Arabs and Muslims. The government has been criticized for employing the same discriminatory practices that law enforcement agencies have been accused of utilizing for decades and for reversing the progress that had been made to end profiling.

Profiling has been exercised by national security and law enforcement agencies for most of the last century in the United States. In September 1901, President William McKinley was assassinated by a white man who was allowed to pass through secret service screening because an agent admitted he was focused on a "dark complexioned man with a moustache." The targeted man, an African American, was a former constable and later apprehended the assassin before he could escape.[2] President Franklin D. Roosevelt signed Executive Order 9066 into law on February 19, 1942 in response to the bombing of Pearl Harbor on December 7, 1941. This order approved the removal of Asians and Japanese Americans from the west coast and the internment of over 120,000 people into detention camps.[3] This action was even upheld as legal by the Supreme Court.[4] There have been countless reports of blacks and Hispanics being profiled during routine traffic stops as part of the war on drugs and illegal immigration. However, profiling has not been limited to minorities. Police admitted that the primary reason it took so long to apprehend the snipers that were terrorizing the Washington, DC area in 2003 was that they were looking for a white man in a white van. They believed white men fit the profile of domestic snipers.

Profiling has been justified as a legitimate law enforcement strategy while being condemned as one of the most reprehensible. Those in favor of its use have defended it as a valuable method to apprehend those most prone to committing certain types of crimes. Those opposed condemn it as a discriminatory practice that ultimately achieves little, if any, of its intended results. The debate is over profiling centers on how it is used to target people of certain races and ethnic groups in the absence of an actual crime. Court cases and police reports detailing how innocent people have been detained, arrested, and even abused have been the catalyst for legal reforms. Law enforcement agencies have also instituted procedural reforms. Still, incidents of profiling continue to be reported across the country. Its use in fighting terrorism has fueled the debate and intensified demands for reforms at every level of government.

Definition of Profiling

Profiling is defined as the practice of law enforcement officials (including security personnel) using race, ethnicity, religion, or national origin as the decisive factor in targeting an individual for suspicion of a wrongdoing. Individuals are targeted because of their believed propensity to engage in a particular crime or types of crimes. The act of profiling occurs when these individuals are then treated in a manner different from others not being targeted. For example, profiling related to traffic stops is identified by first analyzing who gets stopped, then why, and then how they are treated. Profiling can take place in all three or just one of these steps. Even if someone is stopped for a valid reason (such as speeding), profiling occurs if their car is then searched for drugs only because the driver is of a certain race.

Profiling also occurs due to discriminatory omissions. In this case, people of certain races, ethnicities, religions, or national origins are not given equal protection or are ignored. For example, law enforcement officers may purposely not respond to their calls for assistance. Officers could also witness a crime being committed against a member of a certain ethnic group and not take action to protect them or to punish the offender(s).

When race, religion, ethnicity, or national origin is used as part of a description to identify the perpetrator of a specific crime, profiling does not occur. For example, profiling does not occur if police report they are searching for a man of a certain race in connection with a bank robbery. A man of that race can then be justifiably stopped if he meets the perpetrator's reported height, weight, and descriptions of his clothes and vehicle. It does occur, however, if police officers stop men of that race who do not meet any of the other descriptions. Profiling also does not occur if someone is stopped for a valid reason (such as speeding) and the officer then detects other wrongdoings (such as seeing drugs in the car or detecting alcohol on the driver's breath).

Profiling results from the absence of visible or reported wrongdoing. The term DWB (Driving While Black or Driving While Brown) refers to people of color being stopped for no other reason than being of color. Stopped on the pretense of having committed a minor traffic violation, their vehicles are searched or they are subjected to treatment not routinely experienced by all drivers. Profiling can be perpetrated against pedestrians, shoppers, travelers, and even people in their homes. Amnesty International defines profiling as "Driving, Flying, Walking, Worshipping, Shopping, or Staying at Home While Black, Brown, Red, Yellow, Muslim or of Middle Eastern Appearance."[5] With travelers, it often occurs with passengers returning from overseas trips at ports of entry such as airports and docking ports. A March 2000 study by the General Accounting Office found that African American women were more prone to being searched by U.S. Customs agents upon reentering the country than any other group. According to the report, they were "nine times more likely than White women who were U.S. citizens to be x-rayed after being frisked or patted down in fiscal year 1998." However, they were less than half as likely as white women to be found carrying contraband.[6]

Although profiling has been used for decades, demands for reforms have been most recently elevated to national attention for several reasons. First, data has become available to provide quantifiable evidence of profiling. A report from the Department of Justice revealed that of the 16.8 million drivers stopped by police in 2002, 76.5 percent were white, 11 percent were black, 9.5 percent were Hispanic, and 2.9 percent were drivers of other races. On the basis of their percentage of the U.S. population, the report found that the likelihood of drivers of one particular race being stopped did not differ significantly than the likelihood of others being stopped. However, police were more likely to carry out some types of bodily or vehicular search of blacks (10.2 percent) and Hispanics (11.4 percent) than whites (3.5 percent). Among those involved in some type of police contact, blacks (3.5 percent) and Hispanics (2.5 percent) were more likely than whites (1.1 percent) to experience some type of police threat or use of force. Whites (27.4 percent) were more likely to be issued just a warning than blacks (18.3 percent) and Hispanics (18.2 percent), and Hispanics (71.5 percent) were more likely than both whites (56.5 percent) and blacks (58.4 percent) to be issued a ticket.[7]

New Jersey was the first state to officially recognize and use evidence of racial profiling by law enforcement officers in court after a 1999 report by its Attorney General's office. The report highlighted two problems: "(1) willful misconduct by a small number of State Police members and (2) more common instances of possible de facto discrimination by officers who may be influenced by stereotypes and may thus tend to treat minority motorists differently during the course of routine traffic stops, subjecting them more routinely to investigative tactics and techniques that are designed to ferret out illicit drugs and weapons." According to the data in the report, 77.2 percent of recorded traffic stops where searches were conducted involved black or Hispanic drivers, but only 19 percent resulted in arrests.[8]

Second, some of those stopped have been subjected to reported mistreatment at the hands of law enforcement officials. There have been reports of drivers who were detained or even jailed, but then later released without any charges. One of the most common reports has been of mental abuse by officers issuing verbal threats and offensive accusations meant to scare drivers into confessing to involvement in a crime. Others have reported being physically assaulted. In some of the most prominent reports, deaths have resulted from police officers reportedly using extreme and unnecessary force. In the absence of any other evidence, this use of force was attributed to the race or ethnicity of the victim. One reported incident occurred on October 12, 1995, in Brentwood, Pennsylvania, when a 31 year old African American man was killed by police officers after being pulled over while driving the Jaguar of his cousin, Pittsburg Steelers football player, Ray Seals. A tow truck driver reported several officers kicked, hit, and clubbed the victim as he lay on the pavement.[9]

Third, individuals of prominence in their communities have been the victims of profiling, raising the level of awareness of the innocent being subjected to unwarranted targeting, detainment, and even arrests. Those profiled have included lawyers, judges, legislators, doctors, police officers, military officers, and celebrities. African American Harvard law Professor Charles Ogletree perhaps best summed this point by saying that "If I'm dressed in a knit cap and hooded jacket, I'm probable cause."[10] Rather than allowing themselves to be mistreated and then quietly retreating, profiled individuals of prominence have filed lawsuits, published books and articles, and garnered national and international media attention. This has raised the level of awareness of profiling, and put a spotlight on agencies and lawmakers.

Debated Pros and Cons of Profiling

Those that argue against profiling condemn the practice as discriminatory and in violation of the Fourth and Fourteenth Amendments of the Constitution beyond those reasons, it is viewed as an ineffective method to curb drug trafficking, illegal immigration, terrorism, or any of the criminal behaviors it seeks to address. Those in favor of the practice consider it a reliable method to focus law enforcement attention on the groups most likely to commit the aforementioned crimes. The next two sections summarize the main arguments for and against profiling.

Pros

One argument in favor of profiling is that the use of race or ethnicity as a primary factor in targeting criminals is sensible because minorities are most likely to engage in illegal behaviors. As a testament to this, supporters point to the fact that minorities comprise the majority of prison inmates. According to the Department of Justice, in 2004 approximately 8.4 percent of black men between the ages of 25 and 29 were in State or federal prisons, compared to 2.5 percent of Hispanic men and 1.2 percent of white men in the same age group.[11] Hispanics overwhelmingly compromise the majority of illegal immigrants in the United States. According to the U.S. Immigration and Naturalization Service, Mexico's share of the total unauthorized resident population in the United States increased from 58 percent in 1990 to 69 percent in 2000.[12] It is therefore rational to target those with the greatest propensity to break laws.

Those in favor also believe profiling does not violate a suspect's constitutional rights. The constitution and the courts allow profiling where reasonable suspicion exists. In *Terry v. State of Ohio*, the Supreme Court ruled it is not a violation of the Fourteenth Amendment for an officer to detain and search a man's person for a weapon in absence of a search warrant as long as the officer acts upon a reasonable belief based upon articulated objective factors that the man is armed and dangerous.[13]

Additionally, the Fourth Amendment allows for search and seizure where there is probable cause, such as someone acting suspiciously. In *United States v. Brignoni-Ponce*, the Supreme Court ruled that police officers could stop and question passengers in vehicles reasonably suspected of transporting illegal aliens. However, allowing patrols broad and unlimited discretion "to stop all vehicles in the border area without any reason to suspect that they have violated any law, would not be 'reasonable' under the Fourth Amendment. The Fourth Amendment therefore forbids stopping persons for questioning about their citizenship on less than a reasonable suspicion that they may be aliens."[14]

Supporters also argue that prohibiting profiling will hinder the war on terrorism and undermine national security. Terrorism is a real threat and extreme precautions are needed to prevent hostile foreign powers from attacking the country or conducting counterintelligence within U.S. borders. Terrorists will not be deterred by the threat of punishment. Suicide bombers and hijackers are not deterred by serious injury or death. Thus, some believe profiling is needed to discover terrorists before they have the chance to attack.

Cons

The following are common arguments against profiling. Profiling is a violation of the Fourth Amendment. Race or ethnicity alone does not constitute probable cause. Using these factors as in targeting an individual without cause is thus a violation of a citizen's constitutional rights. For example, the Supreme Court has ruled that officers have the right to stop vehicles when there is reasonable cause to believe that a traffic violation has occurred.[15] It also violates the Fourteenth Amendment because those profiled are not being provided equal protection of laws. Even if some stops yield the guilty, many more people that are innocent suffer humiliation, fear, and even trauma. Some people stopped are not even of the targeted race or ethnicity. This error often occurs because stereotypes are used as a means of identification.

For example, Sikhs are neither Arab nor Muslim but are considered so by many Americans because of their turbans and beards.

To protect themselves from being stopped or singled out, some minorities change their style of dress, avoid driving certain vehicles, and even avoid certain routes out of fear. The fear of driving in certain areas impairs both interstate and intrastate commerce. Others will even not exercise their constitutional rights of freedom of speech or freedom to practice their own religion for fear of being targeted. Behavioral and emotional consequences can result and affect victims of profiling and those fearing they will become victims.

Decanters also believe the argument that profiling is justified because more minorities are in prison and thus more prone to commit crimes is flawed and that it becomes a self-fulfilling prophecy. They feel that if more minorities are targeted, more minorities will be convicted of crimes while criminals of other races will get away. Additionally, statistics show that minorities are no more likely to commit crimes than nonminorities. Acts of terrorism have been committed by Americans as well as Middle Easterners. Rates of illicit drug use in 2001 were comparable across the major racial/ethnic groups—7.2 percent for whites, 6.4 percent for Hispanics, and 7.4 percent for blacks.[16] Profiling diverts the attention of law enforcement officials from investigating those who are actually guilty. Those who do not fit a profile could be engaged in crimes or could be used as unknowing accomplices by those who do fit a profile.

Lastly, profiling creates division within the country. Communities become divided, and a division also results between communities and law enforcement agencies, as well as communities and the government. It causes citizens to mistrust the police and courts, not assist law enforcement officials, or report crimes.

Profiling and Terrorism

Profiling has traditionally been justified as a useful tactic to combat drug trafficking, illegal immigration, and gang involvement. Due to the nature of these crimes, blacks and Hispanics have been the primary targets of profiling by law enforcement officers. People of Arab descent and Muslims are profiled for terrorism because they are considered the primary perpetrators of terrorist acts. They were profiled even before 2001 because of international events that created a stereotype of terrorists. Lybian terrorists bombed Pan Am flight 103 over Lockerbie, Scotland on December 21, 1988, killing 259 onboard the aircraft and 11 on the ground. One hundred and eighty-nine of the passengers were Americans.[17] On February 26, 1993, the Islamic terrorist group al-Qaeda first tried to topple the World Trade Center in an underground parking garage with a car bomb by devastating the foundation of the north tower to cause it to collapse onto its twin tower. Six people were killed, more than one thousand were injured, and property damage exceed one half billion dollars.[18] After an Arab suicide bombing of the American destroyer *U.S.S. Cole* on October 12, 2000 in Yemen, 17 sailors were killed and 39 others injured.[19]

Over the past two decades, Arabs and Muslims have been the first suspects in any unnatural disaster on U.S. soil. They were automatically suspected in the Oklahoma City bombing in 1995 and the crash of TWA flight 800 off Long Island in 1996. The first turned out to be a domestic act of terrorism and the second resulted from equipment malfunction. After September 11, 2001, aggressive profiling of Arabs, Arab Americans, Muslims, Sikhs, and South Asians was instituted by the U.S. government as well as state and local agencies. Many of the thousands that were detained, deported, or put in prison by the government were not afforded legal representation. A nationwide campaign was put in place to question Arabs who had entered the country after January 2000 on nonimmigrant visas (student, tourist, or temporary visas). Others, even U.S. citizens, were subjected to extra searches in airports or asked by pilots to get off planes. Some Sikh Americans were asked to remove their turbans in airports, which is a violation of their religious practices. DWB was expanded to DWA (Driving While Arab). Many were subjected to targeted traffic stops for no other apparent reason than their perceived ethnicity or religion. Actions against Muslims were similar to how Japanese Americans and Asians were targeted after the attack on Pearl Harbor by Japan on December 7, 1941.

Because of the events of September 11, 2001, the government has enacted new legislation in the war on terrorism that has elevated fears of profiling. Although none of these Acts were explicitly developed to legalize profiling, they are being debated as laws that may justify the use of profiling. Government officials argue they were not developed for that purpose.

The Patriot Act was passed on October 12, 2001, to greatly enhance the ability of security and law enforcement agencies to deter and punish terrorist acts in the United States and around the world. It also provides for the prosecution of acts that could be connected to terrorism, such as illegal immigration, money laundering, and providing false information regarding terrorism. Earlier acts on these topics were folded into or amended by the Patriot Act. These include the Immigration and Nationality Act, the USA Act, and the Financial Anti-Terrorism Act. The Immigration and Nationality Act, as passed in 1952, outlined laws for the employment of aliens in the United States, including provisions for employment eligibility and employment verification. The Act was modified by the Patriot Act to define terrorist activity and to allow the nonadmission or removal of aliens engaged in terrorist acts even if they possess a valid nonimmigrant or immigrant visa or a green card. The USA Act, passed on October 12, 2001, allowed for terrorists that were not agents of a foreign power to be targets of federal investigations. The Financial Anti-Terrorism Act, passed on October 17, 2001, increased governmental power to investigate and prosecute those who financially support terrorism.

The PATRIOT Act is divided into ten titles, each of which has numerous sections:

Title I: Enhancing Domestic Security against Terrorism
Title II: Enhanced Surveillance Procedures

Title III: International Money Laundering Abatement and Anti-Terrorist Financing
Act of 2001
Title IV: Protecting the Border
Title V: Removing Obstacles to Investigating Terrorism
Title VI: Providing for Victims of Terrorism, Public Safety Officers, and their
Families
Title VII: Increased Information Sharing for Critical Infrastructure Protection
Title VIII: Strengthening the Criminal Laws Against Terrorism
Title IX: Improved Intelligence
Title X: Miscellaneous

The Foreign Intelligence Surveillance Act (FISA) was passed in 1978. It stipulated
that only foreign powers or their agents could be subjected to investigations for such
crimes as espionage or internal terrorism. Investigations could include electronic
surveillance, physical searches, and access to business records. The Act allowed U.S.
government enforcement agencies to utilize pen registers, and trap, and trace devices.
These devices allow for the interception of wire or electronic communications (e.g.,
telephone calls) and identification of their sources (incoming and outgoing). The
Intelligence Reform and Terrorism Prevention Act of 2004 expanded FISA to allow
the government to target "lone wolf" terrorists, i.e., where there is no evidence, they
are members of a terrorist group or agent of a foreign power.

In 2002, the federal government instituted the National Security Entry/Exit
Registration System (NSEERS) program, requiring aliens of certain countries to
become part of a "national registry for temporary foreign visitors (nonimmigrant aliens)
arriving from certain countries, or who meet a combination of intelligence-based
criteria, and are identified as presenting an elevated national security concern."[20]
The program collects information on each registrant's background, purpose of visit
to the United States, and requires periodic verification of their location and activities,
and confirmation of their departure. The program has received criticism because it
only mandates registration by aliens from specific countries, predominantly
Muslim: Afghanistan, Algeria, Bahrain, Bangladesh, Egypt, Eritrea, Indonesia, Iran,
Iraq, Jordan, Kuwait, Libya, Lebanon, Morocco, North Korea, Oman, Pakistan,
Qatar, Somalia, Saudi Arabia, Sudan, Syria, Tunisia, United Arab Emirates, and
Yemen. The majority of those registered are students, and those on extended travel
for business or family visitation.[21]

Efforts to End Profiling

On February 27, 2001 during his State of the Union Address, President Bush
declared "racial profiling is wrong and we will end it in America." During this
joint session of Congress, he directed the Attorney General to implement this policy.
In June 2003, the Department of Justice issued guidance prohibiting racial profiling in law enforcement practices. The guidance stipulates that racial profiling

is prohibited where it does not hinder "the important work of our Nation's public safety officials, particularly the intensified antiterrorism efforts precipitated by the events of September 11, 2001."[22]

The guidance from the Department of Justice, however, is not a law. There have been attempts to pass an End Racial Profiling Act. The latest version in 2005 was introduced by Representative John Conyers Jr. (D-Michigan) and Senators Russell D. Feingold (D-Wisconsin), Arlen Specter (R-Pennsylvania), Hillary Clinton (D-New York), and Jon Corzine (D-New Jersey). The Act, if passed, would prohibit racial profiling at the federal, state, and local levels of law enforcement, as well as on Indian reservations. The act also requires agencies to provide training on racial profiling, collect data, develop procedures for receiving, investigating, and responding meaningfully to complaints alleging profiling by law enforcement agents, and to develop policies to ensure appropriate actions are taken when agents are determined to have engaged in profiling. Federal grants may be given to states, agencies, or even units of local governments to develop and implement best practice devices and systems to eliminate racial profiling. Those that file complaints can be given funds to cover legal fees.[23]

As of October 2004, 29 states require their law enforcement agencies to record the races and ethnicities of motorists during traffic stops. This was an increase of 16 states that required this since March 2001. Twenty-eight states require officers to record statistics for all other officer initiated stops. Most rely on the officer to make a visual determination of race and ethnicity.[24]

The following is a list of agreed upon recommendations by community, civil rights, and government groups to end profiling:

1. The federal government, as well as state and local law enforcement agencies, should ban the use of racial profiling and discrimination via clear, legally enforceable policies and regulations.
2. Agencies should engage in aggressive record keeping and data collection on such topics as traffic stops, incidents of reported profiling, reported acts of discrimination, and reports of discrimination by private citizens (including how they were handled by police). The Department of Justice has developed extensive guidance for law enforcement agencies.[25]
3. Nationwide standards should be developed for the accreditation of law enforcement agencies.
4. Independent bodies should be established to monitor compliance to policies, regulations, and laws. These bodies should also have enforcement authority against noncompliant agencies and individuals.
5. Agencies should promote and strive for racially and culturally diverse workforces.
6. Processes should be put in place so that citizens feel that they can voice their concerns to law enforcement agencies and have confidence their concerns will be taken seriously and acted upon.

7. Training and prevention programs should be provided to law enforcement officials and citizens on such topics as security policies, diversity, and the effects of profiling.
8. Agencies at all levels should team with community groups representing diverse populations.
9. Agencies should ensure that one of their top policies is that everyone is to be treated equally.

Conclusion

While the debate over the use of profiling continues, actions are being taken to end or at least curb its use. There is a growing consensus that the profiling of U.S. citizens is discriminatory and illegal. Agreement on this area may eventually be reached and laws put in place to this effect. However, there remains divided discourse on the profiling of aliens. Illegal immigration continues to be a major area of concern at every level of government. Terrorism is of equal concern. Until a more viable means is developed to combat these two areas, profiling may continue to be executed by law enforcement and security personnel. If this occurs, there will continue to be incidents of innocent citizens being the victims of profiling.

Endnotes

1. Amnesty: War on Terror Sowing Fear, May 28, 2003, Retrieved from the World Wide Web on April 14, 2006, http://www.cnn.com/2003/WORLD/europe/05/28/amnesty.report/
2. Amnesty International, Threat and Humiliation: Racial Profiling, Domestic Security, and Human Rights in the United States, Globe Litho, Ridgefield Park, New Jersey, 2004. p. 23
3. Public Broadcast Station (PBS), Children of the Camps: The Documentary, 1999, Retrieved from the World Wide Web on April 14, 2006, http://www.pbs.org/child-ofcamp/index.html
4. *Korematsu v. United States,* 323 U.S. 214 (1944)
5. Amnesty International, Threat and Humiliation: Racial Profiling, Domestic Security, and Human Rights in the United States, Globe Litho, Ridgefield Park, New Jersey, 2004. p. 2
6. United States General Accounting Office, Better Targeting of Airline Passengers for Personal Searches Could Produce Better Results, Government Printing Office, Washington, DC, March 2000
7. Bureau of Justice Statistics, Contact between Police and the Public: Findings from the 2002 National Survey, U.S. Department of Justice, Washington, DC, April 2005
8. Peter Verniero and Paul H. Zoubek, Interim Report of the State Police Review Team Regarding Allegations of Racial Profiling, April 20, 1999

9. American Civil Liberties Union (ACLU), Racial Profiling May be Hazardous to Your Health, August 15, 2005, Retrieved from the World Wide Web on April 1, 2006, http://www.aclu.org/racialjustice/racialprofiling/19901res20050815.html

10. Ellen Goodman, Simpson Case Divides Us by Race, *Boston Globe*, July 10, 1994

11. Bureau of Justice Statistics, Prisoners in 2004, U.S. Department of Justice, Office of Justice Programs, Washington, DC, October 2005

12. Office of Policy and Planning, Estimates of the Unauthorized Immigrant Population Residing in the United States: 1990 to 2000, U.S. Immigration and Naturalization Service, Washington, DC, January 2003, p. 1

13. *Terry v. State of Ohio*, 392 U.S. 1, 88 S.Ct. (1968)

14. *United States v. Brignoni-Ponce*, 422 U.S. 873 (1975)

15. Michael A. Whren and James L. Brown, *Petitioners v. United States*, 517 U.S. 806 (1996)

16. Office of Applied Studies, National Survey on Drug Use and Health, U.S. Department of Health and Human Services, Washington, DC, September 8, 2005

17. Chebium, Raju, From Lockerbie to Camp Zeist: The Pan Am 103 Trial, Retrieved from the World Wide Web on April 13, 2006, http://www.cnn.com/LAW/trials.and.cases/case.files/0010/lockerbie/overview.html

18. *CNN*, Prosecutor: Yousef Aimed to Topple Trade Center Towers, August 5, 1997, Retrieved from the World Wide Web on April 11, 2006, http://www.cnn.com/US/9708/05/wtc.trial/index.html

19. *CNN*, U.S. Official Sees Similarities between USS Cole Blast and Embassy attacks, October 23, 2000, Retrieved from the World Wide Web on April 13, 2006, http://archives.cnn.com/2000/US/10/23/uss.cole.01

20. U.S. Immigration and Customs Enforcement, Fact Sheet: Changes to National Security Entry/Exit Registration System (NSEERS), December 1, 2003, U.S. Department of Homeland Security, Retrieved from the World Wide Web on April 13, 2006, http://www.ice.gov/graphics/news/factsheets/nseersFS120103.htm

21. Office of Inspector General, Review of the Immigration and Customs Enforcement's Compliance Enforcement Unit, Office of Inspections and Special Reviews, United States Department of Homeland Security, Washington, DC, September 2005, p. 92

22. United States Department of Justice, Guidance Regarding the Use of Race by Federal Law Enforcement Agencies, Civil Rights Division, Washington, DC, June 2003

23. End Racial Profiling Act of 2005, S.2138, 109th Congress, 1st Session, December 16, 2005

24. Bureau of Justice Statistics, Traffic Stop Data Collection Policies for State Police, 2004, United States Department of Justice, Washington, DC, June 2004

25. Office of Community Oriented Policing Services, How to Correctly Collect and Analyze Racial Profiling Data: Your Reputation Depends on It!, United States Department of Justice, Washington, DC, May 23, 2003

Chapter 14

Metropolitan Medical Response Systems: Coordinating the Healthcare Response to Terrorist Incidents

Scott C. Somers and Ronald W. Perry

CONTENTS

During the response to the Pentagon following the terrorist attacks of 9/11, responders benefited from regional mutual aid agreements by being able to receive emergency assistance from neighboring communities. The District of Columbia, Prince George's county, and Montgomery county were just a few of the jurisdictions to send police officers, firefighters, emergency medical personnel, and even a procurement and purchasing specialist to assist Arlington county with managing the consequences of the attack. The events in Arlington on 9/11 clearly demonstrate the need for local communities to establish relationships and joint agreements with governmental agencies and neighboring jurisdictions, as well as private entities to ensure that adequate resources and personnel will be available to assist in mitigating a large-scale natural disaster or act of terrorism.

Providing support to neighboring communities is not a new concept. Many organizations, especially those in the fire service, have already implemented mutual aid agreements similar to that used in Arlington. For example, Phoenix, Arizona, and its metropolitan neighbors have implemented a comprehensive approach to detecting, monitoring, and managing the consequences of a mass-casualty incident involving nuclear, biological, or chemical (NBC) weapons of mass destruction (WMD). Established in 1997 in response to the medical response challenges posed by the Oklahoma City Bombing and the Sarin attack on a Tokyo subway, the Metropolitan Medical Response System (MMRS) provides the operational framework that governs the use of personnel and equipment in situations that result in a multiagency or multi-jurisdictional response. The Phoenix MMRS facilitates the vertical integration of federal, state, county, and municipal resources, as well as the horizontal integration of the public, private, and nonprofit sectors.

Unfortunately, interorganizational communication and coordination of incidents involving numerous patients was not always effective in Phoenix. Although fire departments in the region had long been involved in cooperative planning efforts and operated together on incidents on a daily basis through an automatic aid system, other governmental and private entities had not typically participated in the system. The shortcomings of the narrow focus of these partnerships became evident at an incident in late 1997, when an aircraft arriving from Mexico landed at Sky Harbor International Airport with 28 very sick passengers. The Phoenix Fire Department, which provides fire and emergency medical services to Sky Harbor, arrived on scene and began triaging and treating patients based on standard protocol. Passengers were then transported to area hospitals for clinical evaluations, diagnosis, and definitive treatment. The failure in the system was the lack of communication with Public Health Authority. Without notification of Public Health Authority, there was no screening of passengers. The result could have been the transmission of a highly contagious virus or infectious disease throughout the country carried by asymptomatic patients, who were allowed to transfer to their connecting flights. With the assistance of federal funds through the MMRS program, Phoenix and its partners have built programs and developed a framework dedicated to community planning, epidemiological surveillance, and emergency response to any event involving WMD.

Phoenix, Arizona, provides a case study which describes the organization and operation of the MMRS generally. The state of Arizona has over 5.6 million residents, most of whom live in Maricopa county (Phoenix) or Pima county (Tucson). Maricopa county is located in the central part of the state and is home to 3.3 million people, or about 60 percent of the state's population. The Phoenix metropolitan area serves as the state's population and economic center. The city is also the state's political power base being host to a wide range of federal offices, as well as being the seat of county government and home to the state capital. The utility of describing the MMRS in Phoenix is that emergency managers and planners may use this description as a benchmark to compare terrorism response approaches. In addition, the Phoenix MMRS is highly transportable and elements can be adapted for use in jurisdictions of all types and sizes.

Concept of Operations

The MMRS was originally sought to develop a local system for successfully managing incidents involving 1000 or more patients exposed to a WMD event. This focus shifted after the September 11, 2001, terrorist attacks from a hard patient count to the capability of a NBC agent to generate mass casualties. The MMRS Model is operational in over 125 American cities, with more systems under development. To date, the MMRS is the only operation system for a comprehensive, integrated response to acts of terrorism that has been extensively tested in full-scale exercises. Yet, the MMRS is primarily focused on larger urban centers leaving many small- to mid-sized metropolitan regions at risk. The model, however, has numerous features that are readily exportable, fit large and small cities alike, and can be adapted to a variety of resource levels (Perry and Lindell, 2003).

The U.S. Department of Health and Human Services (HHS) founded the MMRS with a vision of creating a "task force" system of rapid deployment medical assets and personnel similar to the Urban Search and Rescue teams supported by the Federal Emergency Management Agency (FEMA). Metropolitan Medical Strike Team (MMST) concept began in the District of Columbia in 1995 combining resources from DC, Arlington county, Montgomery county, and Prince George's county. A second team was formed in the Atlanta metropolitan region in preparation for the 1996 Summer Olympic Games. Using the MMST Model, only members of the operations team would receive specialized training and equipment needed to deal with a WMD event. This strategy meant that once an incident was determined to involve NBC agents, a team would be notified and dispatched to the region.

Despite rather modest funding, independent positive evaluations of MMST responses to simulated WMD events prompted HHS to expand the MMST concept to an additional 25 cities. Congress appropriated funding for this expansion with the Defense against Weapons of Mass Destruction Act of 1996, more commonly referred to as the Nunn-Lugar-Domenici Act. Phoenix was among the new cities added to the MMST list; however, Phoenix officials deviated from the original strike team approach. Senior officers from the fire department noted that critical time would be lost while strike team members assembled and deployed, while in the meantime, first responders would be exposed to potentially lethal doses of WMD agents. Unlike the military, there are no acceptable losses where police departments, fire departments, and city officials are concerned. The adapted model, although more expensive, reduces risk to first responders, eliminates lost time in responding to an incident, and enhances WMD/NBC surveillance done by local law enforcement officials, fire departments, and public health organizations. In accepting the new model, the HHS changed the name to the MMRS, although the systems in DC and Atlanta maintained their strike team framework. This name change also reflected HHS' ongoing effort to expand beyond traditional first responders to integrate public health officials, laboratories, poison control centers, and mental health professionals, among others.

The MMRS Model begun in Phoenix assumes that first responders are continually alert to potential WMD/NBC incidents and are capable of initiating a safe response. Most municipalities with an MMRS operate under this model. As it is possible that there will be no forewarning of a terrorist incident involving WMD, all first responders receive training in agent recognition and are provided basic equipment to permit safe initial site operations. To accomplish safety and response goals, the system is embedded in the Incident Management System (IMS) to provide the organization to deal with terrorist threats. The response context for virtually all WMD events is that of a hazardous materials incident. Consequently, the Incident Commander (IC) will utilize the IMS to build a flexible response organization that can expand to include additional resources or agencies needed to meet the special needs of such events. The additional resources are built upon special training, equipment, and medical antidotes provided to Hazmat teams. Mutual Aid Systems continue to support the IMS to ensure the availability of adequate resources in both quantity and type. At a minimum, these provisions ensure that (1) no untrained, unprotected personnel will be exposed to an NBC agent and (2) first responders are trained and equipped to safely assess and initiate a response to an incident until more highly trained Hazmat responders make their way to the scene.

WMD incidents may or may not involve a single, geographically defined scene at which response operations might be mounted (Buck, 1998). The Phoenix MMRS IMS Model assumes that if a terrorist event can be defined by a geographic space, such as would be experienced in a chemical or explosive attack on a building then site operations are directed by the IC on scene. This is consistent with the evolution of IMS as a means of organizing local resources for use by the on-scene IC and hence its use by police, fire, and emergency medical personnel (Perry, 2003). If, however, there is no identifiable geographic boundary—as might occur in a biological attack—then the incident is managed from the Phoenix Emergency Operations Center (EOC). Either way, the individuals in command of the response operations are in relative geographic proximity to the incident (Perry, 1991). The principal aim of the IMS Model is to ensure that all resources and MMRS partners are available for every incident, whether an incident turns out to be a routine emergency or WMD mass-casualty incident.

There are two components of a Phoenix MMRS response. The first is inherent in the IMS, represented by highly skilled and well-equipped first responders guided in action by an IC. These responders are the police, firefighters, and emergency medical responders who are always on duty and provide the initial professional response to a wide range of community threats, whether a routine incident or suspected terrorist act. A key advantage to this model is that Phoenix response agencies utilize the IMS on all incidents under the hypothesis that daily use enhances the effectiveness of the system when it has to be used under large scale, more extreme circumstances (Brunacini, 2002). Furthermore, the IMS provides a functional management system that integrates personnel from different emergency response agencies under a single, unified command structure. This is particularly important as the incident expands to incorporate other agencies as needed. The second component of the MMRS IMS Model is the EOC. Activation of the EOC adds special administrative staff to aid in the management of a large-scale terrorist incident. This includes access to technical experts from public, private, and nonprofit organizations who have special knowledge and skills related to NBC agents.

Incident Management System

The IMS is a flexible, scalable structure for marshaling resources and coordinating a multiagency response under a unified command. It is a functionally based approach to management that establishes clear lines of authority, unity of command, an effective span of control, and defined paths for the flow of information. For fire departments operating in the Phoenix mutual (automatic) aid system, the IMS is the way all types of emergencies are handled. The advantage of the IMS lies in its adaptability to incidents of any size, scope, or nature (Brunacini, 2002). Thus, IMS functions equally well for events precipitated by fire, medical, hazardous materials, or rescue demands, and addresses the most routine of incidents as effectively as the large, complex, multi-jurisdictional incidents.

The IMS is built around responsibilities vested in the role of IC. An important strength of the IMS is that it is based upon roles to be executed rather than upon the authority vested in individuals or by virtue of one's rank. Following standard operating procedures, the IC in the field assigns personnel to the relevant roles in a terrorist (or any other) incident. The IMS size and composition can be tailored to the demands of the incident being managed. Thus, the structure begins with the first arriving firefighter establishing command and grows as more experienced officers arrive to assume responsibility for managing the incident. This includes dealing with agent-generated demands that arise from the impact itself and response-generated demands raised by supporting the emergency responders.

In response to the intergovernmental and interorganizational challenges faced by emergency responders during the September 11, 2001, terrorist attacks, President Bush issued Homeland Security Presidential Directive 5 (HSPD-5). HSPD-5 tasked the Secretary of Homeland Security to develop a National Response Plan and oversee the development and administration of the National Incident Management System (NIMS). The NIMS was developed with the intention of creating a national framework for all-hazards response (Perry, 2006).

The 9/11 Commission strongly supported a policy, whereby federal homeland security funding would be contingent upon the "adoption and regular use of ICS and unified command procedures" (National Commission on Terrorist Attacks, 2004, p. 397). Under HSPD-5, all federal agencies are required to adopt and implement NIMS. In addition, the NIMS Integration Center requires state, local, tribal, private sector, and nongovernmental agencies with a direct role in emergency management to train, and certify personnel in NIMS as a condition of receiving federal homeland security funding beginning in FY06. This includes any discipline with emergency responsibilities including law enforcement, fire and emergency medical services, hospitals and public health organizations, and public works and utilities.

The NIMS focuses on the traditional elements of incident command—command, operations, logistics, planning, and administration/finance. Command refers to the overall IC. The IC is responsible for continuous situational assessment, controlling the communications process, developing the overall incident strategy, creating an effective Incident Command organizational structure, and managing the Incident Management plan. Through these duties, the IC builds and maintains the strategy and resources that will be needed to manage the incident (Perry and Lindell, 1992). Operations are responsible for tactical priorities, as well as for the safety and welfare of personnel working on scene. The Logistics Section is the support mechanism for the incident providing supplies and equipment to responders and forecasting future resource needs. The Planning Section gathers, assimilates analyzes, and processes information needed for effective decision making. Planning serves as the IC's "clearing house" for information needed to make long-term strategic decisions. Finally, the Administration or Finance Section evaluates and manages the risk and financial requirements of agencies involved in an incident. Responsibilities include procurement of services, documenting the financial costs of incurred during an incident, and assessing legal risk.

But, NIMS expands beyond the traditional role of incident command to include aspects of preparedness and interoperability. For example, NIMS training materials available from the FEMA specifically address EOCs, multiagency coordination systems, and mutual aid agreements. These sections include (Department of Homeland Security, 2004, p. 4)

- Preparedness—addresses training and exercising, personnel qualifications and certification standards, and publications and management processes and activities.
- Resource Management—defines standardized mechanisms and establishes requirements for processes to describe, inventory, mobilize, dispatch, track, and recover resources over the course of an incident.
- Communications and Information Management—requires a standardized framework for communications and information sharing.
- Supporting Technologies—includes capabilities such as voice and data communications systems, information management systems, and data display systems.
- Ongoing Management and Maintenance—establishes an activity to provide strategic direction for the oversight of the NIMS.

The Phoenix MMRS uses the IMS to resolve some of the interagency coordination problems inherent in large-scale incidents, as demonstrated during the terrorist attacks on 9/11. The strength of the NIMS is its flexibility and thus its ability to adapt to changing incident conditions.

Hospital Incident Management System

The Hospital Incident Command System (HICS) is a form of IMS specifically designed for internal use by hospitals and other healthcare facilities. The HICS includes a core set of response concepts, procedures, and terminology that enable medical staff to fully integrate their activities in a multiagency response environment. This helps hospitals better manage the influx of self-referred patients, family members, and others who converge on medical facilities after a disaster (Macintyre et al., 2000). The HICS has been called a "best practice" by the U.S. Occupational Safety and Health Administration. Fundamental elements of the system are consistent with those of the IMS: predictable chain of command, flexible organizational structure, accountability of operational personnel, and common terminology and interoperable communications. These elements help to advance institutional preparedness within healthcare facilities, while also working to integrate hospitals into the local response system.

The most recent edition of the HICS was published in 2006 in cooperation with the U.S. Department of Homeland Security, the American Hospital Association, and the Joint Commission on Accreditation of Healthcare Organizations. Because HSPD 5 requires hospitals to be NIMS compliant as a condition of receiving federal grants or contracts, HICS was designed specifically to be NIMS-compliant. HICS incorporates operational tools to support hospital planning activities for a myriad of events, including epidemic, natural and civil disasters, and acts of terrorism.

Emergency Operations Center

The Phoenix Emergency Operations Center (EOC) is the city's coordination center for emergency services during any major incident affecting the city, including WMD events. Normally, daily operations are conducted independently from city departments located throughout the city. When a major event occurs, centralized emergency management may be needed to coordinate the activities of various agencies. An EOC provides a central location of authority and information and allows for face-to-face coordination between decision makers. The EOC is the primary focus of policy-making for large-scale incidents and the hub through which information and resources flow. Functions commonly performed in the EOC include

- Receiving information and disseminating warnings and instructions to the public
- Collecting intelligence from and disseminating information to the various EOC representatives as well as federal, state, and county authorities
- Preparing intelligence and information summaries, situation reports, and operation reports as required
- Continuous analysis and evaluation of data pertaining to emergency operations
- Controlling and coordinating the operations and logistical support of resources committed to controlling the emergency condition
- Maintaining contact with support EOCs in other jurisdictions

During a WMD event, the EOC will function in one of two ways. First, if the event occurs in a geographically definable area—as would be expected in a chemical or radiological attack—the EOC provides support to the IC operating on scene by providing specialized information and directing needed resources to the scene. However, if an event unfolds slowly with no definable geographic scene—as a bioterrorist attack might produce—the EOC operates as the command center with the overall IC operating out of that facility.

Similar to on-scene operations, the EOC is organized around the IMS Model and includes the administration, logistics, planning, and operations sections. For WMD events, the functions of command are embodied in three individuals. The MMRS Leader provides special knowledge about WMD threats and is familiar with the IMS used by response personnel. The City Emergency Management Coordinator is knowledgeable about EOC operational capabilities and management.

The third member of the command team, the Emergency Services Director, is a civilian administrative officer representing the City Manager's office and is the liaison with elected officials. Representatives from private and nonprofit organizations may also be represented in the command structure. The personnel and organizations, which are represented in the EOC, will depend upon the type and scope of an incident. However, in the event of a NBC attack, representatives from the County Medical Examiners Office, as well as toxicologists from the Regional Poison Control Center would work in the Operations Section. The Logistics Section would include a representative from the Arizona Healthcare Association. Finally, state and county public health officials are included in the Planning Section.

System Activation

Terrorist events have very different characteristics depending upon the materials used: explosives, chemicals, radiological materials, or biological agents. Because of this, the system for activating the Phoenix MMRS is multifaceted involving public safety dispatchers, first responders, and medical personnel. Dispatchers from the Fire Department Regional Dispatch Center and police dispatchers are the first line of surveillance for possible terrorist activity. Dispatchers may take calls for service, which would indicate an NBC attack is underway such as an explosion or report of multiple people down. Another route for MMRS activation lies in the first responders—police officers, firefighters, and emergency medical technicians—in the field. These responders may come across victims exhibiting the signs and symptoms of exposure to NBC agents. The third route is with hospital or state and county health departments, where epidemiological disease screening is done and outbreak patterns are analyzed.

For all terrorist incidents, the focal point for engaging the Phoenix MMRS are with fire and police dispatch centers. In terms of recent experience, it is expected that most nuclear or chemical incidents will be reported as a hazardous materials incident. Bioterrorism events may also be reported to local emergency services with an increase in "ill person" calls. Local hospitals and laboratories and the state or county health department can confirm that an attack is underway and recommend the activation of the Phoenix MMRS support system for mass vaccinations and assistance with treatment of patients.

Major Functions and Operational Responsibilities

Clearly, terrorist events involving WMD require an integrated, interdisciplinary response from a myriad of healthcare professions and agencies. From a public health perspective, the Phoenix MMRS has two objectives: to conduct epidemiological surveillance for biological threats and to determine if outbreaks of disease may be caused by a terrorist act and to mobilize the healthcare system to effectively respond to incidents associated with a WMD event and provide treatment of patients exposed to NBC agents. Clearly, response to a WMD event would not be effective without strong connections between users of the system, and the Phoenix MMRS IMS program enhances those connections. A Steering Committee manages the medical component of the MMRS and a series of subcommittees, task forces, and planning groups help address specific issues, while serving to build a response network and good working relationships among the various participants by creating a sense of inclusiveness. The Phoenix MMRS operates with a flexible structure designed to reflect and address changes in the threat environment, changes in the state of medicine and technology, and changes in the resources capabilities of MMRS participant agencies. The following discussion addresses the major medical functions of the Phoenix MMRS Model, describes the agencies that have a role in providing public healthcare in the event of a WMD incident, and highlights the interdependencies of these agencies.

Emergency Medical Service Provision

In the Phoenix metropolitan area, fire departments generally serve as the primary provider or pre-hospital advanced life support services. These fire departments use a fully integrated emergency response system utilizing dual-role firefighters (cross-trained as either emergency medical technicians or the higher level of certification of paramedic) in the delivery of both fire suppression and emergency medical services. The fire department has four major responsibilities with regard to the provision of healthcare. The first involves the planning, management, and delivery of emergency medical services. Twenty-six cities are part of a regional dispatch operation and are dispatched as if they were a single fire department; jurisdictional lines are not recognized. All members of the regional dispatch consortium use the same operational policies, procedures, and protocols for communication and emergency scene operations. The IMS is used to fully integrate and support this mix of fire departments during incident operations. This system enables these fire departments to medically manage a mass casualty incident involving NBC agents by drawing upon the collective capabilities and resources of departments in the consortium. It also positions the Regional Dispatch Center to monitor acute trends in call volumes that may be indicative of a biological attack. As the central hub in this regional system, the Phoenix Fire Department serves as a central coordinator for several MMRS IMS functions.

One of the MMRS functions involves review of protocols for patient treatment, medical management policy, and pre-hospital medical scope of practice. The Fire Department Medical Director, the Arizona Department of Health Services

(EMS Section), the Arizona Emergency Medical Systems (AEMS), and the Samaritan Regional Poison Control Center work closely together to ensure that treatment protocols remain current and follow agent-specific guidelines. Paramedic personnel receive recurrent training in toxicology and medical management of patients to include rapid recognition of NBC agent exposure, recognition of toxidromes (toxic exposure symptoms), identification and administration of agent-specific antidotes, and application of poison treatment paradigms. Personnel also receive training to support public health functions such as administration of mass immunizations, support of medical examiner functions, and support of hospital operations.

The Special Operations Section of the fire department maintains a Pharmaceutical Cache, which includes medications, antidotes, and medical supplies in supplies sufficient to treat 1000 civilian casualties of a chemical or radiological incident. The cache also has a sufficient supply of antibiotics to issue prophylactic doses to responder personnel. The EMS Section maintains a current computer listing of local and statewide pharmaceutical wholesalers and retailers who can supply additional antibiotics, vaccines, and other medications needed for the treatment of patients or prophylactic use of citizens or responders. An exercise is conducted biannually to test the capacity of the system to delivery, distribute, and administer these medications. This exercise provides participating agencies with a hands-on experience in real-time, multiagency emergency response simulation.

In the event of an attack involving WMD, actions taken by first responders include those taken by operations responders and those taken by specially trained Hazmat personnel. In the Phoenix MMRS, the first arriving company officer has the responsibility of initiating the IMS by establishing command and beginning to size up the incident. First, arriving companies will begin by conducting a situation assessment, securing the incident area, executing emergency decontamination procedures, and directing casualties to a collection point. Paramedic personnel will then triage patients based on severity of medical need and begin to administer generic treatment of symptoms (assuming that the agent is not yet known). Patients are then transported to appropriate medical facilities for definitive care. In a large-scale incident, it may be necessary to move patients outside of the metropolitan area to prevent overload of local area hospitals. Hazmat team members from the fire department are tasked with entering contaminated areas to extricate incapacitated victims. These members will also attempt to identify the agent involved in the attack. This information is then passed along to on-scene paramedics and forwarded to destination hospitals so that patients may begin to receive agent-specific treatments.

It is also within the purview of EMS to attend to the emergent mental health needs of victims and their families. The Fire Department Community Assistance Program (CAP) is a system of response units composed of one emergency medical technician and one certified behavioral health specialist who has a master's degree in social work or counseling and is trained in crisis management. These units provide on-scene counseling to victims and victim's families and maintain contact information for counseling, hot lines, crisis services, and professional referrals for continued behavioral health support. CAP units operate out of fire stations throughout the Phoenix metropolitan area, and work in partnership with fire departments, police departments, and social service agencies.

Public Health Services

Public health is another function of the Phoenix MMRS. In the United States, local public health departments are centers for medical and epidemiological expertise. Although the role of these organizations is somewhat limited in the event of an explosive, chemical, or radiological event, they do play a significant role in preparedness for and response to biological terrorism. In 2002, the Maricopa County Department of Public Health (MCDPH) established the BioDefense Preparedness and Response Division, which is an active partner in the Phoenix MMRS. Along with the Arizona Department of Health Services (ADHS), MCDPH combats bioterrorism through an effective disease surveillance and identification program. In cooperation with the U.S. Center for Disease Control (CDC) and other partners, information is shared among state and local health agencies, county public health departments, hospitals, and infectious control practitioners through the statewide Health Alert Network system. Surveillance data is collected from these sources allowing for the early identification of public health threats and effective coordination of a healthcare response. The Health Alert Network is supported by local public safety agencies through monitoring of fire and police personnel illness patterns and reporting them to the public health system. If a biological agent is identified, the public health system identifies the agent, provides treatment guidelines, and issues orders for mass prophylaxis.

The need for administration of immunizations or prophylactic medicine to the public may arise with biological agents. In the Phoenix MMRS, the order for mass prophylaxis comes from medical personnel based at the EOC. Medications or vaccines would be obtained through the MMRS Pharmaceutical Cache and the National Pharmaceutical Stockpile. The MCDHS maintains a system of emergency prevention sites where medications would be distributed. A program to use fire department personnel to assist in administering vaccinations has been established and can be run out of local fire stations. Public information regarding the execution of mass prophylaxis/immunizations is managed through the Public Information Officer Section in the EOC.

The Phoenix MMRS provides the impetus for collaborative training and exercises between the public health system and partners in local police and fire departments, hospitals, public schools, the Arizona Department of Emergency Management, the Red Cross, and other private and volunteer agencies. Topics of this training have included use of the IMS, receiving and distribution of materials from the Strategic National Stockpile, simulated chemical attacks, and bioterrorism drills. The lessons learned from these joint exercises have implications for improved communications and a better understanding of the various roles different agencies play in a response to an act of terrorism and what information must be shared with whom. Understanding is a key to relationship building.

Extended Medical Care

Hospitals are focused on providing extended medical treatment to victims of WMD incidents. Preparedness for a terrorist attack requires that hospitals create linkages with governmental agencies, nonprofit organizations, material and pharmaceutical suppliers, behavioral health specialists, and the public health system with the goal of insuring readiness to respond to incidents involving NBC agents. For hospitals, the specific objective is to minimize the negative health consequences of an event while preserving the integrity and resiliency of the clinical healthcare system. Although hospitals have historically undertaken planning individually, the Phoenix MMRS provides opportunities for full participation in collective planning efforts that help to maximize regional treatment capacity and capability for WMD events. Under the MMRS, hospitals prepare to address six issues: internal and external hospital security, lockdown procedures, patient decontamination, patient tracking, treatment protocols, and patient triage. Hospitals are linked through the MMRS hospital subcommittee and the Arizona Hospital and Healthcare Association (AzHHA), a professional association to which all hospitals belong. Through the AzHHA, Arizona hospitals keep current on issues related to the National Bioterrorism Hospital Preparedness Program, the National Incident Command System, and the Hospital Incident Command System, and volunteer activities such as the Medical Reserve Corps and the Emergency System for Advanced Registration of Volunteer Health Personnel. All of these programs provide critical support in the event of a terrorist incident in Phoenix.

In the event of a terrorist incident, hospital security will become a major concern. Hospitals could become a secondary target of terrorists seeking to disrupt the public safety infrastructure of a community in an effort to increase the lethality of their attack. Hospitals may also be inadvertently contaminated by walk-in patients who come directly from the scene of the attack to the hospital without being decontaminated by Hazmat personnel. To guard against these scenarios, hospitals in Phoenix plan to initiate a lockdown procedure upon notification by the Phoenix Regional Dispatch Center. Internal hospital security will be reinforced and supplemental security provided by local police departments when available.

Another major consideration for hospitals is that self-referral of victims can quickly overload area emergency departments while more distant hospitals receive few patients. In March 1995, the Aum Shinrikyo sect—a doomsday religious cult in Japan—released an impure form of sarin in the Tokyo subway system. The St. Luke's Hospital Emergency Department reported an influx of 640 patients within two hours of the incident, 541 of those were self-referred and were never treated or decontaminated on scene by fire/EMS personnel. Fortunately, St. Lukes had planned for such an event. The plan called for postponing routine surgical and outpatient procedures freeing up over 100 physicians and 300 registered nurses and volunteers to handle the influx of patients (Buck, 1998). Treatment capacity is another pressing concern. Within three hours of the 2001 terrorist attack on the Pentagon, Inova Health System's four Virginia hospitals were able to create an additional capacity of 343 beds and 43 operating rooms through early discharge of inpatients with at-home follow-up care by healthcare professionals (Hick et al., 2004). In the days following Hurricane Katrina, the Earl K. Long Medical Center in Baton Rouge doubled its 200 bed capacity by opening several closed wards in the facility (JCAHO, 2006). In conjunction with the AzHHA, Phoenix hospitals have developed plans to operate a Medical Aid Station system staffed by statewide medical personnel recalled by the AHHA hospital representative based in the Phoenix EOC. The Medical Aid Station System expansion includes creation of additional on-site bed space in hospitals as well as the capacity to open, equip, and staff a centralized treatment site at a remote location.

Patient surge may also be addressed by transferring patients outside of the metropolitan area to out-of-area hospitals or even facilities outside of Arizona. Participating healthcare facilities in the region constitute a Hospital Mutual Aid System (H-MAS) that allows for the systematic distribution of patients and the sharing of medical and support staff, supplies and equipment, and pharmaceuticals. A H-MAS is considered a standard of care in the healthcare community and the American Hospital Association has adopted the Model Hospital Mutual Aid memorandum of Understanding as a template for establishing regional intra-agency agreements. In the Phoenix MMRS, patients may also be moved to the National Disaster Medical System (NDMS). The NDMS is a system of military aircraft equipped to sustain patient treatment and move patients anywhere in the United States for extended care. To access NDMS, physicians determine patient suitability for transfer and transported to the NDMS Patient Reception Center located in the Executive Terminal at Sky Harbor International Airport; transportation is accomplished through hospital agreements with private ambulance providers and supplemented by fire department rescue squads when available. Continuity of care is maintained by medical personnel from the Luke Air Force Base hospital and prearranged civilian healthcare providers.

Treatment of patients requires an adequate supply of medications. A pharmaceutical representative located in the Phoenix EOC will coordinate delivery of appropriate medications, antidotes, and medical supplies from the MMRS cache to area hospitals and the Medical Aid Station. The pharmaceutical representative will also work with the representative from the AzHHA to monitor the needs of hospitals and obtain additional drugs through preestablished relationships with local pharmaceutical suppliers and pharmacies. They also help coordinate the delivery of the National Pharmaceutical Stockpile to the Phoenix area. Regional fire departments will aid in the transportation and distribution of these supplies, with necessary security provided by police departments.

Management of the Deceased

The final medical function of the MMRS relates to the handling and disposition of the deceased. In Phoenix, the Maricopa County Medical Examiners Officer (MCMEO) managers this function. The medical examiner's task encompasses seven functions:

- Receive human remains
- Safeguard personal property
- Identify the deceased
- Complete and maintain case files
- Preserve the chain of evidence
- Provide death certificates
- Release remains for final disposition

The medical examiner is responsible not only for handling remains in a manner respectful of family wishes and religious beliefs but also for the important role of photographing, fingerprinting, and collecting DNA specimens to preserve the chain of evidence related to law enforcement proceedings.

In the event that the number of fatalities exceeds the capacity of the MCMEO facility, the Disaster Response Plan is activated. This plan establishes an expanded morgue facility at a hangar at Sky Harbor International Airport that is large enough to accommodate multiple examination stations. The hangar can be partitioned into separate areas for receiving bodies, toxicological chemical laboratory examinations, autopsy examinations, and assignment for disposition. MCMEO personnel and vehicles transfer human remains from an incident to hospitals. Additional equipment and operational support is available from the Arizona National Guard. The Maricopa County Sheriff's Office provides security for all morgue facilities and the Fire Department Special Operations Division will ensure that bodies are decontaminated before being transported to morgue facilities. Further management of the deceased will be overseen by MCMEO, supported by partners from the Arizona Funeral Directors Association.

Conclusion

Preparedness for terrorist events requires solid partnerships and open, timely communication. By virtue of its structure, the Phoenix MMRS is a system that enables participating organizations to build and maintain vertical lines of communication between local, state, and federal responders, as well as horizontal communication links among public, private, and nonprofit response agencies. This system is vested in the everyday use of the IMS; as such, the MMRS structure should operate well because responders are very familiar with and experienced in using this Incident Management System. Indeed, experience using the MMRS to respond to simulated terrorist attacks has demonstrated how well the system works. First responders are trained to observe features indicative of NBC agents and are given the proper PPE appropriate to any threat they might encounter. Thus, the MMRS combines personnel safety concerns with an effective design for managing the consequences of a WMD event. Since its inception, the MMRS has worked to forge working partnerships among public, private, and nonprofit agencies to create a national emergency response infrastructure that protects the country's most populated, and potentially most vulnerable, communities.

References

Brunacini, A.V. 2002. *Fire Command: The Essentials if IMS*. National Fire Protection Association: Quincy, Massachusetts.

Buck, G. 1998. *Preparing for Terrorist*. Del Mar Publishers: Albany, New York.

Department of Homeland Security 2004. *National Incident Management System*. Washington, DC: U.S. Department of Homeland Security.

Hick, J., Hanfling, D., Burnstein, J., DeAtley, C., Barbisch, D., Bogdan, G., and Cantrill, S. 2004. Health care facility and community strategies for patient care surge capacity. *Annals of Emergency Medicine*, 44: 253–261.

Joint Commission on Accreditation of Healthcare Organizations. 2006. *Surge Hospitals: Providing Safe Care in Emergencies*. Joint Commission for Accreditation of Healthcare Organizations: Washington, DC.

Macintyre, A.G., Christopher, G.W., Eitzen, E., Gum, R., Weir, S., DeAtley, C., Tonat, K., and Barbara, J. 2000. Weapons of mass destruction events with contaminated casualties: Effective planning for health care facilities. *Journal of the American Medical Association*, 283: 242–249.

National Commission on Terrorist Attacks. 2004. *The 9/11 Commission Report: Final Report of the National Commission on Terrorist Attacks upon the United States*. New York: W.W. Norton & Company.

Perry, R.W. 1991. Managing disaster response operations in Drabek, T. and G. Hoetmer (Eds.), *Emergency Management*. International City/County Management Association: Washington, DC.

Perry, R.W. 2003. Incident management systems in disaster management. *Disaster Prevention and Management*, 12: 405–412.

Perry, R.W. and Lindell, M.K. 2003. Understanding human response to disasters with implications for Terrorism. *Journal of Contingencies and Crisis Management*, 11(2): 49–60.

Chapter 15

eSAFE: The Knowledge Management System for Safe Festivals and Events

Clark Hu and Pradeep Racherla

CONTENTS

Introduction

For as long as anyone can remember, people have celebrated. The need to celebrate is inherent in everything we do and touches virtually every part of our lives. Over the years, celebrations have evolved from informal and unplanned affairs to well-planned, formal, complex, and reoccurring events. The scales of these events range from small celebrations such as family reunions, to midsized business conferences, to large-scale international sports competitions and festivals.

Event and festival planning has become a business and an industry by itself, with professional standards and expectations. According to an estimate from International Festivals and Events Association (IFEA), the events and festivals produced by its member organizations alone generate a combined economic impact of $25 billion and serve over 400 million event attendees a year. According to the Tourism Industry Association of America (2003), in 2002, 75 percent of U.S. adult travelers attended a cultural activity or event while on a trip. This translates to an estimated 109.8 million U.S. adults. Furthermore, one-fifth of all U.S. travelers in 1999 attended a fair, festival, or other special event during their vacation (Tourism Industry Association of America, 1999). Similar phenomena were also observed in Canada. According to Hill (2002), 12.8 million Canadians (aged 15 or older) attended at least one performing arts event, festival, or public art gallery, and nearly half (6.1 million) attended more than one type of event during 2001. Each year, millions of individuals attend events throughout North America ranging from mega-events, such as international sports events, to large-scale national, to small town festivals and parades. Owing to high media visibility and attention, such events can be characterized as soft targets, being vulnerable to terrorism (International Festivals and Events Association, 2002). Further, there is always a danger of accidents, disasters, and other unwanted hazards that can cause loss of life, property, and eventually destroy the reputation of an event.

Every event has numerous stakeholders such as internal participants (e.g., event planners, sponsors, staff, volunteers, etc.) and external participants (e.g., attendees, guests, governmental agencies, private security agencies, etc.). The well-being of these stakeholders is of primary concern to any event manager. Hence, safety and security constitute the vital aspects of event planning. However, event planning and management professionals face many challenges during the course of their everyday work. How do I manage the crowds attending the event? What is the best way to ensure fire safety during the rock concert? What steps should I take to prevent my signature event from any riots or terrorist attacks? These are some of the many important questions that they face while planning an event. Although the task of ensuring safety and security has always been important to the event planners, the changes and challenges in the industry after the major terrorist attacks have made these issues even more important and salient than ever before.

To ensure the success of an event, an event planner/organizer must deal with multiparty involvements at different times and spaces. This complex nature of the event and festival planning makes the coordination between a host planning committee (or any individual planners) and event stakeholders a knowledge-intensive and exceptionally complicated task. Knowledge about safety and security in the event profession is essential to a safe and successful event (International Festivals and Events Association, 1997). One major challenge is that such knowledge accumulated from an event may not be effectively retained or enhanced after the event is over. Even if such knowledge can be retained or enhanced, another major challenge is how such knowledge can be efficiently communicated and disseminated in a timely manner. There is a need to enhance the overall knowledge of safe and secure events and improve communication efficiency of collaborative networks in event risk management. In such a scenario, it will be extremely beneficial if there is a system that allows event organizers to manage event safety and security knowledge and enables them to share their planning experiences and expertise with other professionals in the field. An information technology enabled knowledge management (KM) system is one such viable solution.

Knowledge Management Approach

The need for better communication and coordination among all the event stakeholders inspired us to develop eSAFE, the online knowledge-based system for safe and secure event planning. This system is specially developed for event management professionals or any other individuals, who are concerned with the safety and security issues of event planning.

eSAFE is based on the concept of KM, a concept that has been gaining increasing importance in the business world during the last one decade (Nonaka and Takeuchi, 1995). Today's economy is fundamentally characterized as a knowledge economy in which organizations emphasize on knowledge learning by building their capacities (e.g., what the organization can do) and human capital (e.g., skills and knowledge learned by the organization's employees).

An organization is not a static entity. It is an organic being that adapts to the environment and generates new knowledge at every step of its functioning. The concept of KM emphasizes on the most efficient and effective methods to identify, transfer, share, renew, and reuse this knowledge to stay competitive in this dynamic world.

Central to this KM concept are the organization's members, who are the major sources of knowledge. The members maintain large amounts of information, which they encounter in the day-to-day operation, assimilate through learning, and turn into new or reusable knowledge. Such knowledge is managed and stored in the tacit (implicit) or explicit forms. Tacit knowledge is kept in one's mind and stored as one's experiences and expertise. When tacit knowledge is written or expressed in the literal or electronic form, it becomes explicit knowledge. For example, an event safety expert publishes his experiences (a form of tacit knowledge) about risk prevention programs in a new book (a form of explicit knowledge) where readers can learn and share their unique experiences. There should be proper systems in place that enable the organization to synthesize this knowledge generated by every member and then ensure that it is effectively transferred, shared, renewed, and reused across the organization whenever and wherever needed.

eSAFE: The Online KMs for Safe Festivals and Events

eSAFE is based on the fundamental concept of KM. It enables event management professionals across the country to have a common platform on which they can search, share, revitalize, and reuse one another's knowledge and expertise. The system attempts to address three aspects that challenge event professionals.

1. Experience/knowledge retention: Much of the unique experience (tacit knowledge) gained by the event planners appears to be lost, leaving a new planner of subsequent or similar events with very little knowledge of the uniqueness of the event planning.
2. Content reprioritization: The attention given to event safety/security has grown tremendously over the past few years. Issues regarding event safety/security/risk management have been reprioritized as significant concerns in today's complex environment.
3. Networking efficiency: Although much of the knowledge involving standard operating procedures (explicit knowledge) has been documented manually, knowledge transformation and intelligence sharing within the network of event professional community have become cumbersome and cost-inefficient to prospective event planners and coordinators.

Event safety and security planning is a complex process that involves inputs from various disciplines and personnel. Further, new knowledge is created at every step of this planning process, which is accumulated with domain experts over a period. These experts are, therefore, in a unique position to create and transfer knowledge because they gain much of their knowledge by working on numerous events and event management organizations. The experts also add value to the current knowledge by leveraging experience to solve problems and provide advice. This knowledge resides in the individual/group of experts, who planned a particular event. As per our earlier classification of knowledge, this can be identified as tacit knowledge. Similarly, any documentation, manuals, books, or reports pertaining to the safety and security planning and procedures can be identified as explicit knowledge.

These resources can be effectively utilized by an event manager to plan a safe and secure event. The KM system we have envisioned for the event industry creates a common platform for industry professionals where they can interact, exchange information and knowledge, and draw on the collective experience of their colleagues as well as other domain experts within the system. The system also enables members to share explicit knowledge in the form of books, reports, journals, and manuals, which provide guidelines while planning the safety and security for an event. The ensuing section will provide details about the design framework and the essential components of the system.

eSAFE System Components

The eSAFE system consists of three major components. Each component is designed to support the major KM processes mentioned in the previous section. The major components of eSAFE are the Knowledge Base, the Advisor, and the ExpertNET (Figure 15.1).

1. Knowledge Base: It manages the explicit knowledge. It is a knowledge repository that allows users to search effectively and retrieve integrated domain knowledge.
2. ExpertNET: A platform for sharing and development of tacit knowledge. It is an expert-driven community of practice that facilitates domain experts to efficiently communicate and network among peers and in the process to share, develop, and transfer individual knowledge.
3. Advisor: A strategic planning tool that provides an expert guided step-by-step planning tool for event managers to plan safety and security issues of an event. An embedded electronic agent within the Knowledge Base generates advisory items (based on user input and organized guidelines and procedures) in safety and security to assist event planning duties.

Knowledge Base

The Knowledge Base is a comprehensive warehouse of knowledge specific to the safety and security aspects of event planning. It consists of policies and procedures, guidelines, etc., that have been synthesized from the various sources (e.g., textbooks and manuals written by experts of the field, government documents, etc.), which provide a structured way to learn the best course of action to be taken while planning an event. The eSAFE Knowledge Base is an online tool for the event planners, organizers, or any individuals concerned with security/safety issues in festivals and events. The process of knowledge acquisition and creation enables continuous

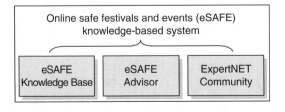

Figure 15.1   The three components of eSAFE.

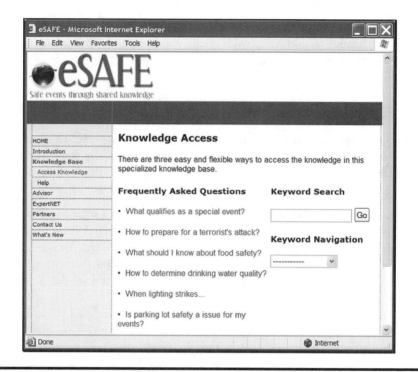

Figure 15.2   Accessing the Knowledge Base.

improvement and enhancement of the Knowledge Base. This component is open for the any user of the system to systematically learn about planning safe and secure events. The Knowledge Base is built using complex text mining software that helps the user navigate through useful information in three ways (see Figure 15.2):

■ Quick access to frequently asked questions (FAQs)
■ Keyword search by the user input
■ Assisted keyword navigation, which guides the user in the search

For example, if one is interested in the information on risk analysis factors, one can either type in the words or go through the keyword navigation to obtain the relevant information. Using the output page, the user can learn from the source and click on the relevant keywords for more information (see Figure 15.3), or even access the contact information of the expert of the source.

eSAFE Advisor

eSAFE Advisor is a strategic planning tool that assists and guides the users to plan a safe and secure event. It is an electronic agent with a dynamic built-in database that

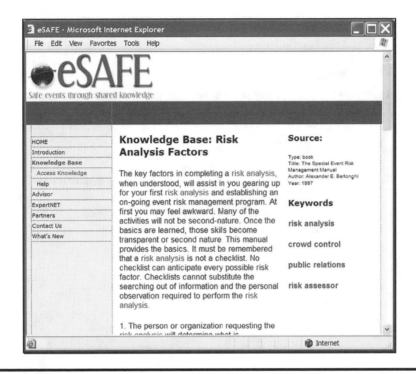

Figure 15.3   Output from the Knowledge Base search.

is regularly updated to keep up with the changing environment and based on the inputs of the members in our expert network (see Figure 15.4).

The basic difference between the previous component (Knowledge Base) and the Advisor is that the former provides general knowledge, guidelines, and tips for all kinds of event management situations whereas the Advisor helps the user get safety and security information specific to the planned event.

For example, an event organizer needs to know the procedures on fire safety planning for a statewide cultural festival in major cities of the state. The Advisor provides a step-by-step planning process wherein the user can input information specific to his or her event. The final report will then list out the relevant guidelines or procedures that are needed to be followed for that particular event. The advice from the Advisor is concise yet covers most important safety and security aspects pertaining to the planned event (see Figure 15.5).

ExpertNET

ExpertNET is a community of experts, who are qualified event professionals and individuals who are recognized as experts in security/safety issues. The secured

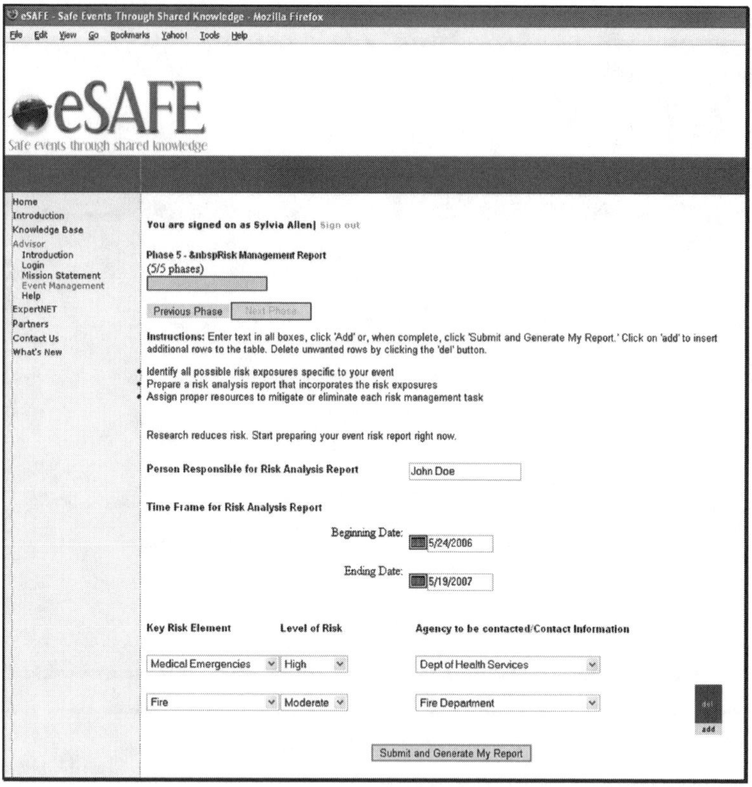

Figure 15.4   A view to access Advisor.

network requires a user name and password to enter. The ExpertNET facilitates its member to

- Search and identify experts as well as access a specialized network of experts across the country
- Participate and share information and knowledge through community forums

The development of ExpertNET involves an analytical method called network analysis. It helps the user to search and identify experts by different criteria such as the expert's name, or area of expertise, etc. (see Figure 15.6).

The member experts are grouped into their respective major areas of expertise such as event safety planning, security planning, and risk management. On the basis of our expert database and analysis, the user will be provided with a useful map in which the shortest and alternative communication routes can be identified to reach particular experts (see Figure 15.7). On the basis of this information, the member can click on the expert members (as nodes presented in the map) to make informed decisions for reaching the final expert source via contacting experts in the communication routes.

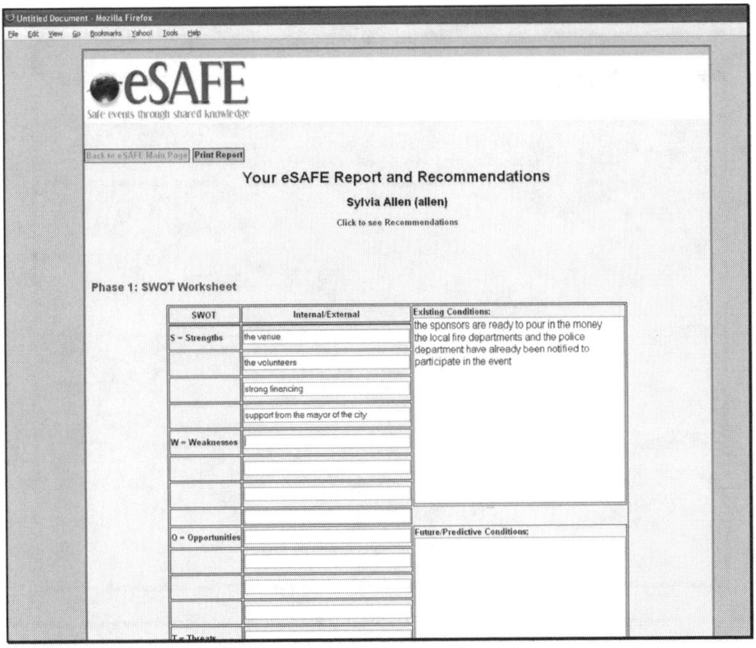

Figure 15.5   A view of advice from the Advisor.

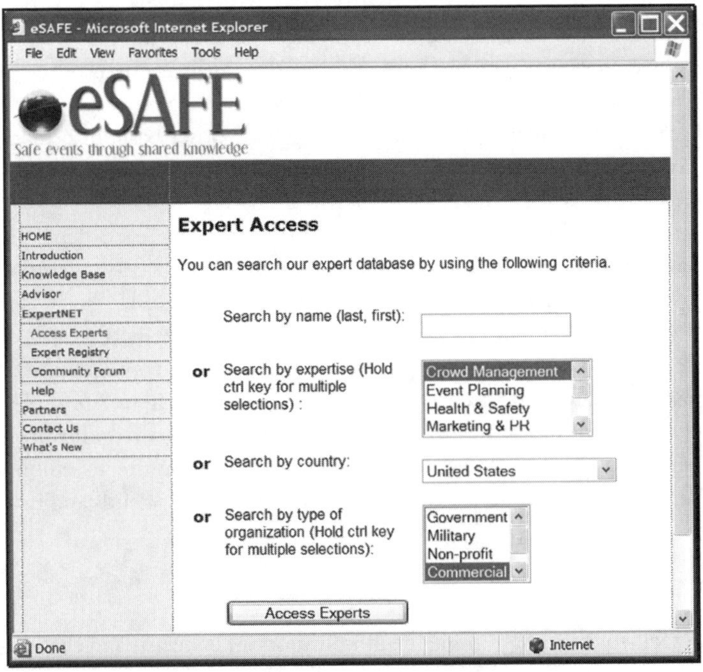

Figure 15.6   Search experts through Access Experts.

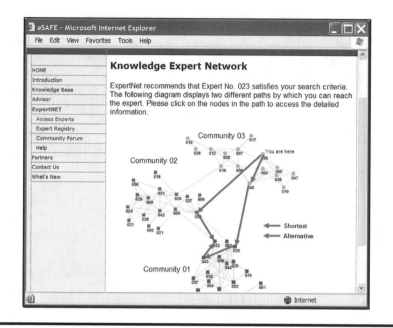

Figure 15.7 Network map of experts.

Another important tool in the ExpertNET is Expert Registry. It is designed to collect important information from qualified experts. A unique feature of this registry is "peer review," which allows an expert to compare with other experts in terms of "knowledge density" (how well an expert knows an area of expertise) on a designed scale. This valuable information along with other basic information (type of expertise, languages, preferred communication channels, etc.) will be used to build the expert knowledge map in the network analysis.

The last tool of ExpertNET is the community forums, each dedicated to the three major knowledge areas of event planning: event safety planning, event security planning, and event risk management (see Figure 15.8). It is a virtual community wherein members participate in communities related to their area of expertise and exchange knowledge. These user-friendly forums help the users discuss and share various safety and security topics of interest (see Figure 15.9). The knowledge discussed can be recaptured to feed in our Knowledge Base for other professionals to learn from and share with even more people. The forums are accessible to every member and help her or him keep up with the latest industry trends and issues.

Summary

Safety and security issues are among the most important concerns and challenges faced by the event industry. The eSAFE is specifically designed for the event management

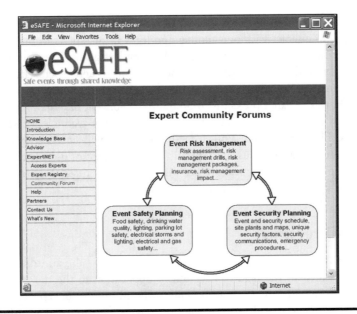

Figure 15.8 Entry page for community forums.

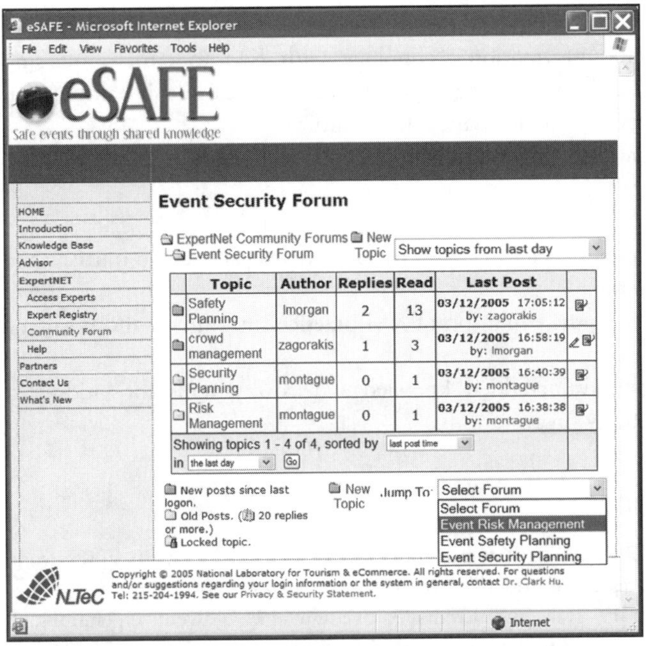

Figure 15.9 Expert communities facilitate sharing of knowledge among the members.

professionals and the event industry. It provides a very useful platform for event stakeholders to interact with one another and learn from experts in this field. This white paper describes basic ideas of the eSAFE system design and its practical benefits.

The system is designed to help the event professionals and experts efficiently use, communicate, and revitalize the knowledge for safe and secure events and festivals. Our goal in this research project is to promote the concept of "safe events through shared knowledge." By integrating KM with information technology, we are confident that this unique online knowledge-based system will significantly contribute to and benefit the event industry in specific and other relevant industries in general. We also hope that this practical project will spur further research into the field of KM and its applications to different industries.

Future Directions

The eSAFE is just not a Web site development project. It is also aimed to encourage extensive research in the field of KM and its application to the tourism industry. This research initiative is aimed to systematically utilize the concepts of KM as an innovative approach to help tourism and hospitality organizations identify, select, organize, and disseminate structured and unstructured knowledge so that it can be used to advance the development of both industries.

The overall goal of our efforts is to develop KM systems and practices that integrate information technology with KM to enrich tourism and hospitality organizations' learning experience and to utilize this value chain to enhance the organizational performance in the future.

As a part of this initiative, NLTeC will engage in the following research activities:

■ Continue developing systems for KM relevant to the tourism and hospitality industries
■ Modeling the evolution of KM practices in tourism and hospitality organizations
■ Building value-added knowledge discovery tools for guiding tourism and hospitality organizations

References

Hill, K. 2002, May. Arts Attendees in Canada. Retrieved May 20, 2005, from http://www. hillstrategies.com/docs/Arts%20attendees%20in%20Canada.pdf.

International Festivals and Events Association. 1997. Event Operations. Port Angeles, Washington: International Festivals and Events Association (IFEA).

International Festivals and Events Association. 2002, Spring. Special Event or Terrorist Target? International Events Retrieved September 14, 2005, from http://www.ifea. com/pdf/TargetArticle.pdf.

Nonaka, I. and Takeuchi, H. 1995. *The Knowledge-Creating Company: How Japanese Companies Create the Dynamics of Innovation.* New York: Oxford University Press.

Tourism Industry Association of America. 1999. Domestic Travel Market Report, 1999 edition. Washington, DC: Tourism Industry Association of America.

Tourism Industry Association of America. 2003. The Historic/Cultural Traveler, 2003 edition. Washington, DC: Tourism Industry Association of America.

Chapter 16

Collaborative Preparedness: The U.S. Department of Homeland Security's Ready Campaign

Heather Getha-Taylor

CONTENTS

An earlier version of this paper was presented at the Association for Research on Nonprofit Organizations and Voluntary Action, November 18, 2005, Washington, DC.

I would like to thank the Campbell Institute for supporting this research as well as the faculty members who assisted me in thinking about this topic, including Professor Mary Tschirhart and Professor Mordecai Lee. I would also like to thank the Ad Council and Christine Neal for providing information about the Ready campaign.

Introduction

In the most significant transformation of the federal government since the merger of the armed forces into the Department of Defense in 1947, President George W. Bush created the U.S. Department of Homeland Security (DHS) as part of the Homeland Security Act of 2002. This cabinet-level organization merged 22 separate entities and over 180,000 employees into one department, committed to protecting the nation against future threats. The merger created a mega-organization that was responsible for a complex and critical mission that included analyzing intelligence, guarding borders, protecting the nation's infrastructure, coordinating emergency response, protecting citizen rights, and enhancing public services.

In addition to the above-mentioned objectives, DHS set preparedness education as a priority. Americans needed to be ready for potential biological, radiological, and chemical threats. Beginning in 2002, the newly created DHS joined forces with the Alfred P. Sloan Foundation and the Advertising (Ad) Council to produce the Ready public information campaign. A combination of radio spots, television ads, print advertisements, and public displays (for use on billboards, bus shelters) were designed to encourage Americans to (1) create a kit of emergency supplies (including water, food, first aid items), (2) formulate an emergency plan, and (3) stay informed.

In addition to the previously mentioned techniques, a Web site (www.ready.gov) was created and a toll-free number was established. This duplication of ads was intended to reach as many people as possible. As noted by Weiss (2002), "with multiple channels, information that reaches people through one channel, such as television advertising, is reinforced by information that reaches people in the workplace or school," (p. 231).

The creation of the ads was an exercise in collaboration: the DHS partnered with the nonprofit Ad Council, which coordinated the efforts of two private advertising firms: the Martin Agency and Ruder Finn Interactive, both of which volunteered their services for the completion of the campaign. In addition to garnering $532 million in donated media support at the time of this writing, there is evidence to suggest that the campaign has changed attitudes and behaviors: in a July 2005 survey conducted by the Ad Council, 58 percent of respondents had taken at least one step to prepare for emergencies. Of the survey respondents who had seen one of the campaign's public service ads, 32 percent had made an emergency plan, compared to 18 percent of respondents who had not seen a Ready ad. Although the campaign was considered a success from almost the beginning of its run, it has evolved over time to include specific messages for the following audiences: Spanish speakers, small-business owners, and children. The evolving campaign has also extended the very definition of readiness. No longer is readiness confined to terrorist threats, but in the wake of Hurricane Katrina in 2005, the redesigned Ready campaign now emphasizes information on how to prepare for natural disasters.

Since its launch, the Ready campaign has been ranked among the most successful public information campaigns in history including those designed to prevent wildfires (the Smokey Bear campaign), prevent pollution (Crying Indian campaign), prevent drunk driving (Designated Driver campaign), prevent crime (McGruff the Crime Dog campaign), and encourage safety belt usage (Crash Test Dummies campaign). After a period, most public information campaigns are quietly retired. In the same fashion, the Ready campaign was initially slated for a two-year run. However, the campaign was deemed so successful—and so relevant to policy needs—that it spurned a long-term preparedness effort that shows no indication of retirement.

In addition to modifying behavior, garnering widespread media support, and reaching diverse target audiences, the Ready campaign highlights the integrated nature of modern governance. The quest for homeland security necessarily spans organizational boundaries. It should be no surprise that this preparedness effort involves a coalition of public, private, and nonprofit partners. What is surprising is the growth in the number of partners who have joined with the DHS and the Ad Council to promote preparedness during National Preparedness Month, a corresponding Ready campaign activity. Since the inception of National Preparedness Month in 2004, the number of partners involved in promoting preparedness has more than doubled, growing from 136 national, state, and local partners in 2004 to 308 partners in 2006.

Given the continued success of the Ready campaign, it is appropriate to examine the development and execution of the campaign to identify important lessons, questions, concerns, and future directions for scholars and practitioners. Homeland security will continue to elicit attention from policymakers, scholars, and citizens in general. Finding appropriate and effective ways to educate and prepare the public for security threats, both artificial and natural, is an evolving task and one that is worth examining.

Public Sector Communication and Homeland Security

Graber (2003) notes that in a democratic society, "accountability and responsiveness are the most important reasons for communication between public officials and citizens," (p. 197). In the case of the DHS, early efforts to communicate with the public faltered (Hall, 2003; Dizard, 2006). Critics claimed that early communications from DHS provided a mixed message: "get ready but don't panic," and were supplemented by somewhat misguided recommendations for preparedness that centered on duct tape and plastic sheeting. These recommendations were subjected to widespread ridicule. Late-night talk show hosts, David Letterman, Jay Leno, and Craig Kilborn, took a swipe at the recommendations. Web loggers even coined the term "duct tape alert" to describe the phenomenon of rising demand for duct tape following then Homeland Security Secretary Tom Ridge's recommendations for preparedness.

In addition to popular culture icons, homeland security experts also criticized Secretary Ridge's recommendations, including the raising and lowering of the color-coded threat level system, as random and of unclear applicability, (Hall, 2003). In response, the DHS identified the need to create a consistent, reliable message of preparedness. The result was the Ready campaign, a collaborative effort created with the help of the Ad Council and the Sloan Foundation. When federal organizations communicate with citizens, says Lee (2005), the purpose of the communication is "tied to implementing the agency's mission," (p. 8). In the case of DHS, there was a general recognition that emergency preparedness must begin at the grassroots level, specifically, in the home. It is not enough for the government to respond quickly and efficiently in the event of a catastrophe. In the hours immediately following any such event, citizens are alone. As a result, they must be prepared to respond appropriately. Educating and preparing citizens, then, is a necessary first step in creating a more prepared homeland.

Role of the Ad Council

The Ready campaign is just the latest chapter in a long line of collaborative public information campaigns that resulted from the relationship between the federal government and the Ad Council. In fact, the federal government and the Ad

Council were once joined at the proverbial hip. The Ad Council was created as a result of combining the private sector advertising firm, the War Advertising Council, with its public sector advertising counterpart: the White House advertising liaison office (see Lee, 2005). The Council's first campaign, the Savings Bond campaign, was deemed a great success. The campaign encouraged Americans to buy savings bonds to support the war effort and it is estimated that nearly 85 million Americans purchased 800 million bonds as a result of the campaign messages (see adcouncil.org).

The federal government has a history of relying on the Ad Council and other public, private, and nonprofit partners to help communicate important public messages as a matter of necessity. This necessity springs from the checks and balances inherent in our federal government. According to Lee (2005), "legislators have an *institutional* interest in minimizing public relations in public administration," (emphasis in original, p. 4). Because public relations are seen as wasteful expenses and opportunities to generate public support for agencies, Lee finds that elected officials generally oppose public information campaigns. As legislators rely upon popularity to survive, they are reluctant to take on strong public agencies. "In that respect," says Lee, "the struggle to control public reporting is the struggle over who will set the agency's destiny," (p. 4).

As an outside entity, the Ad Council's efforts are not tied to election outcomes or budget allocations. However, the success of Ad Council campaigns does rely on support from other organizations, namely media outlets, private foundations, and both public and nonprofit organizations. The Ad Council relies on these collaborative relationships to identify issues, craft advertisements, distribute messages, and evaluate the impact of public service announcements. In addition to addressing social issues through crafted messages, the Ad Council has also worked to bridge the agendas of the public and nonprofit sectors. For example, the Smokey Bear campaign, launched in 1944, connected the USDA Forest Service and the National Association of State Foresters in a collaborative effort to prevent wildfires. The Smokey Bear campaign and the Ready campaign are considered to be two of the most successful collaborative communication campaigns. These initiatives, as well as other notable public information campaigns, including their primary measurable outcomes, are compared in Table 16.1.

One of the common themes that connect all Ad Council campaigns is one of personal responsibility. For instance, the Smokey Bear campaign's foundation is "Only You Can Prevent Forest Fires," and the famous Crying Indian campaign to curtail pollution included the following tagline: "People Start Pollution, People Can Stop It." McGruff the Crime Dog campaign encouraged people to "Take a Bite Out of Crime." It was McGruff the Crime Dog campaign that was credited for shifting public opinion from the notion that crime prevention was the government's responsibility to one that embraced personal action. Research indicated that the campaign was instrumental in inspiring individual-level crime prevention actions (University of Wisconsin, 1993). This theme is reflected in the Ready campaign, which encourages personal preparedness, and is echoed by those involved in homeland security

Table 16.1 Comparison of Selected Notable Public Information Campaigns

Campaign	Launch Date	Sponsors	Goal	Primary Outcomes	Donated Media ($)
Smokey Bear	1944	Public: USDA Forest Service Nonprofit: National Association of State Foresters	Wildfire prevention	1. Loss of forest land from fire has decreased from 22 million acres in 1944 to under 8 million acres in 2004 2. Smokey is #2 most recognized image in America, second only to Santa Claus	1 billion (since 1980)
Crying Indian	1971	Nonprofit: Keep America Beautiful, Inc.	Prevent pollution	1. Catalyst for creation of Environmental Protection Agency and Earth Day 2. Reduced litter by as much as 88 percent in 12 years	1.3 billion
United Negro College Fund	1972	Nonprofit: United Negro College Fund	Promote higher education for minorities	1. More than $2 billion in donations to UNCF 2. 300,000 black college graduates since campaign launch	700 million
McGruff the Crime Dog	1980	Nonprofit: The National Crime Prevention Council	Prevent crime	1. 20 million Americans belong to Neighborhood Watch groups 2. McGruff has been used as an educational tool for police departments across nation	1.3 billion

Table 16.1 (continued) Comparison of Selected Notable Public Information Campaigns

Campaign	*Launch Date*	*Sponsors*	*Goal*	*Primary Outcomes*	*Donated Media ($)*
Designated Driver	1983	Public: U.S. Department of Transportation	Prevent drunk driving	1. Proportion of alcohol-related traffic deaths has dropped from 60 percent in 1982 to 45 percent in 2004 2. 90 percent of adults surveyed were aware tagline: "Friends Don't Let Friends Drive Drunk"	748 million
Crash Test Dummies	1986	Public: U.S. Department of Transportation	Use safety belts	1. Safety belt usage is the law in 49 states 2. 79 percent of Americans regularly buckle up today as compared to 21 percent in 1985	337 million
Ready	2003	Public: U.S. Department of Homeland Security	Emergency prepared-ness	1. 58 percent of Americans have taken at least one step to prepare for emergencies. 2. 32 percent of people who have seen a campaign ad have made a family emergency plan, compared to 18 percent of those who have not seen a Ready ad	532 million
Small Steps	2004	Public: U.S. Department of Health and Human Services	Obesity prevention	1. 30,000 people signed up for quarterly email newsletter 2. 83 percent of Americans believe that taking "small steps" can make a difference in their health	106 million

preparedness education. As noted by American Red Cross President and CEO, Marsha Evans "no community is truly prepared for a disaster until every individual, family and household takes personal responsibility for preparedness" (American Red Cross, 2005). The DHS undersecretary for preparedness George Foresman reinforced this when he said "all Americans have a responsibility to take steps now to be prepared for emergencies, whether they are caused by nature or by man," (Dizard, 2006).

Another theme that has appeared throughout Ad Council campaigns and reappears now in the Ready campaign is the strategic targeting of children. Images such as Smokey Bear and McGruff the Crime Dog are clearly aimed at reaching juvenile audiences, but they have an impact on adults as well. In addition to educating children, targeted messages allow children to educate their parents. Since the Ready campaign's launch in 2003, designers recognized a need to tailor the ads for children. The Ready campaign was significantly redesigned in 2006 to include Ready Kids, a child-friendly approach to preparedness that communicates through a family of mountain lions, including father Rex, mother Purrcilla, and daughter Rory.

Although collaborating to create a common message is a goal in itself, it is not the end goal. The primary goal of the Ready campaign is to enhance preparedness through changing attitudes and behaviors. According to Garnett (1992), attitudinal change is "often a prerequisite" for behaviors to change. Communicating preparedness information is not sufficient. Communication campaigns must be effective in reaching their intended audience(s) and motivating those individuals to action. As Garnett notes, "the greater the involvement government asks of a citizen or group, the greater the perceived benefit to that audience must be relative to costs," (p. 169). Emergency preparedness will continue to be a priority, but whether or not everyone is receiving, and acting on, this message remains to be seen. As illustrated in the next section, Ready campaign designers and supporters have worked to reach the greatest number of people as effectively as possible.

Development of the Ready Campaign

When the Ready campaign was first distributed in 2003, it included prominent, block-style messages, such as "the fight against terrorism begins at home," and bore a patriotic red, white, and blue theme. This design was meant to emphasize the unity of the United States in the aftermath of the 9/11 terrorist attacks. Shortly thereafter, the campaign messages were redesigned to focus on heroes of 9/11, and included images of firefighters as examples of strength under adversity. Now, the campaign has witnessed a third wave of redesign, with a focus on families and preparedness within the home.

The Ready campaign encourages families to do three key things: get an emergency supply kit, make a family emergency plan, and become informed about threats and appropriate responses (DHS Fact Sheet, 2006a). This message has now been extended to reach specialized audiences, such as small businesses, Spanish speakers, and children. According to Dizard (2006), "a well-prepared citizenry can dramatically lighten the burden on first responders." Critics of the early preparedness messages said the campaign did not address the source of the preparedness problem: the capacity to respond. Part of developing that has capacity to respond lies in reaching the right audiences at the right time. The Ready campaign designers have worked collaboratively with a variety of stakeholders to create a multilayered campaign that reaches specific audiences as described below.

Ready Business

The Ready Business campaign was the first specialized expansion of the Ready campaign. Its first messages were distributed in October 2004 and highlighted the dependence of government on small businesses. According to the Small Business Administration, small businesses account for 99 percent of all employers in the United States. Not only must businesses be prepared to protect their assets in the event of an emergency, but they also must prepare their employees for emergencies as well. According to an Ad Council study, 92 percent of business executives agreed that it is important to invest in preparedness, but only 39 percent have made efforts to be better prepared. The Ready Business campaign is intended to "close that gap," said Homeland Security Secretary Michael Chertoff. In the Ad Council's study, businesses cited a lack of time, resources, and funding as reasons for not preparing adequately.

Ready Business was developed and launched collaboratively with 12 organizations representing public, private, and nonprofit organizations, including: U.S. Chamber of Commerce, Small Business Administration, Society of Human Resource Management, The Business Roundtable, The 9/11 Public Discourse Project, ASIS International, Business Executives for National Security, International Safety Equipment Association, International Security Management Association, National Association of Manufacturers, National Federation of Independent Businesses, and Occupational Safety and Health Administration (DHS Fact Sheet, 2006c). Together, these organizations have worked to reach small businesses with less than 1000 employees each. While large organizations were likely to have plans in place for emergency situations, it was small business that suffered from a lack of planning. The ads for this campaign emphasize the message: "becoming a success is hard work; protecting it isn't" (see Figure 16.1).

Ready Kids

Ready Kids is another extension of the Ready campaign and is aimed to educate children ages 8–12. From the beginning, this campaign was a collaborative exercise. Experts from such organizations as the American Psychological Association, American

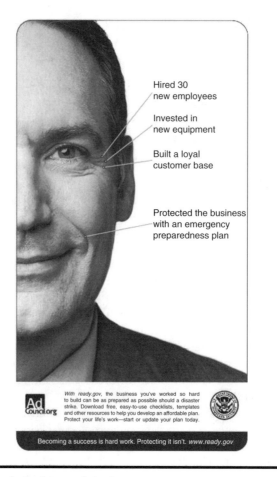

Figure 16.1   Ready Business print ad.

Red Cross, National Association of Elementary School Principals, National Association of School Psychologists, National PTA, National Center for Child Traumatic Stress, U.S. Department of Education, and U.S. Department of Health and Human Services worked together to design materials that would be child-friendly. This campaign does not utilize the typical mix of magazine, newspaper, or TV ads. Instead, Scholastic Inc. developed and distributed materials for fourth, fifth, and sixth grade students. The DHS planned to distribute materials to 135,000 middle school teachers in the 25 largest metropolitan areas in 2006. The materials offer teachers a way to discuss preparedness in the classroom in a way that students can easily understand. The campaign communicates a child-friendly message of preparedness through a family of mountain lions (see Figure 16.2). Kids can continue their learning online through a link that appears on the ready.gov Web site. In just one month after its

Figure 16.2   Ready Kids mountain lion family.

launch, the Ready Kids Web site received more than 2.8 million hits and more than 151,000 unique visitors.

Distributing the Ready Kids information was a collaborative exercise as well. The National PTA, Girl Scouts of the U.S.A., and Boy Scouts of America committed to distributing Ready Kids information and materials to their members. According to the DHS (DHS Fact Sheet, 2006b) the impact of this distribution is substantial. The Girl Scouts count nearly four million members in this country. The Boy Scouts sent material to more than 300 local councils and featured the Ready Kids material on their Web site and in their magazine. Finally, the National PTA planned 26,000 Ready Kids mailings to PTAs across the United States in fall 2006.

Listo

According to Graber (2003): "Communication has become a tougher challenge than ever before in all types of organizations—private and public... The messages that need to be disseminated are increasingly complex at a time when audiences speak different languages and are less in tune with dominant American culture ... " (p. xi). And as the Ready campaign illustrates, this is certainly the case for emergency preparedness. The Listo (Ready) campaign was designed to educate and empower the approximately 37 million Hispanics living in the United States. Like the other iterations of the Ready campaign, the Listo campaign was created as a collaborative effort among Elevación (a bicultural advertising agency), DHS, the Ad Council, and the Alfred P. Sloan Foundation.

This effort is extremely important, given the findings of Weiss (2002): "Citizens who are not literate, who have limited fluency in the native language of the country, who have limited education, who are too poor to afford newspapers, magazines, television, computers, or Internet access have less exposure to information from all sources, have fewer opportunities to benefit from the information, and find it more difficult to use information they do receive," (p. 245). Weiss says it is the information that "offers the opportunity for public policy to correct information gaps, empowering groups that traditionally have had little access to information relevant to their situation."

Interview research conducted in New York in 2004 indicated that even native English speakers found it difficult to comprehend the messages contained in the initial Ready ads. Children, the elderly, and those who were unfamiliar with the Internet found particular difficulty understanding the first set of Ready messages (Getha-Taylor, 2004). The Ad Council's focus groups confirmed this finding and worked to fine-tune the messages. In the case of the Listo version of the Ready campaign, a Guardian Angel icon was added to the messages to make them more relevant to Hispanics in the United States (DHS, 2003). This icon, which is popular in Hispanic culture as a symbol of protection, delivers the message of preparedness (see Figure 16.3).

Ready Campaign Effectiveness

Weiss and Tschirhart (1994), together with Rogers and Storey (1987), define information campaigns as efforts that are intended to generate specific outcomes or effects in a relatively large number of individuals, usually within a specified period, through an organized set of communication activities. Weiss and Tschirhart reviewed the literature to construct a framework of four key tasks that influence campaign effectiveness. These tasks are (1) capturing the attention of the right audience, (2) delivering an understandable and credible message, (3) delivering a message that influences the beliefs or understanding of the audience, and (4) creating social contexts that lead toward desired outcomes. As noted by Weiss (2002), it is difficult to accurately assess the effectiveness of public information campaigns. It is difficult to isolate the effect of the campaign on behavior that is "bombarded by many competing influences" (p. 240). With this in mind, the Ready campaign is examined in light of these criteria below.

¿Terrorismo?

Ayúdate que
yo te ayudaré.

Visita www.listo.gov o llama al 1.800.237.3239

Mantente en Guardia.

Figure 16.3   Listo campaign ad featuring the Guardian Angel.

Criteria 1: Capture the Attention of the Right Audience

According to Garnett (1992), audience segmentation (or disaggregating a mass audience into smaller, more homogenous audiences) "avoids the shotgun approach of sending the same message to everyone via the same medium, a tactic often inefficient, ineffective, or both." Weiss and Tschirhart (1994) agree "campaigns cannot be effective in inducing change in individuals or communities unless they are able to deliver their message to those audiences who are the targets of the campaign designers." This is the very reason the Ready Business, Ready Kids, and Listo campaigns were designed and implemented, and that the design and implementation were collaborative activities.

The Ready campaign began as a broad-brush effort to educate Americans on ways they could prepare for emergencies, especially terrorist threats. As the years have passed since the 9/11 terrorist attacks, the campaign has grown and changed to reflect an expanded definition and approach to preparedness. Preparedness begins at home and is a concern for all Americans—not just politicians or first responders. This expansion in the definition and approach to preparedness also reflects a growing sense of responsibility for homeland security. Given the fact that the extensions of the Ready campaign were designed and implemented in a collaborative fashion, utilizing the input of various stakeholders, there is an evidence of buy-in into the concept that homeland security is a shared priority.

Criteria 2: Deliver a Credible Message That Audiences Understand

Weiss and Tschirhart (1994) find that when the campaign message comes from a credible source, the message itself is considered to be more credible. By creating and implementing the Ready campaign in a collaborative fashion, the DHS and the Ad Council enhance the campaign's validity and credibility. In addition to credibility, Weiss and Tschirhart found that the message needs to be widespread and ongoing. Although most public communication campaigns are retired after a two-year run, the Ready campaign shows no sign of retirement. Further, interest continues to grow among potential coalition members in the National Preparedness Month initiative, which is an output of the Ready campaign. In the years since its inception, the number of private, nonprofit, and public sector partners in the coalition has more than doubled, growing from 136 partners in 2004 to 308 partners in 2006.

Criteria 3: Deliver a Message That Influences the Audience

Public information campaigns crafted by the Ad Council have traditionally attempted to link individual behavior with large social consequences and the Ready campaign continues this effort. In the years since its debut, the Ready campaign has been credited with changing both attitudes toward preparedness and measurable behavior. In a July 2005 survey, 32 percent of respondents who had seen one of the campaign's public service ads made an emergency plan, compared to 18 percent of respondents who had not seen a Ready ad. As the campaign continues, survey findings and focus group feedback will be increasingly important to determine whether or not the messages are as influential over time.

Criteria 4: Create Social Contexts That Lead Toward Desired Outcomes

Although the goal of communication campaigns is to modify individual-level behavior, it should be noted that any single policy instrument, including communication campaigns, is unlikely to create lasting change. Weiss and Tschirhart (1994) note that governments must often rely on mediating institutions to direct changes. By collaborating with public, private, and nonprofit partners to execute the campaigns, the DHS and the Ad Council are creating a community of partners that are committed to preparedness. In the case of National Preparedness Month, coalition members are given latitude in selecting the ways they promote preparedness. In years past, members have distributed brochures, printed messages on employee pay stubs and newsletters, sponsored contests, passed legislation, and sponsored additional promotional activities in conjunction with activities sponsored by the DHS, the American Red Cross, and the Ad Council. This united approach to emergency preparedness ensures that as many people as possible receive the same message from as many organizations as possible. This continuity and consistency is what will contribute to a public context where preparedness is valued.

Motivations for Ready Campaign Collaboration

Preparing the nation for chemical, biological, or radiological attacks requires coordinated effort across the public, private, and nonprofit sectors. Goggin et al. (1990) called attention to the complexity of policy implementation—particularly in policy areas that require the collaboration of organizations across sectors. "Communicating a policy message through the intergovernmental system means creating some shared sense of implementation and some coordinated pattern of activities among many different individuals" (p. 121).

This shared sense of implementation is most evident in the Ready campaign's most obvious output: National Preparedness Month. The first National Preparedness Month was held in September 2004. At that time, 80 national partners joined the DHS and the American Red Cross in educating the public about the importance of emergency preparedness. That figure increased by 137 percent in just one year to 190 total national coalition partners (U.S. Department of Homeland Security, 2005). In addition, all 56 U.S. states and territories are involved in National Preparedness Month, as are the 1770 state and local Citizen Corps volunteer councils and partners across the nation.

This growth in the number and diversity of partners, not only public and nonprofit organizations but also private organizations, speaks to the blurring of sectors. Eikenberry and Kluver (2004) and Ostrander and Langton (1987), note the increasing dependencies, or blurring of boundaries, among the for-profit, nonprofit, and government sectors. This mirrors the emphasis on partnerships in other federal organizations such as the Federal Bureau of Investigation (FBI). Robert Mueller, FBI director, said that "no person, no agency, no company, indeed no country can prevent crime on its own," (Arnone, 2006).

Cooperation, rather than competition, between and among the sectors offers new options for addressing social problems (Eikenberry and Kluver, 2004). Blurring of the sectors is perhaps most evident in federal policy in the form of the National Response Plan. In the National Response Plan, the American Red Cross, a nonprofit organization, is designated as the lead organization for mobilizing and coordinating volunteer response in the event of a national emergency. When necessary, the Red Cross is prepared to mobilize a national network into action, drawing primarily upon its 900 chapters, approximately one million volunteers and 35,000 employees.

In addition to the public and nonprofit sector partners, the private sector has responded to the National Preparedness Month initiative in an unprecedented way. For example, retailers are stocking home preparedness kits; companies are printing readiness statements on their employees' pay stubs; movie studios are sponsoring homeland security creative contests; and corporations are distributing educational materials to school children.

Understanding why these private, nonprofit, and public organizations are committed to homeland security is another question. One explanation may be that the relationship is mutually beneficial. In 2001, Sagawa presented a case study demonstrating a new value partnership, which is a long-term, high-yield alliance and is characterized by several key elements: communication, opportunity, mutuality, multiple levels, open-endedness, and new value (together, these elements comprise the COMMON principle). According to Sagawa, strategic partnerships between nonprofit, private, and public organizations are growing for a number of reasons, including the reputational benefits that may come from aligning with a popular cause or reputable organization. In the case of the Ready campaign and National Preparedness Month, organizational involvement may be viewed as a means to build trust and loyalty with employees, customers, or other stakeholder groups. In addition, coalition members view membership as a way to align their company with important policy goals. Understanding the motivations that drive organizations to join a public policy initiative is important in soliciting support for future efforts that rely on collaboration.

Policy Implications

The Ready campaign may be best understood through the lens of globalization theory. As noted by Stohl (2005), the increase in "global consciousness" may affect the impact of the Ready campaign as a public policy tool. Homeland security is a wicked problem where the cost of failure is enormous and no one organization—or sector—has all the answers. The Ready campaign illustrates the growing interdependence among the private, public, and nonprofit sectors. The growth in the number and diversity of partners involved in the National Preparedness Month coalition helps illustrate this trend.

In addition, the diffusion of the Ready message to the state and local levels illuminates this trend further. The state of New York and the city of Chicago offer two prominent examples. The Ready New York initiative includes a Web site and brochures that echo DHS's goal of preparedness. The Alert Chicago effort includes a partnership of at least ten separate entities working jointly to communicate a message of preparedness that is twofold; visitors to the Web site (alertchicago.org) can learn (1) how to prepare for an emergency and (2) what to do when emergencies happen. An Ad Council executive said that these new iterations of the campaign are appropriate and necessary: "we applaud their efforts because we can't be everywhere." To meet the dual needs of specification and standardization, the DHS is working with the Ad Council to create a Ready "seal of approval." This seal will ensure that citizens are receiving credible preparedness information.

The focus on emergency preparedness each September during National Preparedness Month serves as a reminder, much like the way daylight savings remind people to change their smoke alarm batteries, said an Ad Council executive. The end goal, she said, is creating culture of "a nation prepared." Evidence of reaching this goal can be elusive. "It took us 20 years to convince people to wear seatbelts," she said. Even if attitudes and behaviors are changed at a rate of just 2 percent per year, the Ad Council sees that as progress in meeting this goal. This progress, however, will only be possible through continued involvement of many partners in communicating the preparedness message. The Ready team, including Ad Council executives, ad designers, DHS executives, and National Preparedness Month coalition members, must continue to communicate the message. Natural disasters, such as floods, blackouts, and wildfires, provide teachable moments when the importance of the Ready campaign is most evident.

The Ready campaign is expected to continue indefinitely to communicate the message of preparedness to all Americans, including groups that may have been marginalized in the past. This inclusive approach communicates the message that everyone is important; everyone deserves to be safe; everyone must be prepared. As noted in a Government Executive report (2005), Homeland Security Secretary Michael Chertoff noted that "even under the best circumstances, the government is not going to be able to take care of everybody instantaneously." In addition to the Ready Kids, Ready Business, and Listo specialized campaigns, there are efforts to tailor the message to senior U.S. citizens, people with disabilities, and pet-owners.

As noted by Weiss (2002), information campaigns are particularly useful in instances when the targets of public policy "are very broadly dispersed but not organized," (p. 233). This is particularly applicable to the targets of the Ready campaign. There is no one best way to reach such diverse audiences as those that need to hear the Ready messages. Further, information campaigns are useful when the interests of policymakers and citizens are aligned but there is a lack of information (Weiss, 2002, p. 234). This was a primary concern during the first round of Ready messages. As indicated through interviews with a diverse sample of individuals in New York, the Ready campaign provided some mixed messages. Respondents expressed feelings of patriotism and respect for 9/11 heroes after viewing the ads, but did not necessarily receive the message of preparedness (Getha-Taylor, 2004).

Perhaps most appropriately, Weiss (2002) says that public information campaigns are well suited for public policy problems where there is "broad agreement about desired outcomes," (p. 234). In this instance, campaigns can capitalize on broad social support for the outcome. The Ready campaign benefits from a general interest in preparedness that resonates not only with politicians and federal organizations such as the DHS, but also with leaders of private and nonprofit organizations, families, and even children. This general interest stems not only from the tailored messages delivered through the Ready campaign, but also as a result of highly publicized incidents when preparedness was clearly lacking. The Hurricane Katrina response offers lessons not only for government and small-business owners, but also for the citizenry. In a report issued one year after Hurricane Katrina, Robert Tracinski criticized an apparent lack of preparedness planning among New Orleans residents who were stranded without food, water, or other basic survival supplies. Tracinski said that this event should teach us that it is time to move toward "personal responsibility and private initiative," a theme that is captured in the Ready messages.

Campaign Concerns

Although the number of National Preparedness Month coalition members doubled from 2004 to 2005, there is a marked lack of consistency from year to year. Only 34 coalition members from 2005 continued to support National Preparedness Month in 2006. Further, only 12 organizations, or just 8 percent, of the original coalition members have continued their involvement since 2004. These legacy organizations consist primarily of nonprofit organizations, but also include one business federation and one federal organization. Given the reliance on public, nonprofit, and private organizations to communicate and support the message of preparedness, researchers should investigate the following questions: Why are sponsors dropping out of the coalition? What are the incentives for public, private, and nonprofit organizations to join, and remain involved in, the coalition? How can those incentives be enhanced to support long-term partnerships?

In addition, the term "preparedness" has evolved to include biological and natural threats in addition to terrorist threats. However, that transition has not gone without notice, or criticism. In July 2006, the Federation of American Scientists issued a report that claimed there were factual inaccuracies and gaps in the Ready campaign. Further, the federation's report indicated that advice on the ready.gov Web site was unnecessarily lengthy, repetitive, generic, and generally confusing (Federation, p. 3). The Federation created its own emergency preparedness Web site, ReallyReady.org, as a means to illustrate and correct the inaccuracies. At the time of this writing, neither the Ad Council nor DHS had responded to the claims. As the Ready campaign gains even greater prominence, it will continue to evolve to reflect changing preparedness priorities. Providing clear and accurate information, however, will remain a prerequisite for ongoing campaign support and credibility.

Conclusion and Future Directions

In the wake of the 9/11 terrorist attacks, the public, private, and nonprofit sectors united in the creation and implementation of the Ready communication campaign. Not only has this campaign transferred important messages regarding emergency preparedness to specific audiences using diverse methods, but also serves as an example of cross-sector collaboration toward a common public policy goal. But creating a culture that values emergency preparedness is only just a beginning. The Ready campaign and its subcomponents, including Ready Business and Ready Kids, promise to continue to provide the critical information that Americans need to prepare for emergencies, both man-made and natural.

It is clear that preparedness is not only an advertising theme, but also is a political priority. In October 2005, President Bush nominated George Foresman to be the DHS's first undersecretary for preparedness. The directorate was created to integrate and coordinate DHS's preparedness functions. This emphasis is clearly not lost on the citizenry. As of March 2006, the Ready campaign Web site received more than 1.9 billion hits and 23 million unique visitors; the 800-BE-READY line received over 256,000 calls and more than 5.5 million Ready campaign materials were requested or downloaded from the Web site.

As noted by Garnett (1992), "no other communicator matches government for the quantity, variety, and importance of communications," (p. 15). Government communication, says Garnett, "typically involves more audiences and more diverse audiences," (p. 15). Communicating the importance of preparedness will remain a priority, as will the effort to reach as many Americans as possible. "Multiplicity and diversity of messages and audiences, greater politicization, heightened public scrutiny, and more rigid legal restrictions combine and interact to make government communication more necessary and more difficult," (Garnett, 1992, p. 19, emphasis added). Collaboration, then, is critical to communicating the message of preparedness.

The Ready campaign offers an example of cross-sector collaboration toward a common public policy goal. This shared goal of preparedness has far-reaching implications on the capacity of the federal/state/local government, private businesses, and individuals to respond appropriately in the event of an emergency. Understanding the motivations and incentives that guide such partnerships (as those illustrated in the Ready campaign) merits further investigation. In addition, the effect that the Ad Council's Ready messages have on their intended audiences' attitudes and behavior will require continued investigation as well. Finally, the consistency, credibility, and continuity of preparedness messages delivered by the multiple actors involved in National Preparedness Month activities also deserve long-term study to determine the net impact of the Ready campaign. According to an Ad Council executive, collaborating is critical, but the end result is what really matters: who delivers the message, she said, is not nearly as important as the message itself.

References

American Red Cross 2005. Press Release: Homeland Security and American Red Cross Co-Sponsor National Preparedness Month 2005. Author.

Arnone, M. 2006. FBI chief wants stronger partnerships. Accessed online: www.fcw.com.

(DHS) Department of Homeland Security 2003. Press Release: Department of Homeland Security Launches Listo Campaign.

DHS Fact Sheet 2006a. Ready Campaign. Author.

DHS Fact Sheet 2006b. Ready Kids. Author.

DHS Fact Sheet 2006c. Ready Business. Author.

Dizard, W.P. III. 2006. DHS' Ready.gov: Hold the duct tape, grab the umbrella. *Washington Technology*. July 18.

Eikenberry, A.M. and Kluver, J.D. 2004. The marketization of the nonprofit sector: Civil society at risk? *Public Administration Review*. 64(2); 132–140.

Federation of American Scientists 2006. Full Analysis. Accessed online: www.fas.org/really-ready.

Garnett, J.L. 1992. *Communicating for Results in Government: A Strategic Approach for Public Managers*. San Francisco, California: Jossey-Bass.

Getha-Taylor, H. 2004. Selling Security. Unpublished manuscript.

Goggin, M.L., Bowman, A.O'M., Lester, J.P., and O'Toole, L.J. Jr. 1990. *Implementation Theory and Practice: Toward a Third Generation*. Scott Foresman, Glenview, Illinois.

Government Executive 2005. DHS pushes Ready Business campaign. October 31. Accessed online: www.govexec.com.

Graber, D.A. 2003. *The Power of Communication: Managing Information in Public Organizations*. Washington, DC: CQ Press.

Hall, M. 2003. Get ready for readiness ad campaign. *USA Today*. February 19.

Lee, M. 2005. *The First Presidential Communications Agency: FDR's Office of Government Reports*. Albany, New York: State University of New York Press.

Ostrander, S.A. and Langton, S. 1987. *Shifting the Debate: Public/Private Sector Relations in the Modern Welfare State*. New Brunswick, New Jersey: Transaction.

Sagawa, S. 2001. New value partnerships: The lessons of Denny's/Save the children partnership for building high-yielding cross-sector alliances. *International Journal of Nonprofit and Voluntary Sector Marketing*. 6(3); 199–214.

Stohl, C. 2005. Globalization Theory. In *Engaging Organizational Communication Theory and Research: Multiple Perspectives*. S. May and D.K. Mumby, Eds. Thousand Oaks, California: Sage, pp. 223–261.

Tracinski, R. 2006. The unlearned lesson of Hurricane Katrina. *Fox News*. September 5.

U.S. Department of Homeland Security 2005. Press Release: Coalition Forces More than Double in Size to Join Homeland Security and the American Red Cross for National Preparedness Month 2005. Author.

Weiss, J.A. 2002. Public Information. In *The Tools of Government*. L. Salamon, Ed. Oxford: Oxford University Press, pp. 217–254.

Weiss, J.A. and Tschirhart, M. 1994. Public information campaigns as policy instruments. *Journal of Policy Analysis and Management*. 13(1); 82–119.

CASE STUDIES

Chapter 17

Homeland Security Preparedness and Planning in City Governments: A Survey of City Managers

Christopher G. Reddick

CONTENTS

Chapter is reprinted from Reddick, C.G. (2007). Homeland Security Preparedness and Planning in US City Governments: A Survey of City Managers. *Journal of Contingencies and Crisis Management*, 15(3), 158–167.

Introduction

September 11, 2001, or 9/11, has put extra pressures on local public officials and their agencies to avert and effectively cope with new terrorist threats (Rosenthal, 2003). After 9/11, the idea of homeland security became part of American thinking and behavior (Beresford, 2004). In this new environment that local governments must contend with, it is important to be aware of the scope and effectiveness of homeland security preparedness and planning. This study attempts to address the current state of homeland security preparedness in city governments.

Although resources for homeland security are mainly national, the responsibility to define the situation, initiative a government response, evaluate population needs, plan a relief effort still lies with state and local governments (Wise and Nader, 2002). Therefore, this study uses a survey of city managers in cities serving 100,000 residents or greater in the United States to examine homeland security issues. In this chapter, first there is an examination of the administrative and organizational aspects of homeland security. Essentially, what is the perception of preparedness and planning in terms of resources used and its impact on management capacity for city governments? Second, there is an examination of the extent of homeland security collaboration within local governments and among other levels of governments, which is believed to be one of the key pillars for effective homeland security preparedness and planning. Finally, there is an application of the adaptive management model to homeland security, which calls for continuous learning and collaboration in organizations in preparation for a possible terrorist attack.

To examine these three themes, this chapter is divided into several sections. First is an overview of the existing homeland security literature in public administration, specifically as it pertains to local governments. From this literature, several research questions are derived. This is followed by a discussion of the research methods of this chapter and the results of the survey are presented. A conclusion demonstrates the significance of the key findings.

Literature Review

As mentioned there are three themes explored in this study to determine the scope and effectiveness of homeland security preparedness and planning in city governments. Each of these themes has been derived from the existing public administration literature on homeland security.

Administrative and Organizational Aspect of Homeland Security

In response to emergencies, such as terrorist threats, Carroll (2001) believes that this is shaped by operational, administrative, and sociological components. Operational is the actual service provided by the government; administrative is how government entity is run; and sociological is both internal and external impacts on emergency management. Wise and Nader (2002) describe the organizational aspects of homeland security in terms of areas of intergovernmental complexities, operational, financial, legal and regulatory, and political. Essentially, the literature demonstrates the importance of the surrounding organizational environment, both internal and external, and its impact on homeland security preparedness and planning.

Homeland security mandates from higher levels of government put tremendous pressures on the finances of local governments and dictate intensified administrative oversight (Caruson and MacManus, 2005). In a national survey of American cities, there was evidence that resource capacity, budgetary constraints, and administrative capacity are tied to homeland security preparedness (Gerber et al., 2005). To exemplify this, in a national survey of city officials only around one quarter of respondents believed that there was a likelihood of city residents supporting additional local taxes to fund homeland security, whereas 58 percent believed that this is unlikely (Baldassare and Hoene, 2002). According to a survey of Florida county and city government officials, the largest impacts of homeland security legislation on local governments have been financial and administration (Caruson and MacManus, 2005). Therefore, the administrative environment that city managers face in homeland security is very constrained, with very limited resources and a public unwilling to accept tax increases to fund these important initiatives.

One of the most important administrative aspects of homeland security is the sharing of information between the federal, state, and local governments. The

Government Accountability Office (GAO) conducted a national survey of all levels of government of homeland security information sharing (USGAO, 2003a). The results are that federal, state, and city governments do not perceive the current sharing process of information as effective or very effective because they believe (1) that they are not routinely receiving the information they believe they need to protect the homeland; (2) that when information is received, it is not very useful, timely, accurate, or relevant; and (3) that the federal government still perceives the fight against terrorism to be generally a federal responsibility.

Local officials and first responders in the state of Florida also do not give the federal homeland security advisory system (or the color-coded system developed by the U.S. Department of Homeland Security to provide information on terrorist threat levels) very high marks. More officials tend to rely on information sources other than the federal government for threat data (MacManus and Caruson, 2006). Local government officials tend to rely heavily on state and local outlets for threat information, suggesting that federal sources are not providing the level of specificity desired by local officials (MacManus and Caruson, 2006). The following section provides information on the level of collaboration between and among departments and agencies in homeland security.

Homeland Security Collaboration

One of the most important lessons learned from the events of 9/11 is the importance of coordination among the governmental agencies and organizations, which are responsible for disaster management (Caruson and MacManus, 2006). National terrorism preparedness requires numerous federal, state, local, and private entities to be prepared to operate in close coordination to meet the threat and to mitigate its consequences (Wise and Nader, 2002).

Waugh (1988) explains that this tendency for a lack of collaboration among different levels of governments in emergency preparedness is attributed to three factors. First, vertical fragmentation is due to the dividing of powers between federal and state governments, and the limited powers given to local governments. Second, horizontal fragmentation is due to the jurisdictional issues of all the agencies involved. Finally, there is the unwillingness of the federal government to assume the lead role in disaster preparedness.

This fragmentation is also evident in homeland security grant funding. USGAO (2003b) has reported that mission fragmentation and program overlap are widespread in the federal government and that crosscutting program efforts are not well coordinated in homeland security grants. Therefore, scholars have argued that the federal system inhibits the responsiveness of governments to possible terrorist threats, which is exemplified through the existing grant funding system.

In a national homeland security survey, evidence shows some increased level of collaborations after 9/11. In this survey of city officials, there were high ratings for collaborative efforts of governments, agencies, and other organizations in their region (Baldassare and Hoene, 2002). There were even higher marks given for coordination between departments and agencies within their own city governments. In a survey of county and city officials in Florida, roughly two-thirds of survey respondents reported an improvement in intergovernmental cooperation since 9/11 (Caruson and MacManus, 2006). The change in the homeland security collaboration may be partially explained by the adaptive management model.

Adaptive Management and Homeland Security

The term adaptive management first appeared in the natural resources management literature in the mid-1970s (Hollings, 1978). This theory has been later used to explain homeland security preparedness and planning after 9/11 (Wise, 2006). Adaptive management calls for the integration of science and management and for researchers and managers to work collaboratively with each other and with the public (Graham and Kruger, 2002). Adaptive management attempts to incorporate the views and knowledge of all interested parties. Adaptive management begins with bringing together interested stakeholders to discuss management problems and to develop models to express participants' collective understanding of how the system operates (Johnson, 1999).

In adaptive management, there is citizen and organizational learning whereby professionals learn about the conditions affected by alternative courses of action (Graham and Kruger, 2002). Adaptive management begins with the central tenet that management involves a continual learning process (McLain and Lee, 1996). Indeed, public opinion research has found that the more number of people talk about terrorism, the greater the chance that reason rather than fear will dictate reactions (West and Orr, 2005). This implies that if governments have increased dialogues with citizens on homeland security, this may relieve some of their anxiety about homeland security concerns.

Wise (2006) makes the argument that given the turbulent environment of homeland security, the most suitable approach seems to be the adaptive management model. Adaptive management requires managers to change their approach as new information arrives (Alexander, 2002; Wise, 2006). This mode of management differs from traditional forms of management by emphasizing the importance of feedback in shaping policy, followed by further systematic experimentation and evaluation (Wise, 2006).

Wise (2006) argues that one approach that exemplifies adaptive management is in a report by the GAO that articulates eight factors that facilitate collaboration among agencies (USGAO, 2005). First, there is defining and articulating a common outcome, meaning that collaborating agencies should have a clear and compelling rationale for their work together. Second, establishing a mutually reinforced or joint strategy in which collaborating agencies should establish strategies that work in concert with their partners. Third, collaborating agencies should identify and address their needs by leveraging resources. This implies that by addressing their relative strengths in terms of resource capacity, collaborating agencies can look for opportunities to address resource needs by leveraging each others resources. Fourth, collaborating agencies should agree on roles and responsibilities, meaning that they should work together to define and agree on their respective roles and responsibilities. Fifth, collaborating agencies should establish compatible policies, procedures, and other means to operate across agencies. Sixth, agencies engaged in collaborative efforts should create the means to monitor and evaluate their efforts to enable them to identify areas for improvement. Seventh, collaborating agencies can use their strategic and annual performance plans as tools to drive collaboration with other agencies. Eighth, collaborating agencies can use performance management systems to strengthen accountability for results by placing greater emphasis on fostering the necessary collaboration across organizational boundaries to achieve results.

In this study, to determine the applicability of adaptive management, these eight factors are applied in a survey of city managers. Before this research delves into the survey results, the research questions are stated.

Research Questions

There are three research questions, derived from the previously mentioned literature, that examine city governments' homeland security preparedness and planning.

1. What is the scope and effectiveness of the organizational and administrative aspects of homeland security in city governments?
2. What is the level of cooperation and collaboration between city governments and among other levels of governments in homeland security?
3. How applicable is the adaptive management model at explaining homeland security preparedness and planning in city governments?

To examine these three questions the following section reports on how the survey data was collected.

Survey Data Collection and Research Methods

The study uses data collected from a mail survey of city managers that serve populations greater than 100,000 residents. City managers were chosen for this survey because they hold the highest administrative position in the city and are, therefore, charged with overseeing homeland security. A comprehensive mailing list of cities was obtained from the National League of Cities. Out of 191 cities that were sent a survey 126 responded, giving a response rate of 66 percent. The survey protocols involved sending a cover letter along with the survey to city managers. To get more candid responses, the survey respondents were ensured anonymity. This is especially important given some of the sensitive information asked in the survey. A reminder letter and another copy of the survey were sent one month after the initial mailing for city mangers who did not respond to the first mailing. The response rate for this survey is higher than the typical response rate of around 40 percent for International City/County Management Association (ICMA) surveys of Chief Administrative Officers (CAOs). This high participation rate can most likely be attributed to the timeliness of homeland security at all levels of government since 9/11.

The main research methods used in this chapter are descriptive statistics. In this study, we want to determine the intensity of responses; therefore, many of the questions are constructed on Likert scales. The tables in this chapter provide a summary of the major questions of the survey. Median statistics are used because most of the questions use ordinal data. Cross tabulations were also conducted to determine whether there were differences in responses in cities that have a greater numbers of employees. Essentially, this study examines whether size of the city government has an impact on homeland security issues, which has been done in previous research (Gerber et al., 2005). The following section outlines the characteristics of cities that responded to the survey to see how representative the sample is to the overall population.

Descriptive Characteristics of City Managers and Their Governments

Table 17.1 examines how representative this sample is compared to all the cities in the U.S. serving population of 100,000 residents or greater. In size of city government, this study uses a broad measure of full-time equivalent (FTE) employment. The findings indicate that the typical city that responded to the survey employs between 1000 and 2499 FTE employees. Therefore, the cities that participated in the survey are rather large and should be representative of larger-sized cities in the United States. There were 17 very large cities, responded to this survey, which had 5000 or more FTE employees.

This survey also asked questions on the fiscal capacity, economic development climate, and political climate of each city to gain a better perspective on the environment that these cities operate in (Table 17.1). The fiscal capacity is the ability of the city to raise taxes or fees given political and legal limits that they face. Likert scales with responses ranging from very favorable to very unfavorable were used to represent the capacity issues. The fiscal capacity of a typical city was favorable according to 35 percent of respondents (adding up favorable and very favorable responses).

Table 17.1 also provides information on the economic development climate of the city government. This measures the prospects of the city for job growth, unemployment, and so forth. About three-fourths of city managers believe that the economic development climate of their city is favorable. Only 7 percent of cities believed that their economic development climate was unfavorable.

Table 17.1 Descriptive Characteristics of City Managers and Their Governments

Full-Time Equivalent (FTE) Employees	Frequency	Percent
99 or less	1	0.8
100–499	8	6.3
500–999	24	19
1000–2499	56	44.4
2500–4999	20	15.9
5000 or more	17	13.5
Fiscal capacity		
Very favorable	7	5.6
Favorable	37	29.4
Neither favorable/unfavorable	40	31.7
Unfavorable	31	24.6
Very unfavorable	11	8.7
Economic development climate		
Very favorable	23	18.3
Favorable	71	56.3
Neither favorable/unfavorable	23	18.3
Unfavorable	9	7.1
Very unfavorable	0	0
Political climate		
Very favorable	30	23.8
Favorable	71	56.3
Neither favorable/unfavorable	21	16.7
Unfavorable	4	3.2
Very unfavorable	0	0

Table 17.1 (continued)   Descriptive Characteristics of City Managers and Their Governments

Full-Time Equivalent (FTE) Employees	Frequency	Percent
Gender		
Male	112	88.9
Female	14	11.1
Age range		
25–34	5	4
35–44	24	19
45–54	55	43.7
55–64	39	31
65 or over	3	2.4
Graduate degree		
Yes	82	65.1
No	44	34.9

Table 17.1 also shows the views of city managers on the political climate of their city. The political climate examines the relationship between city council and its citizens. Around 80 percent of city managers believe that the political climate of their city was favorable. Overall, in terms of the environment that city managers find themselves in there is a limited amount of fiscal capacity, but the economic development and political climate are favorable.

The demographic characteristics of the sample showed that 89 percent of city managers are males. There is 44 percent of the sample being composed of city managers in the age range of 45–54. Finally, the majority of city managers have a graduate degree (65 percent). The following section provides the opinions of city managers on possible terrorist threats to local governments.

Possible Terrorist Threats

Table 17.2 provides information on the level of concern that city managers have of different types of terrorist threats over the next year in their municipality. The results in this table indicate that when examining the median responses in the last column, the greatest concerns are an individual/suicide bomb, car or truck bomb,

Table 17.2 Possible Terrorist Threats

How Concerned Are You about the Following Terrorist Threats over the Next Year in Your Locality?	Very Concerned (Percent)	Concerned (Percent)	Neither Concerned/Unconcerned (Percent)	Unconcerned (Percent)	Very Unconcerned (Percent)	Median Response
Individual/suicide bomb	19.8	32.5	31.0	13.5	3.2	1
Car or truck bomb	18.3	51.6	20.6	8.7	0.8	1
Biohazard/biological	15.1	57.1	17.5	8.7	1.6	1
Chemical	15.1	55.6	19.0	8.7	1.6	1
Cyber-terrorism	15.1	47.6	27.0	8.7	1.6	1
Combination (dirty bomb)	13.5	43.7	27.8	11.1	4.0	1
Radiological	9.5	36.5	33.3	13.5	7.1	0
Nuclear	7.9	27.8	38.1	19.0	7.1	0
Airplane used as a bomb	7.1	31.7	38.1	16.7	6.3	0

Notes: Very concerned = 2, concerned = 1, neither concerned/unconcerned = 0, unconcerned = −1, and very unconcerned = −2.

biohazard/biological, chemical, cyber-terrorism, and dirty bomb. There seems to be less consensus among city managers about radiological, nuclear, and airplane used as a bomb. Overall, the findings in Table 17.2 indicate that city managers are concerned about many possible terrorist threats in their municipality. The following section provides information on the equipment that has been purchased to respond to a terrorist attack.

Types of Homeland Security Equipment Purchased

There are various types of equipment that can be used to complete a city government's homeland security goals. Table 17.3 lists the most common equipment that city managers have purchased. Hazmat suits and apparatuses were the most frequently purchased by 89 percent of cities. In addition, χ^2 statistics showed that as the size of the city increases, there would be more purchases made of this type of equipment. Second, communications equipment was purchased by 85 percent of cities to meet their homeland security goals. Information technology, identification technology, and other equipment were also statistically more likely to be purchased by larger-sized cities. There were 15 percent who responded to the other category which included medications, a central command unit, and specialized vehicles. Overall, the results in Table 17.3 are not surprising given the need for more effective communication and related technologies to respond to terrorist threats. The question that city managers must be cognizant of, where is the money coming from to fund their homeland security goals? The following section of this chapter examines this important issue.

Table 17.3 Types of Equipment Purchased to Complete City Government's Homeland Security Goals

	Frequency	Percent
Hazmat suits, apparatuses***	112	88.9
Communications	107	84.9
Information technology**	79	62.7
Surveillance devices	72	57.1
Access control devices	69	54.8
Identification technology***	52	41.3
Other***	19	15.1

*** Significant difference with FTE at the 0.01 level.
** Significant difference with FTE at the 0.05 level.

Homeland Security Funding

Table 17.4 provides information on homeland security funding in city governments. This question specifically asked for information on how homeland security was paid for, the proportion not covered by federal or state government grants. The most common method of paying for homeland security was through the general fund or existing budget of a city with 71 percent of cities using this method. All of the other funds were used less frequently and only 22 percent used asset seizure funds. The smallest number of cities actually raised property taxes to fund homeland security (1.6 percent). Larger-sized cities were more likely to use a special sales tax to fund homeland security, with only 4 percent using this method of payment. Overall, the results in Table 17.4 indicate that most of the cities are paying for their homeland security initiatives (not covered by grants) through the general fund. Not surprisingly, given taxpayer resistance there is much less use of increasing taxes or user fees to fund homeland security.

Figure 17.1 shows the amount of grant funding that cities received in 2005 from federal or state governments. The average amount of grant funding that a city government received was $250,000–$499,000. A small proportion of cities, around 6 percent did not receive any grant funding, although 23 percent of cities received more than one million in federal or state homeland security grants. The χ^2 statistics indicated that larger-sized cities received more in homeland security grant funding than smaller cities.

Table 17.4 How Has Your City Government Paid for its Portion of Homeland Security Costs (i.e., That Portion Not Covered by Federal or State Grants)?

	Frequency	Percent
General fund/existing budget	89	70.6
Asset seizure funds	28	22.2
Reallocate/cut spending	23	18.3
Issue bonds	6	4.8
Dedicate a special sales tax[***]	5	4.0
Raise utility rates	4	3.2
Raise property taxes	2	1.6
Other	1	0.5

[***] Significant difference with FTE at the 0.01 level.

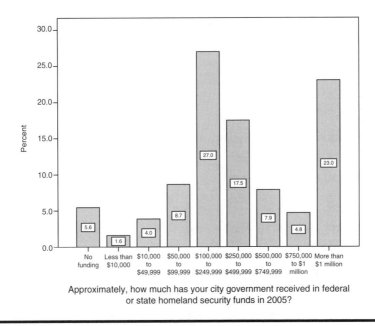

Approximately, how much has your city government received in federal
or state homeland security funds in 2005?

Figure 17.1   Amount of federal or state homeland security grants received.
Note: **Significant difference with FTE at the 0.01 level.**

Organizations/Agencies that City Governments Collaborate with on Homeland Security Issues

Table 17.5 provides information on what organizations/agencies city governments tend to collaborate with on homeland security issues. Not surprisingly, the most common is their state government, with 94 percent of cities collaborating with this level of government. The second highest was 91 percent of cities that collaborated with other local governments. A regional organization was the third most common collaborating entity with 83 percent of cities working with them. Some of the responses for the 9 percent of cities that indicated other were collaborating with the Red Cross, the Department of Energy, and the Center for Disease Control. The χ^2 statistics indicate that larger-sized cities are more likely to collaborate with their state government and with local military installations.

Homeland Security Information Assessment

Homeland security information that cities receive is critical for effective preparedness and response. In terms of the current information received by federal or state agencies on terrorist threats, 48 percent of city managers believed that this was effective (Table 17.6), whereas 24 percent of cities believe that federal or state

Table 17.5   Organizations/Agencies that City Governments Collaborate with on Homeland Security Issues

	Frequency	Percent
Your state government[**]	118	93.7
Other local governments	114	90.5
A regional organization, such as regional planning agency	105	83.3
FBI/Department of Justice	98	77.8
DHS/FEMA	93	73.8
HHS (Health and Human Services)	67	53.2
Nongovernmental organizations	65	51.6
Local military installations[**]	59	46.8
DOD (Department of Defense)	34	27.0
Other state governments	21	16.7
Other	11	8.7

[**] Significant difference with FTE at the 0.05 level.

information received was ineffective. The χ^2 statistics indicate that as the size of the city increases this will have an impact on views of city managers on the effectiveness of information received. The color-coded homeland security advisory system was not viewed by city managers in their planning efforts as extremely effective with only one quarter of them believing this was the case. Indeed, 32 percent actually believe that the advisor system is ineffective. Compared to the responses in some of the previous questions in this chapter, there is a more negative perception of the homeland security advisory system.

Rating Homeland Security Coordination and Collaboration across Governments

Table 17.7 reports on the extent of homeland security coordination and collaboration across governments. City managers generally believe that there is a high level of collaboration among departments and agencies in their city government (87 percent). In addition, collaboration is high across levels of government, agencies, and other organizations in their region (70 percent). A majority of cities believe that

Table 17.6 Homeland Security Information Assessment

For Your City Government, How Effective Is the . . .	Very Effective (Percent)	Effective (Percent)	Neither Effective/ Ineffective (Percent)	Ineffective (Percent)	Very Ineffective (Percent)	Median Response
Current information received by federal or state agencies on terrorist threats?***	4.8	42.9	28.6	19.8	4.0	0
Homeland Security Advisory System (the color-coded system developed by the U.S. Department of Homeland Security) in your planning efforts?	1.6	23.8	42.9	23.0	8.7	0

Notes: Very effective = 2, effective = 1, neither effective/ineffective = 0, ineffective = −1, and very ineffective = −2.

*** Significant difference with FTE at the 0.01 level.

Table 17.7 Rating Homeland Security Coordination and Collaboration across Governments

How Would You Rate the Extent of Homeland Security Coordination and Collaboration . . .	Very High (Percent)	High (Percent)	Neither High/Low (Percent)	Low (Percent)	Very Low (Percent)	Median Response
Among departments and agencies in your city government?	45.2	42.1	7.9	4.0	0.8	1
Across levels of government, agencies, and other organizations in your region?	26.2	43.7	23.0	6.3	0.8	1
Across levels of government, agencies, and other organizations statewide?	14.3	43.7	29.4	11.9	0.8	1

Note: Very high = 2, high = 1, neither high/low = 0, low = −1, and very low = −2.

collaboration on homeland security is high across levels of government, agencies, and other organizations statewide (58 percent). Overall, the results in Table 17.7 indicate that coordination and collaboration is rated the highest in their city, followed by their region, then statewide.

Assessment of Homeland Security Collaboration Using the Adaptive Management Model

Table 17.8 provides an assessment of the level of homeland security collaboration in city government and across other governments in their locality. This provides evidence of the prevalence of the adaptive management model in city government homeland security planning. There was a high level of agreement that homeland security efforts have established a common strategy, addressed the need to leverage resources, established compatible policies and procedures, agreed on roles and responsibilities for planning, developed mechanisms to monitor, evaluate, and report on collaborative efforts. However, there was not as much agreement that homeland security used performance measures, with only 33 percent of cities agreeing to this. Overall, collaboration was high for city governments on homeland security, supporting the adaptive management model. However, actually measuring whether cities were achieving results there was not as much agreement.

Administrative/Management Concerns and Homeland Security

Table 17.9 provides the findings of the survey on the administrative/management concerns of homeland security. The greatest administrative/management concern was lack of money according to 79 percent of cities surveyed. The second greatest concern was personnel limitations with 64 percent of cities believing this was an issue. The χ^2 statistic indicated that as the size of the city increases personnel limitation becomes more of an issue for the city. The third greatest concern was technology/interoperability, with half of city managers citing this as a problem. External cooperation being an administrative/management concern was found in 26 percent of cities. In addition, the lack of clear plan/roles was a problem in 21 percent of cities. One of the responses for the 2.4 percent who responded other was sustaining funding levels for homeland security.

Organizational Aspects of Homeland Security

Table 17.10 shows that there is a very high level of cooperation between city departments and the city managers' office in homeland security planning; with

Table 17.8   Assessment of Homeland Security Collaboration

Homeland Security Collaboration in Our City Government, and across Other Governments, in Our Locality Has …	Strongly Agree (Percent)	Agree (Percent)	Neutral (Percent)	Disagree (Percent)	Strongly Disagree (Percent)	Median Response
Established a common strategy.	22.2	54.0	15.1	8.7	0.0	1
Addressed the need to leverage resources.	18.3	61.9	14.3	5.6	0.0	1
Established compatible policies and procedures.	15.1	51.6	25.4	7.9	0.0	1
Agreed on roles and responsibilities for planning.	14.3	61.9	18.3	5.6	0.0	1
Developed mechanisms to monitor, evaluate, and report on collaborative efforts.	7.9	50.0	31.0	11.1	0.0	1
Reinforced accountability for collaborative efforts through performance systems.	5.6	27.0	45.2	19.8	2.4	0

Note: Strongly agree $= 2$, agree $= 1$, neutral $= 0$, disagree $= -1$, and strongly disagree $= -2$.

Table 17.9   Administrative/Management Concerns and Homeland Security

	Frequency	Percent
Lack of money	100	79.4
Personnel limitations***	81	64.3
Technology/interoperability	63	50.0
Lack of health care capacity	58	46.0
Lack of external cooperation	33	26.2
Lack of clear plan/roles	27	21.4
Lack of internal cooperation	7	5.6
Other	3	2.4

*** Significant difference with FTE at the 0.01 level.

93 percent of cities believing this is the case. There is a similarly high level of agreement that there are open lines of communication on homeland security planning (91 percent). There is less agreement that homeland security planning tends to emphasize preparedness over response (49 percent). Overall, the results in Table 17.10 demonstrate that communication, focusing on long-term issues, and monitoring and evaluating homeland security is very strong in city governments. There is less agreement of an emphasis on preparedness over response in homeland security planning, which would be especially critical for city government since the terrorist attacks of 9/11.

Overall City Government Homeland Security Assessment

Table 17.11 provides information on the overall evaluation by city managers of their city government's homeland security preparedness and planning. City managers believe that their city governments have a high managerial capacity to coordinate and control homeland security, with 81 percent of them agreeing this is the case. Similarly, 73 percent of city managers believe that they have a high level of current homeland security preparedness. The most interesting finding in Table 17.11 is that 35 percent of city managers believe that they have a low probability of being a future terrorist target. Overall, city managers are of the opinion that their cities are well prepared for a terrorist attack, but are not confident that one will take place in the near future.

Table 17.10 Organizational Aspects of Homeland Security

Homeland Security Planning in Our City Government....	Strongly Agree (Percent)	Agree (Percent)	Neutral (Percent)	Disagree (Percent)	Strongly Disagree (Percent)	Median Response
Has a high level of cooperation between city departments and the city managers' office.	57.9	34.9	5.6	1.6	0.0	2
Has open lines of communication.	42.1	48.4	7.9	1.6	0.0	1
Is regularly monitored and evaluated.	31.0	55.6	10.3	2.4	0.8	1
Tends to focus on the long-term issues.	18.3	48.4	21.4	11.9	0.0	1
Includes input from citizens and businesses.	11.9	46.8	25.4	15.1	0.8	1
Has tended to emphasize preparedness over response.	8.7	40.5	31.7	17.5	1.6	0

Notes: Strongly agree = 2, agree = 1, neutral = 0, disagree = −1, and strongly disagree = −2.

Table 17.11 City Government Homeland Security Assessment

How Would You Assess Your City's…	Very High (Percent)	High (Percent)	Neither High/Low (Percent)	Low (Percent)	Very Low (Percent)	Median Response
Managerial capacity to coordinate and control homeland security?	18.3	62.7	15.1	4.0	0.0	1
Current homeland security preparedness?	10.3	62.7	20.6	5.6	0.8	1
Probability of being a future terrorist target?***	4.8	23.8	36.5	22.2	12.7	0

Note: Very high $= 2$, high $= 1$, neither high/low $= 0$, low $= -1$, and very low $= -2$.

*** Significant difference with FTE at the 0.01 level.

Conclusion

This chapter has examined homeland security preparedness and planning in city governments. Some of the most interesting survey results indicate that city managers are concerned about terrorist threats, such as a car or truck bomb, biohazard/ biological, and chemical attack. However, there is less concern about radiological, nuclear, and airplane used as a bomb as possible terrorist attacks. There is no general consensus of the most likely terrorist attack(s) that cities could face.

The two most common types of homeland security equipment purchased by city governments were hazmat suits (and apparatuses) and communications equipment. As existing research shows in terms of paying for homeland security (the portion not covered by grants) most of the cities used their general fund. According to city managers, the possibility of raising taxes is very unlikely. The average amount of grant funding that a city government received was $250,000–$499,000; grant funding increased with the size of the city government.

In terms of collaboration the most common governments that cities work with are their state governments, other local governments, and regional planning authorities. What is interesting is that federal agencies are not near to the top of this list. This is echoed in the views of city managers on the information that they receive from the federal government, with 32 percent of respondents believing that the color-coded homeland security advisory system was ineffective.

According to city managers, there is a very high level of collaboration between and among agencies and different levels of government in homeland security planning. This is somewhat surprising and may be explained by the new type of environment that these city governments are facing post 9/11. A similar result was found in a survey of Florida local government officials of increased collaboration in homeland security (Caruson and MacManus, 2006).

In the application of the adaptive management model to homeland security the results in this study showed that many of the key elements of collaboration identified in the adaptive management literature were supported in this study. The only exception was, performance systems not being as commonly used to gain accountability in city government homeland security. However, the management concerns of homeland security at the top of the list, not surprisingly, were the lack of money and personnel limitations that cities face. Near the bottom of the list was lack of cooperation, which further supports a high level of cooperation and collaboration in homeland security for city governments.

Finally, there is an interesting split between city managers believing that they are well prepared for an attack and the relatively low probability of being a future terrorist target. On a brighter note, city managers believe that the managerial capacity is there in their governments to coordinate and control homeland security.

References

Alexander, D., 2002. *Principles of Emergency Planning and Management.* New York: Oxford University Press.

Baldassare, M. and Hoene, C., 2002. *Coping with Homeland Security: Perceptions of City Officials in California and the United States.* San Francisco, California: Public Policy Institute of California.

Beresford, A.D., 2004. Homeland security as an American ideology: Implications for U.S. policy and action. *Journal of Homeland Security and Emergency Management,* 1(3). Retrieved May 27, 2006, from http://www.bepress.com/jhsem/vol1/iss3/301.

Carroll, J., 2001. Emergency management on a grand scale: A bureaucrat's analysis, in Farazmand, A. (Ed.) *Handbook of Crisis and Emergency Management.* New York: Marcel Dekker, Inc.

Caruson, K. and MacManus, S.A., 2005. Homeland security preparedness: Federal and state mandates and local government. *Spectrum: The Journal of State Government,* 78(2), 25–28.

Caruson, K. and MacManus, S.A., 2006. Mandates and management challenges in the trenches: An intergovernmental perspective on homeland security. *Public Administration Review,* 66(4), 522–536.

Gerber, B.J., Cohen, D.B., Cannon, B., Patterson, D., and Stewart, K., 2005. On the front line: American cities and the challenge of homeland security preparedness. *Urban Affairs Review,* 41(2), 182–210.

Graham, A.C. and Kruger, L.E., 2002. *Research in Adaptive Management: Working Relations and the Research Process* (PNW-RP-538). Portland, Oregon: U.S. Department of Agriculture.

Hollings, C.S. (Ed.), 1978. *Adaptive Environmental Assessment and Management.* New York: John Wiley.

Johnson, B.L., 1999. The role of adaptive management as an operational approach for resource management agencies. *Ecology and Society,* 3(2). Retrieved May 27, 2006, from http://www.consecol.org/vol3/iss2/art8.

MacManus, S.A. and Caruson, K., 2006. Code red: Florida city and county officials rate threat information sources and the homeland security advisory system. *State and Local Government Review,* 38(1), 12–22.

McLain, R.J. and Lee, R.G., 1996. Adaptive management: Promises and pitfalls. *Environmental Management,* 20(4), 437–448.

Rosenthal, U., 2003. September 11: Public administration and the study of crisis and crisis management. *Administration & Society,* 35(2), 129–143.

USGAO (United States Government Accountability Office), 2003a. *Homeland Security: Efforts to Improve Information Sharing Need to be Strengthened.* (GAO-03-760). Washington, DC: U.S. Government Printing Office.

USGAO (United States Government Accountability Office), 2003b. *Homeland Security: Reforming Federal Grants to Better Meet Outstanding Needs.* (GAO-03-1146T). Washington, DC: U.S. Government Printing Office.

USGAO (United States Government Accountability Office), 2005. *Results-Oriented Government: Practices that can Help Enhance and Sustain Collaboration among Federal Agencies.* (GAO-06-15). Washington, DC: U.S. Government Printing Office.

Waugh, W.L., 1988. Current policy and implementation issues in disaster preparedness, in Comfort, L.K. (Ed.) *Managing Disaster: Strategies and Policy Perspectives.* Durham, North California: Duke University Press.

West, D.M. and Orr, M., 2005. Managing citizen fears: Public attitudes toward urban terrorism. *Urban Affairs Review*, 41(1), 93–105.

Wise, C.R., 2006. Organizing for homeland security after Katrina: Is adaptive management what's missing? *Public Administration Review*, 66(3), 302–318.

Wise, C.R. and Nader, R., 2002. Organizing the federal system for homeland security: Problems, issues, and dilemmas. *Public Administration Review*, 62 (Special Issue), 44–57.

Chapter 18

Reorganizing for Homeland Security: The Case of Norway

Per Lægreid and Synnøve Serigstad

CONTENTS

A version of this chapter originally appeared in the *Journal of Management Studies*, 43(5), Sept. 2006, 1395–1413. Reprinted with permission of the journal publisher, Blackwell Publishing, Oxford, UK.

Introduction[1]

Achieving a balance between coordination, specialization, autonomy, and control is an enduring problem both in organizational theory and in administrative practice. This challenge is especially relevant when it comes to the organization of risk management. Organization and reorganization can be seen as a way of managing risk, and hence it is important and interesting how the reorganization is carried out and the result of it, and in particular how the process is affected by how risk is conceived. As part of a fundamental review of homeland security, a reorganization took place in the Norwegian homeland security administration in the early years of the new century. In 1999, the government appointed a public commission to assess the vulnerability of Norwegian society. One of its main proposals was to improve vertical and horizontal coordination in the security administration by establishing a new special ministry for homeland security (NOU, 2000:24). These recommendations were, however, not approved by the government in the White Paper presented to parliament in 2002. Instead, the process resulted in only minor changes in the security administration.

This is somewhat surprising given that this policy field experienced a major external shock in the form of the terrorist attack of September 11, 2001, which took place in the middle of the reorganization process. According to theories of institutional change, such external shocks, catastrophes, or historical junctures, may potentially trigger major change (March and Olsen, 1989; Fligstein, 1991; Hoffman, 1999). We ask why this did not happen in this case, in particular why the Vulnerability Commission's proposal to carry out a radical reorganization by replacing a Network Model with a Hierarchical Model, whose necessity and relevance was strongly underlined by the September 11 terrorist attack, ultimately resulted in a more modest change to a Hybrid Agency Model. Despite the fact that the conditions for radical change were made very favorable by the combination of an external shock, an open policy window, a unanimous proposal by the commission as a matter of urgency, and Norway's status as a member of NATO with a traditionally strong alliance with the United States, little happened.

The concept homeland security is an ambiguous term, which has gained currency since 9/11 (Kettl, 2004c). Covering such concepts as domestic security, civil defense, internal security, society security, and civil emergency, it can be defined in broad or narrow terms. In narrow terms it can be taken to mean intentional or unintentional human activities involving man-made risks that affect the social and natural environment. These include terrorist attacks, drug trafficking, and other criminal behavior. It can, however, also be extended to include unpredictable natural disasters like earthquakes, volcanic eruptions, floods, tsunamis, and hurricanes. In Norway, the tendency is to regard homeland security in broader terms; but, this is controversial, and consensus seminars have been held to try to reach a common definition. In addition, as shown in this chapter, the field of homeland security also straddles the rather blurred boundary between civil society and internal affairs on the one hand and the military and defense sectors on the other. A central challenge in this policy field is to balance the need for increased prevention against the need for a stronger response. Obviously, prevention applies primarily to man-made and manufactured risks, while the response requirement is conditioned by both natural and man-made disasters. Thus, when it comes to reorganizing homeland security the main issue is to frame boundaries around problematic issues (Benford and Snow, 2000; Morrill, in press).

Basically, the field of homeland security is about risk management and the politics of uncertainty, and it can be seen as an expression of the risk management explosion occurring in contemporary public organizations (Power, 2004). Organizing homeland security addresses the question of how to respond to perceived risk. In particular, it confronts the problem of preparing for low-probability and high-impact events (Baldwin and Cave, 1999). Our argument is that organizations and organizational arrangements play a crucial role in the prevention of and response to risk and that reorganization can be seen as means for managing risk. The issue of homeland security is, therefore, to a great extent a question of organization, management, and regulation. The case can be seen as a study of organizational response to change in the risk environment. We are looking at administrative systems that we presume to be tightly organized and designed to operate in high risk environments, but what happens ultimately depends on how organizations frame the problem they are trying to solve by normalizing signals of potential danger so that the chosen path becomes aligned with established goals and practices (Vaughan, 1996; Eden, 2004). We are facing regulatory agencies and organizations that represent variations in the organization of regulation by combining multiple actors in a dynamic risk-regulation regime (Hood et al., 2001).

In this chapter, we address such issues by focusing primarily on the relationships between central government bodies. We start by outlining the problems of specialization and coordination and identify three organizational models: the Hierarchical Model, the Network Model, and the Agency Model. The descriptive part of the chapter traces the process of reorganizing homeland security. The focus is mainly on the proposals concerning horizontal coordination of the central security administration, and the aim is to describe and explain the course of the process and its results. This is done by addressing the relationships, dynamics, and rationales within and between institutions in the field.

This chapter is based on a comprehensive case study of the reorganization process (Serigstad, 2003). It uses public documents from the government and the parliament, internal files from the archives of the Ministry of Justice concerning the ministerial handling of the case, the minutes of meetings of the public commission and other material from the commission's work obtained from the National Archives, and interviews with members of the commission, central officials in the ministries of justice and government administration and members of the parliamentary standing committees of justice and defense, 17 persons altogether. In particular, the use of internal files and interviews and of corroborative data-triangulations strengthens the validity and reliability of the data.

The Problem of Specialization and Coordination

Organizations involved in homeland security must by definition be high reliability organizations in which there is zero tolerance for mistakes (Frederickson and LaPorte, 2002; Kettl, 2004c; LaPort, 1996). At the same time, coordination is a basic challenge and always a central issue in the work of the homeland security bodies (Peters, 2004). The experience of recent accidents and crises has shown that inadequate organization and failure to coordinate, both at lower operative levels and higher administrative levels, is a recurring problem, and several studies and reports have corroborated this finding (NOU, 2000:24; Wise, 2002a; Kettl et al., 2004b). In the fields of safety and security tasks and responsibility tend to be spread between several sectors and levels and involve a large number of actors. Moreover, there is no comprehensive policy or focus.

There may be several explanations for this, the most obvious being that homeland security work is by nature a fragmented, complexed, and disjointed area (Kettl, 2004c). The broad definition of homeland security, as used in the Norwegian case, covers a wide range of issues. In addition, the unpredictable nature of the field obviously makes retrospective learning much easier than learning in advance. Changes, implementation, and improvement are reactive in character, which, in turn, causes considerable diffusion of responsibility between ministries, agencies, and other public and private bodies. The field of homeland security presents intergovernmental complexities and dilemmas along both vertical and horizontal axes (Wise and Nader, 2002). Comprehensive policies or plans for organizational arrangements in the field are not easy to discern.

Generally, it is difficult to coordinate the work of different agencies, and government agencies tend to resist being regulated by other agencies (Wilson, 1989). In the field of homeland security, this problem is enhanced by the critical tasks that the agencies are required to handle. Homeland security is a complex and fragmented area of government, and a growing number of cases and problems do not fit into the traditionally functional structure of polities. In organizational theory, such problems are classified as wicked problems (Harmond and Mayer, 1986). Coordination between these agencies is further complicated by the vertical nature of policymaking. As a rule, modern polities are organized according to the principle of purpose, which makes them vertical in nature and characterized by strong functional sectors and weak coordinating mechanisms (Kettl, 2003). This implies that vertical coordination within specific sectors may be good. When it comes to horizontal coordination, however, these systems face considerable problems. One often runs into the problem of negative coordination (Mayntz and Sharpf, 1975), whereby the wish to coordinate is greater than the willingness to be coordinated. In the case of homeland security, the traditional problems of organizational coordination are multiplied enormously and the stakes associated with success or failure had a vast raise (Kettl, 2004c:66).

The central question becomes how to build effective responses to problems that are never routine and to which systems, therefore, have no standard responses (Kettl, 2003). This study distinguishes between three approaches to coordination, which will be used to classify the different organizational models. The first is a top–down focused approach based on the Hierarchical Model and presumes that the organization of homeland security must begin at the top and be directed downward, implying strong political control. The idea of top–down coordination is derived from the notion that the organizations to be coordinated have already been identified by headquarters coordinators, that the relationship of these organizations to each other is well understood, that agreement has been reached about what objectives will be accomplished by altering certain of these interorganizational relationships, and that the authority and means to alter these relationships exist. In other words, it assumes that having a hierarchy will facilitate implementation. The problem in the context of homeland security, however, is that most of these assumptions are unfounded, and the problems of coordination do not lend themselves well to hierarchical direction (Wise, 2002b:141). This is a model that seems to become particularly popular in the aftermath of major crises (The 9/11 Commission Report, 2004) but which in our case lost its popularity after the September 11 shock.

For complex, unstructured and rapidly changing problems a network approach may be more suitable (Wise, 2002b; Kettl, 2003). This approach builds upon the idea of coordination as a contingent problem. What it is, how it works, and how best to implement it depend on the nature of the issue, the nature of the organization, and the nature of its employees (Lawrence and Lorsch, 1967). The adoption of standard, rational, hierarchical designs and practices is likely to be particularly unsuitable for organizations expected to operate in complex, unstable, and unpredictable environments. Unstable environments require flexibility, rapid decisions, and changes and thus create a need for greater decentralization of authority and less emphasis on formal structure, because it takes too long for information to travel up and down a rigid hierarchy. The key is to create systems that are versatile and flexible. In this approach, the focus is not on strong central control but on better ways of collecting and processing information—from the bottom up and from the outside in (Kettl, 1993).

A third model, the Agency Model, can be labelled (Pollitt and Talbot, 2004; Pollitt et al., 2004). In the Agency Model, a stronger supervisory and regulatory role for semi-independent agencies is supplemented by the principle of integrated responsibility in each public body. Along the vertical dimension the regulatory agencies in this field have a semiautonomous status, which represents more than delegated hierarchy from their parent ministry. Agencies operate on the principle of professional knowledge and should be free from instruction by the cabinet or individual ministers (Christensen and Lægreid, 2006). They carry out regulation using their own delegated regulatory power, resources, and responsibilities. On the horizontal dimension, this model tries to enhance overall responsibility for homeland security by stating that each and every policy field and public organization is responsible for homeland security in its own area. Thus the Agency Model represents a hybrid giving statutory power to homeland regulatory agencies and some coordinating responsibility to a superior ministry and integrating responsibility for homeland security in each and every public organization.

Summing up, the organization of homeland security constitutes a double balancing act because it requires coordination between ministries and agencies and between substantive policy areas and the security field. A substantial dilemma is how regulatory agencies can have enough autonomy to function efficiently but not so much that they become politically uncontrollable. Another dilemma is how responsibility for security matters can be integrated into substantive policy areas without being neglected or relegated to a low-priority issue.

The Norwegian Context: The Network Model and Weak Coordination

The concept of homeland security is rather new in the Norwegian context. Until the mid-1990s the common concept in Norway was civil preparedness, seen as an integrated component of total defense executed by the bodies for civil defense. The Vulnerability Commission changed the concept to society security, signaling a broader definition, less military orientation, and more focus on peacetime issues. In Norway, civil security is traditionally based upon a principle of responsibility built on similarity and proximity. This means that public-sector organizations responsible for a sector or a policy area are also responsible for the safety, security, and preparedness of that sector. Thus, a mainstay in the field of civil security is the idea of internal self-regulation in the various public bodies and policy areas. Until the Ministry of Justice took over the main responsibility for coordinating Norwegian civil security in 1994, there was no superior body in this field. However, even then, the overall responsibility assigned to the ministry was rather weak, both formally and in practice.

In accordance with the principle of responsibility, all ministries must be prepared and able to take charge of coordinating operations. This organizational model is close to the Network Model, which assigns responsibility for security to the sector ministries and individual bodies. The idea is that flexibility and adaptability in the field of security can be guaranteed by making it an integral part of the various substantive policy fields. The reverse side of the coin, however, is that if everybody holds responsibility, nobody does. Accordingly, the central civil security field is quite complex and fragmented, entailing a risk of over-division of responsibility in security matters and ignorance of these aspects in the various policy areas.

Political systems organized in accordance with the principle of ministerial rule, like Norway, often seem to be marked by strong and specialized line ministries and weaker superior ministries. In practice, superior ministries with cross-sectoral responsibility have experienced considerable problems with horizontal coordination between the specialized ministries. This makes it difficult for ministries and agencies to work together (Peters, 2004).

Ministerial organization represents vertical subject-area specialization and a hierarchical system of authority that is highly focused on single ministries as hierarchical units. A study of political and administrative leaders in the Norwegian governmental apparatus revealed that this vertical focus entails a lot of institutional conflict between the ministries. The ministers are judged based on the success of their ministries, and there is a long tradition of ministerial autonomy (Christensen and Lægreid, 2002). This vertical structure and mode of thinking represents a great challenge when it comes to coordination and cross-ministerial cooperation.

Such fragmentation and lack of central coordination may also explain why reform and change in Norway have been characterized by a step-by-step, ministry-specific, and sector-initiated approach (Olsen, 1996). This is also very characteristic for change in the field of civil security. The Ministry of Justice seems to have experienced extensive problems obtaining approval from other ministries for necessary change and reordering. The fact that the civil security field has traditionally not enjoyed a very high priority and has, to a considerable extent, been overshadowed by military defense underlines this.

Added to this, the specific period we examined was characterized by a weak and shifting minority government with a narrow parliamentary basis. The process started when the Bondevik I government was in power. This was a minority center government consisting of the Christian People's Party, the Center Party, and the Liberals. In March 2000 it was replaced by a minority Labour government, and in October 2001 the Bondevik II government came to power as a minority coalition of the Conservative Party, the Christian People's Party, and the Liberals.

The Reorganization of Homeland Security

The process of reorganizing the administration for homeland security started with the establishment of the Vulnerability Commission on society security in 1999 and ended with the parliamentary resolution of December 2002. During this process there were two changes of government as well as the September 11 terrorist attack. We will now describe the process chronologically by distinguishing between four different phases: the initiative, the commission's report, the White Paper, and the parliamentary readings.

The Initiative: An Increased Focus on Civil Security

In Norway, as in the rest of the Western world, the conditions for homeland security have changed dramatically over the last 15 years, especially in the wake of the end of the Cold War. In spite of this, the civil security field has not been subjected to comprehensive review or examination, and it has been difficult to implement measures to improve and modernize the field (NOU, 2000:24). In addition, the field has been dominated by the military, and the defense sector has exerted a strong influence on the terms for homeland security policy. Especially since the end of the Cold War this has been an irritant to the civil security administration, which would like to focus attention on peacetime events and on the challenges associated with the vulnerability of modern society. The need to adapt the field to the new situation was underlined in long-term policy documents during the 1990s. However, little has been done, especially at the level of the central administration.

In an internal ministerial strategy project in 1999, the Department for Rescue and Emergency Planning, which is responsible for civil security, stressed that homeland security should be focused not only on military defense but also on civil security and the vulnerability of modern society. Specifically it recommended that relations between the civil and military security systems should be addressed. The minister of justice agreed to establish a public commission, the Vulnerability Commission, to assess the country's vulnerability and focus attention on the importance of a well-functioning civil security system.

The Commission's Report: Radical Change toward a Hierarchical Model

The Vulnerability Commission soon realized that there were weaknesses in almost all areas of civil security.[2] Closer scrutiny revealed that the field was highly fragmented, lacked an overall organizational principle, and was organized in an ad hoc manner that was to a considerable extent determined by accidents and crises. This caused both diffusion and disclaiming of responsibility. In addition, it became obvious that the Ministry of Justice had considerable problems in exercising its coordination function. Civil security and planning was not one of the Ministry of Justice's core tasks and was performed by a small department with few resources. It was a considerable challenge to the department to devote sustained attention to the field, and it seemed obvious that civil security had been systematically neglected as an everyday priority in the ministries (NOU, 2000:24). It was clear to the commission that what was needed was a stronger central concentration of responsibility, competence, and resources to put civil security on a firm political foundation. This could best be achieved through a new ministry with a responsible and dedicated minister and with the resources to devote all his work to civil security.[3]

In its report, the commission recommended strengthening the vertical and horizontal coordination of the civil security field by establishing a special ministry of homeland security with wide-ranging responsibilities. The commission believed that the division of responsibility and subject areas between ministries, agencies, and other regulatory bodies had caused considerable weaknesses in civil security, which was duplicated at the local level. Added to this, the Ministry of Justice's coordinating responsibility was vaguely defined, had a low priority and was to a considerable extent ignored by the other ministries. Thus, the commission recommended major organizational changes, namely, replacing the integrated Network Model with a top–down Hierarchical Model (NOU, 2000:24).

The commission suggested the new ministry be responsible for assessing national threats and vulnerability, for the preparation of plans, goals and standards, for coordination of emergency measures in the event of terrorism or sabotage, and for the coordination of rescue services, fire departments, civil defense, crisis management and information services. This entailed transferring several administrative bodies to the ministry. The commission suggested merging regulatory bodies responsible for safety and security and organizing them under the special ministry of homeland security to secure their autonomy and achieve a coordinated regulatory policy in civil security. The commission also recommended establishing a coordinating body for the so-called secret services in the ministry of homeland security and putting the National Security Authority under the ministry (NOU, 2000:24).

The Government Report: Toward an Agency Model

The Vulnerability Commission finished its work in June 2000 and the report was sent to the involved parties for comment. Ninety-six different bodies submitted their remarks. Although no one disagreed with the commission's description of the field as highly fragmented or with the problems of coordination and responsibility, only a few supported the idea of establishing a special ministry of homeland security.[4]

The Ministry of Defense supported the commission's description of the field as fragmented and poorly coordinated but expressed the fear that a new ministry of homeland security would bring about a conflict between specialized ministries and the homeland security ministry. In addition, there would be a real danger that the homeland security ministry would lag behind the specialized ministries in technical expertise. To establish a new ministry would, according to the Ministry of Defense, not bring about any improvement, because individual ministers would still be constitutionally responsible for security and safety within their area. A minister of homeland security would not have such responsibility and would therefore not have the authority to make and implement decisions. As an alternative to a ministry of homeland security, the Ministry of Defense suggested revising and broadening the existing guidelines for the Ministry of Justice's coordinating responsibilities. In addition, the Ministry of Defense obviously disliked the idea of moving the National Security Authority from the Ministry of Defense to a new ministry of homeland security, and it strongly opposed the proposed solution on the grounds that it would involve a loss of control over the Security Authority.[5]

In contrast to the other ministries, the Ministry of Justice did not agree with the commission's description of the field. The ministry expressed the opinion that the civil security field had to be fragmented because of the principle of responsibility. Although conceding that flexibility was essential, the Ministry of Justice did not believe this could be achieved by centralizing responsibility. Thus, it defended the existing Network Model.

The Ministry of Defense had by this time decided to prepare a new, long-term military plan and this hastened the Ministry of Justice's work on the White Paper. It feared that if the Ministry of Defense presented a long-term document without the Ministry of Justice doing the same, it would place the Ministry of Justice at a disadvantage. In addition, the ministry feared that the Vulnerability Commission's report would lose its current relevance and that military principles would be allowed to go on dominating the field.[6]

Responsibility for following up the committee's organizational suggestions was delegated to the Ministry of Government Administration. The reason for this was that the government wanted to include the field in a wider political agenda of governmental simplification and coordination. A central goal in the Labour government's modernization program was to improve governmental coordination by establishing a ministry of internal affairs, where homeland security would play a major role in a broad directorate for safety and security.

The follow-up was organized in a working group consisting of representatives from various involved ministries and agencies. The work proved to be very difficult and involved a considerable amount of dissension. However, the group did manage to agree that the focus in the future should be on the Agency Model, i.e., on how to organize the agencies. The ministries differed over whether agencies and other bodies should be merged, given more autonomous positions, or whether the focus should be on clarification of the roles of governmental bodies. Although all agreed that change was necessary, each representative opposed any change that affected his or her own particular ministry or area of responsibility.[7] The working group failed to reach an agreement and finished its work on October 15, 2001. At this point in time it was, however, clear that the Labour government would have to resign, and two days later a new Center-Right government took over.

The new government wanted to focus more explicitly on the coordination responsibility of the Ministry of Justice and, in accordance with this, responsibility for following up the organizational suggestions of the Vulnerability Commission was assigned to the Ministry of Justice. The Bondevik II government wanted to broaden the ministry's responsibility for homeland security and, accordingly, it was decided to establish a new agency for civil protection under the Ministry of Justice by merging the Directorate of Civil Defense and Emergency Planning and the Directorate of Fire and Electricity Safety.

An important proposal from the Vulnerability Commission was to organize the National Security Authority under the proposed ministry of homeland security (NOU, 2000:24). Although the proposal to create the latter ministry was rejected, this suggestion did gain some currency with the Ministry of Justice, which wanted to establish the National Security Authority as an agency under its own supervision, with the aim of broadening its powers. However, the Ministry of Defense was strongly opposed to this solution. This became a highly controversial question and the representatives of both ministries worked hard to defend their interests on the issue. To prevent an open ministerial conflict inside the government, the two ministries reached a compromise by establishing the National Security Authority as an agency with reporting lines to both ministries—to the Ministry of Defense on military matters and to the Ministry of Justice on civilian matters—but administratively subordinated to the Ministry of Defense.[8]

The White Paper on civil security and preparedness was submitted to parliament in April 2002. It had, however, been delayed several times and the Ministry of Justice was still a long way from its goal of presenting the White Paper together with the long-term military plan, which had been submitted by the Ministry of Defense one year earlier. There were two reasons for these delays. The first was the September 11 terrorist attacks in the United States. Although these did not affect Norway directly, the Norwegian central safety and security system was put to the test. However, this incident did not affect the content of the White Paper. The terrorist attacks put the paper in a new light, but the specific content was not changed. On the contrary, the Ministry of Justice regarded the preparatory security work that took place in the wake of the terrorist attacks as confirmation of its view that the field of civil security functioned efficiently and was well organized.[9]

For the progress of the White Paper, the change of government in October 2001 was of far greater importance than the September 11 attacks. Although the Labour government had been working toward a solution that to a certain extent resembled the Vulnerability Commission's proposals regarding hierarchical organization and coordination, the solutions eventually proposed in the White Paper were scaled down, emphasizing integration and the principle of responsibility rather than hierarchical centralization. Thus, the government's proposal to parliament was to abandon the radical solution and instead go some way toward strengthening the coordinating responsibility of the Ministry of Justice by merging the subordinated agencies of civil defense and emergency planning and the agency of fire and electricity safety and by having the National Security Authority report to the Ministry of Justice while continuing to be administratively subordinate to the Ministry of Defense (St.meld. nr. 17, 2001–02).

The Parliamentary Reading: Cultural Collusion but Approval for the Government Report

Although the Ministry of Justice has overall responsibility for civil security, civil security matters in parliament are dealt with by the Standing Committee on Defense, illustrating the dominance of the defense field on these issues. Because, however, the Committee on Justice feared that the military way of thinking would become too dominant if the paper were to be handled by the Committee on Defense only, the White Paper on the Vulnerability Commission's proposals was handled jointly by the two organizations.[10]

The committees were not impressed by the solutions proposed in the government report. All the political parties, including the parties represented in the government, were disappointed, and criticism was along traditional political lines. There was, however, a more important dividing line on the White Paper that was to characterize the rest of the committees' work: the cleavage between the two standing committees. While the Committee on Defense called for more of a military focus, the Committee on Justice stressed that the Vulnerability Commission had been set up to assess the vulnerability and preparedness of society as a whole. These committee disputes were in reality stronger than the party cleavages.

The proposed solution on the National Security Authority was in particular met with criticism and dissent. Supported by the Committee of Justice, the Socialist Left Party and the Center Party suggested establishing this agency under the Ministry of Justice in accordance with the goal of strengthening this ministry's responsibility for coordination. The Committee on Defense strongly opposed this and also took issue with the proposal to give the Security Authority dual lines of reporting. It favored, instead, keeping it under the Ministry of Defense. The solution proposed in the White Paper, however, was a compromise that had already been negotiated between the ministers and they became very defensive when the committees started to question this. Thus, parliament was presented with a fait accompli that it was unable to change.

The conflict between the two standing committees was a central feature of the parliamentary hearing. The explanation for this would appear to lie in the close relationship between the Labour Party and the Christian People's Party. In the Committee of Defense, it seems clear that these two representatives' interests in defending the military sector and securing a military focus were just as strong as their party political loyalties. The reason for this is the framing of the defense committee's work toward an overarching military approach and the downgrading of party political conflicts, the identity crisis in the defense field after the end of the cold war, and the struggle to keep tasks and issues and also the Justice Committee's focus on peacetime issues. The Labour Party had prepared a substantial part of the White Paper while still in office, and the party had a comprehensive plan for organizational arrangements in the field. Yet when it came to discussing the White Paper under the new government, it abandoned its former approach and joined forces with the governing parties. One important explanation for this might be the troubled relationship between the two standing committees. The formation of an ad hoc joint committee led to a considerable amount of sectoral conflict and apparently produced a strong alliance between the representatives of the Labour Party and the Christian People's Party on the Committee on Defense, prompted especially by the Committee on Justice's demand for a say in this area of jurisdiction.

Discussion and Theoretical Reflections—Framing the Field

This chapter is a study in state organizational reform around risk management exemplified by the case of reorganizing for homeland security in Norway with the 9/11 theme as a background. We have revealed that reforms in this field are both encouraged and discouraged by institutions. Both the historical–institutional context of national styles of governance and the regulatory styles of individual institutions, based on specific identities, histories, and dynamics, have made a difference (Olsen, 1997). Of special interest is the role of different organizational fields in the areas of justice and defense and their different ways of framing and reframing the same issue. The challenge is to provide a better understanding of the dynamic relations between the organizational fields of professional expertise, autonomous agencies, and representative democratic bodies in the area of risk management and regulation. A basic point of departure was that reorganization can be seen as a way of managing risk. Accordingly, this must be understood in an institutional manner.

A political-administrative system like the Norwegian one is based on the principle of ministerial responsibility, so there are strong sectoral ministries with their own power bases, which produce conflicts of interest and hence negotiations between actors. Organizational affiliation and sector interests are important in understanding the various problems and solutions the different actors have and the tug-of-war between different parties. The reorganization process changed as a result of bargaining between different actors with different power bases representing different organizational fields. The framing process and negotiations between actors from different organizational fields may explain the reactive response of the justice sector to the initiatives from the defense sector as well as the responses of the various bodies involved in the round of hearings; it also may account for the dispute between the different actors during the policy-formulation and decision-making phases in parliament.

An institutional perspective emphasizes that organizations develop their own values and distinctive characters and thus become institutions. This implies that they develop an intrinsic value and character above and beyond their purely technical and formal characteristics (Selznick, 1957). Over time, a unique culture, a way of perceiving the world and a way of doing things develop, engendering a common normative framework and a kind of received wisdom (Scott, 1995). These values and norms give the institution a distinctive character, which determines how change and reform are conducted. By implication, change will be discreet and gradual, and major changes that are not compatible with institutional values and beliefs will be very difficult to implement (March and Olsen, 1989). The process will be characterized by robustness.

The use of public commissions engaged in a problem-solving strategy followed by a round of public hearings is part of the institutionalized Norwegian policy style of carrying out reorganization processes. Local rationality and institution-based goals motivated by an institution's wish to defend its own identity and ensure its survival can explain both the founding of the public commission and the institutional defense that characterized the statements from affected parties in the public hearings as well as in the ministerial working groups. The historical–institutional roots of ministries with strong internal cultures and traditions constrained the reorganization process, one important characteristic of which was resistance to being coordinated. Although almost everyone agreed that coordination was of the utmost importance and that improvements were necessary, ultimately no one wanted this for themselves. The process can thus be said to be characterized by negative coordination (Mayntz and Sharpf, 1975), where the wish to coordinate was greater than the willingness to be coordinated. It supports the findings from studies of efforts to make policies more coherent that public sector organizations resist coordination (Bardach, 1998; Peters, 2004). The handling of the case by an ad hoc joint committee of the Standing Committees of Defense and Justice can also be seen as a case of cultural collusion between committees with different traditions, cultures, and identities but also as a way to bridge the differences between two organizational fields and to reframe the issue.

Negotiations and institutional constraints can be combined in the concept of an organizational field. The reorganization of homeland security concerns can be framed as a policy field in two different ways: as civil security based on a broad society approach or as civil defense based on a narrow military approach. The two approaches are represented by the ministerial areas of justice and defense, including agencies, ministries, political executives, and parliamentary standing committees in the two fields. How officials within the justice and defense spheres interpreted civil security was crucial for the outcome and this was more affected by path dependencies than by the events of 9/11. The concept of organizational fields also seems to be relevant for understanding the stalemate between justice and defense official (DiMaggio and Powell, 1983; Scott, 1995). What we are experiencing are shifts in field boundaries (Scott et al., 2000) brought about by a weakening of the dominance of the military field and a strengthening of the field of civil society. Fields often form around issues (Hoffman, 1999) and the protection of internal security represents such an issue. Interorganizational cooperation represents a dynamic feature of institutional fields and in this case, the fields eventually came closer together and were able to reach a compromise (Phillips et al., 2000). Initially the two fields interpreted the issue very differently, but in the process of framing and reframing it, the justice and defense organizations found themselves able to work together in spite of their very different conceptual lenses and perceptions of the rules of the game. This case is an example of how actors from different fields depend on each other to reach a decision. The chosen organizational model rejects the radical solution of establishing a new organizational field and builds on existing organizational fields. They manage to work together to find a solution, which, though acceptable to both fields, is rather incremental and not seen as optimal by either side.

Another way of understanding the reorganization is as an adaptation to external shock. What happens has a more temporal than a consequential or strategic logic or logic of appropriateness (Cohen et al., 1972). The reorganization process is subject to randomness and interpretation of unforeseen situations and accidents. An institution can be stable and in relative balance until a historical break, for example a crisis or an external shock, occurs. An external shock can cause a rejection of old norms and values and bring recognition of a need for change.

In our case, however, this way of understanding the decision-making process and its outcome has little explanatory power. In contrast to the assumptions underlying the perspective focusing on adaptation to external shocks, we are unable to identify any significant effect of the September 11 terrorist attack either on the organizational solutions or on the problems of definition concerning the reorganization of Norwegian homeland security. This is somewhat surprising given the close relationship between Norway and the United States in security policy generally, the fact that Norway was on the terrorism hot list, and the Norwegian government's strong and active support of the U.S. government during this crisis. One might have expected Norway, as a small NATO country, to imitate the United States during a period when "everyone was an American," a sentiment expressed by many leading politicians at that time. Also the fact that 9/11 was a critical event with high visibility in the media and carrying strong risks for a government's reputation (Power, 2004) would lead us to expect that such an external shock would have affected the reorganization process. The September 11 attack occurred while the government was in the middle of formulating its White Paper on homeland security, representing an open policy window (Kingdon, 1995), but other factors, like the change of government and the path dependency of the process as well as the institutional constraints exerted by powerful ministries and the reframing of established fields, seemed to have a greater influence on the process than September 11. Although the crisis in the United States and internationally obviously had strong implications for this policy area, it did not affect the question of how to reorganize the Norwegian homeland security administration. Thus, we can say that the organization of homeland security is rather robust, and adaptation to external shocks does not seem to have any significant explanatory power for the reorganization process.

We have revealed a process of bureaucratic politics strongly tempered by institutional constraints based on path dependencies, institutional identities, and historical inefficiency. The dynamics between different organizational fields and their framing of the issue is important to understand the process and its outcome. In view of this, a quick and easy adaptation either to new political signals from the executive or to external pressure and shocks would be unlikely. The process can best be understood from a perspective which takes into account actor-specific interests, institutional identities and traditions, and instrumental choice by political-administrative leaders in a meeting of different organizational fields.

Conclusion

In this chapter, we have discussed how a modern state handles the challenges of risk and regulation. We have revealed that risk management by the state and the organizational response to change in the risk environment can be seen as a process of framing the field of homeland security. A main finding is that a major external shock like 9/11 seems to have little impact on the process of reorganizing the Norwegian homeland security administration. What started life as a relatively comprehensive reorganization process ended with only minor changes being made to the status quo, and this despite the Vulnerability Commission's recommendations for radical organizational changes and the fact that the process coincided with a major external shock. The case illustrates how difficult it is to move responsibility for an agency from one ministry to another, even in a situation where overall agreement exists over what the problems of the field are—namely, fragmentation, weak coordination, and low priority. The Ministry of Justice achieved approval for its view on how to organize the field, and so did the Ministry of Defense to a certain extent. Compared with these two actors, the Vulnerability Commission and the parliament ended up playing rather minor roles. The Ministry of Justice initiated the process because it wanted to upgrade the civil security field and strengthen its role vis-à-vis military security. The process was then taken over by the Vulnerability Commission, which proposed changing organizational arrangements in the field according to the principle of hierarchical top–down coordination in the form of a new ministry for homeland security. Ultimately, however, a Hierarchical Model of this kind turned out to be too radical both for the ministries involved and for the Bondevik II government, which abandoned the idea of a ministry of homeland security in favor of upgrading and strengthening the agencies in the field—partly through mergers and partly by establishing more semiautonomous agencies. At the same time, the principle of responsibility based on similarity, proximity, and internal self-regulation was to be preserved, indicating that the new model is rather ambiguous and represents something of a hybrid. Thus "business as usual" is a better label for the outcome than radical change.

All in all, the process revealed the definition of homeland security and what it should constitute as issues of fundamental dispute. Primarily, the attempt at reorganization constituted a framing process. Does homeland security belong primarily to the field of defense or to that of civil society? Is it just one area among many in the field of general administrative policy and modernization of the public sector or is it a special field with its own particular problems and challenges? This dispute over the basic agenda has important implications for deciding what the relevant problems are, what the good solutions are, and who the legitimate actors and participants are. Thus, the process was not only a decision-making process but also a process of definition, interpretation, developing meaning and a shared understanding, constructing political realities, and negotiating over who is in the best position to advance the field of homeland security (Baumgartner and Jones, 1993; Rochefort and Cobb, 1994; Kettl, 2004a). The political struggle shaped field frames focusing on cultural meaning systems, the process, and its outcome. The broader structure of meaning helped to stabilize the power arrangements and interaction patterns and thus limited the possibilities for substantial change (Lounsbury et al., 2003).

The process also revealed that cleavages are more cross-institutional than inter-institutional. They run between different organizational fields. For example, the disagreement between the justice and defense sectors about how to define safety, security and preparedness, and where to place responsibility for them became most pronounced in the parliamentary reading. The lines of conflict went across institutional boundaries, not along them, in the sense that the distance was greater between the positions of the standing committees on justice and defense than those of the parliament and the government. The dominant conflict was not between the bureaucracy and the government or between the government and the parliament but between different policy fields. In one camp were the ministries, directorates, executive political leaders, and parliamentary standing committees in the policy area of justice, in the other were the corresponding bodies in the field of defense.

One main lesson from this process is that the characteristic features of the tasks and issues in different organizational fields are important (Pollitt et al., 2004) and these must be taken into consideration to understand the reorganization process. On a daily basis, the activities and their outcomes in this policy area are difficult to observe (Wilson, 1989). One of the main tasks of homeland security, however, is to plan for crisis and unforeseen circumstances and to be in a position to handle them. We are in a high-risk area, where timeliness and effectiveness, responsiveness, and flexibility are important features. In such situations, a hierarchical process with clear and stable objectives and top–down instructions might be too rigid and might have to be supplemented by a local security culture and professional ethics and integrity in semiautonomous agencies (Pollitt, 2005).

There is no one best way of organizing homeland security. Organizational structure plays a significant role, but the most critical issues remain unresolved, both theoretically and empirically. We face difficult dilemmas in structural design to which there is no easy or stable solution (Hammond et al., 2003; Hammond, 2007). Different principles for specialization by purpose, process, clients, or area have major

344 ■ Homeland Security Handbook

implications for what is coordinated and what is not. We face the challenge of making responsibility for homeland security part of the everyday business of every public-sector organization. At the same time, there is a need for autonomous professional knowledge and expertise, horizontal coordination between policy areas, and vertical political control. The trade-offs between these needs differ between different institutions and actors and the balance is unstable over time.

The reorganization of the Norwegian administration for homeland security can be seen as a combination of robustness and adaptation. Radical reform initiatives involving the introduction of a Hierarchical Model like that in the United States were rejected and the final solution was a combination of the traditional responsibility model based on a network approach and an Agency Model based on strengthened and partly merged semiautonomous agencies at arms length from the ministry as well as attempts to upgrade the coordinating authority of the Ministry of Justice. In some ways, this solution can be seen as an ambiguous compromise, resulting in a hybrid organization unable to solve the coordination challenges in the field of homeland security. At the same time, though, it might also be regarded as representing a reasonable balance between different considerations. Thus, it might be a robust and flexible solution able to handle the unpredictability and unforeseen character of the tasks in this policy area and thus a promising solution to the coordination challenges of the field. In what direction it will develop in practice remains to be seen.

References

Baldwin, R. and Cave, M., 1999. Understanding Regulation. Oxford: Oxford University Press.

Bardach, E., 1998. Getting Agencies to Work Together: The Art and Practice of Managerial Craftsmanship. Washington DC: The Brookings Institution.

Baumgartner, F.R. and Jones, B.D., 1993. Agendas and Instability in American Politics. Chicago, Illinois: Chicago University Press.

Benford, R.D. and Snow, D.A., 2000. Framing processes and social movements: An overview and assessment. Annual Review of Sociology, 26, 611–639.

Christensen, T. and Lægreid, P., 2002. Reformer og lederskap. Omstilling i den utøvende makt. Oslo: Universitetsforlaget.

Christensen, T. and Lægreid, P., 2006. Agencification and Regulatory Reforms. In T. Christensen and P. Lægreid (Eds.) Autonomy and Regulation. Copying with agencies in the modern state. Cheltenham: Edward Elgar. Paper presented at the Scancor/SOG workshop on Autonomization of the state: From integrated administrative models to single-purpose organizations. Stanford University, April 1–2.

Cohen, M., March, J.G., and Olsen, J.P., 1972. A garbage can model of organizational choice. Administrative Science Quarterly, 17, 1–25.

DiMaggio, P. and Powell, W.W., 1983. Institutional isomorphism and collective rationality in organizational fields. American Sociological Review, 48(4), 147–160.

Eden, L., 2004. Whole World on Fire. Ithaca, New York: Cornell University Press.

Fligstein, N., 1991. The structural transformation of American industry: An institutional account of the causes of diversification in the largest firms. In W. Powell and P. DiMaggio (Eds.) *The New Institutionalism in Organizational Analysis.* Chicago, Illinois: University of Chicago Press.

Frederickson, H.G. and LaPorte, T.R., 2002. Airport security, high reliability, and the problem of rationality. *Public Administration Review*, 62 (Special Issue), 33–43.

Hammond, T., 2007. Why is the intelligence community so different to redesign? Smart Practices, Conflicting Goals and the Creation of Purpose-Based Organizations. Governance, 20(3): 401–422.

Hammond, T., Jen, K.I., and Maeda, K., 2003. Intelligence organizations and the organization of intelligence: What library catalogues can tell us about 9/11. Paper presented at the SOG-Conference, George Washington University, Washington DC, May 22–24.

Harmond, M.M. and Mayer, R.T., 1986. *Organization Theory of Public Administration.* Glenview, Illinois: Scott, Foresman and Co.

Hoffman, A.J., 1999. Institutional evolution and change: Environmentalism and the US chemical industry. *Academy of Management Journal*, 42(4), 351–371.

Hood, C., Rothstein, H., and Baldwin, R., 2001. *The Government of Risk.* Oxford: Oxford University Press.

Kettl, D.F., 1993. Learning Organizations and Managing the Unknown. Paper presented at the Conference on Rethinking Public Personnel Systems, April 16–17, Washington DC.

Kettl, D.F., 2003. Contingent coordination: Practical and theoretical puzzles for homeland security. *American Review for Public Administration*, 33 (September), 253–277.

Kettl, D.F., 2004a. *The States and Homeland Security. Building the Missing Link. A Century Foundation Report.* New York: The Century Foundation.

Kettl, D.F. et al., 2004b. *The Department of Homeland Security's First Year. A Report Card.* Washington DC: The Century Foundation Press.

Kettl, D.F., 2004c. *System Under Stress. Homeland Security and American Politics.* Washington DC: CQ Press.

Kingdon, J.F., 1995. *Agendas, Alternatives, and Public Policies*, 2nd edn. New York: Longman.

LaPort, T., 1996. High reliability organizations: Unlikely, demanding and at risk. *Journal of Crisis and Contingency Management*, 4, 55–59.

Lawrence, P. and Lorsch, J.W., 1967. *Organization and Environment: Managing Differentiation and Integration.* Cambridge, Massachusetts: Harvard University.

Lounsbury, M., Ventresca, M., and Hirsch, P.M., 2003. Social movements, field frames and industry emergence: A cultural-political perspective on US recycling. *Socio-Economic Review*, 1, 71–104.

March, J.G. and Olsen, J.P., 1989. *Rediscovering Institutions: The Organizational Basis of Politics.* New York: The Free Press.

Mayntz, R. and Sharpf, F., 1975. *Policymaking in the German Federal Bureaucracy.* Amsterdam, The Netherlands: Elsevier.

Morrill, C., Institutional change through interstitial emergence: The growth of alternative dispute resolution in American law, 1965–1995. In W.W. Powell and D.L. Jones (Eds.) *How Institutions Change.* Chicago, Illinois: University of Chicago Press (forthcoming).

NOU, 2000:24. Et sårbart samfunn. Utfordringer for sikkerhets-og beredskapsarbeidet i samfunnet.

Olsen, J.P., 1996. Norway: Slow learner or another triumph of the tortoise? In J.P. Olsen and B.G. Peters (Eds.) *Lessons form Experience.* Oslo, Norway: Scandinavian University Press.

Olsen, J.P., 1997. Civil service in transition—dilemmas and lesson learned. In J.J. Hesse and T.A.J. Toonen (Eds.) *The European Yearbook of Comparative Government and Public Administration,* Vol. III. Baden-Baden, Germany: Nomos.

Peters, B.G., 2004. *Are We Safer Today? Organizational Responses to Terrorism.* Unpublished paper. Pittsburgh, Pennsylvania: University of Pittsburgh.

Phillips, N., Lawrence, T.B., and Hardy, C., 2000. Inter-organizational collaborations and the dynamics of institutional fields. *Journal of Management Studies,* 37(1), 23–43.

Pollitt, C., 2005. Ministries and agencies: Steering, meddling, neglecting and dependency. In M. Painter and J. Pierre (Eds.) *Challenges to State Policy Capacity.* London: Palgrave.

Pollitt, C. and Talbot, C. (Eds.), 2004. *Unbundled Government.* London: Routledge.

Pollitt, C., Talbot, C., Caulfield, J., and Smullen, A., 2004. *Agencies: How Governments Do Things through Semi-Autonomous Organizations.* Basingstoke, Hampshire: Palgrave.

Power, M., 2004. *The Risk Management of Everything.* London: Demos.

Rochefort, D.A. and Cobb, R.W. (Eds.), 1994. *The Politics of Problem Definition: Shaping the Policy Agenda.* Lawrence, Kansas: University of Kansas Press.

Scott, W.R., 1995. *Institutions and Organizations.* Thousand Oaks, California: Sage.

Scott, W.R. et al., 2000. *Institutional Change and Healthcare Organizations.* Chicago, Illinois: The University of Chicago Press.

Selznick, P., 1957. *Leadership in Administration.* New York: Harper and Row.

Serigstad, S., 2003. Eit sårbart samfunn. Ein studie av omorganiseringa av den sentrale tryggleiks-og beredskapsforvaltninga i Noreg i perioden 1999–2002. Bergen: Rokkan Centre Report 16, 2003.

St.meld. no. 17 (2001–02) Samfunnssikkerhet. Veien til et mindre sårbart samfunn. The 9/11 Commission Report. New York: W.W. Norton & Company, 2004.

Vaughan, D., 1996. *The Challenger Launch Decision.* Chicago, Illinois: University of Chicago Press.

Wilson, J.Q., 1989. *Bureaucracy. What Government Agencies Do and Why they Do It?* New York: Basic Books.

Wise, C.R., 2002a. Reorganizing the Federal Government for Homeland Security: Congress Attempts to Create a New Department. *Extensions,* Fall 2002:14–19.

Wise, C.R., 2002b. Organizing for homeland security. *Public Administration Review,* 62(2), 131–144.

Wise, C.R. and Nader, R., 2002. Organizing the federal system for homeland security: Problems, issues, and dilemmas. *Public Administration Review,* 62 (Special Issue), 44–57.

Endnotes

1. An earlier version of this paper was presented at the 20th EGOS Conference, Ljubljana July 1–3 2004, Sub-theme 16: Risk and Regulation: Relationships, Dynamics and Rationales within and between Organizations. We would like to thank the participants at the workshop and three anonymous referees for helpful comments.

2. Interview with commission members, internal minutes from the commission's work.

3. Interview with head of commission, internal minutes from the commission's work.
4. Ministry of Justice internal document case number 2000/10065.
5. Ministry of Justice internal document case number 2000/10065.
6. Interview with source from the Ministry of Justice.
7. Interview with source from the Ministry of Labour and Government Administration.
8. Ministry of Justice internal document case number 2000/10065, interview with source from the Ministry of Justice. Another provision of this compromise stipulated that the coordinating secretariat for the secret services should rotate between the Ministry of Justice, the Ministry of Defence, and the Foreign Ministry.
9. Interview with sources from the Ministry Justice.
10. Interview with the leader of the Committee on Justice.

Chapter 19

Behavioral Change and Border Crossing: The Effects of 9/11 on Cross-Border Traffic Five Years Later

Carlos Olmedo and Dennis L. Soden

CONTENTS

Introduction

This chapter assesses the changes in border crossings along the U.S. border in the nearly five years since the events of 9/11. Heightened border security measures after 9/11 were implemented at the primary ports of entry between the United States, Mexico, and Canada. Did the events of 9/11 change the crossing behavior patterns in border regions due to the federal administrative response and, was the socio-economic structure and high level of integration permanently disrupted? If changes in crossing patterns did occur, were they responses to the threat of terrorism or behavior changes due to new crossing procedures? In the end, 9/11 impacts may be issues of relative impacts, the result of turbulence measurable at an economic and individual level, but even more profound on the social structure and exchanges—the behavior—that occurs among residents of the region. The study provides an overview of crossings between the United States, Mexico, and Canada, including detailed analysis on pedestrian, vehicle, and vehicle passenger crossings to determine significant exchanges and movement as a result of the imposed terrorist watch strategy, which was implemented at both U.S. land borders.

Homeland Security Response to 9/11

Despite the bombing of the federal building in Oklahoma City and a previous attack on the World Trade Center, the events of September 11th had a dramatic effect on the American psyche. How the reaction to 9/11 was spread through the nation varied, but on the United States–Mexico border the response was an administrative response, immediately shifting from a policy that was supposed to be incrementally moving toward a seamless border in support of free trade to a view that the border was porous and a contributor to threats to national security. Previously, the southern U.S. border was not considered a serious threat to national security, but more often viewed by many parties as a threat to labor in the form of low-wage earners immigrating, both legally and illegally into the United States. In rapid order, the nature of crossing the United States–Mexico border and the crossing process changed from a bothersome trip with occasional delays to a cumbersome trip that made the border take on attributes of being divided and on permanent alert; an idea more recently associated with Eastern Europe's borders with Western Europe before the decline of the Soviet Union, than to the Western Hemisphere where borders have easily been negotiated for decades.

Although the North American Free Trade Agreement (NAFTA) had intentions of being a step toward economic integration in the Americas, creating in the long term a series of agreements that would remove barriers to moving people, goods, and capital, 9/11 stopped much of the effort in midstream. "Smart and secure borders" became buzzwords not to enhance trade but to present a sense that the policy process was going to develop new mechanisms that would insure trade efficiency between major trading partners and efficient movement of people funneled through major urban ports of entry.

Following the September 11th attacks, all official entry points were, in effect, shut down or responded by deliberately slowing processing as both the U.S. Customs Service and Immigration and Naturalization Service—now reorganized as the Bureau of Customs and Border Protection (CBP) and the Bureau of Immigration and Customs Enforcement (ICE), respectively, under the Department of Homeland Security (DHS)—moved to the highest possible alert. National agencies quickly shifted resources to secure borders rather than expedite entry, going as far as requesting personnel from the National Guard, a recurring theme in homeland security, to better monitor the nation's borders. In the last few months, protocols were being developed by Presidents Bush and Fox to provide for greater latitude in admitting temporary workers and the lessening of some border restrictions, efforts that were immediately shifted to less prominent places on the political agenda, clearly subordinate to the new foreign policy consideration of a war on terrorism. Yet, the reaction to the policy changes, whether viewed as incremental or major shifts, do not appear to have had any real impact on foreign policy between the United States and its North American neighbors. What has been of interest to observers of the border and to students of homeland security is the change in behaviors among border residents in the years since 9/11.

Overall, the post-9/11 changes underscore a shift toward more stringent immigration policies hallmarking a concern under the guise of homeland security that is inherently political at its roots. Immigration, a constant movement that has occurred for centuries is now important to national security and connected to conflict and disorder on a global scale.[1] Before 9/11, media coverage, as well as general American knowledge about the border could be said to be limited with more focus on drug cartels or threats to American labor that might come about from Mexican migration than about any real threat to national security, a term quickly replaced in the United States by homeland security. Moreover, in the case of the northern border, most Americans could be deemed as lacking any real knowledge of the state of affairs with Canada. In the wake of 9/11, closure of the southern border with Mexico was largely an afterthought to reduce the possibility of additional terrorists entering the country, making, perhaps for the first time, entry from Mexico, a threat.

For those living on the border, including many who believe a hardened border is counterproductive to binational relationships and free trade under NAFTA, the de facto lockdown and the subsequent sustained increased time on border crossing, a form of nontrade barrier to entry, has resulted in an inefficient and bureaucratic border setting that has disrupted what Scott[2] refers to as the border business district. The degree to which this business environment has been marked by inefficiencies is a separate issue[3] that does nothing to reverse negative perceptions of the border region. Border crossings and wait times have been significantly altered as the focus has shifted from almost exclusively stopping drugs, contraband, and illegal immigrants, negatives in public perceptions, to securing the nation's borders as part of the Bush administration's war on terrorism, a positive in public perceptions. Although long delays at the border were not new, they had been largely eliminated before 9/11 at many entry points, especially on the northern border with Canada. In the wake of 9/11, border life changed, creating new impacts on cross-border trade and the social–cultural fabric of the region, a reversal to a police mentality, contrary to almost all other efforts occurring globally to open borders through economic liberalization.[4] To a large extent, we explore these conditions largely in the context of El Paso, Texas, and its sister city, Ciudad (Cd.) Juárez, Chihuahua, a border space within the larger area of the U.S. border region that has been a focal point for changes in the way the United States administers its border regime.

El Paso and its Mexican sister city, Cd. Juárez, create one of the largest binational borderplexes[5] in the world, characterized by social and commercial ties unseen in most traditional regional economies. Cd. Juárez is home to the largest concentration of maquiladora[6] employment and payroll in Mexico, cultivating comparative advantages between Mexican labor and U.S. capital. As a result, the region has built itself into a major provider of manufacturing components that are distributed throughout North America. The once remote and unimportant region has become a strategic resource, key to sustaining the greater U.S. and North American economies.[7] In this regard, the region is inherently tied to production sharing technologies and the economies of scale practiced between U.S. and Mexican multinationals, particularly for manufacturing industries related to motor vehicles, vehicle parts, industrial machinery, and computer and electronic and communications equipment.[8] Other unique economic sectors have evolved in El Paso due to the city's border geography, such as transportation, distribution, and professional service industries that serve the manufacturing sector. Also developed are a relatively large retail trade sector that also serves northern Chihuahua, Mexico, and a large federal government sector due to the sizeable military presence, border law and immigration enforcement, and public programs. Because of the high degree of integration, it is important to note that before 9/11, the U.S.-led recession was already being felt in Mexico and in the border region, and a maquiladora slowdown was spreading throughout the various sectors of the metropolitan economy. The 9/11 terrorist attacks not only aggravated the existing economic downturn, they also altered the social characteristics between these international cities, doing so more than casual observers, including policymakers in Washington DC and Mexico City, have observed. If we consider the region as a transition zone,[9] where activities and people straddle national boundaries and cross-border links may in fact be stronger than links to respective nations, then the argument may be made that shifts in managing borders create a series of ripple effects that cannot be fully anticipated or that may have longer-term impacts than expected. In addition, these ripple effects may create demands for additional policy changes as they become permanent or require offsets to existing policies and strategies.

This chapter assesses the effects of the heightened border security measures after 9/11 on the primary ports of entry between the United States, Mexico, and Canada, with discussion related to El Paso, Texas, an area expected to bear pronounced impacts because of its large economic and social integration with Mexico's northern border. This highly integrated region, although beset with problems, has led border communities to seek pragmatic solutions to problems recognizing that globalization has created local problems that can be best solved through cooperation across borders.[10] From a geopolitical perspective, this might be a form of globalization, parallel paths of global (macro) activity in the maquiladora sector with local (micro) strategies and solutions being developed at the expense of the nation-state to maximize regional goals and needs.[11] But, did the events of 9/11 change the region by shifting focus from macroeconomic policy to a federal administrative response and to what degree was the socioeconomic structure and high level of integration permanently disrupted? In some ways, the question of disruptions in the regional economic activities is not new, evidenced by events such as Operation Hold-the-Line in September 1993, which hardened the borders and limited individual exchanges at the same time as transnational economic activities were being touted as strengthening the global position of the America.[12] In many ways, the turbulence of the region is also similar to many areas in transition as nations merge or borders, such as those in Eastern Europe, reemerge with the West.[13] In the end, 9/11 impacts may be issues of relative impacts, the result of turbulence measurable at an economic level, but more profound on the social structure and exchanges that occur among residents of the region, a point to which we shall return.

Mexico and Canada Borders

Differences in border crossing patterns between U.S. southern and northern ports are primarily attributable to city size and geography, and existed long before the passage of NAFTA. Greater people and vehicle flows are expected where a U.S. border city and its neighboring Mexican or Canadian city have a larger combined populace, as in the case of El Paso–Cd. Juárez with roughly 2.2 million inhabitants.[14] In contrast, greater cargo truck crossings will be dictated by geography rather than population size. Trade corridors to the U.S. industrial Northeast and Midwest and other regional markets are well established, primarily as a result of the interstate highway system, so one can expect greater traffic along the entry points closer in distance or connected to well-defined transportation nodes.

Border crossings are compiled as incoming,[15] which in the case of Mexico are compiled as northward crossings, while with Canada they are compiled as southward crossings. In light of the discussion about the effects of 9/11 and homeland security policy impacts, comparisons of 2001 and 2005 annual border crossings between the United States–Canada, and the United States–Mexico are provided in Table 19.1.

Social and familial ties explain the overwhelming ratio in people and vehicle crossings between the United States and Mexico, while the greater ratio of cargo or commercial truck crossings for Canada can be explained by the closer commercial ties between U.S. and Canadian industries that developed from the late 1800s onward.[16] The greater ratio of empty trailer crossings for Mexico are attributed to the more prevalent short-haul drayage transport system between nations developed in conjunction with the maquiladora sector. Overall, we see declines since 2001 in total pedestrian traffic although the percentage of share at each border has remained approximately the same. In addition, we see overall vehicle crossings declining by over 1.7 million with Canadian declines (over 4 million) accounting for all of the contraction and offsetting the increase of over 2.2 million on the Mexican border ports of entry. Passenger declines are of great interest, falling by an estimated 35.6 million overall but with minimal percentage changes. Changes across all three dimensions show that since 9/11, crossings of persons have indeed been reduced (an estimated contraction of 41.4 million), suggesting that 9/11 has forced a degree of change in behavior of border region residents. This behavioral change is supported by analyzing annual crossings since 1994 (Figure 19.1). All three modes show an overall growth trend throughout the 1990s followed by significant declines that are currently below their pre-9/11 peak levels.

Impacts of 9/11 on Crossings at Selected Ports of Entry

Moving a step farther, one approach to considering the effects of 9/11, employs analysis of Mexican and Canadian border crossings by individual ports on a monthly basis for the period before and after the terrorist attacks. By examining monthly totals, the 9/11 immediate impact is the difference between crossings for September and August 2001. Pedestrian, vehicle, and vehicle passenger crossings are analyzed for both over the month (OTM) from August to September 2001, and over the year (OTY) from August 2001 to 2002. August to September 2000, a data point equivalent to one year before 9/11 and August to September 2002, a data point one year later, are considered for monthly changes to provide for reference to the OTM changes occurring in 2001. Last, the values of OTY changes from pre-9/11 in August 2001 through August 2005 are also considered.[17]

Pedestrian Crossings

The five largest ports of entry (San Ysidro, El Paso, Calexico, Laredo, and Nogales), which make up on average over two-thirds of total U.S. incoming pedestrian crossings, experienced significant shifts following 9/11. OTY from August 2001

Table 19.1 2001 and 2005 Incoming Border Crossing Comparisons

Border			Pedestrians	Vehicles	Vehicle Passengers	Cargo Trucks	Trailers (Loaded)	Trailers (Empty)
United States–Mexico	2001	Frequency (percent)	51,501,321 (98.6)	89,526,957 (72.3)	209,105,846 (73.6)	4,304,959 (38.8)	2,372,125 (29.9)	1,916,207 (65.2)
	2005	Frequency (percent)	45,829,612 (98.7)	91,756,403 (75.1)	185,967,448 (74.8)	4,675,887 (40.8)	3,031,474 (34.2)	1,646,088 (63.2)
United States–Canada	2001	Frequency (percent)	749,805 (1.4)	34,308,013 (27.7)	74,971,105 (26.4)	6,776,909 (61.2)	5,570,782 (70.1)	1,020,575 (34.8)
	2005	Frequency (percent)	605,338 (1.3)	30,352,526 (24.9)	62,502,937 (25.2)	6,784,378 (59.2)	5,818,947 (65.8)	956,497 (36.8)
Total	2001	Frequency (percent)	52,251,126 (100)	123,834,970 (100)	284,076,951 (100)	11,081,868 (100)	7,942,907 (100)	2,936,782 (100)
	2005	Frequency (percent)	46,434,951 (100)	122,108,929 (100)	248,470,385 (100)	11,460,265 (100)	8,850,421 (100)	2,602,585 (100)

Source: U.S. Department of Transportation, Bureau of Transportation Statistics, based on data compiled from the U.S. Customs Service.

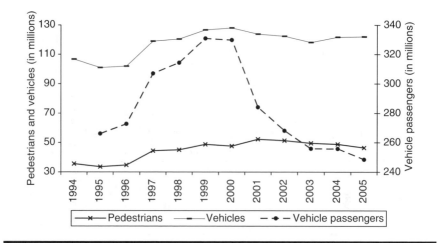

Figure 19.1 U.S. incoming border crossings total: 1994–2005.

to August 2002, persons walking from Mexico into the United States fell at San Ysidro by 377,057, at Calexico by 47,900, and at Laredo by 27,240, and rose at El Paso by 446,638 and at Nogales by 101,176 (Table 19.2). OTM from August to September 2001, the 9/11 events had the greatest negative effect on the California ports of San Ysidro (297,586) and Calexico (75,818) while the Arizona ports of San Luis and Douglas witnessed increases OTM of 63,585 and 26,571, respectively. At Buffalo–Niagara on the northern border with Canada, an initial OTM decline of 66,986, was offset OTY following 9/11 by an increase of 67,118. Compiling all northern and southern U.S. borders together, including smaller ports not included in Table 19.2, we find that pedestrian crossings increased by 5.6 percent OTY or 234,318 and declined by 278,913 or a 6.7 percent reduction OTM.

In the longer period from August 2001 to August 2005, we find the top five ports had quite significant changes in the crossing patterns associated with them. Calexico recorded a drop of 54.2 percent, while San Ysidro followed with a 20.8 percent decline. In Otay Mesa, adjacent to Tijuana, Baja California, and San Diego, there is a significant shift in pedestrian crossings of 117 percent since 2001. In addition, Nogales has experienced an 88.7 percent upward shift and El Paso a 55.1 percent increase for the compared periods. Although this is a mixed record in some ways, it clearly suggests some changes in behaviors associated with crossings have occurred in the post-9/11 period. The extent to which these changes may be offset by other modes is one concern that is important for a variety of local administrative issues (i.e., infrastructure demand, inner city shopping, and subsequent tax consequences) as well as for organization and staffing of federal agencies involved in border crossing–related activities. The shift in pedestrian crossings to avert vehicle crossings that have borne the burden of extended time delays and waits in the border-crossing queue is one substitution effect. As Figure 19.2 illustrates, when

Table 19.2 Pedestrian Crossings Absolute and Percent Changes: 2000–2005

Port	Over the Month						Over the Year			
	Aug. to Sep. 2000	Percent Change	Aug. to Sep. 2001	Percent Change	Aug. to Sep. 2002	Percent Change	Aug. 2001–2002	Percent Change	Aug. 2001–2005	Percent Change
San Ysidro, California	−26,736	−3.9	−297,586	−26.0	−145,690	−19.0	−377,057	−33.0	**−238,034**	**−20.8**
El Paso, Texas	−50,241	−7.6	39,631	9.7	−85,764	−10.0	446,638	108.8	**226,367**	**55.1**
Calexico, California	40,045	5.9	−75,818	−11.9	−16,384	−2.8	−47,900	−7.5	**−345,043**	**−54.2**
Laredo, Texas	−2,424	−0.6	−35,887	−8.3	−26,399	−6.5	−27,240	−6.3	−32,168	−7.4
Nogales, Arizona	−14,895	−4.2	32,506	8.9	−8,449	−1.8	101,176	27.6	**325,361**	**88.7**
Brownsville, Texas	−52,355	−20.9	5,281	1.9	−39,664	−14.2	8,943	3.3	−25,088	−9.3
San Luis, Arizona	38,872	22.2	63,585	35.3	14,659	8.6	−10,391	−5.8	−16,005	−8.9
Hidalgo, Texas	−3,332	−1.5	−8,690	−4.9	−18,550	−11.1	−9,114	−5.2	−18,958	−10.7
Andrade, California	14,739	28.4	9,643	16.7	10,162	17.3	1,018	1.8	6,076	10.5

(continued)

Table 19.2 (continued) Pedestrian Crossings Absolute and Percent Changes: 2000–2005

Port	Over the Month						Over the Year			
	Aug. to Sep. 2000	Percent Change	Aug. to Sep. 2001	Percent Change	Aug. to Sep. 2002	Percent Change	Aug. 2001–2002	Percent Change	Aug. 2001–2005	Percent Change
Progreso, Texas	−9,636	−16.7	−3,127	−4.8	−13,719	−17.9	11,826	18.2	3,450	5.3
Otay Mesa, California	−2,098	−4.0	18,310	31.5	−16,107	−11.8	78,065	134.4	**67,938**	**117.0**
Eagle Pass, Texas	−10,505	−14.3	3,221	4.8	−2,871	−4.8	−8,133	−12.0	−12,767	−18.9
Douglas, Arizona	−6,010	−10.5	26,571	49.3	−4,008	−9.0	−9,386	−17.4	9,800	18.2
Buffalo–Niagara, New York	−14,157	−34.0	−66,986	−73.1	−42,181	−26.6	67,118	73.2	−9,271	−10.1
United States–Canada total	−24,606	−29.6	−69,294	−53.9	−43,849	−23.4	58,892	45.9	−15,444	−12.0
United States–Mexico total	−91,197	−2.3	−209,619	−5.2	−368,255	−8.7	175,426	4.3	−46,259	−1.1
U.S. border total	−115,803	−2.9	−278,913	−6.7	−412,104	−9.4	234,318	5.6	−61,703	−1.5

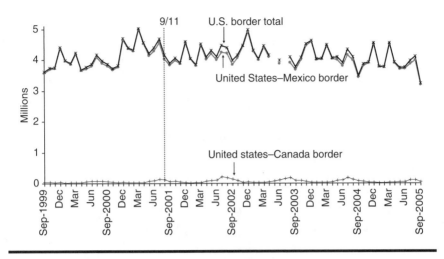

Figure 19.2   Pedestrian crossings borderwide.

both borders are considered, the overall fall in pedestrian crossings during this longer time is primarily a United States–Mexico border phenomena based on headcount.

More detailed examination also reveals some trends that can be disruptive to border administration and must be realized to gauge the full extent of a single phenomenon like 9/11.[18] As an example, in November and December there is a rise in persons walking across at the majority of the southern traversing points, visible in Figure 19.2, and is the result of increased holiday shopping by Mexican nationals in their respective cross-border cities. This seasonal trend is applicable in times of a strong or stable Mexican peso and also affects vehicle and vehicle passenger crossings. Summer and fall months further experience an increase as legal seasonal workers enter from Mexico to tend the U.S. agricultural fields. Extreme variability is also visible at Buffalo–Niagara and other northern crossing points in the summer months and is attributed to seasonal tourism—pedestrian, vehicle, and vehicle passenger crossings rise in the second quarter of the year and fall in the third quarter. Seasonal trends that overlapped with 9/11 may create some uncertainty especially when declines are enhanced by economic conditions such as the pre-9/11 slowdown or a currency crisis.

Vehicle Crossings

Immediately following the September 11th attacks, with the exception of Hidalgo, vehicle crossings fell at all southern and northern border ports (Table 19.3 and Figure 19.3). The August to September 2001 drops varied greatly, from 31,260 at Calexico East to 621,865 at El Paso. Similarly, vehicle crossings fell by close to or more than 100,000 at the ports of San Ysidro, Detroit, Brownsville, Laredo,

Table 19.3 Vehicle Crossings Absolute and Percent Changes

Port	Over the Month						Over the Year				
	Aug. to Sep. 2000	Percent Change	Aug. to Sep. 2001	Percent Change	Aug. to Sep. 2002	Percent Change	Aug. 2001–2002	Percent Change	Aug. 2001–2005	Percent Change
El Paso, Texas	−52,968	−3.6	−621,865	−36.7	−56,429	−5.1	−593,873	−35.0	−291,526	**−17.2**
San Ysidro, California	−118,061	−9.0	−478,136	−31.9	−63,134	−4.1	25,340	1.7	−18,684	−1.2
Detroit, Michigan	−75,337	−9.6	−312,174	−39.9	−75,345	−11.8	−142,463	−18.2	−234,901	**−30.1**
Hidalgo, Texas	−44,287	−6.3	36,982	7.0	−45,031	−6.3	186,508	35.4	24,951	4.7
Brownsville, Texas	−8,324	−1.3	−180,970	−26.3	−29,735	−4.4	−8,918	−1.3	−89,797	−13.1
Laredo, Texas	4,160	0.7	−235,997	−32.2	−41,928	−6.9	−123,511	−16.9	−207,182	**−28.3**
Buffalo–Niagara, New York	−231,469	−24.3	−425,474	−43.7	−283,987	−30.5	−43,065	−4.4	−238,183	**−24.5**
Calexico, California	3,918	0.7	−142,883	−26.1	18,757	3.7	−44,750	−8.2	−19,143	−3.5
Nogales, Arizona	−18,562	−4.6	−99,267	−23.6	−7,001	−2.1	−85,368	−20.3	−154,683	**−36.8**
Otay Mesa, California	−4,633	−1.1	−94,140	−25.8	−6,264	−1.8	−16,751	−4.6	200,315	**55.0**

Eagle Pass, Texas	−5,893	−2.1	−53,272	−18.4	−13,235	−4.2	23,921	8.2	5,152	1.8
Calexico East, California	26,224	12.5	−31,260	−12.3	12,563	4.5	23,899	9.4	5,083	2.0
Blaine, Washington	−42,678	−12.0	−166,711	−46.6	−39,362	−15.6	−105,006	−29.4	−98,511	−27.5
San Luis, Arizona	677	0.3	−65,148	−28.0	−5,589	−1.9	59,493	25.6	26,401	11.3
Port Huron, Michigan	−49,494	−18.7	−103,971	−39.1	−39,401	−14.2	11,607	4.4	−47,780	−18.0
Douglas, Arizona	−3,604	−1.9	−69,000	−33.9	−10,897	−5.4	−246	−0.1	−21,899	−10.7
Calais, Maine	−26,848	−17.4	−33,074	−21.6	−4,433	−5.1	−66,309	−43.3	−30,045	−19.6
United States–Canada total	−718,834	−17.6	−1,577,892	−38.0	−836,677	−22.4	−419,788	−10.1	−857,510	−20.7
United States–Mexico total	−221,691	−2.8	−2,126,136	−25.7	−293,411	−3.8	−493,842	−6.0	−601,475	−7.3
U.S. border total	−940,525	−7.9	−3,704,028	−29.8	−1,130,088	−9.8	−913,630	−7.4	−1,458,985	−11.7

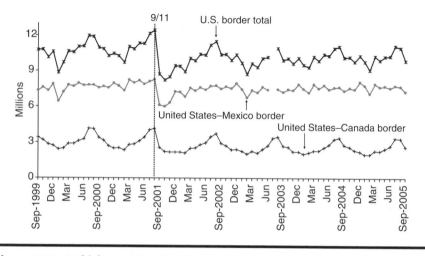

Figure 19.3   Vehicle crossings borderwide.

Buffalo–Niagara, Calexico, Blaine, Port Huron, Nogales, and Otay Mesa (Table 19.3). The 20 days of greater scrutiny after the morning of 9/11 clearly proved to be a deterrence, as persons driving across the U.S. borders reduced by more than 3.7 million—the southern border contracted by roughly 2.1 million while the northern border by 1.6 million. The two largest ports on the southern border for vehicle traffic, El Paso and San Ysidro, and the two largest on the northern border, Detroit and Buffalo–Niagara, accounted for half of this total U.S. border decline. Figure 19.3 also illustrates that both the southern and northern ports of entry have not fully recovered to pre-9/11 levels for incoming vehicle crossings.[19]

The impacts on the 17 largest border ports are summarized in Table 19.3, showing that substantial OTY 2001–2002 and OTY 2001–2005 vehicle declines occurred at El Paso, Detroit, Laredo, Nogales, Blaine, and Calais. In El Paso, this was offset by pedestrian crossings between the sister cities. By contrast Otay Mesa has seen a rise in vehicle traffic, 55 percent between August 2001 and 2005, and is the only port on either borders to have witnessed an obvious and substantial rise in incoming vehicles. Caution is taken about declaring a substantial OTY 2001–2002 increase to Hidalgo due to the unexplained large drop in August 2001 at this port, which skews upward the difference between August 2001 and 2002.

In December 1999, Arizona extended its border zone from 25 to 75 miles, effectively making the Tucson area a border town, meaning Mexican residents no longer need I-94 visas to travel to Tucson from the Nogales, San Luis, and Douglas ports of entry. Nogales is the principal border port connecting Arizona with Sonora's (Mexico) principal city and capital, Hermosillo. Hence, it is highly significant that vehicle traffic through Nogales, as an access point to the interior of Arizona, has contracted to well below pre-9/11 levels. Moreover, between November and

December 2001 all southern ports but one, Nogales, experienced a slight jump in vehicle crossings attributed to holiday purchases made by Mexican nationals.

Looking at the period from August 2001 to August 2005, the largest share of vehicle crossing decline is from the United States–Canada border. The border cities of Detroit–Windsor, Buffalo–Fort Erie, and Blaine–Vancouver saw declines in southbound vehicle crossings of 30.1, 24.5, and 27.5 percent, respectively. Moreover, this decline is linked beyond the immediate border sister cities. Traditionally, vacation travel to Canada had resulted in increases in northern port reported crossings during the summer season. Since 9/11 potential crossings from those in transit through the United States–Canada border during peak vacation periods have declined from pre-9/11 levels.

Vehicle Passenger Crossings

Unlike pedestrian and vehicle crossings data that reports actual units, the number of vehicle passengers is obtained through a random vehicle selection count from which a multiplier is calculated on a month-to-month basis and on a port-by-port basis.[20] The same 17 border crossings for vehicles are analyzed for vehicle passengers, and the data indicates that some ports with lesser vehicle traffic traveled with more individuals in their cars, and vice versa.

With few exceptions (Otay Mesa, Calexico East, and Douglas), vehicle passenger crossings have dropped since 9/11, even more so than vehicles themselves (Table 19.4 and Figure 19.4). As with vehicles, passenger shifts were most evident at the port of El Paso, dropping by 1.3 million OTM August to September 2001, rebounding slightly to a drop of 27.8 percent from 2001 to 2005 (Table 19.4). Buffalo–Niagara witnessed the second largest passenger fall OTY 2001–2005, followed by Detroit, San Ysidro, Hidalgo, and Laredo. Like incoming vehicles, vehicle passengers entering the United States have not recovered to pre-9/11 levels (Figure 19.4). Substantial OTM and OTY vehicle passenger declines are in response to an increase in pedestrian crossings at some ports such as Nogales, El Paso, and Otay Mesa. Local citizens who routinely cross the border have indicated preference to cross and use alternative transportation. In the downtown areas of border cities, this phenomenon is quite observable and recently has been tied to increased bus usage in border cities.[21]

Analysis

Change in Crossing Patterns between Ports of Entry

Behaviors and institutions are often self-perpetuating and subject to change very incrementally. Regime changes more often than not come about as a result of crisis that changes the norms and regulations that govern behavior. As a result, the order

Table 19.4 Vehicle Passenger Crossings Absolute and Percent Changes

Port	Over the Month						Over the Year			
	Aug. to Sep. 2000	Percent Change	Aug. to Sep. 2001	Percent Change	Aug. to Sep. 2002	Percent Change	Aug. 2001–2002	Percent Change	Aug. 2001–2005	Percent Change
El Paso, Texas	−152,608	−3.6	−1,325,860	−38.1	−277,216	−12.0	−1,160,664	−33.4	−966,804	−27.8
San Ysidro, California	−259,734	−9.0	−1,051,899	−31.9	−138,895	−4.1	55,748	1.7	−485,704	−14.7
Hidalgo, Texas	−109,218	−6.2	−279,604	−18.6	−136,683	−8.7	64,629	4.3	−417,329	−27.8
Laredo, Texas	10,398	0.7	−604,293	−36.6	−23,224	−1.6	−221,959	−13.5	−393,868	−23.9
Brownsville, Texas	−20,810	−1.3	−442,173	−29.1	−278,955	−19.9	−114,145	−7.5	−270,346	−17.8
Buffalo–Niagara, New York	−701,380	−31.9	−1,309,350	−51.9	−907,386	−38.5	−167,578	−6.6	−754,392	−29.9
Detroit, Michigan	−12,555	−0.7	−702,271	−46.1	−202,304	−16.7	−309,704	−20.3	−540,134	−35.4
Calexico, California	6,192	0.4	−285,766	−26.1	−14,549	−1.4	−89,500	−8.2	−38,286	−3.5
Nogales, Arizona	−236,451	−23.4	−300,591	−31.6	−102,015	−12.5	−137,786	−14.5	−335,079	−35.2

Eagle Pass, Texas	−14,733	−2.1	−133,180	−18.4	−118,215	−14.9	66,621	9.2	−33,082	−4.6
Otay Mesa, California	−10,192	−1.1	−207,108	−25.8	−13,781	−1.8	−36,852	−4.6	271,304	33.8
Calexico East, California	78,148	12.5	−17,978	−3.5	23,870	4.5	20,010	3.9	36,071	7.1
Blaine, Washington	−94,112	−10.7	−399,858	−46.7	−125,312	−22.0	−287,852	−33.6	−344,031	−40.2
San Luis, Arizona	70,105	12.3	−199,171	−30.6	−100,518	−13.2	108,139	16.6	−159,284	−24.4
Douglas, Arizona	−9,911	−1.9	−138,000	−33.9	−116,288	−15.9	325,180	79.8	28,959	7.1
Port Huron, Michigan	−458,544	−49.7	−258,877	−43.2	−110,441	−21.3	−80,228	−13.4	−119,659	−20.0
Calais, Maine	−59,066	−17.4	−72,763	−21.6	−9,753	−5.1	−145,880	−43.3	−66,099	−19.6
United States–Canada total	−2,308,599	−22.2	−4,026,178	−41.5	−1,426,975	−16.7	−1,138,616	−11.7	−2,401,375	−24.8
United States–Mexico total	−659,430	−3.2	−5,135,561	−27.8	−1,363,053	−7.7	−861,146	−4.7	−2,816,665	−15.2
U.S. border total	−2,968,029	−9.6	−9,161,739	−32.5	−2,790,028	−10.7	−1,999,762	−7.1	−5,218,040	−18.5

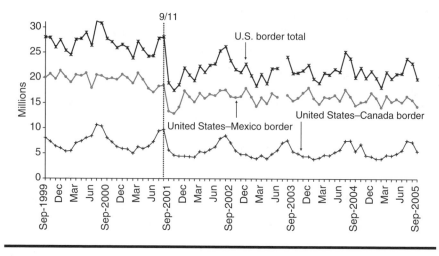

Figure 19.4   Vehicle passenger crossings borderwide.

of activity shifts. The 9/11 impacts on the ports of entry analyzed in this study for pedestrian, vehicle, and vehicle passenger crossings can be separated into three groupings provided in Table 19.5. There is clearly a mix of patterns seen in this table. Some ports such as Laredo, Detroit, and Blaine experienced significant downward shifts in border crossing patterns OTM (August to September 2001) and OTY (2001–2005) in the modes assessed, while others saw declines in two modes, while still others saw a change in only one mode or only short-term OTM versus the longer term. Overall OTM and OTY are mixed for pedestrian crossings

Table 19.5   9/11 Impacts by Border Crossing Types at Selected Ports of Entry: Over the Month (OTM) August to September 2001 and Over the Year (OTY) August 2001–2005

	Pedestrian		Vehicle		Vehicle Passenger	
Port	OTM	OTY	OTM	OTY	OTM	OTY
San Ysidro, California	↓	↓	↓	–	↓	↓
El Paso, Texas	↑	↑	↓	↓	↓	↓
Calexico, California	↓	↓	↓	–	↓	–
Laredo, Texas	↓	↓	↓	↓	↓	↓
Nogales, Arizona	↑	↑	↓	↓	↓	↓
Brownsville, Texas	+	–	↓	↓	↓	↓

Table 19.5 (continued)   9/11 Impacts by Border Crossing Types at Selected Ports of Entry: Over the Month (OTM) August to September 2001 and Over the Year (OTY) August 2001–2005

Port	Pedestrian		Vehicle		Vehicle Passenger	
	OTM	OTY	OTM	OTY	OTM	OTY
San Luis, California	↑	−	↓	+	↓	↓
Hidalgo, Texas	−	−	+	+	↓	↓
Andrade, California	+	+	NA	NA	NA	NA
Progreso, Texas	−	+	NA	NA	NA	NA
Otay Mesa, California	↑	↑	↓	↑	↓	↑
Eagle Pass, Texas	+	−	↓	+	↓	−
Douglas, Arizona	↑	+	↓	−	↓	+
Buffalo–Niagara, New York	↓	−	↓	↓	↓	↓
Detroit, Michigan	NA	NA	↓	↓	↓	↓
Calexico East, California	NA	NA	−	+	−	+
Blaine, Washington	NA	NA	↓	↓	↓	↓
Port Huron, Michigan	NA	NA	↓	−	↓	↓
Calais, Maine	NA	NA	↓	↓	↓	↓
United States–Canada total	↓	−	↓	↓	↓	↓
United States–Mexico total	↓	↓	↓	↓	↓	↓
U.S. border total	↓	↓	↓	↓	↓	↓

Notes: ↑ signifies an observed significant increase for the reference period.

↓ signifies an observed significant decrease for the reference period.

+ signifies that there was an increase, but no or not easily observable substantial increase for the reference period.

− signifies that there was a decline, but no or not easily observable substantial decrease for the reference period.

NA signifies that the port was not analyzed for that particular crossing due to authors' choice of substantial traffic for analysis cutoff.

Observed significant increase (↑) or decrease (↓) is based on the authors' following criteria—for pedestrian a change of 30,000 or 20 percent, for vehicle a change of 50,000 or 20 percent, and for vehicle passenger a change of 100,000 or 20 percent.

since 2001 but a decline is evident in other modes. Moreover, when viewed collectively on an annual basis, the overall patterns on the southern United States–Mexico border and the northern United States–Canada border are the same, both experiencing a shift in behavior as crossings have declined in all modes, particularly in vehicle passengers (Figure 19.1).

Several things are occurring in the border regions during the post-9/11 period. In places such as Otay Mesa, there was a likely effect of day-tourism reduction from Baja California in the short run but a substantial rise in crossings in the long run. The latter coincides with expansion and new 24-hour service at Otay Mesa port facilities necessitated by efforts to reduce wait times at San Diego County ports of entry. This alternative to travelers created an immediate shift in traffic patterns away from San Ysidro toward Otay Mesa. To analyze the likely effect of 9/11 on San Diego County, the aggregate of both ports is then necessary. The result is that in four years time from August 2001 to 2005 total vehicles in both ports have risen by over 181,000, while pedestrians and passengers have contracted by 170,000 and 214,000, respectively. Consequently, over 384,000 fewer personal crossings are being made from Baja California into California through San Ysidro and Otay Mesa since 9/11. In El Paso, daily commuting has changed to a more expedient foot mode over a now lengthier vehicle crossing. However, the increase in pedestrians of over 226,000 at El Paso's port is dwarfed by the reduction of close to 967,000 estimated vehicle passengers. Similar to San Diego, fewer personal crossings, almost three-quarters of a million, are being realized from Chihuahua into El Paso County.

Pedestrian and vehicle crossings have been clearly impacted at the nation's primary ports of entry. Heightened border security increased wait times that were already intolerable before 9/11.[22] In El Paso, vehicle waits of two to three hours to cross over the international bridges was the post-9/11 norm. These times have since diminished, but remain at levels much longer than pre-9/11. In response, people gave up driving, preferring to wait less by walking across, thereby increasing pedestrian crossings both in the immediate period after 9/11 and in the years following.

Days and months after 9/11, vehicle lanes were so congested from the newly implemented security procedures that many Mexican nationals working, studying, visiting, or shopping in U.S. border cities like El Paso walked across and had someone pick them up on the U.S. side or shifted to alternative transportation like bus systems. Even with relatively shorter wait times, pedestrian lines were so long that during the summer months of 2002, INS officials provided some relief by setting up tarps for shade and supplying water to pedestrian crossers to combat dehydration, fatigue, and frustration.[23] The dramatic change in pedestrian travel is also a result from altered southbound travel, realizing that they must cross back which is captured in the incoming northbound crossings. In this regard, El Pasoans, for example, have curbed their social practices of entering Mexico. Like Cd. Juárez residents, El Pasoans walk across when they can. For example, many nightclubs and drugstores are located in downtown Cd. Juárez, just a few minutes walk from El Paso via bridge. Likewise in southern California, forays into Tijuana from

San Diego area have become more difficult and lengthy, curbing some social exchanges. As a result, refusing to travel across and wait in vehicle lines, more individuals park their cars near international bridges, walk across, make their purchases or visit nightclubs, and walk back. On the more extreme side, many individuals have literally stopped going over to enjoy Mexico's restaurants, nightlife, and other entertainment venues because of the time uncertainty in returning. The shift in behavior in the El Paso region as a result of the terrorist attacks is obvious; people are walking across more, driving less, and driving farther distances to cross. When not necessary, they simply are not crossing; a behavior shift that has occurred at the port of Nogales as well. By contrast, at other major entry points such as San Ysidro, Calexico, Laredo, and Brownsville the substantial declines in passenger crossings have only been aggravated by significant declines in pedestrian crossings.

Among the explanations for variability in or substitution between pedestrian and vehicle crossings is that in some instances communities create a contiguous border city, as in the case of El Paso–Cd. Juárez. These cities share one common characteristic—their core downtown areas lie directly on the United States–Mexico international boundary. Between El Paso and Cd. Juárez almost all pedestrian crossings occur downtown. Hence, Cd. Juárez residents have immediate access to their sister city—walking distance for retail purchases and a trolley ride away from El Paso Community College and The University of Texas at El Paso (UTEP) for Mexican nationals studying in El Paso. In addition, there exists a large residential and nonresidential concentration all along the border between El Paso and Cd. Juárez, including both cities' universities (UTEP and la Universidad Autónoma de Ciudad Juárez).[24] Therefore, substitution to walking by foot across the border can be less burdensome than the longer and uncertain vehicle wait times.

In other cases, while the commercial impacts in the larger cites of El Paso and San Diego are to an extent offset by increases and decreases in crossing patterns or by the diversity of their economies, in smaller cities such as Laredo that have experienced substantial declines in all areas and are much more dependent on retail sales from Mexican nationals, the economic impact can be severe. Although the northern ports of Detroit, Blaine, Port Huron, and Calais also witnessed significant declines OTY and OTM in vehicle and vehicle passenger traffic, they hardly have incoming pedestrians by comparison to the southern border.

An Economic Perspective in the Southern Border

The full impact on trade and services to the United States–Mexico border economy is difficult to quantify because none of the traditional sources of data decompose services and trade economic activity into activity generated by U.S. residents versus non-U.S. residents, the daily crossers in the region. Survey instruments performed for the Sonora, Mexico–Arizona, U.S. region have been conducted since the late 1970s to assess these activities.[25] Although restricted to being performed only once per decade, the Arizona exit interviews have provided insight as to what percentage Mexican visitor spending accounts for as a percent of taxable sales by county. Results showed extreme variation, from as little as 3.8 percent to as much as 47.3 percent, dependent on the port and border county under analysis. Other survey-style studies along the San Diego region have also tried to measure the extent of retail sales purchases by Mexican nationals but are by no means definitive.

Similarly, empirical models have tried to assess the effect and extent of retail sales activity captured by Mexican nationals along Texas' border. Again, results differ by region and by model parameters and initial conditions. Under one Federal Reserve study, exported retail sales in Texas ranged from 6 to 22 percent of all retail sales along the border counties.[26] Another impact study on the El Paso region quantified the percent of total retail sales to Mexican nationals at 33 percent.[27] A more recent report suggests that the Texas border MSAs of Brownsville, McAllen, and Laredo move in a more similar fashion to the business cycle in Mexico, while El Paso's economy has become relatively more aligned with cycles in Texas and the United States.[28] This implies that the Texas southern border cities are more tied to movements in the Mexican peso and their impact on local retail sales than many might believe.

Because the southern border retail trade sector is very much dependent on purchases from Mexican nationals, not surprisingly, direct anomalies in border retail sales can be attributed to specific Mexican impacts. In 1995, the year after the massive peso devaluation that crippled the Mexican economy, retail sales witnessed almost no growth borderwide, and fell in Texas border counties.[29] Although sales grew in Arizona and California border counties, their growth was limited by fewer purchases from Mexico. Currency stability clearly plays an important role along the border. As an example, the peso devaluation had a greater negative effect on border retail sales than the 1996 $50 import limit of U.S. goods without declaration instituted by Mexico for its nationals and the 2001 recession that affected both sides of the border.[30]

It could be argued that policy changes that force Mexican and U.S. citizens to change their crossing behavior or causes them to stop crossing at any time can be viewed as great or greater catalyst in crippling border exchange than peso devaluation. The impact from a situation where border wait times create disincentive to cross on both sides has the potential for creating losses that are much greater if one takes into account the money multiplier effect on direct, indirect, and induced economic activity. Hence, the results from Table 19.5 point toward social and business interactions that were altered by the terrorist attacks as various ports witnessed significant contractions in pedestrian, vehicle, and vehicle passenger crossings.[31] Although economists have found it difficult to accurately quantify estimates of border city-pair retail sales derived from Mexican nationals, it runs in the hundreds of millions of dollars using the lowest of estimates, regardless of survey design or empirical method, with the greatest impacts in the areas of San Diego, Nogales, El Paso, and the Texas Lower Rio Grande region.

Social/Health Costs—Southern Border Externalities

The influx of traffic passing through the United States–Mexico border also imposes infrastructure and social costs.[32] Throughout the 1990s, while the increase of illegal activity resulted in greater federal enforcement presence, the surge in populations, commerce, and hence, crossings, led to the construction or upgrade of bridges by the respective governments. However, bridge and highway funding has been outpaced by rapid growth in vehicle and commercial traffic, and consequently congestion at major highways and interchange arteries has been the result. The slower wait times to cross into the United States post-9/11, as well as the increase in vehicle traffic at various ports, have contributed to further congestion at international bridges.[33]

An important congestion cost, air pollution, is increasing in border cities, especially in El Paso, which exceeds air quality standards in many categories and has been declared a non-attainment area by the Environmental Protection Agency. Amaya argues that a key environmental health issue "on the border is poor air quality ordinarily attributed to industrial and automobile emissions. Air pollutant categories include ozone, particulate matter, carbon monoxide, sulfur dioxide, and nitrogen dioxide. These pollutants affect pulmonary function, especially among the susceptible population of children, elders, and those with chronic conditions. Adverse health effects of air pollution include asthma, chronic obstructive pulmonary disease, chronic bronchitis, and coronary artery disease . . . Pollution also threatens water quality on the border. The Rio Grande and the New River near Calexico, California have been designated two of the most polluted U.S. rivers in recent years."[34]

A study performed in 1985 showed that there was more than six times the level of carbon monoxide allowed by the Occupational Safety and Health Administration at the Paso del Norte Bridge and the Bridge of the Americas in the El Paso District. Although the introduction of newer vehicles and oxygenated gasoline has reduced carbon monoxide emissions, the dropped levels per unit have been offset by the tremendous increase in vehicle crossings and currently by the longer wait times.[35]

Ongoing efforts have expanded the number of vehicle crossing lanes at some ports to alleviate the greater scrutiny required by Customs officials. Although these efforts have helped, increased wait times to cross and congestion post-9/11 remain serious social, economic, and environmental health and safety issues for border residents.

Conclusion

The growth of the maquiladora industry in the past 20 years had led to a border that was the most prosperous part of Mexico and a strategic resource to U.S. manufacturing. The drug industry's shift from Miami, Florida, in the 1980s to Tijuana and Cd. Juárez, however, provided the rationale for policing the border to combat the war on drugs and to contain illegal immigration. One could easily make the case that both activities have been futile overall, and in light of 9/11, have no relationship to terrorist attacks.[36]

The 9/11 attacks had different effects on U.S. border regions with Mexico and Canada than on interior places in the country. The political lockdown at the border occurred with greater social and economic impact, more so on the southern border than in the north. Border waits to cross into the United States were already at an all-time high at many ports even before the 9/11 attacks due to the tremendous growth in the volume of trade and traffic. The border region, to reiterate, at least on the United States–Mexico border, had already felt the effects of the economic slowdown well before 9/11. The security measures following 9/11 further increased wait times, causing excessive delays to border populations and affecting local businesses. A hardened border, which is controlled more by a police mentality than with free exchange of goods and persons and the increase from minutes to hours to enter the United States have been the source of considerable frustration to the hundreds of thousands who cross the borders on a daily basis.

For smaller border cities, the decline in individual crossing poses challenges to the important business and social ties that these regions rely upon as part of their commercial base. For larger cities, such as El Paso and San Diego, where the ties are much more integrated, people persist by changing crossing patterns. The data discussed shows that the impact on the border has resulted in shifts between individual vehicles and pedestrian crossings at some ports such as El Paso and Nogales, but overall less people are crossing U.S. international bridges by foot or as passengers, affecting many retailers and service providers in both cities who depend on cross-border sales. Perhaps the greatest impacts resultant from 9/11 are the negative externalities not easily observable or quantifiable, such as greater air pollution from vehicles stranded at the bridges and added pressure to an already underserved infrastructure. Although the war on terrorism is in part to protect our way of life, the social patterns for border populations appear to have already changed. Incrementally, the border has opened up a bit, but may never return to the pre-9/11 level.

This study shows that reaction to 9/11 varied in the border region and that although the role of free trade remains intact individual behaviors altered significantly. Barriers to a seamless border so evident in other parts of the world appear more likely to have gained a more solid base and remain in place for some time to come. Even in the wake of 9/11 Mexico remains no more of a threat to the United States than it did before and the Bush administration's war on terrorism that has made a frontline out of border regions that should be viewed as critical to the nation's well-being, whether from the north or the south. Pragmatic local decisions have been supplanted by administrative fiats from Washington DC. As the world's borders continues to erode and sovereignty by all arguments remains strong, the record of changes in behavior in the case of the U.S. borders suggests 9/11 moved the concept of a seamless border off the political agenda, not just lower on the agenda. Social patterns have dramatically changed and the border has become an additional obstacle to daily activities in many areas. The turbulence of merging borders has dissipated from the primary topic of the region as national boundaries once again seem like walls rather than bridges.

Moving a bit away from the data, one effect that some expected or may have hoped for was a shift in immigration patterns, especially those of unauthorized entrants. No such paradigm shift in immigration has occurred nor was a management shift really implemented. Instead, the shift was a behavioral shift among border crossers and a conversion to a larger administrative effort. Thus, although homeland security is the keyword, the reaction and results have been more administrative, perhaps more local administration than a national policy shift.[37] Overall, it can also be argued that the border crossings that have changed in nature involve a known quality of border residents who would fall onto a low probability radar screen for homeland security purposes. As a result, the processes implemented changed the nature of behaviors but not the existing networks or outcomes and reinforced political positions perhaps more than providing solutions to the issues of homeland security and threats to national well-being.

Endnotes

1. Castle, S. and Miller, M., *The Age of Migration: International Population Movements in the Modern World*, Guilford Press: New York, 1993, p. 283.
2. Houtum, H.V. and Naerssen, T.V., Bordering, ordering and othering, *Economishe en Sociale Geografie*, 93, 2, 125, 2002.
3. Giermanski, J.R., Testimony of Dr. James R. Giermanski, Professor and Director, International Business Studies, Belmont Abbey College, Submitted to: Commerce, Science, and Transportation Committee, U.S. Senate, July 18, 2001.
4. Houtom and Naerssen, 125, 2002.
5. Borderplex is defined as contiguous cities sharing a common international boundary, jointly serving as a traditional urban or metropolitan core. For instance, in El Paso–Cd. Juárez a crossing of the international bridge takes one from one central or core downtown to the other. Similarly, transportation by road, bus, or rail is used to link activity between Tijuana and San Diego's urban cores (roughly 15 miles separate the city of San Diego's downtown and the international boundary with Tijuana—the city of Chula Vista which is part of San Diego County borders Tijuana). Similar borderplexes are emerging in other border areas, especially in Eastern Europe, as pre-World War II relationships re-connect communities.
6. A maquiladora is a Mexican corporation operating under special customs status allowing it to temporarily import into Mexico duty-free, raw materials, equipment, machinery, replacement parts, and other tools needed for the assembly or manufacture of intermediate or finished goods for subsequent export or sale in the domestic market (the latter requires payment of import tariffs on the U.S. raw material used in the production process).
7. Soden, D.L., McElroy, M., and Olmedo, C., *A New Look at Comparative Advantage: Border Areas as Strategic Resources*, Paper prepared for presentation at the International Atlantic Economic Society, Lisbon, Portugal, March, 2004.

8. Olmedo, C., McElroy, M., and Feser, E., The Industry Clusters of Civdad Juárez, Institute for Policy and Economic Development at the University of Texas at El Paso: El Paso, Texas, (http://organizations.utep.edu/iped), IPED Special Report 2007-2, 2007.

9. Glassner, M. and Fahrer, C., *Political Geography*, John Wiley & Sons: Hoboken, New Jersey, 2004, p. 73.

10. Linderking, B., The United States–Mexican border and NAFTA: Problem or paradigm? in *U.S.–Mexico Borderlands: Historical and Contemporary Perspectives*, Oscar J. Martinez, Ed., Scholarly Resources, Inc.: Wilmington, Delaware, 1996, p. 191.

11. Newman, D. and Kliot, N., Introduction: Globalisation and the changing world political map, in *Geopolitics at the End of the Twentieth Century: The Changing World Political Map*, Kliot and Newman, Eds., Frank Cass Publishers: London, United Kingdom, 2000, p. 8.

12. Ackleson, J.M., Discourses on identity and territoriality on the U.S.–Mexico border, in *Geopolitics at the End of the Twentieth Century: The Changing World Political Map*, Kliot and Newman, Eds., Frank Cass Publishers: London, 2000, 155.

13. Ibid.; Rosenau, J., *Along the Domestic-Foreign Divide: Governance in a Turbulent World*, Cambridge University Press: Boston, Massachusetts, 1998.

14. El Paso County 2005 mid-year population estimate—721,598. Source: U.S. Census Bureau. Cd. Juárez Municipality 2005 mid-year population estimate—1,460,660. Source: Consejo Nacional de Población (CONAPO).

15. Source for border crossings: U.S. Department of Transportation, Bureau of Transportation Statistics, based on data compiled from the U.S. Customs Service.

16. Approximately one-fifth of U.S. trade is with Canada versus 12–13 percent with Mexico.

17. Throughout the chapter, OTM refers strictly to the August to September 2001 change. For the OTY analysis August 2001 is chosen because it is the last month unbiased by 9/11. Also note that several ports contain underreported or not reported data creating gaps in respective graphs in order not to bias downward the visual representations.

18. The additional data not published here but part of this discussion is quite voluminous and is available from the authors upon request.

19. Some ports on the southern border have Dedicated Commuter Lanes (DCL), a system approved by dual governments that preclears individuals and vehicles categorized as low risk and allows them to drive through a lane with little interruption. In El Paso for example, the 9/11 disturbance at the international bridges increased the number of persons crossing via the DCL. Between January and September 2002 an average of almost 6000 cars crossed daily through the DCL, an increase of over 140 percent from the daily 2001 average. This increase, however, accounts for only a small percentage of the loss in overall vehicle traffic reported by the Bureau of Transportation Statistics for El Paso. In spite of its advantages, many citizens forego DCL crossings due to the cost and location (in El Paso in 2002 the annual cost was almost $400 and only available at one end of the city). Source for DCL crossings: U.S. Department of Homeland Security, Bureau of Citizenship and Immigration Services (formerly Immigration and Naturalization Services), El Paso Branch.

20. Sprung, M., U.S. Department of Transportation, Bureau of Transportation Statistics, Office of Transportation Analysis.

21. McElroy, M., Sun Bowl fixed route rider survey, Institute for Policy and Economic Development Technical Report 2006–2007, University of Texas at El Paso: El Paso, Texas, 2006.

22. At the port level, general wait times per international bridge can be assessed by monitoring radio stations that provide such information via U.S. Customs or from U. S. Customs directly with the proper credentials. Tracking this information is complex because it varies by bridge, date, time, events, and other factors inherent to the particular cities which are tied together. The Department of Homeland Security, U.S. Customs Web site also provides snapshots of wait times and the number of open lanes for commercial and vehicle crossings for the international bridges at major ports of entry. These data, however, have proven not to be very reliable. For example, the site transmitted from Washington DC can post a five minute delay at a specific bridge in El Paso when it is known for a fact by those living there that the delay is far greater. Furthermore, there exists no historical time series for this data as what is posted is quickly erased after the next time set is posted, thereby limiting comparisons. It should be noted though that recent postings of wait times are far more within the range of being plausible versus past collections. For these reasons mention of specific wait times would be flawed and hence are not provided by the authors—wait times are instead broadly implied or presented in ranges based on first-hand knowledge, personal crossing experience, and information about the individual ports that includes conversations with those who live there.

23. Chavez, A.M., More to visit U.S. to shop, but retailers disappointed, *El Paso Times*, A-1, December 9, 2002.

24. A prime example of the region's integration is the area known as "Chihuahuita" in El Paso. In 1963, Presidents John F. Kennedy of the United States and Adolfo López Mateos of Mexico signed the Chamizal Convention that ended decades of bitter territorial conflict between the two nations. The Treaty of Guadalupe Hidalgo, which officially ended the U.S.–Mexico War, provided that the new international boundary was to be the center of the deepest channel of the Rio Grande River that lies between Texas and Mexico. Flooding and gradual southbound shifting of the Rio Grande left a considerable section of the land on the Texas side of the river. Eventually the land was settled and incorporated as part of El Paso but still claimed by Mexico. With the signing of the Chamizal Convention, Mexico repatriated much of the land it had lost. A man-made channel to prevent the Rio Grande from blurring the international boundary was constructed of concrete and three new bridges were built. The U.S. residents living and businesses on the repatriated land were compensated and relocated northward. The remaining section of land that was previously part of Chihuahua, Mexico and not repatriated is known as Chihuahuita. Another prime example of the region's integration is the night view from Scenic Drive in El Paso's Franklin Mountains (the tail of the Rocky Mountains). If one stares southward it is virtually impossible to locate the international boundary and difficult to differentiate where lights on the U.S. side of the border end and the lights on the Mexican side begin. This is truly one region, two contiguous cities, two countries, separated only by river flow.

25. Charney, A.H. and Pavlokovich, V.K., The economic impacts of Mexican visitors to Arizona: 2001, Economic and Business Research Program, University of Arizona, Arizona, 2002.

26. Phillips, K.R. and Manzanares, C., Transportation infrastructure and the border economy, *The Border Economy*, Federal Reserve Bank of Dallas, Texas, 2001.

27. Peña, S.M., Comercio transfronterizo y su impacto en la región El Paso–juárez: Una propuesta de financiamiento de la planeación binacional, *Frontera Norte*, 14, 29, 2003.

28. Phillips, K.R. and Cañas, J., Business cycle coordination along the Texas–Mexico border, Federal Reserve Bank of Dallas, San Antonio and El Paso Branches, Texas, Working Paper No. 0502.

29. Soden, D.L. and Olmedo, C., At the Cross Roads—U.S./Mexico Border Counties in Transition, Prepared for the Border Counties Coalition by the Institute for Policy and Economic Development at the University of Texas at El Paso: El Paso, Texas, 6–26, 6–33, 2006.

30. In general, a peso drop in value against the dollar means that Mexican firms and consumers find cross-border purchases more expensive. The same peso devaluation increases U.S. purchasing power and stimulates U.S. demand for Mexican goods and services as they become less expensive. Hence, the overall effect of a change in the exchange rate value is somewhat ambiguous on border trade, but currency stability reduces Mexican consumer uncertainty, thereby benefiting U.S. retail trade sales. It is also interesting to note that during times of peso devaluations or inflationary periods, residents of Mexico are known to buy expensive items in the United States to avoid high financing costs in their own country (for the latter, see Jesus Cañas, 2002. "A Decade of Change: El Paso's Economic Transition of the 1990s," Business Frontier, Federal Reserve Bank of Dallas, El Paso Branch, (1), Texas).

31. An example of an economic and multiplier impact is the following: a U.S. citizen foregoes making a trip to Mexico, thereby foregoing the opportunity for a Mexican service provider such as a restaurant to obtain dollars and personal income that may be spent on goods and services in the United States. An example of social impacts is the following: there are greater social and familial ties along the United States–Mexico border that give rise to the large number of people and vehicle crossings. If a friend or relative chooses not to cross to the other side to visit because of wait times, these ties that make the United States–Mexico border region is altered. Social interactions are also changed if one chooses not to cross to see a movie or a play or a theatre act or have a drink.

32. Border regions also bear a greater public health burden from increased trade and immigration in proportion to economic prosperity. These and other demographic and social factors on both sides of the border interact to create health conditions distinct from other areas in the United States, including a higher risk for certain health problems and reduced access to healthcare services. The flow of people back and forth also guarantees efficient transmission of communicable diseases. Additionally, an unknown but significant proportion of the millions of annual border crossings are health-related—medically underserved U.S. residents obtain lower priced prescription and over-the-counter medications as well as basic medical and dental services in Mexico while affluent and indigent Mexican residents obtain improved, specialized or otherwise unavailable healthcare services in the United States, (Amaya, M.A., Health issues on the U.S.–México border, *Dígame, Policy & Politics on the Texas Border*, Brenner, C., Coronado, I., and Soden, D.L., Eds., Kendall/Hunt Publishing Company: Dubuque, Iowa, 2003, chapter 14).

33. Differing operating times between U.S. and Mexican Customs further compounds congestion at the bridges. Cargo trucks begin lining on one side of the border as they wait for the other side of the border to open the inspection gates. Clearly a homogenous schedule would allow those first in line to be inspected before a bottleneck begins. Furthermore, the current inspection system is undermanned at a time when various politicians prefer a policy of "stop and examine everything" without differentiating between what is high risk and what is low risk. Old technologies and compliances from Mexican exporters to preclear cargo before reaching U.S. Customs, and new ones recently implemented should help facilitate the movement of goods.

34. Amaya, M.A., 2003, chapter 14.

35. At least two death have been directly linked to the combination of a long wait and carbon monoxide. In October 2001, a family was driving back to El Paso from Cd. Juárez when two children, ages 13 and 6, fell asleep under the camper in the bed of the family's pickup truck with the back door open. They went to sleep because they had school early the next day. When the family pulled into their driveway after an hour and 45 minutes on the Ysleta-Zaragoza Bridge, they were unable to wake up their two children. They died of carbon monoxide poisoning which entered from small holes, covered by a rug, caused by rust in the lining of the pickup bed. Although the back of the camper had been open, enough air failed to circulate in the idling camper. The family was waved through the inspection booth at the discretion of the inspector who did not try to wake the children up. Authorities did not know whether the two children stopped breathing at the bridge (Louie Gilot, 2 children die after long wait at bridge," *El Paso Times*, A-1, October 23, 2001, and Negligence ruled out in bridge deaths, *El Paso Times*, B-1, October 24, 2001).

36. Axtman, K., Rising tide of border crime and violence, *Christian Science Monitor*, 1, 12, February, 15, 2006.

37. Shirk, D.A., Law enforcement and security challenges in the U.S.–Mexican border region, *Journal of Borderland Studies*, 18, 2, 1, 2003.

Chapter 20

Continuity and Change in Disaster Response: Victim Management in the Case of the World Trade Center Collapse

Steven D. Stehr

CONTENTS

Introduction

On the morning of September 11, 2001, two hijacked commercial aircraft struck the World Trade Center towers (WTCT) in New York City. The towers were hit by Boeing 767s en route from Boston to Los Angeles—each loaded with jet fuel for the cross-country flight. The South Tower, known as World Trade Center 2, collapsed just in under hour after it was hit. The North Tower, or World Trade Center 1, collapsed approximately an hour and a half after impact. The destruction of the towers and surrounding buildings produced an estimated 1.5 million tons of debris concentrated in the approximately 16 acres of the World Trade Center complex of buildings situated in lower Manhattan. Owing to a combination of factors, including the uncertainty regarding the number, identities, and whereabouts of people in the buildings at the time of the collapse, the first official estimates of the number of dead and missing were not issued until September 13.* On that date, 4763 persons were reported as missing and 184 people were confirmed as dead. The number of missing persons would be revised upward (with the highest number—6453— announced on September 24) and then downward in the days and weeks following the tragedy as disaster officials sorted through reports from businesses, family, friends, coworkers, and foreign embassies regarding people thought to have been in or around the WTCT on the morning of September 11. On October 12, four weeks after the event, the number of missing and presumed dead (4715) plus the number of confirmed dead (442) was placed at more than 5100 people. Significantly, only 385 bodies had been identified by this time.

In the immediate aftermath of the collapse of the WTCT, official administrative channels with primary responsibility for locating and assisting victims were overwhelmed or, in some cases, destroyed in the collapse. In the short term, a loosely coordinated network of individuals and organizations formed around the efforts of family, friends, coworkers, nongovernmental agencies, as well as official responders and included the use of relatively new technologies such as patient locator sites on the worldwide web to help identify the location of missing persons. In addition, concerned family members produced and distributed homemade posters and

---

* News sources widely reported on September 11 that approximately 50,000 people either worked in or visited the WTCT on any given week day. Initial reports also estimated that in excess of 10,000 persons had perished in the collapse. The ability of the WTCT to remain standing following the impacts—even for a short time—undoubtedly saved countless lives (Snoonian and Czarnecki, October, 2001).

fliers—most including pictures of the missing and the location where they were last seen—that were attached to the walls outside of hospitals and other publically accessible locations. Over time, as hope gave way to resignation that those who were still missing were most likely fatalities, another set of unique processes were established with the intent of identifying the remains of as many victims as possible (see Table 20.1). This task proved to be daunting. The force of the initial explosion and subsequent collapse, coupled with the searing heat of the fires fed by massive amounts of jet fuel and the contents of the buildings, made locating missing persons and identifying the human remains that were found extremely difficult.

This chapter is designed to enhance our collective understanding of several important aspects of post-disaster response and recovery activities. It focuses on the social and organizational processes at work in the management of mass casualties and victim identification following the collapse of the WTCT. These aspects of disaster response have not been widely studied.* Owing to the enormity of the destruction in New York City and the disruption of normal social and administrative systems, a new and seemingly unprecedented set of mechanisms developed to undertake post-event victim location and identification. The objective of this chapter is to provide initial documentation of the creation and development of these emergent response and recovery systems and to identify the extent to which they converge or diverge with our existing understanding of disaster response.[†]

I argue that not only were there significant differences in the short-term management of the "direct" victims in this case compared to our prior experiences with disasters, but also that there have been significant long-term changes in the management of the "indirect" victims such as surviving family members as well. Thus, this chapter lays the groundwork for a more wide-ranging consideration how the events of September 11 have altered our collective view of disaster victims in general, and the way in which public agencies and charitable relief organizations identify and compensate surviving victims for purposes of providing disaster assistance in particular.

Data for this chapter was gathered in several ways. The author and two additional research team members conducted field research in New York City from September 25–29, 2001.[‡] We conducted semi-structured interviews with

---

* The destruction wrought by Hurricanes Katrina and Rita which devastated several Gulf Coast states in September 2005 and left many dead, missing and dislocated persons in their wake temporarily has renewed interest in the topic of managing large numbers of victims, both living and dead, following catastrophic disasters.

† The initial activities involved in this research effort were supported through the Quick Response Grant Program funded by the National Science Foundation (NSF) (grant number CMS-0090977) and administered by the Natural Hazards Research and Applications Information Center at the University of Colorado and by the University of Louisville. Subsequent work on this and related topics is being supported by NSF grant number CMS-0234100. Any opinions, findings, and conclusions or recommendations expressed in this material are those of the author and do not necessarily reflect the views of the National Science Foundation.

‡ For a more detailed description of these research activities, see Simpson and Stehr, 2002.

Table 20.1 Casualties Following the Collapse of the World Trade Center Towers

Date	Missing Persons	Confirmed Dead	Total Missing and Dead	Bodies Identified
September 13, 2001	4763	184	4947	34
September 17, 2001	4957	190	5147	9
September 20, 2001	6333	233	6566	n.a.
September 24, 2001	6453	261	6714	188
September 27, 2001	5960	305	6265	238
October 1, 2001	5219	314	5533	255
October 3, 2001	5219	363	5582	289
October 6, 2001	4974	380	5354	321
October 9, 2001	4815	422	5237	370
October 12, 2001	4715	442	5157	385
October 15, 2001	4688	453	5141	398
October 18, 2001	4404	456	4860	404
October 21, 2001	4313	461	4774	411
October 24, 2001	4129	478	4607	425
October 27, 2001	3958	506	4464	454
October 30, 2001	3835	529	4364	475
November 2, 2001	3719	542	4261	495
November 5, 2001	3659	542	4201	523
November 8, 2001	3569	600	4169	556
November 11, 2001	3410	632	4042	556
November 14, 2001	3364	632	3996	589
November 17, 2001	3317	636	3953	594
November 20, 2001	3079	673	3752	624
November 23, 2001[a]	1383	2263	3646	
November 26, 2001	1284	2269	3553	

Table 20.1 (continued)   Casualties Following the Collapse of the World Trade Center Towers

Date	Missing Persons	Confirmed Dead	Total Missing and Dead	Bodies Identified
November 29, 2001	879	2321	3300	
December 3, 2001	879	2321	3300	
December 6, 2001	628	2468	3096	
December 9, 2001	588	2469	3057	
December 12, 2001	529	2501	3030	
December 15, 2001	517	2513	3030	
December 18, 2001	517	2513	3030	
December 25, 2001	444	2510	2954	
January 1, 2002	380	2557	2937	
January 8, 2002	314	2581	2895	
January 15, 2002	288	2602	2890	

Note: The number of confirmed dead includes 157 passengers aboard the two airliners.

[a] Beginning on November 21, New York City officials revised their method for tabulating the number of people missing or confirmed dead. After that date, the number of confirmed dead includes both those who have been identified through physical remains or other forms of positive identification as well as those for whom the courts have issued death certificates on the basis of proof provided by a loved one that the individual was at the WTCT at the time of the collapse.

Source: New York Times, various dates.

representatives of the Greater New York Hospital Association, several area hospitals, and other officials involved in identifying and caring for victims. The research team also observed activities at the Family Assistance Center at Pier 94 (the central location to obtain disaster assistance), the City Disaster Command Center, several New York City Fire Department locations, among other disaster-related sites. In addition to direct observation, the research team also analyzed daily news reports published in the *New York Times* and other news agencies, situation reports prepared by the Federal Emergency Management Administration, and two in-depth reports on the activities of the New York City Fire Department and the New York Police Department commissioned by the city of New York and prepared by the McKinsey Company (2002a). Finally, this work relies on research conducted by Louise Comfort, John Harrald, James Kendra, Kathleen Tierney, Tricia Wachtendorf, and others who conducted field research immediately following the disaster.

This chapter proceeds as follows. First, a brief overview of prior research related to the management of mass fatalities and victim identification is provided. Second, some of the unique aspects of the collapse of the WTCT are highlighted that made it a fundamentally different type of disaster when compared to those events with which disaster researchers are more familiar. These unique aspects are important because, as we will see, they provided the initial conditions for disaster response in this case. Third, the results of an analysis of victim management activities in New York City are discussed. The analysis is based on a framework designed to examine key behaviors related to victim management. The framework examines these activities from four levels of analysis (individual, group and family, organizational, and system) in the four phases of victim management (search and rescue [SAR], victim recovery, victim identification, and disposition of the body). This exercise is intended to provide a means of identifying how behavior conformed to what would be predicted from prior studies of disasters, and in what respects behavior deviated from the norm. Finally, I argue that previous conceptions of victim management, which treat these activities as a relatively short and compartmentalized feature of disaster response must be reconceptualized to include longer-term issues, related to disaster assistance and relief programs.

Managing Mass Fatalities and Victim Identification: Previous Research

A common thread running throughout the activities of victim management (and through disaster response activities more generally) is an implicit distinction between the military model and the problem-solving model of response (Tierney et al., 2001, p. 73). The military model assumes that social disorganization will be widespread and that effective response requires the implementation of hierarchically based, command-and-control strategies by formal responding organizations. In contrast, the problem-solving model assumes that the activities of formal organizations during emergencies can be supplemented and enhanced if community members, nongovernmental organizations, and private sector actors develop the capacity to prepare and respond to disasters as well. The presence of these two models highlights what could be called the paradox of disaster management: Emergency planning at all levels of government focuses on the deployment and coordination of formal response organizations, but effective performance often depends on the problem-solving capabilities of those outside of the formal realm.

The most theoretically developed work on the problem-solving model has been done by Louise Comfort. She argues that intergovernmental and interorganizational response to risks and hazards is improved through "auto-adaptation" mechanisms (Comfort, 1999). Auto-adaptation is based on the development of an information transfer infrastructure that enhances individual, organizational, and collective learning in both the short and long term.* Of particular usefulness in Comfort's work is the conceptual distinction drawn between the different levels of response activities. On a continuum from microscopic to macroscopic behavior, Comfort focuses attention on individuals, organizations, and communities.† This scheme is adapted to examine victim management activities in New York City. The levels of analysis examined are individuals, groups (i.e., families, nongovernmental organizations), organizations, and system (i.e., interorganizational and intergovernmental). That said, there has been very little theoretical work done on victim management activities primarily because there have been very few data points to study.

There have been very few mass casualty and fatality incidents in the United States. It is widely believed that the largest number of deaths in an individual event taking place in the United States is between 8000 and 10000 which occurred in 1900 in Galveston, Texas following a category 4 hurricane that produced widespread flooding.‡ Other disasters in the United States that have produced large numbers of fatalities include the San Francisco earthquake in 1906 (approximately 3000), the Johnstown flood of 1889 (approximately 2000), an unnamed hurricane that struck Florida in 1928 (1836), and Hurricane Katrina (1605) (see Table 20.2). Interestingly, several relatively recent high-profile natural disasters such as hurricanes Hugo (1989) and Andrew (1992), and the Loma Prieta (1989) and Northridge (1994) earthquakes in California claimed relatively few lives even while causing billions of dollars in property losses. Historian Ted Steinberg argues that many disasters in the late nineteenth and early twentieth centuries featured incomplete body counts owing to undercounts of poor blacks and the fears of community leaders—particularly in Florida and California—that reports of mass death would hamper tourism (Steinberg, 2000). Indeed, Steinberg estimates that as many as 10–12,000 individuals may have perished in the Galveston flood, and that the San Francisco earthquake and fires probably killed upwards of 3,000 even though the official count well into the 1960s was placed between 500 and 700 (Steinberg, 2000, p. 44).§

---

* For an examination of a similar approach to disaster response using the World Trade Center attacks as a referent see Kendra and Wachtendorf, 2001, 2002.

† For an earlier use of a similar framework, see Drabek, 1986.

‡ In other parts of the world, disasters causing mass fatalities are less rare. For example, it has been estimated that 655,000 people were killed in the earthquake which struck Tangshan, China in 1976, and approximately 500,000 deaths were reported in Bangladesh following a typhoon and flood in 1972. In addition, modern warfare often produces large numbers of sudden deaths. Approximately 78,000 died in the atomic bombing of Hiroshima, Japan and another 37,000 in Nagasaki, Japan (Blanshan and Quarentelli, 1981, pp. 275–277).

§ Erik Larson also places the death toll of the Galveston hurricane and flood at approximately 10,000 people (Larson, 2001).

Table 20.2   Deadliest Natural Disasters in the United States

Type of Disaster	Location	Date	Estimated Number of Fatalities
Hurricane/flood	Galveston (Texas)	1900	8–10,000
Earthquake/fire	San Francisco (California)	1906	3,000
Flood	Johnstown (Virginia)	1889	2,000
Flood	Ohio	1903	2,000
Hurricane	Florida	1928	1,836
Hurricane	Louisiana (Mississippi)	2005	1,605
Hurricane	Charleston (South Carolina)	1893	1–2,000
Hurricane	Louisiana	1893	1–2,000
Tornadoes	Illinois, Missouri, Indiana	1925	747
Hurricane	Florida, Texas	1919	600–900
Hurricane/flood	New England	1938	494
Flood	Ohio	1913	467
Hurricane	Florida Keys	1935	408
Flood	Rapid City (South Dakota)	1972	237
Tornadoes	Tuplelo (Mississippi)	1936	216
Tornadoes	Gainesville (Georgia)	1936	203
Earthquake	Aleutian Islands	1946	165
Earthquake	Anchorage (Alaska)	1964	125

Sources: Adapted from Blanchard, W., 2006. Worst Disasters-Lives lost. Federal Emergency Management Higher Education Project. Accessed at www.training.fema.gov/emiweb/edu/docs/hazdan/ Appendix.

As a consequence of the low number of events involving mass casualties and fatalities, there have been relatively few opportunities for practitioners and researchers to examine the processes and operations utilized to manage these situations. As early as 1959 research was being conducted on death in disasters (Orth, 1959). Beginning in the mid-1970s, researchers at the Disaster Research Center (then at Ohio State University) initiated a series of studies on the handling of mass casualties in disasters. Researchers documented the handling of the dead following the Rapid City, South Dakota flash flood (several hundred fatalities), the Big Thompson Canyon flash flood near Loveland, Colorado where 139 died (another estimated 30 bodies were never found), the Vaiont Dam overflow disaster in Italy (over 1,800 dead), and an earthquake in Iran that killed about 12,000, among other disasters (Blanshan, 1977; Hershiser and Quarentelli, 1979; Blanshan and Quarentelli, 1981).* Other research conducted around this time period examined specific problems such as the role of professional body handlers following disasters (Pine, 1969; Charnley, 1978). More recently, Joseph Scanlon analyzed the management of mass casualties in the aftermath of the Halifax (Nova Scotia) 1917 ship explosion, as well as the Gander air crash, the Zeebrugge ferry disaster, and the Kobe earthquake (Scanlon, 1998).

In general, these studies examine the special problems associated with handling bodies following large-scale disasters, the difference between the procedures associated with "normal" death situations (i.e., isolated deaths that generally take place in hospitals or nursing homes) and death in disasters, and the extraordinary demands that large numbers of casualties and fatalities place on disaster responders. More specifically, these studies focus on two primary areas: (1) activities utilized to recover, identify, and return human remains to families; and (2) the symbolic nature of body retrieval following disasters.

Activities Utilized to Recover and Identify Victims

Immediately following large disasters, several activities related to the management of victims and fatalities take place. The time frame for these activities may be relatively brief or quite lengthy depending on such factors as the scope of the disaster, the number and location of victims, and availability of adequate resources, equipment, and response personnel (Drabek, 1985, p. 86). These activities can be divided into four, sometimes overlapping phases: (1) SAR; (2) recovery of bodies and human remains; (3) identification of victims; and (4) the disposition of the bodies.†

1. *Search and Rescue (SAR).* Immediately following a disaster, official responders, volunteers, and other community members begin the process of locating surviving victims, assisting the injured, and in the course of these activities, finding the bodies of those who did not survive. Research shows that two aspects of the SAR process seem to be particularly important: (1) the interactions between official (e.g., employees of local governments) and non-official (e.g., family members, neighbors, volunteers) personnel, and the related phenomenon of the

---

* For a concise review of this literature, see Drabek (1986) pp. 189–191.

† Blanshan (1977) divides these activities into eleven discreet elements: search, recovery, transportation, clean-up, identification, embalming, storage, positive identification, issuance of the death certificate, distribution of body, and the presentation of body.

development of emergent groups; and (2) the tasks undertaken by established (both governmental and nongovernmental) organizations in the immediate response phase (Drabek, 1986, pp. 158–188). Thus, there is both an informal and formal aspect to SAR activities.

Because SAR actions occur immediately following a disaster event, often as official organizational mobilization is in process, members of the community are usually first on the scene. According to Mileti, "studies have consistently shown that initial SAR work is carried out by persons who are in the impact area and that formal rescue organizations become involved at a later point" (Mileti, 1975, p. 9). This is a significant point because it directs attention to a critical factor in immediate disaster response: the interface between formal organizations and individuals and families who are acting rather autonomously. As discussed below, this interface—and complications stemming from it—was a very important aspect of the initial response following the collapse of the WTCT. When it is not clear which individuals were at the scene of a disaster, family members will expand the SAR function to include filing missing person's reports with local authorities and placing phone calls to area hospitals. A well-established feature of SAR, as well as other aspects of disaster response, is the emergent groups phenomenon (Dynes, 1970). Emergent groups are "private citizens who work together in pursuit of collective goals relevant to actual or potential disasters but whose organization has not yet become institutionalized" (Stallings and Quarentelli, 1985, p. 94). Two distinct types of emergent groups appear to be active in SAR activities: damage assessment groups (who often provide public officials with their first information about the location and extent of the damage); and operations groups (who form to collect clothing, food, water, and medical supplies to distribute to both victims and disaster responders) (Stallings and Quarentelli, 1985). It should be noted that another important SAR activity in some disasters involves pets. A recent study found that 80 percent of persons who reentered evacuated areas did so to rescue their pet, an act that could place the pet owner and disaster personnel at further risk (Heath et al., 2000).

After the immediate post-impact period is past, the primary responsibility for SAR falls to established governmental organizations, typically law enforcement, firefighting personnel, emergency medical teams, and trained SAR teams. Although these official response teams may be assisted by private companies and individuals with access to heavy equipment and other needed resources, local governmental agencies nearly always assume responsibility for the coordination of activities (Drabek, 1985). Official SAR activities have been studied extensively. These studies tend to focus on key operational problems that exist in SAR responses such as poor interagency communications, ambiguity in authority relationships, poor utilization of special resources, and unplanned media relationships (Drabek, 1986, p. 185; Mileti, 1999, p. 225; cf. Stehr, 2001).

2. *The Recovery of Bodies and Human Remains.* Owing to the close spatial link between SAR activities and the casualty recovery phase, it is often family

members, friends, and neighbors who begin the search for victims (Blanshan and Quarentelli, 1981, p. 282). Although the initial, rapid, overall SAR response is largely unplanned, the recovery of bodies and human remains typically assumes an organized form after a short period of time. A division of labor tends to emerge with various professionals and select volunteers (such as members of the clergy) applying their specialized skills. In the case of major accidents, the disaster scene may be controlled by law enforcement and access restricted. Bodies may be marked or photographed before they are moved to aid in identification (Scanlon, 1998, p. 289). Depending on the type and extent of the damage, firefighters, structural engineers, and trained search and recovery teams may be deployed. In cases of widespread flooding (e.g., in the aftermath of the Big Thompson Canyon flood), National Guard helicopters may search for bodies from the air. As bodies are recovered, professional body handlers including medical examiners, coroners, funeral home directors, and morgue attendants begin the initial process of preparing corpses for transportation and searching for identification. In some cases, local morgues and funeral homes may be overwhelmed by the number of bodies leading to improvised solutions such as using refrigerated trucks or school gymnasiums to temporarily house the dead (Scanlon, 1998).

In some major disaster settings, it may be possible to locate bodies relatively quickly but recovery may be difficult and psychologically challenging to recovery personnel. Large amounts of debris or wreckage may make it difficult to gain access to victims and in some cases pose a safety threat to recovery teams. In addition, "these workers must also deal directly with bodies which often seem to be less than human in form and condition" (Blanshan and Quarentelli, 1981, p. 283). But even in these earliest stages of the process, there is the belief that recovery personnel should be aware of the ultimate need to restore identity to the remains that they find. Blanshan and Quarentelli emphasize that there is enormous pressure in many societies for bodies to be recovered and given individual funerals. They quote an Italian General who was overseeing thousands of soldiers who were digging to recover some 1800 victims following the Vaimont Dam disaster: "It's absurd to dig down ten feet of rocks and stones to find a body so we can rebury it in only five feet of dirt" (Blanshan and Quarentelli, 1981, p. 280). This remark, highlights the point that far more is involved than the simple matter of physically finding bodies to bury them again. This point is explained more fully below.

As part of the process of treating the dead as persons, considerable attention is usually given to protecting all identifying evidence on the body and in the surrounding area. Personal effects such as purses, wallets, watches, and jewelry are normally placed in bags or blankets with the bodies so that they can be transported together to a morgue or other body-handling facility.

3. *The Process of Identification of Victims.* Closely linked to the desire that all bodies be recovered is the demand that they be identified. According to Blanshan (1977), it is this demand that distinguishes disaster body handling from normal

death procedures. The victim identification process actually involves two separate tasks. Although one set of workers focus on the task of identifying bodies that have been recovered, another set of workers compile a list of missing persons primarily utilizing information provided by family members and friends. When feasible, bodies are taken to central locations to be cleaned and prepared for the identification process. Blanshan and Quarentelli (1981, p. 284) note that the cleaning of the body is a response to both obvious and subtle needs of the body handlers. The obvious need is to allow the workers to see what they are working on; the subtle need reflects an effort to restore a certain level of humanity to the victims.

For those bodies that are recovered, the identification process first consists of recording physical information such as sex, skin color, height, weight, hair color, and identifying marks such as scars or tattoos. In some cases, the process may then involve sophisticated techniques such as x-rays, dental records, and fingerprints. Family members may be asked to produce pictures, dental records, and medical charts to aid in identification. A noteworthy difference between normal death and death in disasters is that, in most cases, potential identifiers such as next of kin are kept away from the body until the body handlers believe they have match between the information gathered from the body itself and information provided by families (Blanshan and Quarentelli, 1981, p. 285). Even in cases where family members are asked to view multiple bodies, great care is taken to minimize pain and suffering. For example, following the Zeebrugge ferry disaster, bodies were washed, their clothing removed, repaired, dry-cleaned, and then returned to the bodies (Scanlon, 1998).

A close review of the relevant literature shows that the process by which missing persons lists are compiled and disseminated has not been systematically studied to date. However, some studies and media reports of disasters have made passing mention of this activity. The missing persons process involves collection of hundreds or perhaps thousands of names who were reportedly in the area of the disaster. The great difficulty lies in sorting out who is and who is not missing. Apparently, it is usual to find that many people reported to be missing were not at the location of the disaster. Some may have been at the disaster scene but were taken to hospitals or were attempting to get to their homes while the missing persons list was being compiled. Once these people are located, they may not call authorities to ask that their names be taken off the list. Multiple reports of missing individuals from different sources or use of different names when reporting may also cause the initial list of missing persons to swell. Some people may use fictitious names for personal reasons making identification difficult. Finally, some reports of missing persons are hoaxes perpetrated by individuals who gain some vicarious satisfaction by attaching themselves to events that are widely reported by the media.

4. *The Disposition of the Body*. The final steps in the management of mass casualties in the post-disaster response phase begin with a positive identification of the body. In many disasters, there is not an attempt to determine the cause of death.

The cause is usually assumed (Scanlon, 1998). The establishment of positive or legal identity "is perhaps the most significant task in mass casualty body handling [because] at this point the body has once again become a person" (Blanshan and Quarentelli, 1981, p. 285). It is significant not only for the families who no longer have to face the uncertainty about the whereabouts of their loved one, but also for the legal system (a death certificate can now be issued, which begins the process of insurance claims and estate matters) and the funeral professionals (who can now assume a role with which they are more comfortable). At this point, the processes of handling the dead in disasters and normal death converge. The body is transported to a funeral home where the body is prepared and presented, a ceremony arranged, and, finally, internment or cremation.

Symbolic Nature of Body Retrieval

Aside from the practical reasons for locating and retrieving as many disaster fatalities as possible, there is a symbolic aspect of this task that is extremely important. Typically, the management of victims in mass casualty disasters follows a person-to-object-to-person transformation process (Blanshan and Quarentelli, 1981). So, although it may seem expedient to simply provide a simple mass burial of large numbers of bodies following a large-scale disaster, this almost never occurs.* Although rare, mass burials were utilized following a massive earthquake in Mexico City in 1985 and in other major disasters. But research demonstrates that values other than efficiency often prevail. There is a strong need in many cultures to, as Quarentelli noted "bury a person, not an object" (Quarentelli, 1979). Wenger discusses the prevailing attitude in the United States:

> Americans not only value open-casket funerals; more basically, they require that each body be named, buried separately, and some form of ceremony precede the burial. Mass burial, though a highly efficient and expeditious method for handling mass casualties, runs counter to these values (Wenger, 1972, p. 59).

This viewpoint is so firmly entrenched that extensive efforts are nearly always made to dig bodies out from underneath rubble, debris, or earth even if doing so endangers the SAR teams.

---

* Following mass casualties incidents, media reports often emphasize the supposed public health risk associated with dead or decaying bodies. While certainly unpleasant, public health officials do not believe that corpses harbor or spread contagious diseases (de Ville de Goyet, 2001).

Managing Mass Fatalities and Victim Identification Following the Collapse of the World Trade Center Towers

This section describes the processes involved in the management of victims and casualties following the collapse of the WTCT and compares them to our understanding of what typically happens following disasters. The following questions are addressed: To what extent did the experience in New York City conform with what is known about the handling of victims in other disasters? To what extent did the event involving the WTCT elicit responses that are different from what was previously known about the management of disaster victims? Finally, to what extent were preexisting disaster response plans related to managing victims and fatalities implemented, and how were they altered to adapt to new and unprecedented circumstances?

Several observations about the collapse of the WTCT are to provide some context for the discussion that follows. Each of these observations highlight the extent to which this event deviated from what we might call normal disasters.

Nature of the Disaster Site

First, and most importantly, the response activities at what has come to be known as "Ground Zero" were shaped by the fact that the scene was simultaneously considered a disaster area, a crime scene and—it was soon realized–a mass grave. Among other things, this meant that the routinization of recovery activities that typically takes place soon after a disaster was spread out over a much longer period of time as great care was taken to locate bodies and human remains for disposition, and so that each piece of debris could be searched for evidence. The long time frame of recovery also allowed a culture of Ground Zero to develop among the construction workers, engineers, and fire and police personnel (Langewiesche, 2002). Among other things, this culture resulted in conflict and confusion in the long term between and among different official response agencies, nongovernmental organizations, and families and friends of victims as they struggled over competing needs and priorities.

Timing of the Events

The fact that the WTCT remained standing for a short period time following the plane crashes allowed official responders—primarily firefighters from the New York City Fire Department—to mobilize in advance of the main devastation of the subsequent collapse of the buildings. Tragically, this caused many official response personnel to become victims themselves. Although most disasters are of the "hit and run" variety, this event was actually two disasters: the initial impact of the airliners, followed by the collapse of the towers. Other factors related to the timing of the events also played a role in determining the number of the victims. September 11 was both an election day in New York City and the first day of school for New York's public school system. An unknown number of WTCT workers stopped at the polls on their way to work to cast their ballots or to drop their children off at school thus missing the attack. In addition, the observation deck in World Trade Center 2 was not yet open to the public (it was scheduled to be open at 9:30 am) nor were the retail stores in the towers open for business. Finally, a sluggish economy (increasing the vacancy rate in the towers) and extensive renovations taking place on some floors meant that the buildings were not occupied anywhere near their total capacity.

Nature of the Disaster Itself

A combination of factors, including the cause of the disaster (a surprise terrorist attack), the scope of the physical destruction and the enormity of the human losses, the nature of the targets (the WTCT were widely considered to be symbols of American economic might), the ongoing threat of further attacks, and the fact that the events were televised live to a horrified nation, placed considerable pressures on government officials to act swiftly to identify and quantify the missing and the dead. Before September 11, a mass casualty disaster in contemporary America usually involved at most 200 or so victims. The disaster in New York not only produced many more victims, but the destructive forces unleashed were also far worse than any other U.S. disaster experienced in our lifetimes. The jet fuel explosion, extreme heat from fires, and the crushing force of hundreds of thousands of pounds of steel and concrete involved so many body-destroying forces that locating and identifying more than a fraction of the fatalities proved to be impossible.

Continuity and Change in the Response to the World Trade Center Collapse

Kathleen Tierney, Director of the Disaster Research Center at the University of Delaware, has argued that in most respects the disaster response in New York City followed predictable patterns.* In particular, she cited four ways in which the disaster response in this case was similar to that following large-scale natural disasters:

- *Convergence and Emergence.* Following disasters, we typically observe a massive mobilization of people, goods, and services converging on the disaster scene.

---

* Remarks made at the plenary session of the 27th annual Natural Hazards Center Workshop, Boulder, CO; July 2002.

In addition, new groups (most temporary in nature) emerge to assist official responders.

■ *Adaptive Pro-social Behavior.* Many studies have documented the altruistic behavior of individuals (i.e., orderly evacuation, helping individuals escape who may be injured, SAR by people who happened to be in the area of the disaster, volunteers) following disasters.

■ *Organizational Improvisation.* Because large disasters are characterized by complex and nonroutine interactions, new strategies, new tools, new technologies, and new resources are often adopted to solve emerging problems.

■ *Problems in Interagency Coordination.* The same complex and nonroutine interactions, which unleash organizational improvisation also cause coordination problems (such as difficulty in communicating effectively) between response agencies.

There is no question that the many individuals and organizations behaved in predictable ways following the collapse of the WTCT. By all accounts, the individuals evacuating the towers behaved in an orderly manner, groups of volunteers emerged to aid in immediate response (although these activities in this case were limited both by fears of further collapse and security concerns), there was a massive mobilization of people and resources, and problems surfaced in the command-and-control of response agencies and severe communication problems, which tragically led to the death of many first responders. However, an analysis of the events highlights some important differences as well. In brief, the most important differences identified were the following:

1. Owing to the large number of victims and the manner in which they died, and the uncertainty regarding who was in or around the WTCT that morning, an accurate accounting of the number of casualties took a long time to develop. Indeed, the precise number of dead may never be known. A precise accounting of victims is not merely an academic exercise because claims for insurance, government aid, and charitable contributions rely on a medical determination of death. In this case, such a determination was not possible for a large majority of the victims (only 293 "nearly" whole bodies were recovered). Instead, two definitions of "death" were used in this case: medical death that relied on the identification of human remains by a coroner and legal death in which a court declared a victim dead on the basis of the testimony of next-of-kin or others who would testify that the person was at the WTCTs on the morning of September 11. As of August 22, 2002, nearly a year following the attacks, the New York City Office of the Chief Medical Examiner reported that 1373 death certificates had been issued for decedents whose remains had been found and 1361 decedents whose remains had not been found (MMWR, 2002b). The total number of death certificates issued (2734) does not match the official number dead (2823) because some families have not come forward to

request a legal determination of death.* Methods used to identify the bodies or remains that were retrieved include DNA analysis (645), dental radiographs (188), fingerprints (71), personal effects (19), and photographs (16) (MMWR, 2002b).

The confusion regarding the number of dead is attributable to several factors. The intent from the start was to collect missing persons reports centrally through a New York City Police Department (NYPD) hot line. But almost immediately, state and local police departments in New York, New Jersey, and Connecticut, as well as companies with offices in the trade center complex, local relief agencies, and diplomats representing countries from around the world began to compile their own lists (Lipton, 2001). In addition, many missing persons reports were made that included people who were not in fact at the trade center that morning or who had not yet arrived at home.

2. The nature of the victims was also important in this case. Prior research has shown that disaster victims are typically from lower socioeconomic levels and are often members of underrepresented groups (Fothergill et al., 2001).† In the case of the WTC collapse, the victims were disproportionately middle to upper class individuals in the 35–45 age group. According to an analysis of the death certificates that have been issued, 76 percent of the fatalities were white, 15 percent were Hispanic, 8 percent were black, and 6.5 percent were Asian or Pacific Islander (MMWR, 2002b). A majority of the victims were college graduates (68 percent) and males (77 percent). In addition to the 473 uniformed personnel from Fire Department New York (FDNY), NYPD, the Port Authority police, and city Emergency Medical Service (EMS), Cantor-Fitzgerald (a bond trading firm which lost 657 individuals) and Marsh & McLennan (292 dead) contributed the most to the death toll. The fact that most of the victims were educated and otherwise well connected to the social fabric has had a significant impact on the disaster relief and assistance effort as surviving family members have formed sophisticated interest groups (the most active of which is families of September 11) to lobby governmental agencies.

3. The disaster in New York City was in reality two disasters: the impact of the two planes and the ensuing fires, which instantly took many lives; the second disaster was the collapse of the towers. This dual nature of the disaster is important because it allowed a large number of first responders (primarily firefighters) to enter the towers seeking to help evacuate the buildings. When the towers ultimately collapsed, 343 firefighters, 37 Port Authority police, 23 member of the New York Police department, and 2 emergency medical technicians perished. One conse-quence of the large number deaths among the first responders was that animosity

---

* Death certificates for the 10 terrorists on the two planes were not issued and are not included in these data.

† This is not meant to imply that the well-educated and the wealthy are not victimized by disasters. However, these groups are likely to suffer less because they are more likely to have insurance, bank savings accounts, and a family or social network from whom they can receive assistance.

broke out between different uniformed personnel (primarily fire versus police) and between uniformed personnel and civilians over what might be described as a "hierarchy of the dead." William Langewiesche described the situation at Ground Zero in this way:

> Firemen formed most of the recovery teams, and they directed the procedures. Affected no doubt by the isolation of the site as much as by their grief, they treated their own dead with a reverence not afforded others. Because they controlled the emotion-laded retrieval process for the entire site, their attitude bred factionalism on the pile, and in October led to an argument over the body of a Port Authority policeman that foreshadowed more serious confrontations to come. The policeman was discovered in the ruins of the Trade Center's plaza, and although his body was intact, one leg was pinned under a chaos of heavy steel that would obviously take hours to excavate. Because of the instability of the ruins, the excavation would also require shutting down other recovery operations in a wide area at the center of the site. The firemen who were gathering had a better idea: they would free the body instead by cutting off the leg. Amputation may have been the right decision to make, but it was seen by the Port Authority police officers who were arriving on the scene as a solution based on the firemen's relative disregard for non-firemen, and their desire at all costs to keep searching for their own. This was probably unfair. But the police pointed out correctly that no dead fireman would have had his leg cut off. Still, the firemen were unwilling to change their minds. The dispute never got physical, but it took a while to resolve, and it was not forgotten. In the end the Port Authority police won, and the center of the site was shut down for eight hours while they extracted their man. The shutdown became an act of tribute in itself. But increasingly within the inner world of the Trade Center site the dead were seen as members of different tribes (Langewiesche, 2002, p. 75).*

4. The long length of time of the victim recovery effort is also a significant change in this case when compared to the disasters with which we have experience. Typically, the victim management phase of disaster response and recovery is completed within a relatively short period of time and through relatively routine procedures. Among the consequences of this long time frame was the development of a new culture at Ground Zero. This culture rewarded problem solving and swift

---

* William Langewiesche was given nearly total access to Ground Zero and reported on the activities there for nearly a year.

action. Traditional hierarchies were shunned. In fact, the agency that emerged as the focal point for the task of removing and transporting the tons of debris was the little known New York City Department of Design and Construction (DDC). Even though this agency had no statutory responsibility for disaster recovery (this role was supposed to be filled by the city's Office of Emergency Services) and was not even mentioned in the city's emergency response plan, the director of the DDC and his top aid emerged as the main coordinators of the clean-up of Ground Zero (Langewiesche, 2002). A more unfortunate consequence of the suspension of the social order at Ground Zero was widespread looting. Despite commonly held beliefs that looting is common following disasters, it almost never occurs (Drabek, 1986). In this case, many of the shops that were below ground level in the WTCT (including a jewelry store and several bars) and the Banker's Trust building across Liberty Street from the site were systematically looted—apparently by rescue workers or members of construction teams (Langewiesche, 2002, p. 52).

5. Although disasters often induce a change in federal, state, or local governmental policy, these changes are most often incremental in nature (Birkland, 1998). In this case, federal disaster assistance policy underwent a fundamental change. Before September 11, family members who lost a loved one in a disaster were not eligible for compensation beyond Federal Emergency Management Agency's (FEMA) Individual and Family Grants Program, which provide small amounts of funding for temporary housing and other essential needs. In October 2001, the U.S. Congress passed a bill establishing a Victims Compensation Fund. This fund offered cash payments (the average payment was approximately $1.8 million) to surviving family members of the victims. The long-term consequences of this dramatic change in disaster relief policies remain to be seen.

Concluding Remarks

This chapter has identified some of the ways in which victim management changed in the immediate aftermath of the disaster at the World Trade Center. A natural extension of this research is to consider the management of the indirect victims (family members of the fatalities and others whose lives were negatively affected by the disaster). In the days, weeks, and months following the events in New York, a massive mobilization of disaster assistance and relief efforts took place. According to the FEMA, in the 12 months following September 11 over 55,000 people affected by the disaster had registered with that agency for state and federal disaster assistance and more than $5 billion had been expended in the New York area by federal and state governments for disaster recovery and assistance. These monies, administered through approximately 50 separate programs, provided aid to individuals and communities for, among other things, housing assistance and repair, food stamps, disaster unemployment insurance, crisis counseling, burial expenses, criminal victim grants, and the removal of debris. In addition to these governmental efforts, over

$1.5 billion was raised by over 200 nonprofit charities to provide aid to the victims of September 11.

These relief efforts raise a number of questions that have both practical and theoretical importance particularly with regard to the organizational and administrative processes employed by the agencies and groups involved in delivering disaster assistance. For example, how did these agencies and groups process large numbers of requests for assistance? How were victims identified and who was made eligible for aid? Who among the victims "fell through the cracks" of the relief system and how might they be identified? To what extent did pressures to render aid quickly affected decision making processes? What role have web-based technologies played in the disaster assistance system? What problems have disaster relief officials encountered and how have they been resolved? As the potential for large scale, mass casualty events increases in the United States, these questions will become increasingly important elements of public policy debates (Stehr, 2006).

Beyond the practical questions of who got what from whom, the implementation of these relief and assistance programs also provides an opportunity to examine and test a number of questions regarding our collective understanding of disaster recovery and theories of organized response. For example, to what extent have the many public agencies, private nonprofit organizations, and emergent groups of victim's families coordinated their relief efforts? If they have coordinated their efforts, has this coordination been attempted through relatively formal mechanisms (i.e., formal agreements, contracts, legal requirements) or through informal means (i.e., sharing of information, emergent relationships, preexisting networks of contacts). Has the level of coordination affected the ways in which decisions are made and how benefits were distributed? More generally, which theories of organization best describe the interorganizational activities and social processes related to disaster assistance that continue to unfold in the aftermath of the attacks of September 11.

Bibliography

Adler, J., 2001. Ground zero. *Newsweek*, September 24, pp. 72–87.

Adler, J., 2002. Five who survived. *Newsweek*, September 11, pp. 21–29.

Baker, A., 2002. After 9/11, a question of command. *New York Times*, October 9, p. A1.

Birkland, T., 1998. *After Disaster: Agenda Setting*, Public Policy, and Focusing Events. Washington, DC: Georgetown University Press.

Blanchard, W., 2006. Worst Disasters-Lives Lost. Federal Emergency Management Higher Education Project. Accessed at www.training.fema.gov/emiweb/edu/docs/hazdem/Appendix.

Blanshan, S., 1977. Disaster body handling. *Mass Emergencies*, 2:249–258.

Blanshan, S. and Quarentelli, E.L., 1981. From dead body to person: The handling of fatal mass casualties in disaster. *Victimology*, 6:275–287.

Charnley, M., 1978. The temporary morgue and the identification of bodies. *The Police Chief*, pp. 285–288.

Comfort, L., 1999. *Sharing Risk: Complex Systems in Seismic Response*. New York: Pergamon.

de Ville de Goyet, C., 2001. Stop propagating disaster myths. *The Lancet* (August 26), 356:762–764.

Drabek, T., 1985. Managing the emergency response. *Public Administration Review*, 45:85–92.

Drabek, T., 1986. *Human System Response in Disaster: An Inventory of Sociological Findings*. New York: Springer-Verlag.

Dwyer, J., 2002. Before the towers fell, fire department fought chaos. *New York Times*, January 30, p. C1.

Dwyer, J., Flynn, K., and Fessenden, F., 2002. 9/11 exposed deadly flaws in rescue plan. *New York Times*, July 7, p. A1.

Dynes, R., 1970. *Organized Behavior in Disaster*. Lexington, Massachusetts: Heath Lexington Books.

Fothergill, A., et al., 2001. Race, ethnicity and disasters in the United States: A review of the literature. *Disasters*, 23(2):156–173.

Heath, S.E., Voeks, S.K., and Glickman, L.T., 2000. A study of pet rescue in two disasters. *International Journal of Mass Emergencies and Disasters*, 18:361–381.

Hershiser, M.R. and Quarentelli, E.L., 1979. The handling of dead in a disaster, in Kalish, R.A. (Ed.), *Death and Dying: Views from Many Cultures*. Farmingdale, New York: Baywood Publishing, pp. 132–144.

Kendra, J. and Wachtendoft, T., 2001. Elements of Community Resilience in the World Trade Center Attack. Paper presented at the 48th North American Meetings of the Regional Science Association International, Charleston, South Carolina, November 2001.

Kendra, J. and Wachtendorf, T., 2002. Creativity in Emergency Response After the World Trade Center Attack. Paper presented at the Ninth Annual Conference of the International Emergency Management Society, Waterloo, Canada, May 2002.

Langewiesche, W., 2002. *American Ground: Unbuilding of the World Trade Center*. New York: North Point Press.

Larson, E., 2001. *Isaac's Storm: a Man, a Time, and the Deadliest Hurricane in History*. New York: Crown.

Lipton, E., 2001. Taking account of the dead, feeling the weight of history. *New York Times*, October 6, p. A1.

McKinsey Company, 2002a. Report On the New York City Fire Department.

Mileti, D.S., 1975. *Disaster Research and Rehabilitation in the United States: A Research Assessment*. Boulder, Colorado: Institute of Behavioral Science, The University of Colorado.

Mileti, D.S., 1999. *Disasters by Design: A Reassessment of Natural Hazards in the United States*. Washington, District of Columbia: Joseph Henry Press.

MMWR (Morbidity and Mortality Weekly), 2002a. Rapid assessment of injuries among survivors of the terrorist attack on the World Trade Center—New York City, September 2001, January 11, 51:1–5.

MMWR (Morbidity and Mortality Weekly), 2002b. Deaths in World Trade Center Attacks—New York City, 2001, September 11, 51:16–20.

Orth, G.L., 1959. Disaster and the disposal of the dead. *Military Medicine*, 124:509.

Perez-Pena, R., Trying to command an emergency when the emergency command center is gone. *New York Times*, September 12, p. B1.

Pine, V.R., 1969. The role of the funeral director in disaster. *The Director*, 39:11–23.

Quarentelli, E.L., 1979. The Vaiont dam overflow: A case study of extra-community responses in massive disasters. *Disasters*, 3:199–212.

Scanlon, J., 1998. Dealing with mass death after a community catastrophe: Handling bodies after the 1917 Halifax explosion. *Disaster Prevention and Management*, 7:288–304.

Simpson, D. and Stehr, S., 2002. Investigating the disaster in New York City: Notes on doing field research following the collapse of the World Trade Center Towers. *Natural Hazards Review*, May, 7(2):1–4.

Snoonian, D. and Czarnecki, J.E., 2001. Robust towers succumb to terrorism. *Architectural Record*, October, 189(10):22.

Stallings, R.A. and Quarentelli, E.L., 1985. Emergent citizen groups and emergency management. *Public Administration Review*, 45:93–100.

Stehr, S.D., 2001. Community recovery and reconstruction following disasters, in Farazmand, A. (Ed.), *Handbook of Crisis and Emergency Management*. New York: Marcel Dekker.

Stehr, S.D., 2006. The political economy of urban disaster assistance. *Urban Affairs Review*, 41:492–500.

Steinberg, T., 2000. *Acts of God: The Unnatural History of Natural Disasters in America*. New York: Oxford University Press.

Tierney, K.J., Lindell, M.K., and Perry, R.W., 2001. *Facing the Unexpected: Disaster Preparedness and Response in the United States*. Washington, District of Columbia: Joseph Henry Press.

Walsh, E. and Nichols, R.A., 2001. Thousands of volunteers come to aid of New York: Hope of finding more survivors in the wreckage declines. *Washington Post*, September 13, p. A18.

Wenger, D., 1972. DRC studies of community functioning, in Proceedings of the Japan–United States Disaster Research Seminar: Organizational and Community Responses to Disaster. Columbus, Ohio: Disaster Research Center, The Ohio State University, pp. 29–73.

Wong, E. and Fritsch, J., 2001. Firefighters dash into towers; many do not return. *New York Times*, September 12, p. B1.

FINANCIAL AND ECONOMIC IMPACTS

Chapter 21

Homeland Security Administration and Finance: A Survey of Texas County Officials

Christopher G. Reddick and Howard A. Frank

CONTENTS

Chapter reprinted from Reddick, C.G., and Frank, H.A. (2006). Homeland Security Administration and Finance: A Survey of Texas County Officials. *Journal of Homeland Security and Emergency Management*, 3(3), 1–21.

This chapter examines homeland security administration and finance in Texas county governments in the United States. A survey was conducted in the spring of 2006 to determine the extent of funding sources for homeland security and the perception by county officials on the effectiveness of financing homeland security. First, the results of this study indicate that as the size of the county government increases, the various aspects of homeland security finances also increase. Second, county officials have indicated that increased funding for homeland security will come from existing revenue sources; raising property taxes is not a feasible option. Third, there is a belief by county officials that there has not been a radical change in the existing county budget as a result of homeland security initiatives. Counties feel that they are well prepared in their financial management systems to deal with a possible terrorist attack.

Introduction and Background

The terrorist attacks, in the United States, of September 11, 2001, or 9/11 have put extra pressure on public officials and their agencies to avert and effectively cope with new threats (Rosenthal, 2003). Since 9/11, there remains considerable fear and anxiety about future attacks. After 9/11, the idea of homeland security became a part of American ideology (Beresford, 2004). These emotions force public officials, especially those at the local level who are primarily responsible for public safety, to devote large sums of money to homeland security (West and Orr, 2005). Counties across the United States have been bearing a considerable portion of the burden of financing and managing homeland security in their locales (Caruson and MacManus, 2005).

The purpose of this chapter is to investigate the scope of homeland security, in particular focusing on its impact on administration and finances in county governments in Texas. This is done through a survey of Texas county government officials. In addition, there is an examination of the perceptions by county public officials on the effectiveness of the existing financial management system to meet the current and future demands of homeland security. This is a relatively unexplored area that has a substantial impact on local governments' homeland security preparedness (Caruson and MacManus, 2005).

For the purpose of this study, homeland security refers to domestic governmental actions designed to prevent, detect, respond to, and recover from acts of terrorism. This chapter focuses on counties because these governments typically have closer political and administrative ties with state governments than do cities. Counties are representative of a broader electorate than cities, which enables them to better mediate conflict (Waugh, 1994). Therefore, county governments may in fact be the most logical choice for homeland security functions because of their unique roles in state and local governance. While the federal government has a lead role in establishing national priorities and policies for homeland security, local governments arguably have the best knowledge of their territory and are best suited to address specific, localized needs (Wise and Nader, 2002).

Adaptive management is a theory that can be used to explain the impact of homeland security on county government finance and administration (Wise, 2006). Adaptive management calls for the integration of science and management, where public officials work collaboratively with each other and with the public and learn together (Graham and Kruger, 2002). Adaptive management attempts to incorporate the views of all interested parties to discuss management problems and then to develop models that express participants' collective understanding of how the system operates (Johnson, 1999). This approach differs from traditional forms of management by emphasizing the importance of feedback in shaping policy, followed by further evaluation (Wise, 2006). Adaptive management may be a possible route for counties to pursue to be more responsive to their stakeholders, at the same time meeting homeland security needs.

This chapter is divided into several sections to explore the scope and effectiveness of homeland security and financial management in Texas county governments. The following section specifies the research questions that will frame the discussion of the survey results. This is followed by a detailed illustration of the survey methods and results. The conclusion provides a reexamination of the research questions of this study, limitations, and future research.

Research Questions

There are three research questions addressed in this study, which have been derived from the existing literature. These questions deal with county government size, funding methods and sources, and effectiveness of homeland security finance and administration.

1. Does the size of the county have an impact on homeland security funding in Texas counties?
2. What are the common methods of financing homeland security in Texas counties?
3. How effective are financial management policies on homeland security in Texas counties?

The first research question deals with county government size as a possible factor identified in the literature that can be used to explain homeland security initiatives (Baldassare and Hoene, 2002; Gerber et al., 2005; MacManus and Caruson, 2006). The literature has maintained that larger local governments will be more advanced in their homeland security preparedness. For example, a survey of Florida cities' and counties' officials showed that larger jurisdictions reported federal or state information sources as a critical outlet for terrorist threat data than smaller cities (MacManus and Caruson, 2006). In a national survey of homeland security preparedness, it was found that large cities had a greater perceived likelihood of attack on their locality than smaller and medium-sized cities (Gerber et al., 2005).

The second question examines sources of homeland security funding, which has been examined in previous research of Florida cities and counties (Caruson and MacManus, 2005). The last question deals with an application of the adaptive management model to homeland security (Wise 2006). This study specifically applies this theory to county government administration and finances. Before this chapter addresses these important research questions, it examines the survey data collection methods.

Survey and Methods

The authors of this study conducted a Web survey of Texas county treasurers and county judges in the spring of 2006. To get more candid responses, the public officials were assured confidentiality of their responses. Because county judges and treasurers are actively involved in county government finances, they were a logical choice to send a survey to.

A county judge is the chief elected official in county government in Texas. His or her position is defined according to the Texas Association of Counties (http://www.county.org) as having broad judicial and administrative powers over the county government. This official presides over a five-member commissioners' court, which has budgetary and administrative authority over county government operations. In terms of financial management, the county judge has a significant role in the preparation of the county budget.

The county treasurer, also an elected official, is the county's banker and the chief custodian of county finances. This official receives all monies belonging to the county, keeps an account of all monies in a designated depository, and pays disbursement of all monies as directed by commissioners' court. Both officials, given their respective roles, have an important impact on county finances.

A comprehensive mailing list of county treasurers and judges, including their e-mail addresses, was provided by the Texas Association of Counties. This research surveyed only counties serving populations of 10,000 or greater, because of the desire to focus on medium- to large-sized governments and their adoption and views on homeland security issues.

First, a cover letter was e-mailed introducing the project with a Web link to the survey. In three weeks, this was followed by a reminder e-mail sent to county officials who did not respond to the initial mailing. Out of 166 officials who were sent a survey, 95 counties responded, which is a response rate of 57 percent. This is an above-average response rate compared to International City/County Management Association (ICMA) surveys of local government officials, which usually is around 35 percent.

The methods used in this chapter were descriptive and summary statistics of the survey responses. The coding for the questions are located on the top of the columns in the tables and the average response category is the mean value of the coded responses. Analysis of variance (ANOVA) statistics was conducted to determine whether there were statistically significant differences between being a larger-sized county government and the responses to the survey questions. Before we can explore the research questions of this study, the following section summarizes the characteristics of the counties, their governments, and the officials surveyed.

Texas Counties, Their Governments, and Officials

To gain a better perspective of the counties that participated in the survey, Table 21.1 presents summary statistics with this information. In terms of the fiscal capacity of Texas counties, which is defined as the ability of the county government to raise taxes given political and legal limits (such as a balanced budget law), there was an average response of −0.47. This was calculated by averaging the scaled responses to whether county officials believed that they had a favorable to unfavorable fiscal capacity (2 points assigned for very favorable, 1 point for favorable, −1 point for unfavorable, and −2 points for very unfavorable). This implies, because of the negative score, that Texas counties may not have a lot of resources for activities such as homeland security. However, the county officials have a more favorable view of economic development in their locality, which is defined as job growth and its impact on the county, with an average response of 0.36. In addition, the political climate is favorable, which is the political relationship between county commission and its citizens having an average response of 0.68.

There was also information in the survey on the size of counties surveyed in terms of full-time equivalent (FTE) employees. This is a measure of size that can be used to determine whether larger-sized counties have differing views on homeland security-related issues. The results in Table 21.1 showed that 77.4 percent of counties surveyed had less than 499 employees. In addition, 50 percent of the counties surveyed were in the 100–499 FTE employment range. There was only one very large county that responded to the survey having 5000 or more FTE employees. There were ten counties that responded having 1000–4999 employees. The results show that this study is more representative of small to medium-sized counties. Therefore, the findings should be interpreted with caution given the types of counties in the sample.

ANOVA was used to determine whether FTE employment size had an impact on many of the measures examined in this study. A more favorable economic development climate was statistically related to being a larger-sized county government. This may be explained by smaller counties typically being more fiscally restrained than larger county governments because of lack of resource capacity to attract and retain businesses.

Table 21.2 shows that the typical county treasurer or county judge who responded to the survey was in the age group of 45–64 years. In the sample, 58.8

Table 21.1 Information on Counties and Their Governments

Full-Time Equivalent (FTE) Employees	Frequency	Percent
99 or less	23	27.4
100–499	42	50
500–999	8	9.5
1000–4999	10	11.9
5000 or more	1	1.2

County Characteristics	Very Favorable Percent (2)	Favorable Percent (1)	Neutral Percent (0)	Unfavorable Percent (−1)	Very Unfavorable Percent (−2)	Average Responses
Fiscal capacity	2.4	16.9	27.7	37.3	15.7	−0.47
Economic development climate[a]	12	41	22.9	19.3	4.8	0.36
Political climate	9.8	59.8	19.5	11	0	0.68

[a] Significant difference of employee size and this variable at the 0.01 level; for average response calculation the coding is in parenthesis.

Table 21.2   Information on County Government Officials

	Frequency	Percent
Age range		
25–34	2	2.4
35–44	12	14.5
45–54	26	31.3
55–64	32	38.6
65 and over	11	13.3
Gender		
Male	47	58.8
Female	33	41.3
Graduate degree		
Yes	17	20.7
No	65	79.3
Position		
County judge	53	55.8
County treasurer	42	44.2

percent composed of males. Only 20.7 percent of officials who responded to the survey had a graduate degree. Finally, of officials who responded to the survey, 55.8 percent were county judges and the remainder treasurers.

With this information on the counties that were surveyed, and officials who responded to the survey, the following section provides data on the extent of homeland security preparedness and planning in Texas county governments.

Homeland Security Preparedness and Planning

The degree of homeland security preparedness and planning information provides the extent to which counties view themselves as being prepared for a possible terrorist attack (Table 21.3). In terms of county governments' current homeland security preparedness, the average response was 2.44, which implies that counties are

Table 21.3 Homeland Security Preparedness and Planning

How would you Assess your County's	*Very High Percent (4)*	*High Percent (3)*	*Low Percent (2)*	*Very Low Percent (1)*	*Nonexistent Percent (0)*	*Average Response*
Current homeland security preparedness**	4.5	47.7	38.6	5.7	3.4	2.44
Probability of being a future terrorist target***	5.7	14.8	45.5	26.1	8	1.84
Managerial capacity to coordinate and control homeland security spending	10.1	57.3	23.6	4.5	4.5	2.64

Your County Government	*Strongly Agree Percent (2)*	*Agree Percent (1)*	*Neutral Percent (0)*	*Disagree Percent (−1)*	*Strongly Disagree Percent (−2)*	*Average Response*
Has employed a set of performance measures that allow county decision makers to know if they are improving homeland security preparedness	4.5	39.3	29.2	22.5	4.5	0.17
Is more secure against homeland security threats than it was before September 11, 2001	16.9	52.8	16.9	9	4.5	0.69
Has benchmarks for progress in improving homeland security preparedness	4.5	40.4	34.8	16.9	3.4	0.26
Has coordinated its homeland security planning with the cities and counties within its region**	21.3	52.8	16.9	6.7	2.2	0.84

Notes: Significant difference of employee size and this variable at the (**) 0.05 level or (***) 0.01 level; for average response calculation the coding is in parenthesis.

in the range of low to high in terms of their perception of preparedness. Firstly, this shows that as county size increases, the perception of being more prepared rises as well. Secondly, in terms of the probability of being a future terrorist target, there is a perception of this being a low probability for most counties. However, as the size of the county increases, there is a belief in a greater likelihood of being a future terrorist target. Finally, the managerial capacity to coordinate and control homeland security spending is viewed favorably with an average response of 2.64, which is in the low-to-high range. In terms of preparedness of counties in Texas, officials believe that they are prepared. There is the perception of a low probability of a terrorist attack within their county. Counties have high managerial capacity to coordinate and control homeland security spending.

Delving further into the theme of homeland security preparedness and planning, this research found that only 39.3 percent of counties have performance measures that allow for the improvement of homeland security preparedness (Table 21.3). However, 52.8 percent of county officials believe that they are more secure against a terrorist attack than before September 11, 2001. In addition, 40.4 percent of respondents are in agreement that they have benchmarks for progress in improving homeland security preparedness. The results show that 52.8 percent of counties have actually coordinated homeland security planning with cities and counties in their respective region.

What do the results mean overall for homeland security preparedness and planning in Texas counties? First, there is a perception that Texas county officials are more secure against a terrorist attack than before 9/11. Counties have coordinated homeland security planning in their respective region. However, there was less agreement of having performance measures and benchmarks in place to evaluate homeland security preparedness. Although current homeland security preparedness and planning of Texas county governments are critically important, the following section provides information on where the homeland security funds are coming from and where they are going.

Homeland Security Funding

A core issue of this chapter is the examination of homeland security finance. As an illustration of its importance, the greatest homeland security concern was lack of money according to 73 percent of county officials who responded to the survey (Table 21.4). Personnel limitations were cited by 65 percent of counties as a major concern. Technology interoperability was viewed as a concern by 53 percent of Texas county officials. Of the governments surveyed, larger counties have greater concerns over lack of internal cooperation within their organization than smaller counties.

Another question that was asked was how the county government will pay for its portion of homeland security costs not covered by homeland security grants

Table 21.4 Homeland Security Funding

What are your county government's greatest homeland security concerns?	Percent
Lack of money	73
Personnel limitations	65
Technology/Interoperability	53
Lack of health care capacity	33
Lack of clear plan/roles	27
Lack of external cooperation	18
Lack of internal cooperation**	7
We do not have concerns	4
How will your county government pay for its portion of homeland security costs (i.e., that portion not covered by federal or state grants)?	
Existing budget/revenue funds	53
General fund	49
Reallocate/cut spending	34
Raise property taxes	24
Asset seizure funds	7
Other***	5
Issue bonds	1
Which, if any, of the following types of equipment has your county government purchased to complete its homeland security goals?	
Communications	76
Hazardous material suits, apparatuses*	40
Information technology**	24
Surveillance devices	16
Identification technology	15
Access control devices*	8
Other	7

Table 21.4 (continued)   Homeland Security Funding

Has your county government requested federal or state funding for any of the following homeland security-related programs and needs?	Percent
Equipment**	38
Disaster response***	27
Disaster mitigation/preparedness	25
Drills and training exercises**	17
Physical surveillance/security systems**	15
Medical public health surveillance systems	11
Staffing	11
Public education*	9
Information technology	8
Cyber security	2
Other	1

Notes: Significant difference of employee size and this variable at the (*) 0.10 level, (**) 0.05 level, or (***) 0.01 level.

(Table 21.4). To cover homeland security costs, 53 percent of counties would pay through existing budget/revenue funds, while 49 percent of counties would use the general fund. Only a few counties would actually raise property taxes (24 percent). Therefore, most of the funding for homeland security, not coming from grants, is from the existing budget line items. Raising taxes does not seem to be a popular choice among county officials.

An open-ended question at the end of this survey supports this conclusion, with many county officials noting that there is no political appetite for tax increases to fund homeland security. Therefore, other programs may have to be cut to fund homeland security spending. This perception of lack of support for new taxes and fees to fund homeland security is not just an artifact of Texas counties; it is pervasive across cities of all sizes and regions in the United States (Baldassare and Hoene, 2002).

What kinds of equipment has the county government purchased to reach its homeland security goals (Table 21.4)? The results for this question indicate that communication devices are most commonly purchased by counties (76 percent). These local governments are trying to address one of the most frequent problems in responding to a terrorist attack, having a good communications network. Finally,

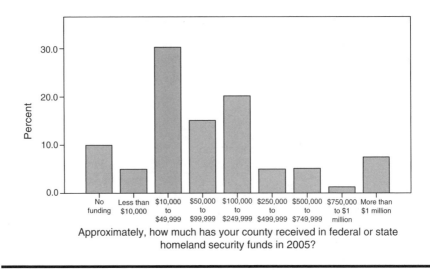

Figure 21.1   County government received federal or state homeland security funds.

hazardous material suits and apparatus were purchased, according to 40 percent of counties.

Table 21.4 provides information on the requests for grant funding for homeland security. The most commonly requested external funding was for equipment according to 38 percent of county officials. Disaster response funding was the second most frequently requested grant. There were statistically significant differences with larger counties being more likely to request money for equipment, disaster response, drills and training exercises, physical surveillance/security systems, and public education. As the statistical results indicate, the size of the county has a direct bearing on many homeland security initiatives.

Figure 21.1 provides information on how much these counties actually received in homeland security grant funding from federal or state governments. The average amount of funding received was very small, between $10,000 and $49,999. Very few counties received more than one million dollars in external funding. There were around 20 percent of counties that received an amount from $100,000 to $249,999 in grant funding. The amount of grant funding received by Texas counties was very highly correlated with size of county government at the 0.01 significance level (not shown). Not surprisingly, larger counties typically received more grant funding.

Intergovernmental Aspects of Homeland Security

A major dilemma posed with homeland security is the vast number of agencies involved at all levels of government (Wise and Nader, 2002). Table 21.5 provides

Table 21.5 Intergovernmental Aspects of Homeland Security

	Strongly Agree Percent (2)	Agree Percent (1)	Neutral Percent (0)	Disagree Percent (−1)	Strongly Disagree Percent (−2)	Average Response
Homeland security from federal or state grants						
Fail to recognize the importance of county coordination	17	37.5	22.7	22.7	0	0.49
May improve security against terrorist acts at the expense of traditional emergency preparedness concerns	9.1	46.6	23.9	20.5	0	0.44
Should not be used to make up for pre-existing shortfalls in police, fire, rescue, and hospital capabilities	11.4	47.7	19.3	18.2	3.4	0.45
Shortchange high-population, high-risk areas by overfunding low-population, low-risk ones*	4.5	21.6	25	39.8	9.1	−0.27
Do not provide enough funds for overtime expenses*	9.2	39.1	40.2	11.5	0	0.46
Are too easily commingled with traditional first responder funding to assess their impact on homeland security preparedness	3.4	36.4	35.2	23.9	1.1	0.17

(continued)

Table 21.5 (continued) Intergovernmental Aspects of Homeland Security

	Strongly Agree Percent (2)	Agree Percent (1)	Neutral Percent (0)	Disagree Percent (−1)	Strongly Disagree Percent (−2)	Average Response
In their respective regions						
Counties are the logical choice for coordinating homeland security	23	55.2	10.3	10.3	1.1	0.89
Nongovernmental entities such as hospitals and the Red Cross would prefer coordinating homeland security activities with counties rather than individual cities	7	48.8	38.4	4.7	1.2	0.56
Security sensitive activities such as airports, seaports, and power generation should come under the homeland security purview of counties rather than cities	9.3	39.5	37.2	11.6	2.3	0.42
Intragovernmental service agreements can minimize only a small portion of the increased homeland security outlays county governments will need to make in future years	4.6	64.4	24.1	6.9	0	0.67

Notes: Significant difference of employee size and this variable at the *0.10 level; for average response calculation the coding is in parenthesis.

information on the intergovernmental aspects of homeland security in Texas counties. County officials believe that traditional emergency preparedness functions may be shortchanged because of homeland security funding. Counties are of the opinion that they are the logical choice for coordinating homeland security. According to county officials, nongovernmental entities, such as the Red Cross, would prefer to coordinate with counties rather than cities. In addition, intergovernmental service agreements can only do so much to mitigate a small portion of the homeland security funding issues. There was disagreement that low-population and low-risk counties were being shortchanged in terms of homeland security grant funding.

The results in Table 21.5 showed that counties believed that they have become an integral part of the homeland security equation. However, non-homeland-security projects are getting shortchanged in funding. There is agreement that having an intergovernmental service agreement can only do so much to minimize homeland security costs.

County Government Financial Impacts and Homeland Security

Table 21.6 provides information on the perception of county officials on the effectiveness of the financial management impacts of homeland security. There was an average response of −0.08 that capital budgeting priorities have changed as a result of September 11, 2001, implying that counties believe that it has not occurred. There was also a divergence in views that homeland security expenditures are displacing outlays in traditional civilian functions. There was disagreement that county residents are willing to pay for increased homeland security. In addition, a disagreement was found for county residents being willing to pay increased taxes to fund homeland security spending.

There was general agreement that homeland security had an impact on financial management in Texas counties (Table 21.6). One of the most interesting findings showed that according to half of county officials, homeland security expenditures were being tied to strategy and risk assessment rather than specific threats. This supports the long-term strategic view of the adaptive management model. According to 52.6 percent of county officials, there is a high level of consensus of the need for infrastructure to coordinate homeland security activities. Over half of respondents believe that homeland security preparedness is the primary responsibility of the federal government, and should be funded accordingly. This finding was also confirmed by a General Accounting Office (GAO) survey, which indicated that state and local governments perceived that the fight against terrorism to be generally a federal government responsibility (GAO, 2003). There were 49.5 percent of officials who are of the opinion that they have provided good oversight of homeland security preparedness spending.

Table 21.6   County Government Financial Impacts of Homeland Security

	Strongly Agree Percent (2)	Agree Percent (1)	Neutral Percent (0)	Disagree Percent (−1)	Strongly Disagree Percent (−2)	Average Response
As a result of September 11, 2001, or 9/11						
Capital budgeting priorities in my county have significantly changed	3.2	27.4	33.7	29.5	6.3	−0.08
Overtime outlays for first responder (i.e., emergency personnel called to the scene of a crisis) training and deployment have increased dramatically	5.3	31.6	36.8	22.1	4.2	0.12
Homeland security expenditures are displacing outlays in traditional civilian functions, such as general government services*	4.2	25.3	29.5	35.8	5.3	−0.13
Homeland security expenditures are being tied to strategy and risk assessment rather than to specific threats or special events (e.g., VIP visits, national holidays, etc.)	12.6	50.5	24.2	9.5	3.2	0.6
In my county government						
Homeland security funding should be focused more on disaster/terror prevention than response and recovery	9.5	28.4	32.6	27.4	2.1	0.16
Accounting and financial reporting facilitate comprehensive analysis of homeland security preparedness**	4.2	36.8	36.8	18.9	3.2	0.2

There is the infrastructure (e.g., equipment, IT, and communications) needed to coordinate homeland security activities	12.6	52.6	13.7	15.8	5.3	0.52
Our county residents					
Are willing to pay for significantly increased homeland security outlays because of a heightened concern over terrorism**	2.1	9.6	24.5	50	13.8	−0.64
Are willing to accept county government tax increases to fund homeland security preparedness**	1.1	9.6	21.3	48.9	19.1	−0.76
Believe homeland security preparedness is the primary responsibility of the federal government and should be funded accordingly*	20.2	53.2	16	10.6	0	0.83
Our county elected officials					
Are providing good oversight of homeland security preparedness spending	15.8	49.5	21.1	10.5	3.2	0.64
Have the expertise needed to oversee homeland security outlays	8.4	38.9	23.2	24.2	5.3	0.21
Are willing to invest in critical homeland security infrastructure*	3.2	34	36.2	21.3	5.3	0.09

Notes: Significant difference of employee size and this variable at the (*) 0.10 level or (**) 0.05 level; for average response calculations the coding is in parenthesis.

The results in Table 21.6 show overall that traditional functions in the county budget have not substantially changed because of homeland security spending. There is a general agreement that residents are unwilling to have their property taxes increased to fund homeland security. These officials believe that they are good stewards of homeland security resources, but question why the federal government is not taking on more responsibility for homeland security funding.

Conclusion

The purpose of this chapter was to examine the scope and effectiveness of homeland security with a particular focus on administration and finance. Returning to the three research questions outlined earlier in this chapter, the results confirmed that size of the county did have a bearing on various aspects of homeland security initiatives. For instance, the perception of being more prepared for a possible terrorist attack increases in larger counties. Lack of internal cooperation is more prevalent in larger counties than in smaller counties. Residents are more willing to pay for and accept tax increases to fund homeland security in larger-sized counties.

In terms of methods of funding homeland security, the most pressing issues here are lack of money and personnel limitations that counties face. The funding sources for homeland security will not come from increased property taxes or other fees. Existing budget lines have been reallocated to pay for homeland security. Equipment is the most common homeland security purchase for Texas counties. External homeland security grant funding is surprisingly small with an average in the range of only $10,000–$49,000.

Finally, the adaptive management model was applied to homeland security administration and finance. There is a very high level of collaboration and coordination of homeland security planning with cities and counties in their regions, which is one of the key components of this model. However, the extent of providing benchmarks and performance measures to improve homeland security preparedness was not as prevalent. Most importantly, there seems to be an agreement among county officials that homeland security expenditures are being tied to an overall strategy and risk assessment, a significant sign of progress using an adaptive management approach.

There are some limitations of this study that should be noted. First, this research uses a survey to collect information and opinions about homeland security and there is no independent verification of the claims made by these public officials. Second, this is a study that relies on data from a single state and, therefore, the results may not be generalizable to all counties in the United States. However, despite these limitations, this research has provided a basis for future studies of financial and administrative aspects of homeland security in local governments. This is an especially important issue given the large amount of resources devoted toward this area and the critical role that counties play in homeland security.

References

Baldassare, M. and Hoene, C., 2002. *Coping with Homeland Security: Perceptions of City Officials in California and the United States*. San Francisco, California: Public Policy Institute of California.

Beresford, A.D., 2004. Homeland security as an American ideology: Implications for U.S. policy and action. *Journal of Homeland Security and Emergency Management*, 1(3). Retrieved May 27, 2006, from http://www.bepress.com/jhsem/vol1/iss3/301.

Caruson, K. and MacManus, S.A., 2005. Homeland security preparedness: Federal and state mandates and local government. *Spectrum: The Journal of State Government*, 78(2), 25–28.

Gerber, B.J., Cohen, D.B., Cannon, B., Patterson, D., and Stewart, K., 2005. On the front line: American cities and the challenge of homeland security preparedness. *Urban Affairs Review*, 41(2), 182–210.

Graham, A.C. and Kruger, L.E., 2002. *Research in Adaptive Management: Working Relations and the Research Process (PNW-RP-538)*. Portland, Oregon: U.S. Department of Agriculture.

Johnson, B.L., 1999. The role of adaptive management as an operational approach for resource management agencies. *Ecology and Society*, 3(2). Retrieved May 27, 2006, from http://www.consecol.org/vol3/iss2/art8.

MacManus, S.A. and Caruson, K., 2006. Code Red: Florida City and county officials rate threat information sources and the homeland security advisory system. *State and Local Government Review*, 38(1), 12–22.

Rosenthal, U., 2003. September 11: Public administration and the study of crisis and crisis management. *Administration and Society*, 35(2), 129–143.

United State General Accounting Office (GAO), 2003. Homeland Security: Efforts to Improve Information Sharing Need to be Strengthened (GAO-03-760). Washington, DC: U.S. Government Printing Office.

Waugh, W.L., 1994. Regionalizing emergency management: Counties as state and local. *Public Administration Review*, 54(3), 253–258.

West, D.M. and Orr, M., 2005. Managing citizen fears: Public attitudes toward urban terrorism. *Urban Affairs Review*, 41(1), 93–105.

Wise, C.R., 2006. Organizing for homeland security after Katrina: Is adaptive management what's missing? *Public Administration Review*, 66(3), 302–318.

Wise, C.R. and Nader, R., 2002. Organizing the federal system for homeland security: Problems, issues, and dilemmas. *Public Administration Review*, 62(Special Issue), 44–57.

Chapter 22

Border Closures in the Southern United States: Measuring the Economic Impact of a Sustained Crisis

Mathew McElroy and Dennis L. Soden

CONTENTS

Introduction

In many ways, the movement of goods and people between the United States and Mexico has been cumbersome for years, but a total slowdown or even a lockdown of the border was never fully understood until 9/11. At one level, the entire scope of security changed, and at another level, the value of trade between the two nations was reassessed leading to a simple question, what happens if the border was closed for an extended period of time?

In this chapter, we examine this question. The border is first framed in the context of the comparative advantage it provides to the American industry. Then using an economic model designed for the border region, the impacts of a closure are considered across three scenarios or levels of severity.

Comparative Advantage and the United States–Mexico Border

Increasingly, nations and regions are finding that the factors that make up comparative advantage in an era of globalization are ever changing. Moreover, the assumptions of classical economics, namely the immobility of capital and labor, no longer seem to bear themselves out. Simply put, things are not static and factors of production are used in a competitive gamesmanship to maximize local opportunities in global markets that are also ever changing. As a result, contemporary analyses of economies at all levels are often confused, and developing a niche in international trade has become increasingly difficult.[1] However, there has been a boom in global trade in almost all parts of the world. Growth in international trade has been reported as growing three times that of national economies.[2] Growth in North America trade has also been accelerated by the North American Free Trade Act (NAFTA) signed in January 1994, between the United States, Canada, and Mexico.

In 2005, 36.6 percent of total U.S. exports went to Canada and Mexico, making them the United States' number one and two trading partners, respectively. As a result, the economic dependence between the United States, Canada, and Mexico is perhaps greater than any other in the world. The dependency is more than just Canada and Mexico relying on the U.S. market. It has also become a dependency for the United States at two levels. First is the obvious trade volume from a monetary perspective. Second is the dependency that the U.S. industrial sector has developed. The extent of the flow of goods and services across the U.S. border with Mexico is, to a large extent, the focus of this chapter. However, more importantly, we ask what would happen if this trade flow was disrupted as a result of a September 11th type of event. The degree to which American industry and manufacturing require a stable and constant flow of components and parts to build a range of products has made the southern border a strategic resource in the calculus of the American economy; and a secure border is more than just a concern about terrorism, it is a concern about the impacts on American industry. In this chapter, we focus on the southern U.S. border with Mexico, examining the economic impacts of a security breach that would shut down trade between the two nations.

The United States and Mexico Border: September 11th, China, and Port Disruptions

The United States–Mexico border region extends nearly 2000 miles and is home to a highly integrated social and economic system. With a wide range of problems ranging from low incomes and higher-than-average poverty levels, low education levels, environmental and health concerns, the two sides of the border have developed symbiotically, solving or at least "satisficing" many problems.[3] Regardless of NAFTA, it is safe to say that the integration along the border would have continued as part of the daily exchange that marks the region.[4] Yet, border communities have been at the periphery of their national economies, and even farther a field politically as the Distrito Federal and District of Columbia operate toward them with benign neglect at one level (i.e., economic development, education, social programs), and intrusion and a police mentality at another (border crossing, trade impediments). The events of September 11th, however, immediately turned eyes to border regions, especially the southern border, which one could argue, had no role in September 11th events, but is the focus of antiimmigration efforts for those who use homeland security as a platform for their plans.

In an era of global trade, and the fierce competition between nations it has engendered, securing borders to insure the free flow of goods and services has become a major priority.[5] This priority has become even greater since September 11th. Under NAFTA and the trade growth it fostered, the new imperative of moving goods and services to insure the economic stability of North America has also come to include concerns for homeland security, a phrase new to discussions of borders and international trade since September 11th.

Immediately following the September 11th attacks on the United States, the U.S. Customs Service and Immigration and Naturalization Service moved to the highest possible level of alert (these agencies have been reorganized since and are combined into the agency of Immigration and Customs Enforcement, ICE). National agencies quickly shifted resources to better monitor the nation's borders. As a political victim, the protocols that Presidents Bush and Fox were developing to provide for guest workers and loosening of some border restrictions were dismissed as the war on terror began. For those living on the border and those who believe a hardened border is counterproductive to binational relationships, the change has been an inefficient bureaucratic response that has hindered the border economy and rekindled negative perceptions of the border region, conditions many free-trade advocates oppose to this day. Border crossings and wait times have been significantly altered as the focus shifted from almost exclusively stopping drugs, contraband, and illegal immigrants to securing the nation's borders and would appear unlikely to change under current congressional suggestions (Migration Policy Institute, 2005; *The Kansas City Star*, 2006)[6,7] and programs, such as U.S. VISIT which to date have not registered any efficiencies in crossing times.[8] It could be easily argued that reactive politics has been the post-September 11th response, but that would be a bit misleading because most American politics is, in fact, reactive. The response is somewhat expected as one considers that terrorism is new to the American psyche when compared to the rest of the world.

Returning to the economic question, it is only fair to note that before September 11th the U.S.-driven recession was already being felt throughout the border region as a maquiladora[9] slowdown spread throughout various sectors of the border economy on both sides. The September 11th attacks not only aggravated the existing economic downturn, but they also altered the social characteristics between the international cities that lie on the border. Measurements of this impact are the records of employment and border crossings that are seen in Figures 22.1 and 22.2. Both figures confirm that a decline was already underway and was clearly accelerated after September 11th. Another point that gives more perspective is that in the

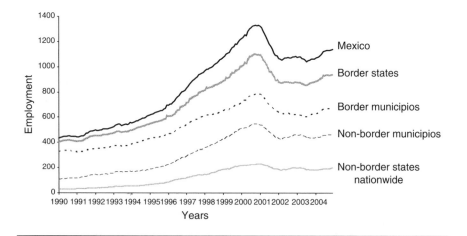

Figure 22.1 Maquiladora employment, 1990–2004. (From Indistria Maquiladora de exportacion, Instituto de Estadistica Geografoa e Informatica (INEGI), seasonally adjusted by IPED.)

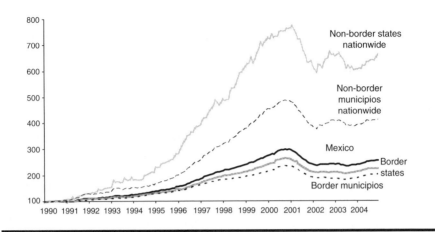

Figure 22.2 Pedestrian crossings at top ports (in thousands). (From Indistria Maquiladora de exportacion, Instituto de Estadistica Geografoa e Informatica (INEGI), seasonally adjusted by IPED.)

20 days of greater scrutiny after the morning of September 11th, persons driving across all U.S. borders took a dip of more than 3.7 million.[10]

Similar to other regional systems, national and state components drive the economy of the southern border in a multidirectional manner. However, unlike interior markets, the southern border is more prone or sensitive to international shocks and by economic activity in Mexico. In the same fashion, Mexico's northern border is disproportionately affected by economic activity in the United States and states on the southern border. More precisely, maquiladora output is predominantly exported to the United States, and, as a consequence, U.S. consumption patterns have a significant influence on manufacturing activity in Mexico, namely the maquiladora-manufacturing sector. Hence, U.S. economic growth is a primary driver to individual cities and states that make up the United States–Mexico border region. Maquilas make up over 60 percent of total nonfarm employment in Northern Mexico[11] and have a strong positive correlation to economic activity in southern U.S. border states. For example, employment regression equations for the four large southern border cities (San Diego, El Paso, McAllen, and Brownsville) estimate the elasticity between maquila output and U.S. border city manufacturing employment to be between 0.13 and 0.21, for retail employment between 0.12 and 0.14, and for transport between 0.04 and 0.10. In other words, a 10 percent rise in export manufacturing in a Mexican border city leads up to a 2.1 percent, 1.4 percent, and 1.0 percent rise in employment, respectively, in the neighboring U.S. border city.[12]

The importance of a region's economic base has also been measured by calculating location quotients over time to identify areas of specialization.[13] A location quotient (LQ) is defined as the local share of jobs in an industry divided by the national share of jobs in the same industry. Industries with a higher share of employment (LQ > 1) than those in the national economy are considered basic industries and drivers of the local economy. This approach assumes that basic industries generate sufficient employment to cover local needs, and all extra industry employment results from external demand (production for consumers outside the local area). In the border region, calculations for the El Paso area indicate that manufacturing, transportation services and trucking and warehousing, retail trade activity, and federal civilian jobs have location quotients well above the national reference point. Consequently, El Paso and other border cities function both as a land port for transshipments and as a binational regional production network for the North American market.[14] Using El Paso as a case in point, like other border cities it plays a key role to the drayage and logistics component of the just-in-time system between the two nations. Almost all trade and truck traffic that passes through El Paso are related to in-bond processing. The port of El Paso is the second largest southern port behind Laredo in import and export trade value. In 2005, $25.8 billion in imports and $19.2 billion in exports passed over El Paso's international bridges,[15] representing 18.3 percent of total trade through the southern U.S. customs districts. The importance of international trade in the states of southern border has resulted in a substantial number of jobs related to trucking, warehousing, customs brokerage, freight forwarding, and other related services. Total employment in these industries peaked in the third quarter of 2000, and began to drop off in the fourth quarter, also coinciding with a decrease in cross-border maquila activities, and suffering further declines after September 11th.[16] Since September 11th, and more importantly as a result of the recession, maquiladora employment has rebounded to 230,895 in December of 2005, but is still short of pre-September 11th number.

Data reflects that, although it was not business as usual for commercial truck traffic, border disruption and longer wait times did not significantly deter cargo transportation across borders to conduct daily business. On the southern side, truck crossings were similar to what was expected given the integration of the two nations and the United States–Mexico business cycle. More clearly, although the September 11th events further weakened business and consumer confidence, it was ultimately demand drops related to the recession that forced changes in truck crossings not the events of September 11th. And although longer wait times at the border have created disequilibria in the just-in-time system that the manufacturing process is dependent upon, goods continue to flow to support U.S. manufacturing.[17]

Hence, the extent to which September 11th affected our transportation system is really a question of how much the events affected product demand and seemingly "seamless" just-in-time supply chain. One thing is for certain: transaction costs increased, whether through changes in transport modes, greater inventory costs, communications costs, or distribution delays.[18]

The growth of the maquiladora industry in the past 20 years has led to a border that was the most prosperous part of Mexico and an undeniable strategic resource to U.S. manufacturing, especially in the electronics and automotive sectors. The illegal drug industry's shift from Miami in the 1980s to Tijuana and Ciudad Juárez, however, provided the rationale for policing the border to combat the war on drugs and to contain illegal immigration. One could easily make the case that both activities have been futile overall, and in light of September 11th have no relationship to the terrorist attacks. Although the increase of illegal activity along the southern border resulted in greater federal enforcement, the rise in crossings and commerce led to the construction or upgrade of bridges and new industries growing, including a significant service sector that had previously been marginally successful.[19]

The September 11th attacks had differential effects on U.S. border regions with Mexico and Canada than on interior places in the country. The lockdown of the border resulted in both social and economic impacts. Border waits to cross into the United States were already at an all-time high at many ports due to the tremendous growth in trade and traffic. The border region, to reiterate, at least on the Mexico–United States border, had already felt the effects of the economic slowdown well before September 11th. The security measures implemented following September 11th further increased wait times, causing excessive delays to the border population who routinely cross, which had a major affect upon local businesses. Although the added wait times have not deterred commercial truck crossings, the greater transaction costs of wait times for trucks add to the costs of production, a spillover ultimately paid for by consumers. An undermanned customs agency and agents working longer hours aggravated the process. A hardened border, which is controlled more by a police mentality than with free exchange of goods and persons, and the increase from 20–30 minutes to three hours to enter the United States have been the source of considerable frustration to the hundreds of thousands of daily crossers who travel between the United States and Mexico. Incrementally, the border has opened up, but may never return to the pre-September 11th level. However, for commercial ties in the region, a perspective that reinforces the concept of a strategic resource can be the basis for repositioning the border. The comparative advantage that exists needs to be reconsidered, not as an advantage in labor, but a geopolitical advantage that can ensure the continuation of activities in the North American manufacturing sector when global events force halts in international trade that supports manufacturing.

Strategic Resources

The attacks on the World Trade Center and the Pentagon on September 11th took most Westerners by surprise. It showed that the threat of a terrorist attack is very real and that control of global security has become a matter of paramount importance to the United States, as well as other democratic countries.[20] The question of security of shipping (trade and transportation) lanes has often been discussed in connection with political and military developments worldwide and instantly gained attention.

In this regard, we ask, what about borders? The borders between the United States and its two continental neighborhoods are the source of a huge economic force including three of the world's largest economies.[21] In fact, it is safe to say they are so linked and integrated that they coexist and would independently be less significant. Can we think of borders as strategic resources? The term is often used, but is it a way to redefine the comparative advantage of the region, especially the Mexico–United States border that has previously defined its comparative advantage as cheap labor.

Historically, minerals and energy resources have held the position of the most desirable strategic resources in national security, world politics, and economics.[22] However, in light of the September 11th attacks it seems that borders, in general, and the U.S. borders, in particular, garnered a heightened position as strategic resources, in that, although world travel, trade, and transportation basically stopped, the borders were able to maintain travel, trade, and transportation activities after a few hours, albeit with more regulations and restrictions, but also with the implementation of the highest level of national security procedures. Thus, the economic activities were not vanquished but subdued given that the borders continued to operate under extreme events, thereby designating the borders as having the major characteristic of being a strategically solvent resource.

It seems relatively clear that some resources are more important than others. Resources essential to the economy of a country are called critical or strategic resources, and the definition of critical or strategic may vary from country-to-country or time-to-time. Change in a resource's value occurs in response to social, economic, and technological changes and the importance of a resource is related to the demand for its product or products.[23]

Historically, the United States has viewed minerals, such as oil and the like, as strategic resources. Task forces have been set up to evaluate mineral efficiency; bilateral and multilateral agreements have been developed between importers and exporters; price agreements have been negotiated to ensure access and delivery of strategically defined resources.[24] When countries become significantly dependent upon exports of resources they become strategically important to the economies of those countries. What is determined to be a critical or strategic material may vary among industries and within any given nation. A country's economic structure and status as a political and military power will determine the resources that are considered strategic to the nation as a whole and the resources that are critical to the existence of specific industries.[25] In addition, factors, such as the existence of mineral deposits, availability of capital and technology, sufficient energy production, industrial and military demand, transportation infrastructure, and export capabilities, determine what is strategic and what is not.[26] It is the last two that allow us to reconsider the strategic value of the border.

Nations no longer depend on a single factor of production to meet critical needs but rather on a plethora of inputs and processes to sustain prosperity (Cammarota, 1984).[27] In this regard, the ability to keep the U.S. economy protected from threat includes ensuring the free flow of goods between manufacturing and assembly plants in Mexico and final production activities in plants in the United States. In the event of a war or a national emergency created by terrorism, the old industrial practice of stockpiling, which has given way to just-in-time delivery needs, is no longer viable. The flow of factors of production from maquiladoras becomes critical to maintaining economic stability, thus free flow of goods across national boundaries, in turn, makes these borders strategic resources.

Curlin[28] notes that: "No one can doubt that the problem of dependency of the United States upon strategic minerals is serious, important, and complex. In many respects the ready availability of strategic resources is a key to national economic welfare and security. Yet, definitions of strategic are uncertain, with different standards coming from different sources both private and governmental, and expectations of domestic production, substitutability, and foreign supply gyrate from moderate optimism to cataclysmic pessimisms." In this line of thinking, realization that national economic security (jobs, flows of goods, supply chains) is linked to borders creates an opportunity to examine the comparative advantages that border trade creates for the United States. The danger of an interruption of trade between the United States and Mexico places the U.S. economic security at a high danger level. A point we believe can be demonstrated through an examination of the current economic growth in China based on comparative advantage in cheap labor, and the port strikes and shutdowns in 2003 in the western United States, which is the transportation access point for China's manufacturing exports.

China and Cheap Labor

It is no fault of the Chinese that they currently have become the awakened economic giant. The loss of jobs in the maquiladora sector of Mexico clearly makes this evident in the border region, although it has not been as catastrophic as some foretold. Complaints by border business interests that China is undercutting the region with cheap labor are no more a viable way to protect the region than Ross Perot's contention that NAFTA would create "a giant sucking sound" as American jobs went to Mexico. Job loses of over 33,000 maquiladora workers (from peak in October 2000: 264,241 to 230,895 at end of 2005) and significant concerns about investment declines in the region have had a measurable impact. Yet, in a world where Wal-Mart prices are demanded, Mexico's labor costs are three times higher than China's[29] and its political system has indirectly thwarted foreign direct investment by ignoring infrastructure needs and modernization, both political and economic, that industries demand and are able to obtain in other nations.

However, the argument can be made that China too will see its comparative advantage decline in favor of central Africa or other parts of Asia. The world of multinational manufacturing is one of entrance and exit based on cheap labor (Marquand, 2002).[30] The United States–Mexico border needs to shed the view that cheap labor in Mexico will recreate opportunities that are beneficial to both the United States and Mexico economies. The key to the region and protecting broader North American manufacturing may well be in location, location, location, location! Geopolitically, there is a need to rethink the border's comparative advantage, viewing it as a strategic resource that will ensure and protect the manufacturing base of the continent. As an illustration, the shutdown of the seaports of the United States, by terrorism or another event, can serve as a means for understanding the strategic value of our southern borders.

The contract dispute between members of the International Longshoreman and Warehouse Union (ILWU) and the Pacific Maritime Association (PMA) in 2002 effectively proved the vulnerability of seaport operations and the serious implications that disrupted port activity can have on the American economy. As a starting point, it is important to note that ocean cargo represents more than 7 percent of U.S. gross domestic product, a figure which is adversely affected when major events directly affect the nation's ports.

The contract between ILWU and PMA controls the flow of goods through America's 29 major Pacific ports, a dollar volume of $260 billion in 2001. The *San Francisco Chronicle* reported that, "a 10-day shutdown at West Coast ports could strip $19.4 billion from the U.S. economy...after 20 days, the price jumps to $48.6 billion." The longshoremen's strike of 2002 at west coast ports serves to make the case for viewing the nation's southern border trade as a strategic resource. Manufacturing facilities dependent on delivery of components through seaports were reported as having to shut down in seven days or less, a proverbial closing of a pipeline.[31] These numbers reflect the adverse effects of a labor strike and not a larger event like an act of terrorism, which can also greatly impact the economic progress of the United States. Terrorism and other global events can impede international trade in ways we still do not understand. Proximity among trading partners, coupled with trust and systems that can insure movements of goods between nations, thus become even more critical than ever.

From another view, the *North County Times* (California) reported that a simulated port security drill under the direction of former CIA Director James Woolsey exposed a breakdown of communication and coordination between the agencies. The simulation involved the smuggling of a "dirty bomb" into the Port of Los Angeles. Those participating in the simulation included personnel from the Transportation Security Administration, Office of Homeland Security (now DHS), the Customs Service, and the port authorities of New York, New Jersey, and Georgia. This exercise determined that it would take 92 days to work through the backlog of cargo lost by such an event, costing the U.S. economy $58 billion. In the simulation, ships were stranded, importers and exporters lost money due to spoilage and lost sales, and manufacturers began to close plants. With this in mind, there is little doubt that the economic impact of disrupted port activity would be sizeable, estimated by the president of the Federal Reserve Bank of San Francisco to exceed $2 billion a day.[32]

In addition to these estimates, a study conducted by the Anderson Economic Group suggested that the personal income losses might be somewhere between the one and two billion dollar mark. Their report, "Flash Estimate: Impact of West Coast Shutdown," considered only reduction in earnings to U.S. persons, which includes lost wages and other earnings to workers, consumers, and producers in the United States. Thus, the total economic damage of the shutdown was approximately $1.67 billion, for a period of 12 days, and in the event of a four week shutdown, they estimated that personal income would be reduced by $4.79 billion.[33]

While it can be argued there are disparities between media reports and studies like the one conducted by Andersen Group, the indications clearly show the tremendous impact that a slowdown or disruption of port activity can have on the economy. Thus, the implication is that dependency on American seaports creates a distinct vulnerability in the event of violence or a domestic event, such as a labor strike. Restarting operations takes considerable time and transshipment stoppage has a snowball effect on manufacturing that has been disrupted. Proximity and the availability of alternative ports of entry between the United States and Mexico can offset this form of crisis.

Southern Border Security: The Impacts of a Shutdown on Regional Economies

Since September 11th, the Institute for Policy and Economic Development has been involved in a variety of studies examining numerous economic conditions in the border region. The institute has developed economic modeling capability to address these issues known as The Border Model. We will not deliberate the model here, but point out that it allows for analysis of impacts on both sides of the border at the same time and covers the six Mexican states and all counties on the U.S. side (see Figure 22.3).[34]

Using The Border Model, three scenarios were developed that examined the economic impacts of a border closure on the regional economy.[35] Our three scenarios are tested using the transportation matrix that is incorporated into the model, allowing for changing the crossing times, which are converted to commuting (labor) costs, transportation costs, and accessibility costs (access to goods for production). We also limited our first examination of this problem to El Paso, Texas. The model allowed us to examine both gross regional product (GRP), a measure of the overall economic impact, and the loss of employment as a result of these scenarios. The following are the three scenarios considered:

Policy change 1 (low): A minor localized but significant policy change, such as U.S. VISIT with no long-term closure but a likely lengthening of time to traverse the border. The impact has the effect of increasing El Paso–Chihuahua commuting, accessibility, and transportation costs two percent each.

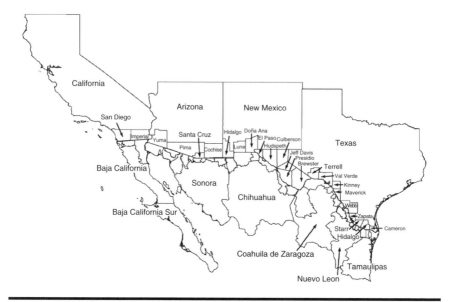

Figure 22.3   The Border Model interactions.

Policy change 2 (medium): A major, but localized, policy change, such as a bridge failure or loss of a port of entry. The impact has the effect of increasing El Paso–Chihuahua commuting, accessibility, and transportation costs by 20, 10, and 9 percent, respectively.

Policy change 3 (high): A major, systemwide slowdown throughout the border region, but only on goods and people moving out of Mexico, which is typical of the bottlenecks after September 11th, with a six month "test" duration. The impact has the effect of increasing El Paso–Chihuahua commuting, accessibility, and transportation costs by 40 percent each.

The scenarios were run using a period of 2003 to 2010 to determine the impacts across time. On the basis of the model in Figure 22.4, we see that employment from a low-impact scenario deviates little from the baseline projection, but in the first year up to 330 jobs would be lost in El Paso. A medium scenario would result in approximately 1,450 jobs lost in the first year, while a high scenario would impact close to 23,000 employees in the first year or 6.5 percent of the workforce. From the baseline, shown in white, we can see that both the low and medium scenarios would be deemed manageable in the regional economy. In fact, they are likely to be barely felt in the long run as employment opportunities opened up. A high-impact scenario, however, creates a major effect. In the seven year period following a security event that closed the border for an extended period of time, more than 31,000 jobs would be lost, 8.25 percent of the workforce. The secondary and tertiary effects of these job loses are not readily observable, but any 8 percent loss

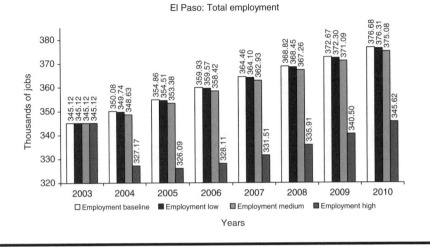

Figure 22.4 Total employment impact for El Paso, Texas, for three security scenarios.

of jobs in any location is a serious problem and is not recoverable in the same way as the low and medium scenarios are by baseline growth. To put it in a different perspective, the long-term impact would stagnate the 2010 economy at the original 2003 baseline.

Figure 22.5 provides another view of these scenarios by reporting the impact on GRP as a result of the three scenarios. Once again, the low and medium scenarios deviate only slightly from the baseline as adjustments in the economy are made or

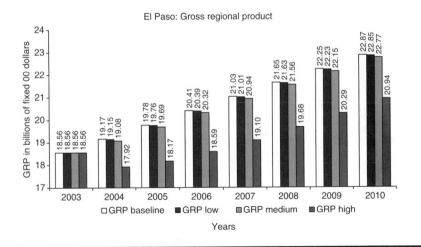

Figure 22.5 Impact on gross regional product in El Paso, Texas, for three scenarios.

the impacts absorbed by other forms of growth. Looking at 2007, the mid-year of the scenarios, the most dramatic effect is the high scenario. GRP falls more than 9 percent from the baseline in the fourth year after the closure, to a point near the original 2003 baseline, a loss of $1.93 billion. By 2010, the decline is at $1.93 billion, meaning that effect sets the economy back four years in terms of matching the baseline. These impacts neither tell us what the secondary and tertiary effects may be nor do they give us a full assessment of what would occur borderwide.

Figure 22.6 goes to the next level providing regionwide or borderwide impacts for employment and GRP, for both the United States and Mexico, or the combined border economy. Employment borderwide is calculated for a high scenario and indicates that the loss of jobs would approach 800,000 to 1 million. This is, however, probably overestimated due to inclusion of Mexican states in the model not just border areas due to the nature of data collection in that nation, but three-fourths of this loss is likely to be in border communities.

Gross regional product borderwide sees a major impact dropping from approximately $290 billion to $269 billion or a loss of more than $20 billion as seen in Figure 22.6. Put into perspective, this 7 percent drop would equal the economy of the entire El Paso area, in essence eliminating what is equal to a city of 700,000 people. Moreover, as the trend lines go out, the "shock" to the economy is permanent and the region as a whole does not appear to ever recover to its original position.

Although this data is preliminary, it clearly indicates that economic security is related to the border being fluid. The next step is to determine to what degree what further effects (forward linkages) would trickle through the economy, if just-in-time deliveries halted and if recipients of border products see their assembly lines closed because components cannot cross into the United States from Mexico.

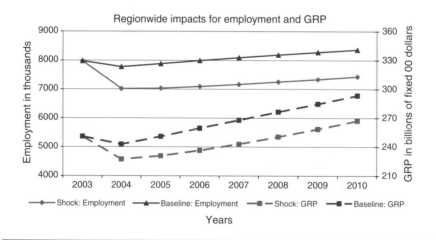

Figure 22.6 Borderwide impacts from three scenarios.

These tests of economic border security suggest at minimum a severe or high-impact event will impact stability of the region within which it may occur. The west coast dock strike, for example, played havoc on the nation's supply chain as 47 percent of supply chain managers reported considerable serious and negative effects that harmed their operations.[36] Closure of over 200 maquiladoras in the El Paso region that services inland facilities would be the "tip of the iceberg," as the border is considered for its role in the larger economic system.

This data also suggests that commercial and political interests should recognize the symbiotic nature of the peripheries of each nation in which they reside, and make strides to help others overcome ignorance and neglect. The Midwest auto industry alone, for example, would succumb without the production that comes through southern ports. What were thought of as sleepy border villages rested in the tradition of the siesta is a far cry from the reality and economic activity that comes from the border and feeds the need of the industrial heartland. Nor in many ways is this thinking new. Herzog,[37] along with others, has pointed out that the trans-frontier area is a single functional domain. However, policy and decision makers neither have treated it as such nor have they used it to their advantage. Thus, the map of the borders with its lines demarcating the states, cities, and counties should be viewed as a myth. A border security breakdown will create a series of billiard ball–like events that will undeniably demonstrate the high level of integration and dependency that exists.

This discussion now returns to comparative advantage. Under globalization, a lengthy literature records how the world has indeed changed.[38] Consistent with, or perhaps parallel to, globalization new regional actors have emerged. Unlike their old-war predecessors who were linked through national security threats, these subregional economic zones transcend political boundaries in new and unique ways, linking industries and processes at multiple levels.[39] Constituent states, such as the United States and Mexico in this discussion, become recipients of ties that are commercial, political, and socially beneficial to a subsystem, in our case, the border. The payoff to the constituent states is security in the trade flows between the two nations, a security complex that protects the economic prowess of leading world economies.

Reducing risks is no longer about traditional national security issues, but has made economic insulation, not isolation from crisis, a priority. Overall, the problems of weapons of mass destruction are less critical than economic collapse, which can be offset by free trade among neighbors with complimentary inputs into the production processes of goods and services.

International boundaries, thus, are not places of fighting and protection but artificial zones created by governments for a variety of reasons that today may not hold true. It is, however, unlikely that they will disappear even in the context of successful integration, if it occurs, of the European Union. The natural occurrence of United States–Mexico trade is based on the comparative advantage of the factors of production of labor (Mexico) and capital (United States). The border then is a function in national well-being that defines the character of each nation's internal elements in much the same way sea power defined strategic thinking for the British, Dutch, and other empires along the lines of Mahan's sea power doctrine.[40]

The function of the boundary between the United States and Mexico could be different in that proximity and mutual economic need create a strategic response that ensures the boundaries function is stable and not likely to rapidly change in time of crisis as much as in other locales.[41] Subsequently, a strategic resource concept of the border becomes a risk reduction strategy. Risk reduction, in both a military and economic sense, based on commerce is contributing to the strength of ties between nations, creates common interests that create an intertwined system that lessens military tensions between nations, and draws them together against other common threats while building economic strength for both partners. This risk reduction allows two nations to maintain activities when threats to the global economic system would force closure or greatly reduce activities, thus, reducing risk within the territory of North America and creating a new response to a crisis of security which Beck has explored (Beck, 1992).[42]

This results, as well, in a de-territorialization amenable to trans-boundary activities, such as commerce, and is the reverse of programs, such as "Hold the Line," and perhaps U.S. VISIT, which many contend, is unlikely to halt external threats.[43] In addition, it views the boundary between nations differently, in a dynamic sense that can enhance regional activities rather than thwart them, a view that would likely be considered the antithesis of U.S. border management that is more militaristic than democratic societies and a neutral political partner in Mexico requires. Subsequently, a geoeconomic perspective in terms of cooperatively protecting resources and jointly using national comparative advantages to compete in the global market emerges using a view that the border can be managed to expedite and benefit nations, thereby creating a commercial fusion.

The case to extend this fusion stems from the success of NAFTA itself, the lessons of the west coast seaport strikes, September 11th, and the findings we have shared here. Trade between the United States and Mexico exceeds $250 billion per year, with 85 percent of Mexico's exports to the United States being manufactured goods, many of which are part of other production activities in the interior of the nation (Hakim and Litan, 2002, pp. 4–5).[44] The strategic resources view is not about institution building, but implies an initiative that uses the advantages of geography to enable broader economic interests. It requires greater coordination to stabilize transaction costs and the political economy of the region, broadly defined. In doing so, it will buffer the economies of the partners against external shocks, such as September 11th and further the agenda of integration within the hemisphere.

Conclusion

In many ways, the bottom line is that border security in an economic context is important and requires maximization on a number of fronts outside the range of this chapter. However, it allows us to envision the economic stakes and remarket or reconceptionalize the border as a North American subset that can be the model for other integration purposes related to border security.

In closing, H.J. Mackinder[43] perhaps best captured the idea that underscores the values associated with this discussion. He writes:

> They (policy makers) must have a global outlook and a quick readiness to meet emergencies, for it was never more true than in this newly "closed" world that our stability is but balance, and wisdom lies in the masterful administration of the unforeseen; they must also have a trained power of judging values and be capable of long views in framing policies for the future; and they will, of course, still need an understanding of the momentum with which both Man and his environment come to the present from the past (Mackinder, 1942, p. 129–130).

Endnotes

1. Caporaso, J.A., The international division of labor: A theoretical overview, in *A Changing International Division of Labor*, Capraso, J.A., Ed., Lynne Reinner Publishers: Boulder, Colorado, 1987.
2. Fry, E.H., North American economic integration. *Policy Papers on the Americas*, XIV: 8, 2, 2003.
3. Soden, et al., At the crossroads: US/Mexico border counties in transition, prepared for the US/Mexico Border Counties Coalition by the Institute for Policy and Economic Development at the University of Texas at El Paso: El Paso, Texas, 2006, March.
4. Linderking, B., The U.S.–Mexican border and NAFTA: Problem or paradigm? in *U.S.–Mexico Borderlands: Historical and Contemporary Perspectives*, Martinez, O.J., Ed., Wilmington, Delaware: Scholarly Resources, Inc., 1996, p. 191.
5. Rozental, A., Integrating North America: A Mexican perspective, in *The Future of North American Integration*, Hakim, P. and Litan, R.E., Eds., Washington, DC: The Brookings Institute, 2002, p. 84.
6. Mohar, G. Mexico-United States Migration: A Long Way To Go *Special Source Issue: US Mexico Migration*. 2004. Migration Policy Institute. Available online at: http://www.migrationinformation.org/special_mexico.cfm.
7. Montgomery, D. Americans speaking out against illegal immigration. *Kansas City Star: Reprinted form McClatchey Newspapers 2007–08–19, Page A1, Kansas City Star, The (Mo)*.
8. See Department of Homeland Security Web site, www.dhs.gov for discussion of the U.S. VISIT prior to implementation; Walker, K.C. U.S. VISIT: enhancing border security or exemplifying optical solutions in our post 9/11 universe, Unpublished manuscript, 2004; Fisher, D., New DHS border scrutinized, *E-Week Enterprise News and Reviews*, http://www.eweek.com/print_article/0,3048,a=116133,00asp; Shoop, T., Plan for new entry-exit system falls short, report says, *Government Executive*, June 9, 2003.
9. A maquiladora is a Mexican corporation operating under a special U.S. Customs and Border Protection status that allows it to temporarily import from the United States into

Mexico duty-free, raw materials, equipment, machinery, replacement parts, and other tools needed for the assembly or manufacture of intermediate or finished goods for subsequent export to the United States or sale in the domestic market (the latter requires payment of import tariffs on the U.S. raw material used in the production process). A maquiladora is also referred to as maquila and twin-plan.

10. Olmedo, C. and Soden, D.L., Terrorism's role in re-shaping border crossings: 11 September and the US borders, *Geopolitics*, 10, 1, 2005.

11. McElroy, M., The emergence and evolution of the maquiladora industry in Mexico, in *Digáme!: Policy and Politics on the Texas Border*, Brenner, C., Coronado, I., and Soden, D.L., Eds., Kendall Hunt: Dubuque, Iowa, 2003, p. 137; Olmedo, C., Impacts of September 11th on the U.S. border with Mexico and Canada, *Border Business Review*, 1, 5, June, 2003.

12. Hanson, G.H., U.S.–Mexico integration and regional economies: Evidence from border city pairs, *Journal of Urban Economics*, 50, 250, 2001.

13. Cañas, J., A decade of change: El Paso's economic transition of the 1990s, *Business Frontier*, Federal Reserve Bank of Dallas, El Paso Branch, (1), 2002.

14. Hanson, G.H., 2001. U.S.–Mexico Integration and Regional Economies: Evidence from Border-City Paris. *Journal of Urban Economics*. Volume 50, Issue 2, September 2001, pp. 259–287.

15. Source for port trade: http://texascenter.tamiu.edu.

16. Statistics compiled by the U.S. Customs Service show that in 2001, the port of El Paso was the third highest in northbound truck crossings behind Laredo and Otay Mesa/San Ysidro. This represents a substantial drop in truck traffic from 2000 in El Paso when 720,000 trucks crossed northward through its international bridges. El Paso also ranked second in pedestrian crossings and first in vehicle and vehicle passenger crossings.

17. Just-in-time inventory management requires that Mexican and Canadian suppliers make their deliveries to the United States at predictable intervals upon demand. From the transport perspective, every delivery is a payment, so the wait times are not deterrence, only a burden that ultimately can lead to a reduction in income through a reduction in deliveries. But from the inventory perspective, delays can cause production line shut-downs, creating a backlog of orders. Multinationals have turned just-in-time delivery into just-in-case inventory and, in some cases, switched production lines to other assembly plants or source from other suppliers.

18. Comparing pedestrian crossings alongside vehicle crossings, the impact had definite implications at various key entry points. Heightened border security increased wait times that were already intolerable before September 11th. In response, people engaged in substitution, giving up driving, preferring to wait less by walking across the border, thereby increasing pedestrian crossings (See: Olmedo, 2003; Olmedo and Soden, 2005).

19. Cañas, J., and Coronado, R. 2002. Maquiladora Industry: Past, Present and Future. *Business Frontier*. Federal Reserve Bank of Dallas. 2002:1.

20. Rogers, P., *Losing Control*, Pluto Press: London, 2002.

21. Fry, E.H., 2, 2003.

22. Santini, J.D., Congress and strategic minerals policy, in *Strategic Minerals and International Security*, Ra'anan, U. and Perry, C.M., Eds., Pergamon-Brassey's International Defense Publishers: New York, 1985, p. 50.

23. Cohen, S.D., *The Making of United States International Economic Policy*, Praeger: Westport, Connecticut, 1994; Henning, D.H. and Mangun, W.R., *Managing the Environmental Crisis*, Duke University Press: Durham, North Carolina, 1989.

24. Pirages, D., *The New Context for International Relations: Global Ecopolitics*, Duxbury Press: North Scituate, Massachusetts, 1978.

25. Szuprowicz, B.O., How to avoid strategic materials shortages; dealing with cartels, *Embargoes and Supply Disruptions*, John Wiley & Sons: New York, 1981.

26. Ibid.

27. Cammarota, V.A., America's dependence on strategic minerals, in *American Strategic Minerals*, Mangone, G.J., Ed., Crane, Russak & Co., Inc.: New York, 1984.

28. Curlin, J.W., The political dimensions of strategic minerals, in *American Strategic Minerals*, Mangone, G.J., Ed., Crane, Russak & Co., Inc.: New York, 1984.

29. Fry, E.H., 14, 2003.

30. Marquand, R., China Coast as factory of the world, *The Christian Science Monitor*, 1, 7, December 16, 2003.

31. Baker, D.R., Economy may sink if strike shuts ports, http://www.sfgate.com/cgi-bin/article.cgi?file+/chronicle/archive/2002/08/28/BU88270, 2002.

32. Isidore, C., Hope in west coast port talks, http://money.cnn.com/2002/10/02/news/economy/ports, 2003.

33. Anderson, P.L. and IIhan K. Geckil, I.K., Flash estimate: Impact of west coast shutdown, www.andersoneconomicgroup.com, October 15, 2002.

34. We are currently in our second iteration of the model as a result of some software changes; subsequently, the data reported here comes from our first version.

35. In a sense, these are incomplete because the earlier version of the model did not allow for measuring the impacts throughout the U.S. and Mexico economies, a reason for development of the second version.

36. Kioa, K., How did the west coast dock strike affect the nation's supply chains? Institute for Supply Chain Management, www.ism.ws/aboutISM/MediaReleases/pr120502West CoastDock.cfm, 2002.

37. Herzog, L.A., *Where North Meets South: Cities, Space, and Politics on the U.S.–Mexico Border*, University of Texas Press: Austin, Texas, 1990.

38. Mittelman, J.H., *The Globalization Syndrome: Transformation and Resistance*, Princeton University Press: Princeton, New Jersey, 2000.

39. Chia, S.Y. and Lee, T.Y., Subregional economic zones: A new motive force in Asia-Pacific development, in *Pacific Dynamism and the International Economic System*, Bergsten and Noland, Eds., Institute for International Economics: Washington, DC, 1993, p. 226; Mittelman, 2000, p. 113.

40. Livezey, W., *Mahan on Sea Power*, Oklahoma Press: Norman, Oklahoma, 1947, p. 316.

41. Dalby, S., Critical geopolitics and the world order models project, Paper presented to the Inaugural International Conference in Critical Geography, Vancouver, 146, August, 1997.

42. Beck, U., *Risk Society*, Sage: London, 1992.

43. Walker, K.C., U.S. VISIT: Enhancing border security or exemplifying optical solutions in our post 9/11 universe, Unpublished manuscript, 2004.

44. Hakim, P. and Litan, R.E., Eds., *The Future of North American Integration*, The Brookings Institute: Washington, DC, 2002.

45. Mackinder, H.J., Geography, an art and a philosophy, *Geography*, 27, 129, 1942.

Index

443

N

P